Organizational Science Abroad

Constraints and Perspectives

Organizational Science Abroad
Constraints and Perspectives

Edited by
Chimezie A. B. Osigweh, Yg.

Plenum Press • New York and London

Library of Congress Cataloging in Publication Data

Organizational science abroad: constraints and perspectives / edited by Chimezie
A. B. Osigweh, Yg.
    p.   cm.
Bibliography: p.
Includes index.
ISBN 0-306-42969-1
    1. Comparative management. 2. Comparative organization. 3. Management—Cross-
cultural studies. I. Osigweh, Chimezie A. B., 1955–
HD30.55.O735   1988   88-28572
658—dc19   CIP

© 1989 Plenum Press, New York
A Division of Plenum Publishing Corporation
233 Spring Street, New York, N.Y. 10013

To my special family:

Dr. Arthur ("Sir") Hougland
Dr. Magaret ("Madam") Hougland

Amy Hougland
Chris Hougland
John Hougland

Contributors

Nancy J. Adler, Faculty of Management, McGill University, Montreal, Canada

Wiktor Askanas, Faculty of Administration, University of New Brunswick, Fredericton, New Brunswick, Canada

William Aussieker, Department of Management, California Polytechnic State University, San Luis Obispo, California

Schon L. Beechler, Graduate School of Management, The University of Michigan, Ann Arbor, Michigan

Kim S. Cameron, Graduate School of Business Administration, University of Michigan, Ann Arbor, Michigan

Cary L. Cooper, Manchester School of Management, University of Manchester, Institute of Science and Technology, Manchester, United Kingdom

Charles J. Cox, Manchester School of Management, University of Manchester, Institute of Science and Technology, Manchester, United Kingdom

Robert Doktor, Department of Management and Industrial Relations, College of Business Administration, University of Hawaii, Manoa, Hawaii

Dexter Dunphy, Australian Graduate School of Management, University of New South Wales, Kensington, New South Wales, Australia

Sarah J. Freeman, Graduate School of Business Administration, University of Michigan, Ann Arbor, Michigan

W. Harvey Hegarty, Graduate School of Business, Indiana University, Bloomington, Indiana

Richard C. Hoffman, College of Business and Economics, University of Delaware, Newark, Delaware

Myung Un Kim, Graduate School of Business Administration, University of Michigan, Ann Arbor, Michigan

Yasumasa Kondo, Department of Commerce, Doshisha University, Kyoto, Japan

Chimezie A. B. Osigweh, Yg., Department of Management, School of Business, Norfolk State University, Norfolk, Virginia

Vladimir Pucik, School of Business Administration, The University of Michigan, Ann Arbor, Michigan

S. Gordon Redding, Department of Management, University of Hong Kong, Hong Kong

Fritz Rieger, Department of Management, University of Windsor, Windsor, Ontario, Canada

Rolf E. Rogers, Department of Management, California Polytechnic State University, San Luis Obispo, California and Department of Management, University of Hawaii, Honolulu, Hawaii

Uma Sekaran, Department of Management, College of Business and Administration, Southern Illinois University, Carbondale, Illinois

Jeannette Shi, Australian Graduate School of Management, University of New South Wales, Kensington, New South Wales, Australia

Coral R. Snodgrass, Department of Management, College of Business and Administration, Southern Illinois University, Carbondale, Illinois

Richard M. Steers, Department of Management, Graduate School of Management, University of Oregon, Eugene, Oregon

Jeremiah J. Sullivan, Department of Marketing and International Business, Graduate School of Business Administration, University of Washington, Seattle, Washington

Teruhiko Suzuki, Department of Commerce, Doshisha University, Kyoto, Japan

Rosalie L. Tung, School of Business Administration, University of Wisconsin-Milwaukee, Milwaukee, Wisconsin

Durhane Wong-Rieger, Department of Management, University of Windsor, Windsor, Ontario, Canada

Foreword

Organizing consists of making other people work. We do this by manip-
ulating symbols: words, exhortations, memos, charts, signs of status.
We expect these symbols to have the desired effects on the people concerned. The success of our organizing activities depends on whether the
others do attach to our symbols the meanings we expect them to.
Whether or not they do so is a function of what I have sometimes called
"the programs in their minds"—their learned ways of thinking, feeling,
and reacting—in short, a function of their culture. The assumption that
organizations could be culture-free is naive and myopic; it is based on a
misunderstanding of the very act of organizing. Certainly, few people
who have ever worked abroad will make this assumption.

The dependence of organizations on their people's mental programs does not mean, of course, that we do not find many similarities
across organizations. Some characteristics of human mental program-
ming are universal; others are shared by most people in a continent, a
country, a region, an industry, a scientific discipline, or even a gender.
A global, rather than national, organizational science weighs both similarities and differences. The two are each other's inseparable comple-
ments. Similarities are only of interest for traits that could also have been
different, differences only for what could have been similar. Weighing
similarities and differences is not a matter of numbers: Mr. Fujisawa's
dictum, which heads Chapter 2 of this book, represents the voice of
common sense (or of wisdom, which is the same thing) and reminds us
that one difference, if overlooked, may offset nineteen similarities.

Research in multinational organizations, including my own work,
has shown that people in similar positions but in different countries
often do the same things, but attach quite different meanings to what
they do. Daily practices vary less than underlying values. This also
means that across national borders practitioners will cooperate more
easily than theorists. Those of us involved in organizational science

often tend to forget that we, too, are children of our national and professional cultures, and that our minds have also been programmed by this background. Being theorists by profession, we operate precisely in the area where consensus across borders is most difficult to obtain. Paradoxically, what applies least abroad is our theories, not our practices.

In human history, countries or areas that for a period wielded considerable political and economic power have usually, with some delay, also exported ideas to other parts of the world. This has been true in the West for, successively, the Mesopotamian civilizations, Greece, Rome, the Arabs, the Renaissance Italians, Western Europe, and the United States. We are presently witnessing a shift toward Japan, and, as this book shows, China may be the next country to watch. Asia, from India eastward, had its own internal transfers of ideas in the past millennia, but now, for the first time in human history, East and West seem to meet in an integration of ideas. In the meantime, we should realize that a dominant country's ideas frequently are built upon those of its predecessors in the history of domination. U.S.-dominated organization science had inherited from Europeans: Durkheim, Fayol, Marx, Freud, Lewin, Weber. Chapter 7 of this book illustrates to what extent Japanese organizations have been influenced by U.S. examples.

What is probably also new to the present era is the fact that no country will ever again on its own exercise as much domination as some did in the past: neither politically nor economically nor ideologically. We will have to live in an interdependent world whether we like it or not. For organizational science, this means that the field will become a very different game from the mainly U.S.-centered discipline of the past decades. Contributions of people with quite varying mental programs will have to be recognized. This is no less than a paradigmatic shift, in the sense of Thomas Kuhn's *The Structure of Scientific Revolutions* (University of Chicago Press, 1970). In fact, it is a shift not toward one but toward a whole series of new paradigms. Paradigmatic shifts, as Kuhn has shown, are not smooth transitions, and those educated in the old ways may experience such a shift as nonsensical, irrelevant, threatening— anyway, it will meet with considerable resistance.

The book in front of you represents a courageous attempt at supporting such a paradigmatic shift. Across its chapters, it interestingly illustrates various stages of transition from a U.S.-centered to a globally interdependent approach. Its authorship, while predominantly North American, includes many persons who are in some way bi-or multi-cultural: It is the marginals, both in countries and in disciplines, from whom basic innovations can be expected.

One striking feature of the U.S. organizational science paradigm is its fascination with the role of management. "Management" is an American invention. The assumption that there should be a special class of people who are needed in order to make other people work, and the assumption that these managers represent the vital core of the organization, that they "are" the organization much more than all the other members, are by no means universal. They are not shared by, for example, most Japanese, nor were they held by the German fathers of organizational science. I have been amused by the number of times I have seen my own research described in U.S. sources as "a comparative study of managers' values"—whereas in fact I studied employees' values. I happen to believe that management and managers can only be understood in relationship to the kind of people managed. For example, I believe that Japanese management without Japanese employees is like the sound of one hand clapping.

The editor, Professor Chimezie A. B. Osigweh, should be congratulated for a timely and stimulating volume, composed of chapters by some of the best experts in the field. As the book's subtitle emphasizes, it represents work in process, in a field in which I sincerely hope that work will always remain in process. May it help many readers along on the road toward a truly global, multiparadigm organizational science.

Geert Hofstede

Maastricht, The Netherlands

Preface

There is no evidence yet that the phenomenal surge of business activities into the global economy following World War II shows any signs of abating. Rather, the conduct of business intercourse by for-profit and nonprofit entities is spectacularly breaking out of prevailing domestic parochialism, as large and small firms become more involved in international business relations. Apparently, there seems to be an increasing realization among organizational leaders that the growing innovations in technology, communication, and transportation systems are transforming the contemporary world into a small global marketplace.

Not surprisingly, the amount of organizational research and its application, both within individual countries and on a worldwide scale has also been growing dramatically over the years. Yet, what is known worldwide about organizational science, or management theory and practice, is mostly based on experience garnered from or inquiry conducted in the United States of America. Even where the investigation or experience-based learning emanates from a different country, it is nonetheless likely to be significantly founded on United States organizational science precepts. And, where the organizational science precepts, research, and practices are truly indigenous to some other country, to the extent that they were originally developed elsewhere by non-American nationalities, they are, like their United States counterparts, imported by other countries and championed by scholars and practitioners alike, often with little or no adaptation at all. One major example is what William G. Ouchi describes as the Japanese management system in his widely received 1981 book *Theory Z* (Reading, Massachusetts: Addison-Wesley). Underlying such unchecked exportation and importation of organizational research and practices is the implicit, if often fictional, assumption that they possess universality and, by that virtue, are entirely transferable across national boundaries and may expect to encounter the same level of success originally recorded at home.

There is something myopic about any perspective that asks only if "our way," the indigenous way, will work abroad in today's culturally variegated global business environment. Recognizing that, this book is written for anyone concerned with or interested in transnational organizational research and practice. Its basic premise is that organizational science activity should be disciplined by careful, indeed meticulous, and sustained attention to country-specific particularities, especially those relating to social, political, technological, and economic cultures. Its object is to examine through various perspectives the constraints and other issues dealing with the predominant practice of constructing and investigating organizational research and application in one country, and utilizing elsewhere (in nonindigenous settings) the body of knowledge so produced.

Accordingly, the book is segmented into five parts. Part I introduces the volume, providing an analysis of myths in (transnational) organizational science and the universality misconception, while providing an incisive review of the field. Part II provides various perspectives and insights from Europe, based on data from countries such as Czechoslovakia, Hungary, Poland, and the USSR in Eastern Europe, and France, The Netherlands, Sweden, Switzerland, the United Kingdom, and West Germany in Western Europe. Part III emphasizes Asia, with particular attention to the People's Republic of China and Japan. Part IV offers some perspectives and insights from Latin America (specifically, Brazil) and the international airline industry. Data for the latter were obtained from airlines in 35 countries. A culture-relative model for achieving organizational effectiveness as well as a future research agenda that emphasizes changes in our approach to organizational research are offered in Part V. (See Chapter 1, "The Issues and Perspectives," for more detailed descriptions of the contents of each chapter.)

I am grateful to the following individuals for their comments and various degrees of insight: Mark L. Chadwin (Old Dominion University), Cary L. Cooper (University of Manchester), Robert Doktor (University of Hawaii), Michael R. Czinkota (Georgetown University), Gary Oddou (San Jose State University), Daniel Ondrack (University of Toronto), and Jeremiah J. Sullivan (University of Washington). Joseph L. Boyd and Edgar L. Williams, Jr., offered a supportive institutional climate. Tonya A. Long and Zachary Johnson provided the needed research assistance. Aretha R. Harris prepared the final manuscript.

Chimezie A. B. Osigweh, Yg.

Norfolk, Virginia

Contents

PART I. INTRODUCTION

1. **The Myth of Universality in Transnational Organizational
   Science** 3

   Chimezie A. B. Osigweh, Yg.

   I. Organizational Science in a Transnational Business
      World 4
   II. Myth and Meaning: On the Role of Myth in
       Organizational Science 7
   III. The Universality Myth in Transnational
        Organizational Science 9
   IV. The Challenge Illustrated in a Parochial-Ethnocentric
       Management Context 13
   V. The Issues and Perspectives 16
      A. Insights and Perspectives from Europe 16
      B. Insights and Perspectives from Asia 17
      C. Other Specific Insights and Perspectives 19
      D. Conclusion 20
   VI. Summary 21
   VII. References 22

2. **From the Atlantic to the Pacific Century: Cross-Cultural
   Management Reviewed** 27

   Nancy J. Adler and Robert Doktor, with S. Gordon Redding

   I. Cross-Cultural Management: Some Major Debates ... 29
      A. Cross-Cultural Variance 29
      B. Cultural Determination 30
      C. Convergence versus Divergence 33

D. Beyond Comparison: Intercultural Interaction 36
E. Synergy from Cultural Diversity 37
II. From the Atlantic to the Pacific Century 39
A. Single-Culture Management Studies 40
B. Comparative Management Studies 41
C. Sociological Studies 42
D. Developmental Psychology Studies 43
E. Causes of Misinterpreting Data across Cultures .. 44
III. Implications for the Practice of Management 47
IV. Implications for Future Research 48
V. References 48

PART II. INSIGHTS AND PERSPECTIVES FROM EUROPE

3. **Applying American Organizational Sciences in Europe and
the United Kingdom: The Problems** 57
Cary L. Cooper and Charles J. Cox

I. Differences, Similarities, and Implications 59
A. Different Social Science Traditions (Europe—
Cognitive and Psychoanalytic; America—
Behavioral and Humanist) 59
B. Differences in Managerial Models (Europe—
Cognitively Complex; America—Action-Oriented
and Behaviorist) 59
C. Belief in the Notion of Human Complexity
(Europe—Human Complexity; America—Rational
Man) 60
D. Belief in Tradition (Europe—Tradition Is Valued
and Change Regarded with Suspicion; America—
Change Seen as Positive) 61
E. Suspicion of Things Foreign (Europe—
Conservative and Strongly Influenced by Own
Culture; America—Many Cultural Influences) 61
F. Suspicion of Experts (Europe—Value on Wide
Education and Cultured Background, "Gifted
Amateur"; America—Value on Technical Expertise
and "Self-Made Man") 62
G. Political Orientation versus Openness (Europe—
Political Values; America—More Open Values) ... 62
H. Class Structure (Europe—Strong Class Structure
[Particularly United Kingdom]; America—More
Classless) 63

I. Economic Situation (Europe—Pessimistic;
America—Optimistic) 63
J. Management Education (Europe—Institutional;
America—Stimulus–Response) 64
II. Conclusion 64
III. References 65

4. The Failure of Management Techniques in Central
Planning Economies 67

Wiktor Askanas

I. Systems Management Techniques and Their
Limitations 67
A. Process of Decentralization 71
B. Process of Restructuralization 73
C. Process of Computerization 75
II. Conclusion 78
III. References 79

5. Union–Management Participation in Corporate Decision-
Making: A Comparative Analysis of Codetermination in
West Germany and the United States 81

Rolf E. Rogers and William Aussieker

I. Conceptual Framework 82
II. *Mitbestimmung* 85
A. Effectiveness 87
B. The Harzburg Model 88
III. Union or Employee Participation 89
IV. U.S. Codetermination 90
A. Effectiveness 92
V. Summary and Conclusions 93
VI. References 94

6. Convergence or Divergence of Strategic Decision Processes
among 10 Nations 97

Richard C. Hoffman and W. Harvey Hegarty

I. National Culture as a Dimension of Organizational
Context 98
II. Comparative Research in Strategic Management 99
III. Strategic Decision-Influence Processes 100
IV. Research Design 102
A. Sample and Data Collection 102

B. Variables and Measures 103
C. Data Analysis 104
V. Findings 105
A. External versus Internal Organizational Context
and Strategic Decision Activities 105
B. Strategic Decision-Influence Process 109
VI. Summary and Conclusions 111
VII. References 114

PART III. INSIGHTS AND PERSPECTIVES FROM ASIA

7. The Diffusion of American Organizational Theory in Postwar Japan

7. The Diffusion of American Organizational Theory in
Postwar Japan 119

Schon L. Beechler and Vladimir Pucik

I. Diffusion Stages 120
A. Stage 1: The New Theology 122
B. Stage 2: Empirical Guide 123
C. Stage 3: Culturalist Rollback 125
D. Stage 4: New Directions 126
E. Stage 5: Integration 128
II. Conclusion 130
III. References 131

8. Rational Man Theory in American and Japanese Performance Control

8. Rational Man Theory in American and Japanese
Performance Control 135

Jeremiah J. Sullivan, Teruhiko Suzuki, and Yasumasa Kondo

I. Experiment 1 136
A. The Fundamental Attribution Error (FAE) 136
B. Attribution Theory 136
C. The Availability Hypothesis 137
D. The Culture Hypothesis 139
E. Research Design 140
F. Method..................................... 141
G. Results 143
H. Discussion 144
II. Experiment 2 145
A. The Performance Control Process 145
B. Group versus Individual Focus 146
C. Hypotheses 149
D. Research Design 150

    E. Method   150
    F. Results   153
    G. Discussion   155
  III. Conclusion   158
  IV. References   159

9. Chinese Enterprise Management **161**
  Rosalie L. Tung

    I. Economic System   162
       A. Central Planning   162
       B. Types of Ownership   164
       C. The Four Modernizations   164
   II. Sociopolitical Systems   165
  III. The Cultural System   166
       A. Power Distance   167
       B. Uncertainty Avoidance   168
       C. Individualism   168
       D. Masculinity   168
  IV. Enterprise Management Systems   169
       A. Recruitment of Workers   169
       B. Promotion to Managerial Level   170
       C. Role of Factory Director   170
       D. Worker Participation in Management   170
       E. Trade Unions   171
       F. Motivational Devices   172
       G. Reprimands   176
   V. Conclusion   177
  VI. References   178

**10. A Comparison of Enterprise Management in Japan and the
   People's Republic of China** **179**
  Dexter Dunphy and Jeannette Shi

    I. The Significance of Japan and China for
       Management Theory   179
   II. Is There a Single East-Asian Cultural Cluster?   182
  III. Differences in Values between Japan and China   187
  IV. Some Implications   187
       A. Societal Objectives   187
       B. Value Differences   196
   V. Conclusion   197
  VI. References   199

PART IV. OTHER SPECIFIC INSIGHTS AND PERSPECTIVES

11. **Contradictions between Brazilian and U.S. Organizations:
    Implications for Organizational Theory** **203**
    Kim S. Cameron, Myung Un Kim, and Sarah J. Freeman

        I. Introduction 203
       II. Brazilian Context 205
           A. Political Conditions 206
           B. Economic Conditions 206
           C. Demographic Conditions 207
           D. Social Conditions 207
           E. Religious Homogeneity 208
           F. Summary 208
      III. Similarities between Brazilian and U.S. Institutions .. 208
      IV. Surprises regarding Brazilian Higher Education
          and Culture 210
           A. Summary 217
       V. Explanation Based on Hofstede's Brazil 220
      VI. Discussion 222
     VII. Implications 224
    VIII. Conclusion 225
      IX. References 226

12. **The Influence of Societal Culture on Corporate Culture,
    Business Strategy, and Performance in the International
    Airline Industry** **229**
    Durhane Wong-Rieger and Fritz Rieger

        I. Introduction 229
           A. Societal Culture 229
           B. Industry Culture 230
           C. Corporate Culture 231
           D. Societal Culture Configuration Model 231
       II. Study 1—Field Research 234
           A. Method 234
           B. Results and Discussion 235
      III. Study 2—Quantitative Analysis 238
           A. Clustering Analysis 238
           B. Industry Performance Analysis 240
           C. Size, Operating Strategies, and Performance 241
           D. Determinants of Performance 250

      E. Corporate Culture 256
  IV. Implications and Conclusions 263
   V. References 264

PART V. CONCLUSION

13. **Organizational Effectiveness and Its Attainment: A
     Cultural Perspective** 269

Uma Sekaran and Coral R. Snodgrass

    I. A Brief Review of Organizational Effectiveness
       Literature 270
   II. The Cultural Relativity of Organizational Effectiveness 273
  III. Hofstede's Cultural Dimensions: Organizational
       Effectiveness (OE) and Integrating Systems (IS) 275
       A. Masculinity–Femininity 275
       B. Individualism–Collectivism 276
       C. Power Distance 276
       D. Uncertainty Avoidance 276
       E. OE and the Masculinity–Femininity Dimension ... 277
       F. Integrating Structures and the Other Three
          Cultural Dimensions 277
   IV. Cultural Dimensions and OE Connections 280
       A. Organizations in the Masculine–Individualism
          Quadrant 280
       B. Organizations in the Feminine–Individualism
          Quadrant 282
       C. Masculine-Collectivistic Organizations 282
       D. Feminine-Collectivistic Organizations 282
    V. Does Such a Theory Hold Water?—A Preliminary
       Test of the Model 283
       A. Yugoslovia 284
       B. Sweden 285
       C. The United States 286
       D. Japan 286
   VI. Implications 287
       A. A Word of Caution regarding Managerial
          Implications 288
       B. Implications for Research 289
  VII. Conclusion 289
 VIII. References 290

**14. Organizational Science in a Global Environment: Future
 Directions**   293

 Richard M. Steers

    I. Prologue   293
   II. Culture as an Explanatory Variable in Organizational
     Science   296
      A. Culture and Problem Identification   296
      B. Culture and Approaches to Problem-Solving   298
      C. Culture and Problem Resolution   299
  III. A Proposed Agenda for Internationalizing
     Organizational Science   300
  IV. Concluding Remarks   303
   V. References   304

Bibliography   305

About the Authors   327

Index   335

Organizational
Science Abroad

I
INTRODUCTION

1

The Myth of Universality in Transnational Organizational Science

Chimezie A. B. Osigweh, Yg.

The purpose of this chapter is to examine, from a transnational perspective, the universality myth in applied organizational science. Accordingly, the first section considers the notion of organizational science in a transnational business environment. The second explores the concept of myth and the meaningfulness of any knowledge underpinned by it in organizational science. The third focuses on the myth of universality in organizational science, in general, and transnational organizational science, in particular. The fourth section uses the parochial-ethnocentric management context to illustrate the challenge of the universality myth in transnational organizational science. The fifth presents some of the emerging issues and perspectives reflected by this chapter and detailed by the other chapters in this volume. A summary follows as the final section of the chapter. Throughout, the discussion points to, or focuses on, important research and practice issues, perspectives, and implications for management in the international, cross-cultural, multicultural world of organizations.

Chimezie A. B. Osigweh, Yg. • Department of Management, School of Business, Norfolk State University, Norfolk, Virginia 23504.

I. ORGANIZATIONAL SCIENCE IN A TRANSNATIONAL BUSINESS WORLD

Like human beings in any other facet of life, managers in organizations have specific sets of preferences, assumptions, beliefs, or values to which they subscribe (Adler & Jalinek, 1986; Guth & Tagiuri, 1965; Kets de Vries & Miller, 1986; Locke, 1976; Maruyama, 1961, 1984; Mendenhall & Oddou, 1986; Schein, 1985; Zaleznik & Kets de Vries, 1980). These values provide premises that nurture the managers' ideas on how to effectively seek attainment of the organization's objectives. With time, the various value premises, and the specific ideas associated with them, are translated into: (1) particular systems of values, behaviors, policies, and practices that may alter or reinforce the original ideas, and (2) sets of practice-related performance or behavioral expectations that may, in turn, change or reinforce the existing policies. This complex process of interaction among ideas originating from the managers' immediate (local/domestic) environment results in certain preferred ways of achieving organizational objectives through other people and through the application of the available knowledge base. The meaningful body of knowledge emerging, in some organized fashion, from this complex interaction process is what we variously describe as management, organizational behavior and theory, or organizational science (Miner, 1984, p. 296; see also Blunt, 1983, pp. 2–3; Negandhi, 1983, p. 19; Osigweh, 1985b, pp. 4, 105). Experts have traditionally examined, refined, and conceptualized this body of knowledge to provide useful research and practice insights for improving how organizations are managed within the domestic business context.

With the emergence of big business and global commerce as a contemporary economic phenomenon (see, e.g., Barnet & Müller, 1974; Osigweh, 1985a), more and more firms are confronted with issues of managing organizations internationally, given the rising eminence of transnational interactions. If transnational interaction is defined as "the movement of tangible or intangible items across state boundaries when at least one actor is not an agent of a government or an intergovernmental organization" (Nye & Keohane, 1971, p. xii; Rosenberg, 1967), it becomes more obvious why a transnational perspective on managing organizations within the broadening international business horizon is of some significance. Consider that "tangible or intangible" items can include commodities or services to which monetary value can be attached, such as money itself, goods, information, ideas, or expertise regarding how these can be effectively managed in organizations to efficiently produce additional tangible and intangible items. This suggests that the dramatic growth of international business relations that began soon after

World War II can be better understood in terms of three underpinning occurrences.

First is the enormous intangible exchange in ideas, information, expertise, and cultural horizons, as industry transcends geography and the world becomes more integrated geographically and economically (see, e.g., Kobrin, 1984; Kumar, 1979; Samiee, 1984). This occurrence, as well as those described later, have been heralded by the growing innovations in communication, information processing, transportation, and other technologies to which individuals are exposed worldwide; these have jointly reduced spatial and temporal distances almost to a vanishing point. Second is the tremendous growth of international nongovernmental organizations. About 3,000 nonprofit, international nongovernmental organizations were recorded in 1971, whereas only 1,012 existed in 1954 (Skjelbaek, 1971). The magnitude of increase in the number of profit-making international business organizations (e.g., multinational corporations) is estimated at a much higher level for the same period, in the absence of comprehensive data to that effect, considering that there were more than 4,289 U.S. international companies in 1976 (U.S. Department of Commerce, August 1977, p. 39). The activities of these profit and nonprofit organizations range from mining, cultural exchange, and information sharing, to manufacturing, wholesaling/ retailing, and legalistic and technological regulation. They span every conceivable field, from commerce and industry to medicine, religion, agriculture, sports, education, and transportation. Examples are Exxon and the Royal Dutsch/Shell Group (energy), Anaconda (mining), Mitsubishi Corporation (wholesaling), Sears Roebuck (retailing), International Business Machines (IBM), the World Federation of Trade Unions (WFTU), International Olympic Committee (IOC), World Council of Churches (WCC), International Commission of Jurists (ICJ), and the International Air Transport Association (IATA). Within the institutional frameworks provided by these organizations, individuals in one country are able to share ideas with others in different countries, in ways that transcend or even defy national boundaries. Third, and perhaps the most widely noticed occurrence deals with tangible items. These are strictly economic goods and services possessing precisely determinable monetary values (Morse, 1971). They include major economic indicators of internationalization such as foreign direct investment, international sales, and profits earned abroad (Adler, 1984; Kobrin, 1984). For example, it has long been recognized—at least, since 1780 when Jeremy Bentham first coined the term *international*—that the economies of most countries of the world are no longer strictly domestic (see, e.g., Osigweh, 1983); this is even more so today. Direct investment abroad by U.S.

companies increased about 14 times from $11.8 billion to $168 billion between 1950 and 1978 (Eiteman & Stonehill, 1979, p. 12; U.S. Department of Commerce, August 1979, p. 56), and may be currently estimated at around $250 billion. Exports as a percentage of the U.S. gross national product (GNP) increased from 4.8% to 9.6% between 1960 and 1981 (International Monetary Fund, 1982; Kobrin, 1984). Sales by majority-owned overseas subsidiaries of U.S. corporations increased to over $450 billion in 1975 from $100 billion in 1966 (Adler, 1984, p. 36; U.S. Department of Commerce, February 1977, p. 29). Other countries are, like the United States, expanding their business activities abroad. For example, direct investment in the United States by foreign companies increased from $26.5 billion in 1974 and $40 billion in 1978 to over $100 billion in 1983 (Eiteman & Stonehill, 1979, p. 15; U.S. Department of Commerce, August 1979, p. 56; October 1984, p. 38).

These three occurrences point to the fact that underlying the transnational perspective is the premise that "international" business interactions go beyond the simplistic "inter-*nationes*" interpretation (i.e., transactions only between and among countries). They include interactions that may be nonterritorial, nongovernmental, subnational, local, interpersonal, or organizational and may involve the exchange of techniques, commodities, services, and data-based information (Osigweh, 1983). Today, leaders of big business organizations, themselves individuals from the corporate homes of the businesses, are frequently involved with other individuals of diverse backgrounds in political-economic and sociocultural systems quite different from their own. The organizational decisions they make may, for instance, follow interaction patterns that: (1) transcend national boundaries (e.g., a policy decision affecting a foreign subsidiary made by an executive in the home office) or (2) may be localized within the host country (e.g., a policy decision made by an expatriate manager transferred from the home office to run the overseas subsidiary). This additionally underscores that the transnational perspective covers the areas variously known as international, cross-cultural, cross-national, or comparative management. Thus, *transnational organizational science* as a term suggests that products of organizational research can be generated in one or more countries but adapted, modified, or simply applied elsewhere in one or more other countries, beyond the borders of the country(ies) where the research-based knowledge was originated. Accordingly, the focus here is on issues dealing with the prevalent practice of developing and testing management/organizational theory, research, and practice in one country (e.g., Japan) and applying the resulting body of knowledge—or more precisely, (pre)determining its applicability—elsewhere in one or more nonindigenous settings (e.g., Argentina or the United States). Because the United States has historically led the way in the development of organizational science knowledge (see, e.g., Adler, 1983; George, 1972; Osigweh, 1985b; Wren, 1979), this work treats organizational science as a predominantly American construction—except where it is specified otherwise.

This suggests that the advantages of the conceptual and applications-oriented advances in traditional, domestic-based, predominantly American organizational science needs to be extended or made available to firms operating in the global, transnational environment (see, e.g., Brossard & Maurice, 1976; Child, 1981; Neganchi, 1983), while addressing and taking into practical consideration the problems and concerns of such an endeavor. For if, at a minimum, organizational science research is to remain relevant to managers "and not become an ivory tower aside" (Adler, 1983, p. 231), it must begin to substantially include work that goes beyond the purely domestic perspective. It must also begin to address transnational problems and issues, because there are major impacts of culture (viewed in terms of social, political, economic, technological, demographical, and environmental heritage and location) on how individuals and groups work within organizations across countries (Brossard & Maurice, 1976; Child, 1981; Hofstede, 1983, 1980). Understanding these will help separate myth from practical reality in organizational science.

II. MYTH AND MEANING: ON THE ROLE OF MYTH IN ORGANIZATIONAL SCIENCE

Applied organizational science deals with the management of meaning (Culbert & McDonough, 1980; Dowling, 1978; Frost, 1985; Gray, Bougon, & Donnellon, 1985; Smircich & Morgan, 1982). This recognition cues researchers and practitioners to the view that happenings in organizational settings cannot be understood without recognizing the symbolic nature of organizations and the meanings underpinned by that nature. It further acknowledges that much that is of importance, in terms of management's understanding of the attitudes and actions of persons within organizations, is found in the shared or conflictual meanings created, questioned, and maintained within the organizations. Of course, management itself participates to originate, change, or sustain any symbolism that may be said to mean something. Indeed, as a primary responsibility, organizations and their leaders (or managers) must serve as shapers of meaning for organizational participants. This was noted long ago by Chester I. Barnard (1938), the influential American executive, author, and management pioneer (see also, Osigweh, 1987; Peters & Waterman, 1982; Scott, 1982; Smircich, 1983).

The centrality of myth to the notion of meaning has been explicity or implicity documented (Benson, 1983; Cummings, 1983; Mitroff, 1983; Osigweh, 1988; Pondy, 1978; Scott, 1985). Meaning is sought in organizational contexts by generating symbolic constructions (Gray *et al.*, 1985; Pondy, 1978; Schwartz, 1985) or, simply, *myths* (Mintzberg, 1975; Peters & Waterman, 1982; Schwartz, 1985; Scott & Mitchell, 1986) that provide for all persons accepting the myth, a basis for self-confident action. Knowledge underpinned by myth, thus, provides a framework for meaningful action. It is in this respect that myths are both important and, as some experts would argue (see, e.g., Becker, 1971; Schwartz, 1985), quite necessary in the social construction of organizational reality.

It may be useful, at this point, to distinguish between two ways in which socially constructed organizational reality may be said to "mean" something, as a prelude to differentiating two meanings of myth. Gray *et al.* (1985, pp. 84–88) would describe these in terms of conceptual and valuative meaning, what we would refer to as "cognitive meaning" and "evocative meaning" (using Schwartz's, 1985, more descriptive terminology). Within the cognitive orientation, the meaning of reality is understood from the standpoint of the world of fact—that is, by differentiating actual experiences and assigning meanings to empirical facts. The "reality" that is constructed is one of fact, not values or judgmental dispositions. Within the evocative orientation, the emphasis is on the world of values (Pfeffer, 1982; Schwartz, 1985). Meaning is viewed in terms of affective behavior and the strength of responses evoked evoked by symbols and implicit beliefs (Epstein, 1979). The constructed "reality" flows from a process of valuing in which "judgements of value give meaning to judgements of reality" (Vickers, 1965, p. 40).

The foregoing distinction suggests that myths in organizational science have cognitive and evocative meanings. If myths had only cognitive meanings, they could be treated with precision in specific situations; they could be objects of dispassionate reflection, and we could apply them as if they were theories of science. They could be precisely compared, and objectively so, with a view to discovering their merits and demerits in various specific environments. Admittedly, we sometimes do compare myths, but not with cognitive dispassion. For example, we compare one Third World country's myths with another's concerning how a shifting away from capitalism to Marxism will assuredly achieve economic progress and somehow solve all, or at least, most of the country's organizational and management problems; we do this while holding dear to our own myths. Or, we compare the Lilliputian's myths of size with those of the Trojans, if any such myths exist. However, we hardly do this with our own myths—because the symbolic system that guides our own self-confident action is not easily given to this cognitive dispassion. Its meaning is evocative. Thus because someone else's national anthem has no evocative meaning for us, it is simply a piece of music. Of course, ours, with its affective or valuative meaning, is "a call very dear to the heart!"

This suggests that the evocative meaning of myth is a desperate claim to being fundamental, infinite, immortal, powerful, et cetera, et cetera, by virtue of being a unique or vital kind, whose essentiality and power is indeed what is being posited by the myth. The despair results from the fact that myths are "vehicles of repression" or "instruments of denial" (Becker, 1971; Schwartz, 1985). They repress other ideas and (even) meaningful knowledge by simply denying them. Their evocative meaning and vitality derive from denying that which they deny. Hence, the act of denial (e.g., of truths or falsehoods, of the unsound or the fictional) cannot be part of the cognitive meaning of myths. ("[T]hat would be to assert what is denied; and it was precisely to deny what is denied that the myth was started" [Schwartz, 1958, p. 35]). In an implicit way, therefore, myths in transnational organizational science challenge us to unearth and confront the experiential world of fact (i.e., within the cognitive meaning). They exist that the brave among us may demystify and demythologize them. But this challenge is only apparent after we first succeed in recognizing a myth as what it is (within the evocative meaning).

Thus the significance of myths and the meaningfulness of the knowledge they substantiate cannot be realized without understanding that the first truth about a myth is that it is a myth, a self-deception, and that what myths are intended to conceal need to be understood in order to demythologize the sphere of knowledge. Demythologizing organizational myths by recognizing and understanding their existence helps destroy their capacity for being taken as facts they are not.

III. THE UNIVERSALITY MYTH IN TRANSNATIONAL ORGANIZATIONAL SCIENCE

The traditional belief in the universality of organizational science precepts can be quite misleading, especially in a transnational context. Indeed, that this belief is a myth has been widely suggested (see, e.g., England, 1975; Hofstede, 1980, 1983, 1984; Laurent, 1983; Mintzberg,

1975; Sethi, Namiki, & Swanson, 1984; Steele, 1976; Triandis, Malpas, & Davidson, 1973). Yet its pervasiveness in applied organizational science is unmistakable (Adler, 1983; Adler & Jalinek, 1986; Barrett & Bass, 1976; Carroll & Grillen, 1987; Haire, Ghiselli, & Porter, 1966; Hemphill, 1959; Lau, Newman, & Broedling, 1980; Mahoney, Jerdee, & Carroll, 1965; Miner, 1982, 1984; Negandhi, 1983; Roberts, 1970; Sekeran, 1981). Apparently, old paradigms never die (Osigweh, 1983, p. 19). And myths never easily relinquish power, but dare the brave to dismantle them.

The modern history of the universality myth may be traced back to 1916 when Henri Fayol, the French industrialist and management pioneer, published his seminal work on general management (see Fayol, 1916/1949; also Fayol, 1937). Fayol believed that management activity is common to all human undertakings and involves the performance of a finite set of activities, which he defined as the basic elements or fundamental functions that "[e]veryone has a greater or lesser need for" (quotation translated and cited by Breeze, 1985, p. 47). He further propagated his belief in the universal applicability of management precepts by offering 14 "general" principles of administration meant to serve as guideposts for managers—to show them the "indispensable" ways of performing the basic management functions (Fayol, 1916/1949, pp. 19–41; see also, George, 1972; Osigweh, 1985b; Wren, 1979).

Although Fayol's teachings flowered only briefly in Europe and North America during the 1920s and 1930s (due partly to the limited distribution of his book, the popularity of Frederick Taylor's scientific management movement, and to the onset of World War II), a number of developments continued to cultivate ideas concerning the universality of management theory and practice. In France, some followers, particularly Joseph Carlioz, the junior Henri Fayol, Antonin Franchet, Leon Franchet, and Henry Verney, published major works sustaining Fayol's ideas (see Breeze, 1985). These individuals proceeded from a basic premise epitomized by Carlioz's underlying theme: that management "involves a small number of functions that are recognizable everywhere" (translated and quoted by Breeze, 1985, p. 50). In the United States, leading management scholars and practitioners (e.g., Davis, 1928, 1935; Gulick, 1937; Mooney & Reiley, 1931) were paying increased attention to the emerging focus on "managerial functionalism," concerned with distinguishing the various kinds of duties performed by managers everywhere. For example, Ralph C. Davis, the Ohio State University professor who was the first American to clearly express the functional tenets of management (he could not read French and was not familiar with Fayol's work—Osigweh, 1985b) proposed the distinctive functions of planning, organizing, and controlling (see Davis, 1935, pp. 12–13).

Two years later, Luther Gulick (1937 p. 13) offered his POSDCORB, an acronym that stood for planning, organizing, staffing, directing, coordination, reporting, and budgeting. This early management argot became instantly famous, to the extent that if you asked a manager or business student to describe the manager's functions in the 1940s and early to mid-1950s, he or she would have been most likely to respond by the simple statement: POSDCORB.

The publication of Constance Storr's English translation of Fayol's (1916/1949) work made it more readily available in North America and thus stimulated additional interest (among traditional organization and management/organization theory departments) in the process of organizational management, particularly in the United States, during the 1950s and 1960s. Many books appeared, preaching the universality of principles and techniques of managing organizations (e.g., Davis, 1951; Elliott, 1959; Koontz & O'Donnell, 1955; Newman, 1951, Terry, 1953; Urwick, 1952). This period (1950s and 1960s) also corresponds to the decades during which large-scale transnational studies on organizational functioning were conducted at four major universities—M.I.T., Chicago, California, and Princeton—resulting in the initial efforts that extended traditional organizational theory into the areas of comparative/cross-cultural management (Harbison & Meyers, 1959; Negandhi, 1975, 1983).

These transnational organizational science studies followed what may be described in terms of three interrelated research and practice directions. First, an economic development emphasis (Farmer & Richman, 1965; Harbison & Myers, 1959; Narain, 1967; Negandhi & Prasad, 1971; see also Osigweh, 1985a) was oriented toward indentifying and noting the importance of management inputs and development trends (e.g., managerial techniques, practices, methods) that are significant in helping underdeveloped nations achieve rapid industrialization. Second, an environmental orientation (Farmer & Richman, 1965; Schöllhammer, 1969) investigated management effectiveness and practice in the context of impinging environmental (legal, social, political, cultural) variables. Third, a behavioral thrust (Davis, 1971; Haire, Ghiselli, & Porter, 1966; Ryterband & Barrett, 1970) focused on interrelationships between management practice and effectiveness and concepts such as beliefs, need hierarchies, value systems, and individual attitudes within specific cultures. By examining environmental, behavioral, and development variables, the practice of these three transnational organizational science approaches recognized the role of culture in the social, behavioral, and economic environments of organizations worldwide. Nevertheless, the approaches reflected the dominant belief of American schol-

ars (e.g., Negandhi & Estafen, 1965; Schöllhammer, 1969) in the
universality of organizational science precepts. Moreover, the widely
held belief in Europe was also that management was something universal in all cultural environments (Gonzalez & McMillan, 1961; Hofstede,
1980).

As a result, scholars and pracitioners resisted what they viewed as
the danger of "letting the environment crowd the comparative analysis," because the belief in the universality of management precepts created mental maps that urged researchers and organizational professionals "not to throw out the management baby with the environment
bath" (Boddewyn, 1966, p. 12). That is, it was widely believed that
universal management principles and techniques should be protected
from being smothered by blankets of social or cultural contexts. The
underlying argument (see, e.g., Farmer, 1968; Hofstede, 1980, 1983;
Negandhi & Prasad, 1971) was that sound management principles and
techniques existed irrespective of national or local environments. A local
or national practice that deviated from the principles or techniques
should be immediately realigned to them. If this process is sustained,
by applying sound universal organizational science percepts abroad,
societies will begin to "converge," looking more and more alike. Effective managment would result, producing organizational (economic) effi-
ciencies that would enable even the very poor countries of the world to
become as wealthy as the rich.

During the 1970s and 1980s, transnational organizational studies
have increasingly pointed to the fact that the universality thesis is too
obviously in conflict with the reality we see around us (England, 1975;
Hofstede, 1983; Laurent, 1983; Steele, 1976). The suggestion is that the
universality of an applied organizational science is a myth, as more and
more experts are asking questions such as, Are American organizational
concepts and measures transferable to other cultures? Is "organizational
culture" culture-bound? Is organizational development work (based on
American conceptions) truly possible in Europe? Does a universal model
of organization truly exist? (see, e.g., Adler & Jalinek, 1986; Brossard &
Maurice, 1976; Child, 1981; Laurent, 1983; Sekaran, 1981; Steele, 1976).
These suggest that, although the universality myth is still in power (see,
e.g., Adler, 1983; Barrett & Bass, 1976; Negandhi, 1983), there is an
increased and more pragmatic recognition that management needs to be
thoroughly sensitive to the local or national environment in which the
organization operates. This is because management reality is a social
construction of its particular cultural environment. As a result, its effectiveness cannot be separated from its environment. The difficulty for
applied organizational science stems from the fact that cultural dif-

ferences exist even within various localities or regions of a nation and only more so among countries or beyond national environments. In addition, other (non-American) nations seem to be increasingly developing their own management concepts and practices that may or may not be workable abroad (see, e.g., England, 1983; Ouchi, 1981; Sethi, Namiki, & Swanson, 1984). Thus a dilemma is confronted: *whether* or *not* to let the local environment check the application of organizational science in a transnational management context. The magnitude of the challenge underscored by this dilemma may be illustrated in the context of parochial and ethnocentric management studies.

IV. THE CHALLENGE ILLUSTRATED IN A PAROCHIAL-
ETHNOCENTRIC MANAGEMENT CONTEXT

A review of the major approaches for creating transnational organizational science knowledge (Adler, 1984) reveals that parochial studies constitute the most common approach. Studies of the United States conducted by Americans predominate. Ethocentric studies (e.g., those that attempt to replicate American-based management research elsewhere, in another country), constitute the second most common approach. These two approaches, the parochial and the ethnocentric, account for well beyond 80% of the available transnational organizational science knowledge (Adler, 1983). Hence our focus on them for illustrative purposes.

A study is produced within a parochial context if it is orginally designed, conducted, and applied in a particular culture, by researchers and pracitioners from that cultural environment, in the hope of transferring to other cultures the results of the study and its original applications. Studies of this nature assume universality, even if only implicitly, by neglecting other cultural environments in the belief that similarity pervades all of the world's industrialized cultures. But this belief is fictional. It cannot be concluded that all, or even any, studies conducted in one culture (e.g., the United States) is equally applicable to other cultures (e.g., Africa, Europe, Latin America, the Middle East, or the Orient) unless so proven. In effect, the local or cultural environment cannot be considered a constant in the process of attempting to produce transnational organizational science knowledge "within a 'black box' labelled 'management,' without much concern for the external environment in which the firm may operate" (Farmer & Richman, 1964, p. 56). Of course, there is no problem with this as long as the external environment is about the same for all firms. However, in cases where the environment differs significantly, the body of knowledge so produced will, in all likelihood, be grossly inadequate for explaining any comparative differentials in organizational or managerial effectiveness.

In short, most studies conducted in parochial contexts may be only applicable to their indigenous homes, to the culture in which the research was originally conducted. One reason for this is that the rules and requirements for successful or effective organizational management may differ so greatly across specific national and cultural boundaries as to render futile, or meaningless, any effort to generalize management precepts defined as "universal" by researchers in one culture (see, e.g., Berry, 1969; Lammars, 1976; Miller & Simonetti, 1974; Oberg, 1963). To simply confine management research to one cultural environment, in the contemporary transnational world of business, is to constrain the resulting management knowledge in both theory construction and practical application.

Turning now to the second most predominant approach for producing transnational organizational science knowledge, ethnocentric studies are those resulting in contexts in which research originally designed, conducted, and applied in a particular culture, by individuals from that culture, are subjected to replication in a second culture. Studies of this nature do not explicitly assume universality; they question it. Nevertheless, their general purpose is to extend the universality of specific sets of research results and their implications for organizational practice, inasmuch as their "interpretations are generally stated in terms of the second culture being *less* [or more] *than* the first culture" on some critical dimension (Adler, 1984, p. 40). These studies primarily search for similarities across cultures to validate any attempts to extend their theoretical frameworks to the second culture. They would essentially like to increase the predictive scope of their hypotheses, by extending to other cultures theories that can be applied in their own culture (Adler, 1984; Brislin, Lonner, & Thorndike, 1973).

In this spirit, ethnocentric studies address questions such as, Can researchers conclude that this theory may be extended to France, even though it was originally developed and applied in China? Is that theory culture-dependent, or is it culturally universal? Can managers use American home culture approaches (or approaches developed and applied in American settings) abroad? Is this American management theory workable in, say, Argentina? As a result of this orientation, factories owned communally in Yugoslovia can be used via ethnocentric research to test theories on stockholder corporations developed in North America (see, Triandis, 1968, 1972). The ethnocentric researcher is, in this way, able to incorporate patterns of behavior not present at home or to find in the

second culture treatments not available in the home culture. One problem is that the approach, when it uncovers differences, does not necessarily provide clues as to why such differences exist (see, e.g., Roberts,
1970). Rather, the differences are explained away as indicative of some
defect in research design. Another problem arises from the myopic scope
and too limiting nature of this approach. There is something quite stifling, something of a tunnel vision, about an orientation that mainly seeks
to address the management problems of today's transnational world of
business by simple asking if the indigenous way (i.e., if "our own way,"
if home country perspectives and approaches) will work overseas. Consider that only one country, the United States, has produced most of the
available organizational science knowledge. This suggests that the "indigenous way," in such a question, almost invariably translates to our
way, the "American way," in a business world where others (e.g., the
Arabs, Brazilians, Britons, Chinese, French, Germans, Russians, Tanza-
nians) are not only increasingly active participants but also possess
and are evolving their own principles, practices, and distinct rules of the
game. The underlying belief that management and organizational effectiveness abroad only requires a good track record in America or the
mastery of esoteric expertise prescribed and defined in the United States
(or in any other one particular country for that matter) is a myth—the
universality myth.

In sum, the vast part of contemporary organizational science knowledge is either explicit or implicit in the assumption that organizational
and management practices developed in one country can be extended
universally with similar results in organizational effectiveness. The se-
duction of this thesis cannot be understated. Even efforts that purport to
question it (e.g., those based on ethnocentric research) have also sought
mostly to extend the universality of their results. This poses a dilemma,
the challenge of which urges us to reexamine our perspectives on applying indigenous organizational science abroad. No doubt, the universality view is in power. Nevertheless, there is the unequivocal suggestion that the view is suspect and ought to be questioned. First,
organizational science scholars and practitioners are increasingly pointing to equifinality in the transnational development and application of
management precepts, in the sense that specific management objectives
can be achieved in many culturally distinct ways (Bennett, 1977; Negandhi, 1975). Second, there is increasing suggestion that the foreign application of organizational science should be based on cultural relativity—or on the understanding that no cultural lense or practical
approach is necessarily better than any other (see, e.g., Hofstede, 1980,
1983, 1984). It is within this background that the current work focuses on

issues emphasizing some of the various constraints and perspectives on applying organizational science abroad.

V. THE ISSUES AND PERSPECTIVES

As argued, organizational research and practice worldwide have continued to rely primarily on American concepts and theories. Although this reliance has been successful in some cases, there is also some evidence of weakening competitiveness (see, e.g., Ricks, 1983) or lessened effectiveness among organizations that have seemingly not seriously recognized the universality myth and, therefore, have not vigorously adapted to the cultural traditions of their host countries. This suggests much caveat about applying indigenous organizational science abroad. Nancy J. Adler, Robert Doktor, and S. Gordon Redding carry forth the introductory analysis provided by Chapter 1 in this regard. They emphasize the impact of cultural diversity and the cognitive aspects of culture on international organizational behavior. These scholars review the development of comparative and cross-cultural management, identifying five major issues confronted by each approach. Included are issues of cross-cultural variance, cultural determination, worldwide organizational and sociocultural convergence/divergence, intercultural interaction, and using cultural diversity for synergistic organizational purposes. Discussion of these issues provides a backdrop that substantiates the Occidental heritage of transnational organizational science, while documenting the emergence and increasing evidence of at least one other organizational science tradition, which is more Oriental in its perspective.

A. Insights and Perspectives from Europe

To simply say that transnational organizational science has an Occidental history may unintentionally understate, or even blur, the fact that prior to the 1970s, much of Europe's organizational and management research and practice came across the Atlantic, from the United States. Indeed, it was not until the mid-1970s that it became increasingly obvious that many of the American organizational science precepts were irrelevant to the problems and concerns of European managerial and organizational life. Cary L. Cooper and Charles J. Cox explore the irrelevance of American organizational science to the United Kingdom, in particular, and to other countries of (Western) Europe in general. These scholars conclude, in part, that the apparent failure of American organizational science in Europe is not due to any proven ineffectiveness of the concepts, principles, and theories, but is the result of local (European) resistance stemming from significant cultural differences and traditions. Based on the analysis of data obtained primarily from Eastern Europe (Poland, Czechoslovakia, Hungary, U.S.S.R., and Cuba), Wiktor Askanas adds some dimensions to the argument by Cooper and Cox by examining the failure of management techniques in centrally planned economies. He defines a number of specific American organizational science techniques and explores why they have failed in central planning economies. The failure, suggests Askanas, is largely traced to an ideological heritage that warrants inadvertent inverse interpretations of the "imported" organizational science ideas, while occasioning cultural resistance to the management techniques.

Rolf E. Rogers and William Aussieker examine labor–management relations and codetermination in West German and American firms, thus focusing on human resource strategies, particularly worker participation in organizational decision-making. They find strong differences in West German and American practices, which they explain in terms of specific cultural attitudes and sociopolitical concerns. Their exploratory case study further illustrates, in a concrete way, the "failure" underpinned by Askanas, and Cooper and Cox, tracing it to constraints deriving from different and specific patterns of development and environmental conditions. Richard C. Hoffman and W. Harvey Hegarty focus on convergence and divergence issues while providing a study of scanning and planning procedures, using 505 top managers in the United States and nine Western European countries including France, the United Kingdom, West Germany, Switzerland, the Netherlands, Sweden, Denmark, Norway, and Finland. Unlike Askanas and Rogers and Aussieker, these scholars find strong similarities between the American and European countries and also among the European countries themselves. Where differences exist, the study explains them in terms of specific organizational practices rather than by environmental context (national culture). The study also seems to support the suggestion by Cooper and Cox that where American organizational science has failed in Europe, it is due to reasons other than any proven ineffectiveness of particular (American) concepts or theories—such as the immediate application of the transferred precepts, without necessary conceptual modification or appropriate adaptation to the corporate/local culture.

B. Insights and Perspectives from Asia

The emergence of various Asian perspectives is becoming more obvious, as transnational organizational science reveals what can be described as symptoms of a gradual movement from the Atlantic to the Pacific century (see Chapter 2). Yet it is important to note that Asian organizational theory and practice, like those of Europe, had been traditionally American or "Western," but have grown more and more distinctively Oriental as they become modified and infused with various distinctive conceptions of the Asian spirit. Thus, Schon L. Beechler and Vladimir Pucik view organizational science in Japan as a unique and complex, if curious, mixture of American (or "Western") concepts and Japanese essence. These scholars review the flow of ideas about management and organizations between the United States and Japan, focusing on the differences in the diffusion patterns over time and across different classes of adopters. They illustrate the principal stages in the diffusion of the imported American organizational theories in Japan, and examine their linkage to (1) transformations of socioeconomic conditions, (2) changes of economic priorities on micro- and macrolevels, and (3) changes in interests and needs of any distinct (e.g., Japanese) approach to (the traditional American-originated) organizational theory. Two related experiments by Jeremiah J. Sullivan, Teruhiko Suzuki, and Yasumasa Kondo identify the theory of group functioning held by Japanese and American managers. Some specific similarities and dissimilarities were found by the experiments. For example, the results suggest that both American and Japanese managers have a similar theory of performance control as a rational process that focuses on the individual rather than the group. Managers in both cultures approach the performance control process in terms of the rational-man model of organizational behavior. Furthermore, when both sets of managers violate parts of the rational-man model, they do so in a similar manner, employing the fundamental attribution error. Japanese managers demonstrate only a modest commitment to the social group model often used to characterize their attitudes and behavior. However, Japanese and American managers do differ in their theories concerning the function of work groups in the performance control process.

Many experts will agree that China is the neglected Asian giant in transnational organizational science literature. Rosalie L. Tung examines the role of various economic, sociopolitical, and cultural variables as constraints on the management of industrial organizations in the People's Republic of China. In the process, she discusses several facets of organizational processes and management practices in China, paying particular attention to some similarities and differences between Chinese enterprise management and the predominantly American-based Western organizational science. Dexter Dunphy and Jeannette Shi explore the basic underlying value similarities and dissimilarities between

Japan and the People's Republic of China (PRC), arguing that organizations and their managers must ultimately reflect and express the prevailing values of the cultural context in which they operate. They show that shared value assumptions support similar enterprise practices in the two countries, whereas value differences underline some of the striking dissimilarities in organizational practices and productivity. These scholars conclude that Japan and the PRC are very close on the key value dimensions that divide East Asian countries from Western countries and that they represent a distinctive subset of an East Asian cultural cluster. Although they are closer to Western values than other East Asian countries, Dunphy and Shi further conclude that both countries are developing distinctively East Asian management designs that may be, at least, as viable as designs based on Western organizational science in supporting the future economic and enterprise development of technologically sophisticated societies.

C. Other Specific Insights and Perspectives

Additional evidence from other continents, such as Peter Blunt's (1983) investigation of organizational theory and behavior in some African countries, also reveals that a growing number of management designs or practices different from U.S.-based conceptions are steadily, if slowly, emerging in other cultures of the world. Kim Cameron, Myung Kim, and Sarah Freeman take us to Latin America for further insight in this regard. These scholars study organizational theories and practices in Brazil, with particular attention to the organizations constituting the Brazilian system of higher education. They find that the basic frameworks of many organizational science theories developed in the United States seem to apply to institutions in Brazil's higher education system. However, the specific organizational variables, applications, and relationships within those frameworks are inapplicable in Brazil. Their analysis identifies 10 characteristics that appear to contradict commonly accepted, United States-based organizational theories. For example, Brazilian characteristics such as the political process surrounding decision making and those relating to the centralization and formalization of the system appear to stand at variance with common organizational science theories of motivation, distributive justice, and the contingency theories of organizational design. Furthermore, the study finds that the Brazilian higher education institutions are very effective organizations within their own environment. They are at least as effective as their United States counterparts even though many of their practices are contradictory to traditional U.S.-based organizational science precepts and management designs thought to be universally applicable.

Two related studies by Durhane Wong-Rieger and Fritz Rieger produce some complementary results. These researchers investigate the interrelationships among societal culture, corporate culture, business strategy, and performance, using international airlines from 35 countries. The findings suggest that societal, regional, or local/domestic culture as well as industry culture have a significant influence on the organization's strategies but not on the effectiveness of its functioning in the external international arena. Viewed in conjunction with the results of the study by Cameron, Kim, and Freeman, this finding further suggests that societal culture primarily influences organizational and management effectiveness within its local environment. In essence, the effectiveness of organizational approaches is culturally specific, in the sense that effectiveness can only be viewed relative to performance in the particular cultural setting.

D. Conclusion

Altogether, the pieces of work collected in this volume point to the fact that with the internationalization of business and industry and the globalization of competition, a culturally relative approach to understanding the concept of organizational effectiveness and the means by which it can be attained has become both desirable and imperative. Such an understanding will not only aid managers of multinational and transnational corporations to manage more effectively but will also enable researchers to engage in fruitful hypothesis testing in this area. The underlying premise is that an overriding object of organizational science is to generate conceptual, theoretical, and applied knowledge, as a vehicle for improving organizational performance through effective managerial practices.

Uma Sekaran and Coral R. Snodgrass help address this objective by developing a conceptual scheme for defining and attaining organizational effectiveness, using the four cultural dimensions empirically established by Geert Hofstede (1980). The usefulness of the four Hofstede dimensions is examined, whereas his classification of countries across the four cultural dimensions is also compared to other available classification schemes. The applicability of the resulting Sekaran–Snodgrass model is demonstrated by examining four different countries, which lie along the four different cultural quadrants delineated by Hofstede, and on which published data are available.

Following the general and specific contours of this book, Richard M. Steers makes a final case for a better understanding of culture and cultural variations as they relate to organizations at work. Certainly, because of the centrality of this variable in managerial problem identification and problem-solving, culture permeates most, if not all, aspects of organizational behavior. In addition, Steers suggests a future agenda, focusing on how we might change the ways we conduct research in organizational settings. His underlying intent is to facilitate increased efforts to incorporate the international dimension into future organizational research.

VI. SUMMARY

The task of this chapter was to examine the myth of universality in an applied transnational organizational science context. Organizational science deals with the systematic body of knowledge involving certain preferred, or meaningful, ways of achieving organizational objectives through other people and through the utilization of the available base of knowledge. The transnational perspective recognizes that results of organizational research and experience in one or more countries may be simply adopted or modified for application in any other country or countries beyond the national boundaries where they originated. It incorporates the areas of management and organizational studies variously described as comparative, cross-national, international, or cross-cultural. Because applied organizational science deals with the management of meaning (e.g., meaningful performance and effectiveness), our transnational perspective acknowledges the importance, for management, of understanding the culture-based attitudes and actions of persons within organizations. Much that is important in the nature of these attitudes and actions is rooted in the shared or conflicting meanings created, questioned, and maintained by the organization and its local culture.

Myths are symbolic constructions by which organizations underpin meaning. They provide a basis for meaningful organizational action. Yet they are self-deceptive by their very nature. They construct reality by building upon the evocative meaning of meaning. This way, they effectively conceal that which they conceal, while daring the brave among us to demystify them within the cognitive meaning of reality. If, as argued, cognitive meaning is reflective of the world of scientific fact, then myths exist in organizational science in general and transnational organizational science in particular so that they may be demystified through the pursuit of cognitive meaning. Once demythologized, by recognizing and understanding their existence as what they are, the capacity of the myths for being taken as the facts they are not is destroyed. This, in an applied organizational context, translates to more meaningful performance, improved productivity, or to the effective management of organizational phenomena.

It is within this background that the origins, nature, and challenge of the universality myth in transnational organizational science is explored, and a dilemma posed by the myth is identified. The magnitude of the challenge underpinned by the dilemma is illustrated in the context of parochial and ethnocentric management studies.

Finally, a general assessment of this volume is presented, and the various issues and perspectives being offered are spotlighted. The relationships among the various parts are highlighted, with brief reviews of chapters included.

VII. REFERENCES

Adler, N. J. (1983c). Cross-cultural management research: The ostrich and the trend. *Academy of Management Review, 8*(2), 226–232.
Adler, N. J. (1984). Understanding the ways of understanding: Cross-cultural management methodology reviewed, In R. N. Farmer (Ed.), *Advances in international comparative management: A research annual* (Vol. 1, pp. 31–67). Greenwich, CT: JAI Press
Adler, N. J. (1986). *International dimensions of organizational behavior.* Boston: Kent Publishing.
Adler, N.J., & Jalinek, M. (1986, Spring). Is "organizational culture" culture bound? *Human Resource Management, 25*(1), 73–90.
Barnard, C. I. (1938). *The functions of the executive.* Cambridge, MA: Harvard University Press.
Barnet, R.J., & Müller, R. E. (1974). *Global reach: The power of the multinational corporations.* New York: Simon and Schuster.
Barrett, G. V., & Bass, B. M. (1976). Cross-cultural issues in industrial and organizational psychology. In M. D. Dunnette (Ed.), *Handbook of industrial and organizational psychology* (pp. 1639–1686). New York: Rand McNally.
Becker, E. (1971). *The birth and death of meaning* (2nd ed.). New York: Free Press.
Bennett, M. (1977). Testing management theories cross-culturally. *Journal of Applied Psychology, 62*(5), 578–581.
Benson, J. K. (1983). Paradigm and praxis in organizational behavior. In L. L. Cummings & B. M. Staw (Eds.), *Research in organizational behavior* (Vol. 5, pp. 3–56). Greenwich, CT: JAI Press.
Berry, J. W. (1969). On cross-cultural comparability. *International Journal of Psychology, 4*, 119–128.
Blunt, P. (1983). *Organizational theory and behaviour.* New York: Longman Group, Ltd.
Boddewyn, J. (1966). *Comparative concepts in management administration and organization.* Mimeo, New York Graduate School of Business Administration.
Breeze J. D. (1985). Harvest from the archives: The search for Fayol and Carlioz. *Journal of Management, 11*(1), 43–54.
Brislin, R. W., Lonner, W. J., & Thorndike, R. M. (1973). *Cross-cultural research methods.* New York: Plenum Press.
Brossard, M., & Maurice, M. (1976). Is there a universal model of organization structure? *International Studies of Management and Organization, 6*(3), 11–45.

Carroll, S. J., & Gillen, D. J. (1987, January). Are the classical management functions useful in describing managerial work? *Academy of Management Review, 12*(1), 38–51.

Child, J. (1981). Culture, contingency and capitalism in the cross-national study of organizations. In L. L. Cummings & B. M. Staw (Eds.), *Research in organizational behavior,* (Vol. III, pp. 303–356). Greenwich, CT: JAI Press.

Culbert, S. A., & McDonough, J. J. (1980). *The invisible war: Pursuing self-interests at work.* New York: Wiley.

Cummings, L. L. (1983, October). The logics of management. *Academy of Management Review, 8*(4), 532–538.

Davis, R. C. (1928). *The principles of factory organization and management.* New York: Harper & Brothers.

Davis, R. C. (1935). *The principles of business organization and operation.* Columbus, OH: L. H. Hedrick.

Davis, R. C. (1951). *The fundamentals of top management.* New York: Harper & Brothers.

Davis, S. M. (1971). *Comparative management: Cultural and organizational perspectives.* Englewood Cliffs, NJ: Prentice-Hall.

Dowling, J. B. (1978). *Organizational legitimacy: The management of meaning.* Unpublished doctoral dissertation, Palo Alto, Stanford University.

Eitman, D. K. & Stonehill, A. I. (1979). *Multinational business finance.* Reading, MA: Addison-Wesley.

Elliott, O. (1959). *Men at the top.* New York: Harper & Brothers.

England, G. W. (1975). *The manager and his values: An international perspective from the USA, Japan, Korea, India and Australia.* Cambridge, MA: Ballinger.

England, G. W. (1983, Fall). Japanese and American management: Theory Z and beyond. *Journal of International Business Studies, 14*(2), 131–142.

Epstein, S. (1979). The ecological study of emotions in humans. In P. Pliner, K. R. Blankenstein, & I. M. Spigel (Eds.), *Advances in the study of communication and affect: Vol. 5. Perception of emotions in self and others* (pp. 47–247). New York: Plenum Press.

Farmer, R. N. (1968). *New directions in management information transfer.* Bloomington: Cedarwood Press.

Farmer, R. N., & Richman, B. M. (1964, Winter). A model for research in comparative management. *California Management Review, VII*(2), 55–68.

Farmer, R. N., & Richman, B. M. (1965). *Comparative management and economic progress.* Homewood, IL: Irwin.

Fayol, H. (1916/1949). *General and industrial management* (Constance Storrs, Trans.). London: Pitman.

Fayol, H. (1937). The administrative theory of state. (Sarah Greer, Trans.). In L. Gullick & L. Urwick (Eds.), *Papers on the science of administration.* New York: Institute of Public Administration, Columbia University.

Frost, P. J. (1985, Summer). Special issue on organizational symbolism: Introduction. *Journal of Management, 11* (2), 5–10.

George, C. S. (1972). *The history of management thought.* Englewood Cliffs, NJ: Prentice-Hall.

Gonzalez, R. F., & McMillan, C. (1961). The universality of American management philosophy. *Academy of Management Journal, 4* (1), 33–41.

Gray, B., Bougon, M. G., & Donnellon, A. (1985, Summer). Organizations as constructions and destructions of meaning. *Journal of Management, 11*(2), 83–98.

Gulick, L. H. (1937). Notes on the theory of organization. In L. H. Gulick & L. F. Urwick (Eds.), *Papers on the science of administration.* New York: Institute of Public Administration, Columbia University.

Guth, W. D., & Tagiuri, R. (1965, September-October). Personal values and corporate strategy. *Harvard Business Review,* 123–132.

Haire, M., Ghiselli, D. E., & Porter, L. W. (1966). *Managerial thinking: An international study.* New York: Wiley.

Harbison, F., & Meyers, C. (1959). *Management in the industrial world.* New York: McGraw-Hill.

Hemphill, J. K. (1959). Job descriptions for executives. *Harvard Business Review, 37*(3), 55–67.

Hofstede, G. (1980). *Culture's consequences: International differences in work related values.* Beverly Hills, CA: Sage Publications.

Hofstede, G. (1983, Fall). The cultural relativity of organizational practices and theories. *Journal of International Business Studies, 14*(2), 75–89.

Hofstede, G. (1984). The cultural relativity of the quality of life concept. *Academy of Management Review, 9*(3), 389–398.

International Monetary Fund. (1982). *International financial statistics yearbook.* Washington, DC: Author.

Kets de Vries, M. F. R., & Miller, D. (1986, April). Personality, culture, and organization. *Academy of Management Review, 11*(2), 266–279.

Kobrin, S. J. (1984). *International expertise in American business: How to learn to play with the kids on the street.* I. I. E. Report Number 6. New York: Institute of International Education.

Koontz, H., & O'Donnell, C. (1955). *Principles of management.* New York: McGraw-Hill.

Kumar, K. (1979). *Bonds without bondage: Explorations in transnational cultural interactions.* Honolulu: University Press of Hawaii.

Lammers, C. J. (1976). Towards the internationalization of the organizational sciences. In G. Hofstede & M. S. Kassem (Eds.), *European contributions to organization theory.* Assen, The Netherlands: Van Gorcum.

Lau, A. W., Newman, A. R., & Broedling, L. A. (1980). The nature of managerial work in the public sector. *Public Management Forum, 19,* 513–521.

Laurent, A. (1983). The cultural diversity of Western management conceptions. *International Studies of Management and Organization, XIII*(1-2), 75–76.

Locke, E. A. (1976). The nature and causes of job satisfaction. In M. D. Dunnette (Ed.), *Handbook of industrial and organizational psychology* (pp. 1297–1349). Chicago: Rand McNally.

Mahoney, T. A., Jerdee, T. H., & Carroll, S. J. (1965). The jobs of management. *Industrial Relations, 4,* 97–110.

Maruyama, M. (1961, First Quarter). The multilateral mutual causal relationships among the modes of communication, sociometric pattern and the intellectual orientation in the Danish culture. *Phylon: The Atlanta Review or Race and Culture,* 41–58.

Maruyama, M. (1984). Alternative concepts of management: Insights from Asia and Africa. *Asia Pacific Journal of Management, 1*(2), 100–111.

Mendenhall, M. E., & Oddou, G. (1986, September). The cognitive, psychological and social contexts of Japanese management. *Asia Pacific Journal of Management, 4*(1), 24–37.

Miller, S. W., & Simonetti, J. L. (1974). Culture and management: Some conceptual considerations. *Management International Review, VII*(6), 87–101.

Miner, J. B. (1982). *Theories of organizational structure and process.* Chicago: Dryden Press.

Miner, J. B. (1984). The validity and usefulness of theories in an emerging organizational science. *Academy of Management Review, 9*(2), 296–306.

Mintzberg, H. (1975, July-August). The manager's job: Folklore and fact. *Harvard Business Review,* 49–61.

Mitroff, I. (1983). *Stakeholders of the organizational mind.* San Francisco, CA: Jossey-Bass.

Mooney, J. D., & Reiley, A. C. (1931). *Onward industry!: The principles of organization and their significance to modern industry.* New York: Harper & Row.

Morse, E. L. (1971, Summer). Transnational economic processes. *International Organization, XXV*(3), 23–47.

Narain, D. (1967, March). Indian national character in the twentieth century. *Annals,* 124–132.

Negandhi, A. R. (1975, June). Comparative management and organization theory: A marriage needed. *Academy of Management Journal,* 334–344.

Negandhi, A. R. (1983). Cross-cultural management research: Trend and future directions. *Journal of International Business Studies, 14*(2), 17–28

Neghandhi, A. R., & Estafen, B. D. (1965). A research model to determine the applicability of American management know-how in different cultures and/or environments. *Academy of Management Journal, 8,* 309–318.

Negandhi, A. R., & Prasad, S. B. (1971). *Comparative management.* New York: Appleton-Century-Crofts.

Newman, W. H. (1951). *Administrative action: The techniques of organization and management.* New York: Prentice-Hall.

Nye, J. S., & Keohane, R. O. (1971). Transnational relations and world politics: An introduction. In R. O. Keohane & J. S. Nye, Jr. (Eds.), *Transnational relations and world politics* (pp. ix–xxix). Cambridge, MA: Harvard University Press.

Oberg, W. (1963). Cross-cultural perspective on management principles. *Academy of Management Journal, 6*(2), 129–143.

Osigweh, C. A. B. (1983). *Improving problem-solving participation: The case of local transnational voluntary organizations.* Lanham, MD: University Press of America.

Osigweh, C. A. B. (1985a, December). International business and the growth model. *Journal of Economic Development, 10*(2), 123–142.

Osigweh, C. A. B. (1985b). *Professional management: An evolutionary perspective.* Dubuque: Kendall/Hunt Division of W. C. Brown Co.

Osigweh, C. A. B. (1987). *Management as if rights mattered: The challenge of employee rights and management responsibilities.* Working paper, Norfolk, VA: Norfolk State University School of Business. Presented to the First Industrial Congress of the Americas, Quebec, Canada, August 21–27, 1988.

Osigweh, C. A. B. (1988). The challenge of responsibilities: Confronting the revolution in workplace rights in modern organizations. *The Employee Responsibilities and Rights Journal, 1*(1), 5–25

Ouchi, W. G. (1981). *Theory Z: How American business can meet the Japanese challenge.* Reading, MA: Addison-Wesley.

Peters, T. J., & Waterman, R. H. (1982). *In search of excellence: Lessons from America's best run companies.* New York: Harper & Row.

Pfeffer, J. (1982). *Organizations and organization theory.* Marshfield, MA: Pitman.

Pondy, L. R. (1978). Leadership is a language game. In M. W. McCall & M. M. Lombardo (Eds.), *Leadership: Where else can we go?* (pp. 87–99). Durham, NC: Duke University Press.

Ricks, D. A. (1983). *Big business blunders.* Homewood, IL: Richard D. Irwin.

Roberts, K. (1970). On looking at an elephant: An evaluation of cross-cultural research related to organizations. *Psychological Bulletin, 74*(5), 327–350.

Rosenberg, A. (1967, November). International interaction and the taxonomy of international organization. *International Associations, 19*(11), 721–729.

Ryterband, E. C., & Barrett, G. V. (1970). Managers' values and their relationships to the management of tasks: A cross-cultural comparison. In B. M. Bass, R. C. Cooper, & J. A. Hass (Eds.), *Managing for accomplishment*. Lexington, MA.: D. C. Heath.

Samiee, S. (1984). Transnational data flow constraints: A new challenge for multinational corporations. *Journal of International Business Studies, XV*(1), 141–150.

Schein, E. H. (1985). *Organizational culture and leadership: A dynamic view*. San Francisco, CA: Jossey-Bass.

Schöllhammer, H. (1969). The comparative management theory jungle. *Academy of Management Journal* (March), 81–97.

Schwartz, H. S. (1985, Spring). The usefulness of myth and the myth of usefulness: A dilemma for the applied organizational scientist. *Journal of Management, 11*(1), 31–42.

Scott, W. G. (1982). Barnard on the nature of elitist responsibility. *Public Administration Review* (May/June), 197–201.

Scott, W. G. (1985, August). Organizational revolution: An end to managerial orthodoxy. *Administration and Society, 17*(2), 149–170.

Scott, W. G., & Mitchell, T. R. (1986, Autumn). Markets and morals in management education. *Selections: The Magazine of the Graduate Management Admission Council, III*(2), 3–8.

Sekaran, U. (1981). Are U. S. organizational concepts and measures transferable to another culture? An empirical investigation. *Academy of Management Journal, 24*(2), 409–417.

Sethi, S. P. Namiki, N., & Swanson, C. L. (1984). *The false promise of the Japanese miracle: Illusions and realities of the Japanese management system*. Marshfield, MA: Pitman.

Skjelsbaek, K. (1971, Summer). The growth of international nongovernmental organizations in the twentieth century. *International Organization, XXV*(3), 70–92.

Smircich, L. (1983). Organizations as shared meaning. In L. R. Pondy, P. Frost, G. Morgan, & T. Dandridge (Eds.), *Organizational symbolism* (pp. 160–172). Greenwich, CT: JAI Press.

Smircich L., & Morgan, G. (1982). Leadership: The management of meaning. *Journal of Applied Behavioral Science, 18*(3), 257–273.

Steele, F. (1976). Is organizational development work possible in the UK culture? *Journal of European Training, 5*(3), 105–110.

Terry, G. R. (1953). *Principles of management*. Homewood, IL: Irwin.

Triandis, H. (1968). Factors affecting employee selection in two cultures. *Journal of Applied Psychology, 47*(2), 89–96.

Triandis, H. (1972). *The analysis of subjective culture*. New York: Wiley-Interscience.

Triandis, H. C., Malpas, R. S., & Davidson, A. R. (1973). Psychology and culture. *Annual Review of Psychology, 24*, 355–374.

Urwick, L. F. (1952). *Notes on the theory of organization*. New York: American Management Association.

U.S. Department of Commerce. (1977, February). *Survey of current business*. Washington, DC: U.S. Government Printing Office.

U.S. Department of Commerce. (1977, August). *Survey of current business*. Washington, DC: U.S. Government Printing Office.

U.S. Department of Commerce. (1979, August). *Survey of current business* (Table 3, p. 56). Washington, DC: U.S. Government Printing Office.

U.S. Department of Commerce. (1984, October). *Survey of current business*. (p. 38). Washington, DC: U.S. Government Printing Office.

Vickers, S. G. (1965). *The art of judgement*. London: Chapman and Hall.

Wren, D. A. (1979). *The evolution of management thought*. New York: Wiley & Sons.

Zaleznik, A., & Kets de Vries, M. F. R. (1980). *Power and the corporate mind*. Boston: Bonus Books.

2

From the Atlantic to the Pacific Century
Cross-Cultural Management Reviewed

Nancy J. Adler and Robert Doktor

In collaboration with S. Gordon Redding

*Japanese and American management is 95 percent
the same, and differs in all important respects.*
T. Fujisawa,
Co-founder of Honda Motor Corporation

International commerce is vital to national prosperity. According to
Robert Frederick, chairman of the National Foreign Trade Council, 80%
of United States industry now faces international competition. The
growing interdependence of national economies has created a demand
for managers sophisticated in international business and skilled in working with people from other cultures. Just to remain competitive, the

Reprinted with permission from the *1986 Yearly Review of Management*, J. G. Hunt and
J. D. Blair (Eds.), *Journal of Management*, 12(2), 295–318. Copyright 1986 Southern Management Association.

Nancy J. Adler • Faculty of Management, McGill University, Montreal, Canada H3A
1G5.   **Robert Doktor** • Department of Management and Industrial Relations, College
of Business Administration, University of Hawaii, Manoa, Hawaii 96822.   **S. Gordon
Redding** • Department of Management, University of Hong Kong, Hong Kong.

27

world of business is asking international questions and demanding global answers.

The field of comparative management developed to increase our understanding of worldwide business. A relatively recent phenomenon, it has paralleled the internationalization of the firm and the rise of the multinational corporation (MNC) following World War II. Only a decade ago, Evans (1976) anticipated the potential of this new field:

> Thus far, the field of organization theory has failed to come to grips with the cultural component of the environments in which organizations are embedded. This is not at all surprising because there are formidable conceptual and methodological obstacles to overcome. The fact that MNCs operate in a multitude of cultural and societal settings not only poses a challenge to executives but also provides an opportunity for organizational researchers to use this worldwide organizational phenomenon as a vehicle for research. (p. 241)

Today, the move from the multinational to the global corporation marks yet another fundamental change in perspective. Corporate structures will no longer be primarily multidomestic, but rather truly global in their strategy, structure, markets, and resource bases.

For years, scholars have called for research that would explain and analyze the relationship between management and culture (e.g., Roberts, 1970; Sorge, 1983; Weinshall, 1977). Others have argued that the growing body of organization theory literature (research conducted within one country, usually the United States) should be integrated with the comparative management literature (research conducted in more than one country) (Joynt, 1985). Cross-cultural management research has attempted to do just that: inform people working in organizations whose employees or clients span more than one culture. Cross-cultural management studies the behavior of people interacting within and between organizations around the world. It describes and compares organizational behavior across cultures, and, perhaps most important for managers, seeks to understand and improve the effectiveness of people interacting with colleagues from different cultures. Cross-cultural management thus expands domestic management knowledge and practice to encompass international, global, and multicultural spheres.

This article documents the development of the comparative and cross-cultural management fields through a discussion of the major issues each has addressed. That development has focused primarily on Western research traditions and paradigms. Paralleling the shift of business from the Atlantic to the Pacific Basin, we move from the field's conceptually Occidental history to an Oriental perspective. This shift, both geographical and conceptual, foreshadows the move from the Atlantic to the Pacific century.

I. CROSS-CULTURAL MANAGEMENT: SOME MAJOR DEBATES

The fields of comparative and cross-cultural management address five central questions. First, does organizational behavior vary across cultures? Second, how much of the observed difference can be attributed to cultural determinants? Third, is the variance in organizational behavior worldwide increasing, decreasing, or remaining the same? Fourth, how can organizations best manage within cultures other than their own? Fifth, how can organizations best manage cultural diversity, including using diversity as an organizational resource? This includes a macrolevel question: the implications for government and economic policy of one form of organization being found to be more efficient than others in a given environment. Although more research has been done on the first three questions, scholars in the field have considered all five. We review each separately.

A. Cross-Cultural Variance

Does organizational behavior vary across cultures? Or, perhaps more important, do the relationships between organizational factors (e.g., work climate, leadership style, decision-making processes, degree of formalization) and organizational outcomes (e.g., performance, satisfaction, commitment of organizational members) vary from one nation to the next? Crozier (1964) contended that the research community has often ignored cultural differences altogether:

> Intuitively . . . people have always assumed that bureaucratic structures and patterns of action differ in different countries. . . . Men of action know it and never fail to take it into account, but contemporary social scientists . . . have not been concerned with such comparisons. (p. 210)

1. Single-Culture Studies

Single-culture studies have attempted to document aspects of organizational behavior in many countries, but they are not designed to identify similarities and differences. Almost half (47.2%) of all recent cross-cultural management articles report on single-culture studies (Adler, 1983b). Examples include such articles as "Politics, Bureaucracy, and Worker Participation: The Swedish Case" (Albrecht, 1980), "Cultural and Situational Determinants of Job Satisfaction Amongst Management in South Africa" (Blunt, 1973), "Early Chinese Management Thought" (Chang, 1976), and "Managerial Attitudes of Greeks: The Roles of Culture and Industrialization" (Cummings & Schmidt, 1972).

2. Comparative Studies

Comparative studies have focused on whether there is a difference among organizations operating in two or more cultures. About a third (34.2%) of all cross-cultural management articles report findings from comparative research (Adler, 1983b). Examples of comparative research include such articles as "Worker Participation Contrasts in Three Countries" (Foy & Gadon, 1976), "The Impact of Culture upon Managerial Attitudes, Beliefs and Behavior in England and France" (Graves, 1972), and "Social Performance Goals in the Peruvian and the Yugoslav Worker Participation System" (Hoover, Troub, Whitehead, & Flores, 1978). Although some studies find more similarities and others more differences, it is clear that neither the behavior of people in organizations nor the relationships between behavior and organizational outcomes are identical worldwide.

3. Nation versus Culture

In both single-culture and comparative studies, nation and culture have been used as if they were synonymous, with national boundaries separating one cultural group from another. Rarely have more specific definitions of culture been used, nor has domestic cultural heterogeneity been considered. In essence, the majority of these studies should be labeled *cross-national* rather than cross-cultural.

B. Cultural Determination

Given that differences exist, can they be explained by cultural determinants? In other words, can organizational characteristics that influence or determine human behavior in work situations be explained by cultural factors? Are the relationships between organizational behavior and organizational outcomes, whether similar or different across countries, contingent upon cultural variables? As a number of authors have indicated, the question is not merely whether organizations differ across cultures but whether the differences are caused by cultural factors.

1. Culture

Culture and cultural influences are concepts that neither anthropology nor management has defined consistently. Tylor (1877) defined culture as "that complex whole which includes knowledge, belief, art, law, morals, customs and any capabilities and habits acquired by a man as a member of society" (p. 1). Linton (1945) described culture as "the configuration of learned behavior and the results of behavior whose component elements are shared and transmitted by members of a particular society" (p. 32). Barnouw (1963) wrote that "a culture is a way of life of a group of people, the configuration of all of the more or less sterotyped patterns of learned behavior, which are handed down from one generation to the next through the means of language and imitation" (p. 4). Kroeber and Kluckhohn (1952), in cataloging more than a hundred definitions of culture, gave one of the more comprehensive and generally accepted:

> Culture consists of patterns, explicit and implicit of and for behavior acquired and transmitted by symbols, constituting the distinctive achievement of human groups, including their embodiment in artifacts; the essential core of culture consists of traditional (i.e., historically derived and selected) ideas and especially their attached values; culture systems may, on the one hand, be considered as products of action, on the other as conditioning elements of further action. (p. 181)

Culture is, therefore, (a) something that is shared by all or almost all members of some social group, (b) something that the older members of the group try to pass on to the younger members, and (c) something (as in the case of morals, laws, or customs) that shapes behavior or structures one's perception of the world (Carrol, 1982, p. 19).

In Hofstede's (1980) more recent work, culture is defined as:

> The collective programming of the mind which distinguishes the members of one human group from another, . . . the interactive aggregate of common characteristics that influence a human group's response to its environment. (p. 25)
>
> Culture is not a characteristic of the individual; it encompasses a number of people who were conditioned by the same education and life experience. When we speak of the culture of a group, a tribe, a geographical region, a national minority, or a nation, culture refers to the collective mental programming that these people have in common; the programming that is different from that of other groups, tribes, regions, minorities, or nations. (p. 48)

Such a definition implies a clear and important distinction between (a) the shared ideas that shape and influence social action and (b) the action itself as played out in the social system. Culture appears to be increasingly, agreed upon by theorists as being the former (Child, 1981, p. 324; Keesing, 1974; Kroeber & Parsons, 1958, pp. 582–583; Parsons, 1973, p. 36), although this convenient analytical distinction does not show how ideas and action are connected in real life. Theorists concerned primarily with such a sociological question agree that even though cultural patterns are observable in the realm of social action, culture itself exists at another level of analysis.

The idea of culture as mind-state raises the problem of reductionism and an explanatory cul-de-sac, whereas using social patterns for explanation removes the understanding of their determinants. A past review of the sociological literature on culture (Wuthnow, Hunter, Bergesen, & Kurzweil, 1984) stresses the embryonic nature of the discipline. Even so, fruitful progress may be marked, and more predicted, with culture being accepted as an observable aspect of human behavior, manifest in social interaction and tangible objects like organizations, but resting on symbolic frameworks, mental programs, and conceptual distinctions in people's minds (Hicks & Redding, 1983; Redding, 1982).

These collective mental programs may be termed *cognitive maps.* Because cognitive maps vary across cultures, their effects upon managerial action can also vary and at times even become severely dysfunctional. Although the number of analytic dimensions needed to describe and classify cultural similarities and differences is unknown, recognizing the existence of each culture's unique set of cognitive maps and their potential impact upon managerial action, however measured, is extremely important.

2. Culture's Influence

However defined, culture influences people's values, attitudes, and behaviors, which in turn collectively define their culture. Culture influences organizations through societal structures such as laws and political systems and also through the values, attitudes, behavior, goals, and preferences of participants (clients, employees, and especially managers). The circular nature of culture has made it difficult, if not impossible, to separate cultural causation from determination by other societal factors. Is the influence of the educational system a cultural influence? The influence of the legal system? The influence of the political system? The answers have depended on various researchers' definitions of culture. From our perspective, culture is certainly not identical to other primary societal structures, but it strongly influences their form and function. Specific educational, political, legal, and economic systems exist in a given society partly because of their cultural heritage.

From the viewpoint of organizational culture, the question becomes: Do organizational culture and structure determine people's behavior in organizations, or does national or ethnic cultural conditioning limit the organization's influence? Does the culture that enters the organization through employees limit the influence of management-created organizational culture and structure (Adler & Jelinek, 1986)? Apparently, yes.

However, it may be that our Western cognitive conditioning leads us to separate culture from other societal influences and the organization from its environment. Westerners tend to see categories, distinctions, and separateness, whereas people conditioned by Eastern cultures are more likely to see continuity and connectedness (Maruyama, 1980, 1982, 1984).

In 1982, M. Solange-Perret conducted a particularly important dissertation research at the University of Western Ontario, under the guidance of Professor Joseph de Stefano. The study attempted to distinguish between national and cultural impacts on management. She used Kluckhohn and Strodbeck's (1961) five dimensions to identify the underlying cultural variance between American and French managers working in United States- and French-based subsidiaries of a major American corporation. The five dimensions used were relationship to self, others, external environment, activity, and time. Using observation and interview techniques, she documented fundamental differences in managerial styles and control systems between the two subsidiaries. Her data revealed parallels between the variance in fundamental cultural orientations and the actual work behavior and attitudes of the two groups. Solange-Perret is currently replicating the study.

C. Convergence versus Divergence

Is the diversity of behavior in organizations across cultures increasing, decreasing, or remaining the same? Trying to resolve what is commonly labeled the *convergence/divergence dichotomy*, scholars ask whether organizations worldwide are becoming more similar (convergence) or are maintaining their culturally based dissimilarity (divergence).

1. Convergence

Adherents of the convergence (or universalist) perspective argue that organizational characteristics across nations are mostly free of the particularities of specific cultures (e.g., Cole, 1973; Form, 1979; Hickson, Hinnings, McMillan, & Schwitter, 1974; Kerr, Dunlop, Harbison, & Myers, 1952; Negandhi, 1979, 1985). This position suggests that as an outcome of "common industrial logic"—most notably of technological origin—institutional frameworks, organizational patterns and structures, and management practices across countries are converging.

For example, Child (1981) and Child and Tayeb (1983) concluded that organizational variance today depends much more on contingencies other than culture than it has previously:

> Contingencies of technological development, market and geographical diversification, large-scale production and close interdependence with other organizations . . . impose a logic of rational administration which it becomes functionally imperative to follow in order to achieve levels of performance sufficient to ensure the survival of the organization. . . . It is argued that this logic is in all societies, irrespective of culture, economic or political systems, steadily pervading the design and management of organizations which are subject to high performance requirements either because of competitive pressure or because of external demands for their effectiveness. Cultural differences are therefore of diminishing importance. (Child & Tayeb, 1983, p. 27)

In full agreement, Levitt (1983) declared that:

> A powerful force drives the world toward a converging commonality, and that force is technology. It has proletarianized communication, transport, and travel. It has made isolated places and impoverished peoples eager for modernity's allurements. . . . The result is a new commercial reality—the emergence of global markets for standardized consumer products on a previously unimagined scale of magnitude. Corporations geared to this new reality benefit from enormous economies of scale in production, distribution, marketing, and management. By translating these benefits into reduced world prices, they can decimate competitors that still live in the disabling grip of old assumptions about how the world works.
>
> Gone are accustomed differences in national or regional preference. (p. 92)

He added that "different cultural preferences, national tastes and standards, and business institutions are vestiges of the past" (p. 96). Similarly, based on their comparative analysis of organizations, Hickson, McMillar, Azumi, and Horvath (1979) concluded that although organizations worldwide are far from identical, the key relationships among organizational variables remain constant across cultures.

2. Divergence

By contrast, other scholars argue that organizations are culture-bound, rather than culturally free, and are remaining so (e.g., Hofstede, 1980; Laurent, 1983; Lincoln, Hanada, & Olson, 1981; Meyer & Rowan, 1977). These scholars conclude that the principle of *equifinality* applies to organizations functioning in different cultures (Negandhi, 1973) and that many equally effective ways to manage exist. The most effective depend, among other contingencies, on the culture(s) involved.

For example, Bass and Eldridge (1973) found distinct differences in managerial objectives among the 12 countries they studied. England (1975), although finding differences, found more similarities than expected in managerial values across the United States, Japan, Korea, India, and Australia. Heller and Wilpert (1979) identified several important country-specific differences in their 8-country comparative study (including the United States, the United Kingdom, Germany, Sweden, the Netherlands, France, Spain, and Israel) of managerial attitudes and decision-making behavior. Similarly, Laurent (1983) documented fundamental differences in managers' assumptions and conceptualizations among 9 Western European countries and the United States.

Whereas the previously mentioned studies found countries using distinctly different managerial styles, other studies have identified clusters of similar countries. This difference has much to do with the particular variables and sets of countries studied. For example, Haire, Ghiselli, and Porter (1966), in studying the managerial attitudes of 3,641 managers in 14 countries, clustered the countries into five groups: Nordic European (Denmark, Germany, Norway, Sweden), Latin European (Belgium, France, Italy, Spain), Anglo-American (England and the United States), developing countries (Argentina, Chile, India), and Japan. Of all the attitudinal differences they observed, 25% of the variance was associated with national differences, leading them to infer that although "cultural influence is present and substantial, it is not overwhelming" (p. 9).

Hofstede (1980), in a landmark study of 160,000 employees working in 40 countries for a major American multinational, identified four dimensions on which styles of work differ: power distance, uncertainty avoidance, individualism/collectivism, and masculinity/femininity.

Convergence or divergence? The studies are inconclusive. Perhaps, instead of asking whether there are similarities or differences, we should be asking when there are similarities and when differences. And if differences exist, when are there consistent patterns of cultural clustering as opposed to individual expressions of distinct cultures?

Accordingly, this third-level question should perhaps be: When do organizations converge and when do they maintain their cultural specificity? In surveying the cross-cultural management literature, Child (1981) observed that reputable scholars using equally reputable methodologies were forming opposite conclusions—some finding convergence, some divergence. Analyzing the studies, he discovered that the majority of those focusing on macrolevel variables were finding few differences across cultures, whereas those examining microlevel variables were observing many significant differences. Similarly, Aiken and Bacharach (1979) have suggested that cultural effects are more manifest in the "various patterns in organizational members" (p. 216) than in such areas as structure, procedures, and rules. Perhaps, as suggested by the Fujisawa quotation that opens this article, our organizations are becoming more similar in terms of structure and technology, whereas people's behavior within those organizations continues to manifest culturally based dissimilarities.

Although culture may continue to affect the formal institutional level, the increasing prevalence of common technology tends to reduce its impact. Because culture is in part defined at the level of cognitive maps, we should probably expect to observe the most profound differences at the informal rather than the formal organizational level.

D. Beyond Comparison: Intercultural Interaction

Management, as a profession, is not an academic discipline. For managers, understanding cultural similarities and differences and their causes, although interesting and necessary, is not sufficient. International managers need to know how to act when working in foreign cultures. Interaction, not merely comparison, is the essence of most managerial action. What happens when people from different cultures work together? In what ways do people modify their within-culture styles when working with people from other cultures? What are the most effective ways to approach foreign colleagues and clients? International managers' jobs involve a high level of cross-cultural interaction, which has been largely overlooked by management researchers. Fewer than one-fifth (18.6%) of all cross-cultural management research articles have focused on interaction (Adler, 1983b).

1. Interaction

The cross-cultural communication and psychology literature suggests that people behave differently with members of their own culture than they do with members of foreign cultures. Research in nonbusiness contexts has demonstrated that when people from various cultures interact, the differences among them become salient (Bouchner & Ohsako, 1977; Bouchner & Perks, 1971). Moreover, when people confront actual differences in interpersonal situations, they tend to exaggerate those differences (Sherif & Hovland, 1961; Vassiliou, Triandis, Vassiliou, & McGuire, 1980). In addition, perceived similarity, not difference, predicts satisfaction with work relationships (Bass, Burger, Doktor, & Barrett, 1979; Polakos & Wexley, 1983; Wexley, Alexander, Greenwalt, & Couch, 1980).

In international exchanges, "the greater the cultural differences, the greater is the likelihood that barriers to communication will arise and that misunderstandings will occur" (Mishler, 1965, p. 555). Peterson and Shimada (1978) have even questioned whether "managers from significantly different cultures such as Japan and the United States can ever completely understand each other" (p. 803). Moreover, research suggests that the relationships among managers may deteriorate when differences become very apparent (Stening, 1979).

Current studies comparing intracultural and intercultural negotiating behavior document that Japanese and American business people modify their within-culture styles when negotiating internationally (Graham, 1985). Likewise, English and French-Canadian business people alter their intracultural negotiating behavior when bargaining across cultures (Adler & Graham, 1986). An interesting study of such areas of subtle tension, this time in an entirely Asian geographical context (although in a largely Western intellectual one), is reported by Everett, Krishnan, and Stening (1984). They studied the stereotypes of one another held by groups of Southeast Asian and Japanese managers in subsidiaries of Japanese companies and concluded that there were "serious limitations to the exportability of the Japanese style of management" (p. 149). This recent research shows that we cannot assume that managers behave identically in within-culture and cross-cultural situations.

E. Synergy from Cultural Diversity

Managers must learn to use cultural diversity as an advantage, rather than as a disadvantage, to the organization. Although a sizable body of literature describes the impacts of diversity on small-group processes, decision making, and creative problem solving, few researchers have focused on intercultural interaction within work settings. Even fewer have asked proactive, action-research questions investigating the creation of organizational benefits from cultural diversity.

Because culture tends to be invisible and, when visible, is usually seen as causing problems for the organization, the phrasing of this fifth question is particularly important. Only infrequently do people view cultural diversity as benefiting the organization. For example, international executives attending management seminars at the European Management Institute (INSEAD) in France were asked to list the advantages and disadvantages of cultural diversity to their organizations. The data, collected by Andre Laurent and Nancy J. Adler and summarized in Adler (1986, pp. 76–98), indicate that although every executive could list several disadvantages, only 30% of them could list even one advantage. Similarly, in a Canadian study, only 1 of 60 organizational development consultants surveyed mentioned an advantage to the organization from cultural diversity, whereas all 60 mentioned disadvantages (Adler, 1983c). Likewise, all of the 52 corporate and academic experts attending the 1981 McGill International Symposium on Cross-Cultural Management could identify several problems but few benefits of diversity (Adler, 1983a).

Sufficient research on cultural synergy in organizational settings has yet to be conducted, but Maruyama (1973, 1980, 1982, 1984) has given us one of the best paradigms both for thinking about the potential benefits of diversity and for understanding our historical blindness to its possibilities for organization and management. Maruyama proposes four metatypes of causality: nonreciprocal causal models, independent event models, homeostatic causal-loop models, and morphogenetic causal-loop models. The four correspond respectively to the organizational approaches of international, multidomestic, multinational, and global firms. Each is discussed briefly in terms of its conceptualization of cultural homogeneity and heterogeneity.

In nonreciprocal causal models, causality is linear and unidirectional (A→B→C→D→E). Homogeneity is considered natural, desirable, and good, and heterogeneity an abnormality or error. Cultural diversity is viewed as the source of all conflict, inconvenience, and inefficiency. The parts are subordinated to the whole. Under this assumption of nonreciprocal causality, homogeneity is viewed as basic and natural, and change is seen as evolving through a competitive survival-of-the-fittest model. The organizational analogy is the international firm, in which the headquarters' culture is assumed to apply universally and management believes that there is one best way to manage. The culture of top management dominates all parts of the organization. This approach is in accordance with the insistence on a strong organizational culture for international as well as domestic firms.

In independent event models, events are seen as random. Therefore, the question of causality lacks explanatory power. Management views the organization as an aggregate of individuals who think and act independently. Thus, cultural conditioning is either ignored or treated as an irrelevant myth. The organizational analogy is the multidomestic firm, an organization with highly independent operations in many countries. Multidomestic firms recognize cultural differences, and, unlike international firms, reject attempts to have everyone working the same way. Multidomestic firms regard each national unit as independent and fairly autonomous, with random rather than planned interaction among the parts. Management makes no attempt to create mutually beneficial combinations among domestic operations. When necessary, consensus is expected to cancel out differences and allow for concerted action. Multidomestic firms recognize cultural diversity, although harboring no illusion that they can control it or benefit from it.

In homeostatic causal-loop models, causal relations form stable loops. Organizational structures (patterns of heterogeneity) are maintained in equilibrium by causal loops. The organizational analogy is the multinational firm. Diversity (or geographic differentiation) is basic, indispensable, and desirable, whereas homogeneity is the source of competition and conflict. Cultural interaction and heterogeneity are considered beneficial. Change and evolution can come only from external forces causing the organization to adapt to new, stable patterns of equilibrium.

In morphogenetic causal-loop models, causal relations form loops, but heterogeneity goes beyond homeostasis and generates new patterns of mutually beneficial relations among the interacting elements, thus raising the level of sophistication of the whole system. Unlike homeostatic models, in which external forces cause change, morphogenetic models can internally generate their own evolution: They constantly create new, improved, mutually beneficial systems of interaction. The organizational analogy is the global firm, which considers heterogeneity essential and indispensable. The global firm constantly seeks and generates new patterns through international interaction, which is developmental, evolutionary, and, as is necessary for evolution, degenerative.

In moving from international, multidomestic, and multinational firms to the era of the global corporation, our approach to recognizing, understanding, modeling, and using cultural diversity is changing. Research is required on organizational uses of morphogenetic causal-loop models to create synergy from cultural diversity. It is no longer valuable to ask if cultural diversity is salient. The global organization needs to develop ways to create and manage evolving systems of cultural synergy.

II. FROM THE ATLANTIC TO THE PACIFIC CENTURY

As the world enters the Pacific century, the differing impacts of Occidental and Oriental culture on managerial interaction have become highly significant. Yet, most management scholars to date have focused on the Atlantic rim rather than on the Pacific rim. Existing research on Asian managers is based on Western theoretical models that fail to account for differences between Occidental and Oriental cultures and mind-sets. (We note here that although the term *American* refers to all peoples of North and South America, we use it as a shorthand and writing convenience to refer to the citizens of the United States of America.)

Questioning the universal applicability of theories developed and tested in the West, Azumi (1974) suggested that "if the perspective of social science as developed in the West is inadequate, that must be demonstrated by the creation of a new and better social science instead of developing separate social sciences for different societies" (p. 527). Such a new social science, including the science of management, would account for cultural diversity rather than assume a monocultural perspective. More important, it would recognize differences between Oriental and Occidental mind-sets and their implications for international managerial action. In other words, it would form a solid theoretical base for comparative studies that would examine cultures and their cognitive maps and predict their impact on organizational behavior.

A. Single-Culture Management Studies

Espousing an admittedly simplistic mechanical model, observation alone reveals differences in the behavioral characteristics of managers from various Asian countries. Single-culture studies on Japanese, South Korean, and Chinese management practices have documented these differences.

Studies have shown that Japanese managers and workers have a sense of identity with their work groups (Befu, 1983b; Cole, 1979; Doi, 1962; Gibney, 1982; Kumagai, 1981; Tung, 1984), an ethic of cooperativeness (Befu, 1983a; Kawai, 1981; Ouchi & Jaeger, 1978), a high dependence on the larger entity (Abegglen, 1984; Cole, 1979; Conner, 1976; Doi, 1973; Minami, 1980), a strong sensitivity to status (Cole, 1979; Dore, 1978; Hofstede, 1980; Pascale, 1978), and an active respect for the interests of individuals and for each individual as a person (Deutsch, 1984; DeVos, 1973; Graham & Sano, 1984; Moran, 1985).

South Korean managers have been observed to exhibit the Confucian virtues of familism, filial piety, and loyalty and obedience to authorities, including their leaders (Chung, 1978; Nam, 1971). They desire to contribute to the national well-being (Chung, 1978; England & Lee, 1971), tend to hold strong personal opinions (Nam, 1971), and are uninclined to adopt systems of shared management, or power equalization within the organization (England & Lee, 1971; Harbron, 1979).

Ethnic Chinese managers, whether from the People's Republic of China (PRC) or from Taiwan, Hong Kong, or Singapore, have been shown to honor a tight set of business rules, many of them unwritten (Benedict, 1946; Chui, 1977; Tung, 1981a). They possess what Redding (1977) has referred to as a "siege mentality," characterized by excessive anxiety, especially concerning material security (Chui, 1977). They see money as a security surrogate, emphasize hard work, thrift, and competitiveness (Chui, 1977; Lemming, 1977; Nevis, 1983; Silin, 1976), and believe in Confucian familism (Redding & Wong, 1986; Sterba, 1978; Tung, 1981b; Yang, 1973).

B. Comparative Management Studies

Of the few comparative studies of organizations, the majority focus on comparisons between Japan and the West. The Japanese view of conflict between the whole and its parts and conflict among parts is different from that of the West (Kawai, 1981; Kumon, 1984; Minami, 1980; Suzuki, 1976; Yamauchi, 1974). The Japanese also tend to see more complementarity and interconnectedness in opposites than do Westerners, who tend to see only conflict between opposites (Mendenhall & Oddou, 1986).

Keys and Miller (1984) suggested three "underlying factors at the heart of the Japanese system that foster the development of the various management theories and models" (p. 349): a long-range planning horizon, commitment to lifetime employment, and collective responsibility. Noting that these factors were rooted in Japanese culture, they hypothesized a causal relationship between cognitive maps (implicit cultural views of the world) and specific management practices. Similarly, Doktor (1983a), comparing differences in behavior and time-use patterns between Japanese and American chief executive officers (CEOs), identified cognitive maps as a primary explanatory variable. He found that Japanese CEOs tended to be more deliberate, more planning oriented, and less frenetic in their behavior than their American counterparts.

Although few comparative management studies focus on Asian countries other than Japan, those that do are important because they pay attention to cognitive factors. For example, in comparing American managers with those in the PRC, Nevis (1983) noted the strong relationship between mind-sets and productivity. The Cultural Revolution brought about two major attitudes or mind-sets that affected productivity in the PRC. First, great caution about standing out in any way became the norm. Second, in order to reward loyalty to the work unit and to the nation, the idea of equal sharing became prevalent. It was better to have everyone share equally what little there was than to give extra rewards to those who stood out as highly productive workers. Thus, poor performance and good performance were rewarded equally.

Investigators studying organizations in Hong Kong (Lau, 1977; Redding, 1980; Redding & Hicks, 1983) and Taiwan (Silin, 1976) have reported that although work itself is highly individualized and competitive, official positions are only loosely designated. Apparently, ethnic Chinese people's subjective environment has enough authority to make explicit demarcation of official positions and roles less necessary than in the West. Consistent with these findings, Hofstede (1980) found that managers in Hong Kong prefer low levels of uncertainty avoidance.

Scholhammer's (1969) survey of approaches to comparative management showed researchers' tendency to concentrate on socioeconomic variables or managerial attitudes but not on cognition. Robert's (1970) survey of cross-cultural management research indicated the relevance of studies on meaning, communication, and perception but failed to refer to any single study on cognition *per se*. Likewise, Weinshall's (1977) edited collection of works on the linkages between culture and management, for all its strengths, contained not a single study of cognition.

Within Asia, most research has been done on Japan. Dunphy and Stening (1984) compiled a comprehensive annotated bibliography of over 400 Japanese research articles on organizational behavior and management, published in English. Of the Japanese studies, very few (4%) are comparative studies that consider the impact of the cognitive aspects of culture on managerial practice.

Notable among those scholars who consider cognition is Kumon (1984), who, as cited by Mark E. Mendenhall and Gary R. Oddou (1986), has summarized the differences between the cognitive processing of information by Japanese and Westerners, observing that:

> The nature of Japanese reasoning is "analytical" whereas that of Westerners can be characterized as "comprehensive." Thus the cognitive process of Japanese, in most cases, goes from the whole to its parts. For them to understand something is to divide it into parts. . . . [T]he cognitive process of Westerners tends to proceed from individual elements to a larger whole. . . . [W]hen individual objects which were first taken separately are put together forming one whole, Westerners say they comprehend it. Comprehension is just the opposite of division. (pp. 8–9)

C. Sociological Studies

As indicated earlier, sociological literature, unlike most management literature, generally supports both the importance of the subjective environment's influence on organizational behavior and the need for organizational analysis at the individual level, both within cultures and across cultures. Silverman (1970), in arguing that the unique role of sociologists is to understand the subjective logic of social situations, stressed the importance of this understanding to comparative management research. He identified five issues that foreshadowed comparative management's current methodological dilemma: (a) the nature of the predominant meaning structure and its associated system in different organizations and the extent to which they rely on varying degrees of coercion or consent; (b) the characteristic pattern of involvement of the actors' differing attachment to rules and to definitions of their situation; (c) the typical strategies used by the actors to attain their ends; (d) the relative ability of different actors to impose their definition of the situation upon others; and (e) the origin and pattern of change of meaning structures in different organizations.

All these issues emphasize individuals' definitions of the situations they are in, an emphasis reflected in the emergence of such approaches as ethnomethodology (Cicourel, 1972; Garfinkel, 1967) and the action frame of reference (Harre & Sekord, 1972; Silverman, 1970). Bougon, Weick, and Binkhorst (1977) gave more specific attention to cognition as a factor in organizational analysis and presented an empirically based picture of organizational participants' "cause maps." They concluded that:

> Social settings are defined and must be analyzed in terms of the participant's epistemology: organization problems are mind-environment problems. . . . Cause maps will help us find that by a non-logical, but highly intelligent mental process, organization participants perform translation from the world of experience to the world of mind. (p. 23)

Supporting the concept of mind–environment problems and focusing attention on the informal side of organizational behavior, Lammers and Hickson (1979), in their review of the comparative organization theory literature, concluded that "there are grounds to suspect that specific traditions, value patterns, ideologies, and norms (originating, for example, in cognitive maps) are bound to differentiate as much or even more than structural factors, between societies" (p. 275).

That there are major differences between the cognitive processes of Orientals and Occidentals often comes as a surprise to both sides. Each side is inherently unable to step outside its own world view to see the possibility of alternatives. Yet, the Western literatures of psychology, philosophy, and anthropology that describe and analyze Oriental peoples consistently refer to such cognitive differences.

D. Developmental Psychology Studies

Research concerned with the development of cognitive styles has demonstrated a relationship between elements of socioeconomic status and the propensity for cognitive differentiation or what is often termed *field articulation* (Witkin, Dyke, Faterson, Goodenough, & Karp, 1962). As a cognitive style dimension, individuals have been shown to vary from low field articulation (being intuitive, holistic, socially dependent, other directed, and motivationally diffuse) to high field articulation (being analytical, systematic, emotionally self-controlled, perceptually discriminating, socially independent and self-reliant, and motivationally focused). Poverty of the socioeconomic environment has been shown to be related to a focus on security and biological needs, immediate gratification, and obedience to well-tried methods of coping with daily needs. These conditions are inimical to the development of field articulation. Therefore, cultures in areas of high national economic development and modernization are more likely to demonstrate the cognitive characteristics of high field articulation (Gruenfeld & MacEachron, 1975). Triandis (1973) has expanded this view by suggesting that the level of economic development both affects and is dependent on the ability of members to respond and adjust to increasing environmental complexity. Gruenfeld and MacEachron (1975) have demonstrated that the degree of field articulation among managers and technicians correlates with their respective countries' economic development indices. Thus, cognitive aspects of culture appear to be somewhat developmentally related to national economic conditions, and finding major differences in cognitive functioning among regions of the world with significantly different economic histories, traditions, and levels of development ought not to be surprising.

E. Causes of Misinterpreting Data across Cultures

To understand our cultural myopia, we may consider Needham's (1978) explanation of how the idea of causation developed via one route in the West, beginning with the ancient Greeks and culminating in Newtonian physics, while taking a totally different route in China:

> We are driven to the conclusion that there are two ways of advancing from primitive truth. One was the way taken by some of the Greeks: to refine the ideas of causation in such a way that one ended up with a mechanical explanation of the universe, just as Democritus did with his atoms. The other way is to systematise the universe of things and events into a structural pattern which conditioned all the mutual influences of its different parts. In the Greek world view, if a particle of matter occupied a particular place at a particular time, it was because another particle had pushed it there. In the other view, the particle's behavior was governed by the fact that it was taking its place in a "field of force" alongside other particles that are similarly responsive: causation here is not "responsive" but "environmental." (p. 166)

Another aspect of cause-and-effect relations is what might be called the building blocks of explanation. When thinking about a problem,

Westerners normally use abstract concepts such as "productivity," "morale," and "leadership style." By contrast, the Oriental mind tends to use more concrete ideas such as, "How can we improve product quality and thus increase export sales?" (Redding, 1980). Nakamura (1964) identified the following contrasting characteristics as typical of Oriental thinking: (a) an emphasis on perception of the concrete, on the particular rather than the universal, and a lack of development of abstract thought; (b) a central focus on practicality; and (c) a concern for reconciliation, harmony, and balance.

Some Westerners tend to denigrate Orientals' style of thinking as nonspecific and therefore primitive, but Needham (1978) has defended its richness and strength. He has noted that many Western scholars embrace "total system" and "contingency" concepts in most branches of science, including management, but that they rarely associate these approaches with Oriental cognitive processes. Nonetheless, these frameworks reflect an approach that is fundamental to the Oriental perspective. The striking validity of Oriental thinking for dealing with complexity was elegantly argued by Capra (1975) in the context of post-Heisenberg physics.

Maruyama (1985), in relating cognitive issues to comparative management, has expanded upon similar points:

> The principles, styles and methods of management are affected by mind patterns, which may vary from individual to individual and from culture to culture. As the cultural heterogeneity increases, managers become aware of some new phenomena:
>
> 1. That management principles and methods must be adapted both to the cultural heterogeneity within the office and to the local culture;
> 2. That there are significant individual differences within each culture;
> 3. That some managers and workers from the local culture may look excellent if judged by the criteria of the superior from a foreign culture, but they may be cultural deviants who reject their own culture, and whose credibility may be very high among foreigners but very low among their compatriots;
> 4. That those who appreciate both local and foreign cultures are a valuable asset.
>
> It is posited here that in any larger culture there are all types of individual mind patterns, but that cultural differences exist in the distribution of various individual types as well as in the social dynamics of the interaction among different types: some types are officially accepted or encouraged while others are relegated to the social periphery, ignored, institutionally suppressed, individually repressed, latent or nonverbalized. (p. 126)

In considering Maruyama's implications, we note that the foundation of all managerial interaction, especially in the less-prescribed domain of the informal organization, is ultimately the unique set of cognitive maps in the manager's head. These maps are the basic components of culture and may become organizationally dysfunctional when differences among interacting cultures become more salient. As the world moves out of the Atlantic century into the Pacific century, cultural differences are likely to become far more significant. Some of the East–West cognitive differences outlined here must therefore be considered in future comparative management research.

Clearly, methodologies relying on data collected without attention to cognitive dimensions will lack reliability in the Pacific century. Earlier attempts to deal with these methodological issues (Adler, 1984; England & Harpaz, 1983; Sekaran, 1983) have addressed the fundamental question of measurement validity. For example, a questionnaire designed for cross-cultural equivalence may be used to compare managers' values or attitudes across various European and North American cultures. The questionnaire itself, however, may contain an implicit Western paradigm of causality. Simple translation, reverse translation, and other procedures for maintaining equivalence of literal meaning do nothing to address Orientals' alternative paradigm of causality. For example, rating a leadership dimension in order to measure an organization's climate presupposes a causal link between individual initiative and results, a link not accepted in Japanese mind-sets. This lack of causal equivalence plagues almost all methodologies using interpretive data rather than strictly observed behavior. In East–West managerial comparisons, data interpreted and filtered either by the subject or by the researcher are always suspect because of the potential impact of differing cognitive maps of causality.

Precautions must also be taken in interpreting and drawing implications from analyzed data in Oriental/Occidental comparisons. For example, one major theme within the popular literature comparing the decision making of American and Japanese managers has been that the Japanese are more "holistic," the Americans more "segmented" (Ouchi, 1981). But "segmented" may not be a bipolar opposite of "holistic." The Japanese may be segmented and holistic simultaneously. This very combination of cognitive patterns may be a significant dynamic in Japanese managerial success.

Another recurring theme in the literature on Japanese management, especially on the decision-making process, is the importance of the group. However, a crucial difference between Japanese and Western conceptions of the group is often overlooked. In the United States, people frequently associate the concept of group with affiliation. In Japan, however, affiliation is not the main subliminal perception. Grouping implies a sense of interrelatedness among all natural elements—including, in this case, group members. Interrelatedness is coupled with a blurring of physical barriers, including those among individual human bodies. It is interrelatedness—with everything being a part of everything else—that results in strong social cohesion, not, as frequently hypothesized by Westerners, a powerful need for affiliation among organizational members. For example, Ouchi and Jaeger (1978) argued that their Type Z organization would be appropriate where it could fulfill a need for stability and affiliation, as in the segment of American society adversely affected by urbanization and a geographically mobile work force. Apparently, these authors inferred that the strong dynamic of "groupism" in Japan means the same as a greater sense of American-style affiliation needs.

Ouchi and Jaeger's (1978) causation map may be an accurate description of Japanese dynamics. It may be that Japanese workers are cognitively more similar to American workers than different from them. Perhaps Japanese sociocultural values are similar to American values, and differences in managerial practice account for higher Japanese productivity. On the other hand, it may be that decision-making behavior in Japan and the United States differs quite markedly, and, moreover, that one culture's behavior is inappropriate for use in another culture.

Furthermore, differences in cognitive modeling behavior among cultures suggest that researchers and managers belonging to one culture may misinterpret the meaning of another culture's decision-making behavior. Therefore, even in cases where one culture's decision-making techniques seem to be appropriate for another, misapplication may occur due to erroneous analysis of the underlying way of seeing the world implicit in each culture, as illustrated by the example of equating Japanese groupism with a need for affiliation.

III. IMPLICATIONS FOR THE PRACTICE OF MANAGEMENT

A key element in the process of management anywhere in the world is being able to anticipate future actions of colleagues and competitors. Much of the research reviewed and analyzed in this article addresses this issue through the metaphor of cognitive style. Often, when we have trouble understanding and predicting the future behavior of our colleagues, peers, or competitors, we attribute these difficulties to language problems or to idiosyncracies in their behavior. But these prediction and understanding problems may arise from lack of appreciation of the thought processes manifested by foreigners in our managerial environment. Part of our inability to understand or predict the future behavior of our peers, colleagues, and competitors may be caused by our inability to understand how they are modeling the world and what kind of causal dimensions they use to see the world. The question, "Shall we do business with these people or not?" is really the question, "Do we understand how they are thinking about the world?" (Williamson, 1986). Finally, our ability to present our view of the world so that it can be understood and appreciated within the cognitive paradigms held by significant foreign colleagues determines, in large measure, our own acceptance by and relevance in an increasingly multicultural managerial environment.

IV. IMPLICATIONS FOR FUTURE RESEARCH

The forces of technological rationality drive organizations toward common work flows, operating procedures, and structures. On the level of interpersonal interaction, particularly in the informal organization, national culture mediated through cognitive maps results in a variety of behaviors among members. Therefore, understanding the demands of rational technology is insufficient for understanding organizational behavior across cultures; we must also understand the realities constructed by the respective participants. Progress in cross-cultural management research depends as much upon our understanding of the relationship between culture and cognition as it does upon our understanding of any other set of variables in the complex world of management research in the Pacific century.

V. REFERENCES

Abegglen, J. C. (1984). *The strategy of Japanese business.* Cambridge, MA: Ballinger.
Adler, N. J. (1983a). Cross-cultural management: Issues to be faced. *International Studies of Management and Organization, 13*(1-2), 7–45.
Adler, N. J. (1983b). Cross-cultural management research: The ostriche and the trend. *Academy of Management Review, 8*(2), 226–232.
Adler, N. J. (1983c). Organizational development in a multicultural environment. *Journal of Applied Behavioral Science, 19*(3), 350–365.
Adler, N. J. (1984). Understanding the ways of understanding: Cross-cultural management reviewed. In R. N. Farmer (Ed.), *Advances in international comparative management* (Vol. 1, pp. 31–67). Greenwich, CT: JAI Press.
Adler, N. J. (1986). *International dimensions of organizational behavior.* Boston: Kent Publishing.
Adler, N. J., & Graham, J. L. (1986). Cross-cultural interaction: The international comparison fallacy. Working paper, McGill University, Faculty of Management, Montreal.

Adler, N. J., & Jelinek, M. S. (1986). Is "organization culture" culture bound? *Human Resource Management, 25*(1), 73–90.

Aiken, M., & Bacharach, S. B. (1979). Culture and organizational structure and process: A comparative study of local government administrative bureaucracies in the Walloon and Flemish regions of Belgium. In C. J. Lammers & D. J. Hickson (Eds.), *Organizations alike and unlike* (pp. 215–250). London: Routledge & Kegan Paul.

Albrecht, S. L. (1980). Politics, bureaucracy, and worker participation: The Swedish case. *Journal of Applied Behavioral Science 16*(3), 229–317.

Azumi, K. (1974). Japanese society: A sociological review. In A. D. Tiedemann (Ed.), *An introduction to Japanese civilization* (pp. 515–535). New York: Columbia University Press.

Barnouw, V. (1963). *Culture and personality*. Homewood, IL: The Dorsey Press.

Bass, B., & Eldridge, L. (1973). Accelerated managers' objectives in twelve countries. *Industrial Relations, 12,* 158–171.

Bass, B. M., Burger, P. C., Doktor, R., & Barrett, G. V. (1979). *Assessment of managers.* New York: Free Press.

Befu, H. (1983a). Giri and Ninjo. In *Kodansha Encyclopedia of Japan* (Vol. 3, p. 34). Tokyo: Kodansha.

Befu, H. (1983b). Groups. In *Kodansha Encyclopedia of Japan* (Vol. 3, p. 63). Tokyo: Kodansha.

Befu, H. (1983c). On. In *Kodansha Encyclopedia of Japan* (Vol. 6, p. 105). Tokyo: Kodansha.

Benedict, R. (1946). *The chrysanthemum and the sword.* New York: Houghton Mifflin.

Blunt, P. (1973). Cultural and situational determinants of job satisfaction amongst management in South Africa. *Journal of Management Studies, 10*(2), 133–140.

Bouchner, S., & Ohsako, T. (1977). Ethnic role salience in racially homogeneous and heterogeneous societies. *Journal of Cross-Cultural Psychology, 8,* 455–492.

Bouchner, S., & Perks, R. W. (1971). National role evocation as a function of cross-cultural interaction. *Journal of Cross-Cultural Psychology, 2,* 157–164.

Bougon, M., Weick, K., & Binkhorst, D. (1977). Cognition in organizations: An analysis of the Utrecht Jazz Orchestra. *Administrative Science Quarterly, 22*(4), 1977.

Capra, F. (1975). *The tao of physics.* New York: Bantam.

Carrol, M. P. (1982). Culture. In J. Freeman (Ed.), *Introduction to sociology: A Canadian focus* (pp. 19–40). Scarborough, Ontario: Prentice Hall.

Chang, Y. N. (1976). Early Chinese management thought. *California Management Review, 19*(2), 71–76.

Child, J. (1981). Culture, contingency and capitalism in the cross-national study of organizations. In L. L. Cummings and B. M. Staw (Eds.), *Research in organizational behavior* (Vol. 3, pp. 303–356). Greenwich, CT: JAI Press.

Child, J., & Tayeb, M. (1982–1983). Theoretical perspectives in cross-national organizational research. *International Studies of Management and Organization, 7*(3-4).

Chui, V. C. L. (1977). *Managerial beliefs of Hong Kong managers.* Unpublished master's thesis, University of Hong Kong.

Chung, K. H. (1978, October). *A comparative study of managerial characteristics of domestic, international, and governmental institutions in Korea.* Paper presented at the Midwest Conference in Asian Affairs, Minneapolis, MN.

Cicourrel, A. V. (1972). *Cognitive sociology: Language and meaning in social interaction.* London: Penguin.

Cole, R. E. (1973). Functional alternatives and economic development: An empirical example of permanent employment in Japan. *American Sociological Review, 38,* 424–438.

Cole, R. E. (1979). *Work, mobility, and participation: A comparative study of American and Japanese industry.* Berkeley, CA: University of California Press.

Conner, J. W. (1976). Joge kankei: A key concept for an understanding of Japanese-American achievement. *Psychiatry, 39,* 266–279.

Crozier, M. (1964). *The bureaucratic phenomenon.* Chicago: University of Chicago Press.

Cummings, L. L., & Schmidt, S. M. (1972). Managerial attitudes of Greeks: The roles of culture and industrialization. *Administrative Science Quarterly 17*(2), 265–272.

Deustch, M. F. (1984). *Doing business with the Japanese.* New York: New American Library.

De Vos, G. A. (1973). *Socialization for achievement: Essays on the cultural psychology of the Japanese.* Berkeley, CA: University of California Press.

Doi, T. (1962). Amae: A key concept for understanding Japanese personality structure. In R. J. Smith & R. K. Beardsley (Eds.), *Japanese culture* (pp. 253–287). Chicago: Adline.

Doi, T. (1973). *The anatomy of dependence.* Tokyo: Kodansha.

Doktor, R. (1983a). Culture and the management of time: A comparison of Japanese and American top management practice. *Asia Pacific Journal of Management, 1*(1), 65–71.

Doktor, R. (1983b). Some tentative comments on Japanese and American decision making. *Decision Science, 14*(4), 607–612.

Dore, R. P. (1978). *Shinohata: Portrait of a Japanese village.* New York: Pantheon Books.

Dunphy, D. C., & Stening, B. W. (1984). *Japanese organization behavior and management.* Hong Kong: Asian Research Service.

England, G. W. (1975). *The manager and his values: An international perspective from the USA, Japan, Korea, India and Australia.* Cambridge, MA: Ballinger.

England, G. W., & Harpaz, I. (1983). Some methodological and analytic considerations in cross-national comparative research. *Journal of International Business Studies, 14*(2), 49–59.

England, G. W., & Lee, R. (1971). Organizational goals and expected behavior among American, Japanese, and Korean managers: A comparative study. *Academy of Management Journal, 14*(4), 424–438.

Evans, W. M. (1980). *Organization theory.* New York: Wiley.

Everett, J. E., Krishnan, A. R., & Stening, B. W. (1984). *Through a glass darkly: Southeast Asian managers' mutual perceptions of Japanese and local counterparts.* Singapore: Eastern Universities Press.

Form, W. (1979). Comparative industrial sociology and the convergence hypothesis. *Annual Review of Sociology, 5,* 1–25.

Foy, N., & Gadon, H. (1976). Worker participation contrasts in three countries. *Harvard Business Review, 54*(3), 71–84.

Garfinkel, H. (1967). *Studies in ethnomethodology.* Englewood Cliffs, NJ: Prentice-Hall.

Gibney, F. (1982). *Miracle by design: The real reasons behind Japan's economic miracle.* New York: Times Books.

Graham, J. L. (1985). Cross-cultural marketing negotiations: A laboratory experiment. *Marketing Science, 4*(2), 130–146.

Graham, J. L., & Sano, Y. (1984). *Smart bargaining: Doing business with the Japanese.* Cambridge, MA: Ballinger.

Graves, D. (1972). The impact of culture upon managerial attitudes, beliefs and behavior in England and France, *Journal of Management Studies, 10,* 40–56.

Gruenfeld, L. W., & MacEachron, A. E. (1975). A cross-national study of cognitive style among managers and technicians. *International Journal of Psychology, 10*(1), 27–55.

Haire, M., Ghiselli, E. G., & Porter, L. W. (1966). *Managerial thinking: An international study.* New York: Wiley.

Harbron, J. (1979). Korea's executives are not quite "the new Japanese." *The Business Quarterly, 44*(3), 16–19.

Harre, R., & Sekord, P. F. (1972). *The explanation of social behaviour.* Oxford: Blackwell.

Heller, R. A., & Wilpert, B. (1979). Managerial decision making. An international comparison. In G. W. England, A. R. Negandhi, & B. Wilpert (Eds.), *Functioning organizations in cross-cultural perspective*. Kent, OH: Kent State University Press.

Hicks, G. L., & Redding, S. G. (1983). The story of the East Asian economic miracle: Part 2, the culture connection. *Euro-Asia Business Review, 2*(2), 18–22.

Hickson, D. J., Hinnings, C. R., McMillan, C. J. M., & Schwitter, J. P. (1974). The culture-free context of organization structure: A tri-national comparison. *Sociology, 8*, 59–80.

Hickson, D. J., McMillar, C. J., Azumi, K., & Horvath, D. (1979). Grounds for comparative organization theory: Quicksands or hard core? In C. J. Lammers & D. J. Hickson (Eds.), *Organizations alike and unlike* (pp. 25–41). London: Routledge & Kegan Paul.

Hofstede, G. (1980). *Culture's consequences: International differences in work-related values*. Beverly Hills, CA: Sage.

Hoover, J. D., Troub, R. M., Whitehead, C. J., & Flores, L. G. (1978). Social performance goals in the Peruvian and the Yugoslav worker participation systems. In J. Susbauer (Ed.), *Academy of Management Proceedings '78*, (pp. 241–246). San Francisco, CA.

Joynt, P. (1985). Cross-cultural management: The cultural context of micro and macro organizational variables. In P. Joynt & M. Warner, *Managing in different cultures* (pp. 57–68). Oslo, Norway: Universitetsforlaget.

Kawai, H. (1981). *Crisis of the Japanese "hollow structure"* [Nihonteki chuku kozo no kiki]. Tokyo: Chuo Koron.

Keesing, R. M. (1974). Theories of culture. *Annual Review of Anthropology, 3*, 73–97.

Kerr, C. J., Dunlop, T., Harbison, F., & Myers, C. A. (1952). *Industrialism and industrial man*. Cambridge, MA: Harvard University Press.

Keys, J. B., & Miller, T. R. (1984). The Japanese management theory jungle. *Academy of Management Review, 9*, 342–353.

Kluckhohn, C., & Strodbeck, F. L. (1961). *Variations in values orientations*. Evanston, IL: Row, Peterson.

Kroeber, A. L., & Kluckhohn, C. (1952). *Culture: A critical review of concepts and definitions*. Cambridge, MA: Harvard University Press.

Kroeber, A. L., & Parsons, T. (1958). The concepts of culture and of social systems. *American Sociological Review, 23*, 582–583.

Kumagai, H. (1981). A dissection of intimacy: A study of bipolar posturing in Japanese social interaction—*amaeru* and *amayakasu*, indulgence and deference. *Culture, Medicine and Psychiatry, 5*, 249–272.

Kumon, S. (1984). Some principles governing the thought and behavior of Japanists (contextuals). *Journal of Japanese Studies, 8*, 5–28.

Lammers, C. J., & Hickson, D. J. (1979). Towards a comparative sociology of organizations. In C. J. Lammers & D. J. Hickson (Eds.), *Organizations alike and unlike* (pp. 3–20). London: Routledge & Kegan Paul.

Lau, S. (1977). *Managerial style of traditional Chinese firms*. Unpublished master's thesis, University of Hong Kong.

Laurent, A. (1983). The cultural diversity of Western management conceptions. *International Studies of Management and Organization, 8*(1-2), 75–96.

Lemming, F. (1977). *Street studies in Hong Kong*. Hong Kong: Oxford University Press.

Levitt, T. (1983). The globalization of markets. *Harvard Business Review, 83*(3), 92–102.

Lincoln, J. R., Hanada, M., & Olson, J. (1981). Cultural orientations and individual reactions to organizations: A study of employees of Japanese-owned firms. *Administrative Science Quarterly, 26*, 93–115.

Linton, R. (1945). *The cultural background of personality*. New York: Appleton-Century.

Maruyama, M. (1973). Paradigmatology and its application to cross-disciplinary, cross-professional and cross-cultural communication. *Dialectica, 29*(3-4), 135–196.
Maruyama, M. (1980). Mindscapes and science theories. *Current Anthropology, 21*(5), 389–600.
Maruyama, M. (1982). New mindscapes for future business policy and management. *Technology Forecasting and Social Change, 21,* 53–76.
Maruyama, M. (1984). Alternative concepts of management: Insights from Asia and Africa. *Asia Pacific Journal of Management, 1*(1), 100–111.
Mendenhall, M. E., & Oddou, G. (1986, September). The cognitive, psychological and social contexts of Japanese management. *Asia Pacific Journal of Management, 4*(1), 24–37.
Meyer, J. W., & Rowan, B. (1977). Institutionalized organizations: Formal structures as myth and ceremony. *American Journal of Sociology, 83,* 340–363.
Minami, H. (1980). *Encyclopedia on human relations of the Japanese* [Nihonjin no Ningen Kankei Jiten]. Tokyo: Kodansha.
Mishler, A. L. (1965). Personal contact in international exchanges. In H. C. Kelman (Ed.), *International behavior: A social-psychological analysis* (pp. 555–561). New York: Holt, Rinehart & Winston.
Moran, R. T. (1985). *Getting your yen's worth: How to negotiate with Japan, Inc.* Houston, TX: Gulf Publishing.
Nakamura, H. (1964). *Ways of thinking of Eastern peoples.* Honolulu, HI: East-West Center Press.
Nam, W. S. (1971). *The traditional pattern of Korean industrial management.* ILCORK Working Paper No. 14, University of Hawaii, Social Science Research Institute.
Needham, J. (1978). *The shorter science and civilization in China.* Cambridge: Cambridge University Press.
Negandhi, A. R. (1973). *Management and economic development: The case of Taiwan.* The Hague: Martinus Nijhoff.
Negandhi, A. R. (1979). Convergence in organizational practices: An empirical study of industrial enterprise in developing countries. In C. J. Lammers & D. J. Hickson (Eds.), *Organizations alike and unlike* (pp. 323–345). London: Routledge & Kegan Paul.
Negandhi, A. R. (1985). Management in the Third World. In P. Joynt & M. Warner, *Managing in different cultures* (pp. 69–97). Oslo, Norway: Universitetsforlaget.
Nevis, E. C. (1983). Cultural assumptions and productivity: The United States and China. *Sloan Management Review, 24*(3), 17–28.
Ouchi, W. G. (1981). *Theory Z: How American business can meet the Japanese challenge.* Reading, MA: Addison-Wesley.
Ouchi, W. G., & Jaeger, A. M. (1978). Theory Z organization: Stability in the midst of mobility. *Academy of Management Review, 3*(2), 305–314.
Parsons, T. (1973). Culture and social system revisited. In L. Schneider & C. M. Benjean (Eds.), *The idea of culture in the social sciences.* Cambridge, England: Cambridge University Press.
Pascale, R. T. (1978). Zen and the art of management. *Harvard Business Review, 56*(2), 153–162.
Peterson, R. B., & Shimada, J. Y. (1978). Sources of management problems in Japanese-American joint ventures. *Academy of Management Review, 3,* 796–805.
Polakos, E. D., & Wexley, K. N. (1983). The relationship among perceptual similarity, sex and performance ratings in manager-subordinate dyads. *Academy of Management Journal, 26,* 129–139.
Redding, S. G. (1977). Some perceptions of psychological needs among managers in

South-East Asia. In Y. H. Poortinga (Ed.), *Basic problems in cross-cultural psychology* (pp. 338–344). Amsterdam: Swets and Zeitlinger.

Redding, S. G. (1980). Cognition as an aspect of culture and its relation to management processes: An exploratory view of the Chinese case. *Journal of Management Studies,* *17*(2), 127–148.

Redding, S. G. (1982). Thoughts on causation and research models in comparative management for Asia. *Proceedings of the Academy of International Business Conference on Asia Pacific Dimensions of International Business* (pp. 1–38), University of Hawaii.

Redding, S. G., & Hicks, G. L. (1983). *Culture, causation and Chinese management.* Unpublished manuscript, University of Hong Kong, Mongkwok Ping Management Data Bank.

Redding, S. G., & Wong, G. (1986). The psychology of Chinese organizational behavior. In M. H. Bond (Ed.), *The psychology of Chinese people.* Hong Kong: Oxford University Press.

Roberts, K. H. (1970). On looking at an elephant: An evaluation of cross-cultural research related to organizations. *Psychological Bulletin, 74*(5), 327–350.

Schöllhammer, H. (1969). The comparative management theory jungle. *Academy of Management Journal, 12*(1), 81–97.

Sekaran, U. (1983). Methodological and theoretical issues and advancements in cross-cultural research. *Journal of International Business Studies, 14*(2), 61–73.

Sherif, M., & Hovland, C. I. (1961). *Social judgment: Assimilation and contrast effects in communication and attitude change.* New Haven, CT: Yale University Press.

Silin, R. H. (1976). *Leadership and values: The organization of large scale Taiwanese enterprises.* Cambridge, MA: Harvard University Press.

Silverman, D. (1970). The theory of organizations. London: Heinemann.

Solange-Perret, M. (1982). *Impact of cultural differences on budget.* Unpublished doctoral dissertation, University of Western Ontario, London, Ontario, Canada.

Sorge, A. (1983). Cultured organizations. *International Studies of Management and Organization, 12,* 106–138.

Stening, B. W. (1979). Problems in cross-cultural contact: A literature review. International Journal of Intercultural Relations, 3, 269–313.

Sterba, R. L. A. (1978). Clandestine management in the Imperial Chinese bureaucracy. *Academy of Management Review, 3*(1), 69–78.

Suzuki, H. (1976). *The transcendents and the climate* [Choetsusha to fudo]. Tokyo: Taimedo.

Triandis, H. C. (1973). Subjective culture and economic development. *International Journal of Psychology, 8,* 163–182.

Tung, R. L. (1981a). Management practices in China. *China International Business,* 64–105.

Tung, R. L. (1981b). Patterns of motivation in Chinese industrial enterprises. *Academy of Management Review,* 481–489.

Tung, R. L. (1984). Business negotiations with the Japanese. Lexington, MA: Lexington Books.

Tylor, E. B. (1877). *Primitive culture: Researches into the development of mythology, philosophy, religion, language, art and custom* (Vol. 1). New York: Henry Holt.

Vassiliou, V., Triandis, H. C., Vassiliou, G., & McGuire, H. (1980). Interpersonal contact and stereotyping. In H. C. Triandis (Ed.), *The analysis of subjective culture* (pp. 89–115). New York: Wiley.

Weinshall, T. D. (1977). *Culture and management.* London: Penguin.

Wexley, K. N., Alexander, R. A., Greenwalt, J. P., & Couch, M. A. (1980). Attitudinal congruence and similarity as related to interpersonal evaluations in manager-subordinate dyads. *Academy of Management Journal, 23,* 320–330.

Williamson, O. E. (1986). *The economic institutions of capitalism*. New York: The Free Press.
Witkin, H. A., Dyke, R. B., Faterson, H. F., Goodenough, D. R., & Karp, S. A. (1962). *Psychological differentiation*, New York: Wiley.
Wuthnow, R., Hunter, J. D., Bergesen, A., & Kurzweil, E. (1984). *Cultural analysis: The work of Peter L. Berger, Mary Douglas, Michel Foucault, and Jurgen Habermas.* London: Routlege & Kegan Paul.
Yamauchi, T. (1974). *Logos and lemma* [Rogosu to remma]. Tokyo: Iwanami Shoten.
Yang, H. L. (1973). *The practice of nepotism: A study of sixty Chinese commercial firms in Singapore.* Unpublished manuscript, University of Singapore.

II
INSIGHTS AND PERSPECTIVES FROM EUROPE

3

Applying American Organizational Sciences in Europe and the United Kingdom
The Problems

Cary L. Cooper and Charles J. Cox

Until the 1970s, much of European thought, research, and action in the organizational sciences came across the Atlantic from the United States. Graduate students and scholars in the fields of management and organizational behavior from England, France, Holland, West Germany, and many other countries, internalized American concepts of "participation," organizational development, and so forth, without seriously considering their transplantation and applicability to European culture. This was in parallel with a general increase in American influence in Europe, after World War II, in all aspects of life—economic, cultural, and particularly entertainment. By the mid-1970s, however, it was becoming obvious that many of the concepts in American organizational sciences were irrelevant, particularly in their American format, to the problems, concerns, and cultures of organizational life in Europe. Although many of the conceptualizations and action plans from U.S. organizational and management scientists have "face validity," they have not proved to be

Cary L. Cooper and Charles J. Cox • Manchester School of Management, University of Manchester, Institute of Science and Technology, Manchester M6O 1QD, United Kingdom.

the radical alternatives that Europe needed to solve its most pressing problems.

Even in Britain, which, it is often assumed, has many cultural similarities with America (indeed, Haire, Ghiselli, & Porter, 1966, found that the attitudes and orientations of British managers were more similar to American than to other European managers), a number of writers have, more recently, pointed to cultural differences as explanations of the resistance to American ideas in the social sciences being applied, for example, in U.K. organizations. Steele (1976) lists seven assumptions that he considers "fundamental and necessary" for providing a context for organizational development (OD) activities (these are, of course, based on an American concept of OD), and then goes on to discuss a number of factors within the U.K. culture that are incompatible with these assumptions. These include: (1) valuing security and stability; (2) adherence to tradition; (3) legitimacy of hierarchical authority; (4) intellectual tradition of rationality; (5) mistrust of professionals and tradition of the "gifted amateur"; (6) strong value placed on privacy and the inviolability of one's person and one's home.

Greiner (1977), also talking about OD, compares the similarities and the differences that he saw in America and Britain. He sees the cultural characteristics of the British as (1) strong inclination for intellectualizing; (2) appreciation of, and patience for, the historical flow of events; (3) persistence in elaborating concepts that began years before; (4) willingness to describe events in the most clinical terms; (5) tolerance for great complexity; (6) strong sense for structural and individual differences. Whereas, he views the American approach as characterized by (1) shooting first and asking questions later; (2) a desire for more simple terminology and concepts; (3) assembly line approach to training; (4) here and now optimism—belief that just about any change is possible; (5) willingness to shrug off or even forget; (6) quest for objective "hard" result; and (7) enthusiasm to convert people and organizations to an ideal model.

Greiner (1977) does suggest a number of similarities as well: (1) focus on behavioral processes and relationships; (2) concern for improving behavioral capacities to cope with the future; (3) and a value orientation toward participative method.

It is possible that this approach of Greiner's in looking for both similarities and differences provides the key to the problem. There are some very obvious similarities between American and European cultures, particularly between America and the United Kingdom. That this is particularly true in managerial culture is shown by Haire, Ghiselli and Porter (1966). However, it may be that the differences are even more important. The similarities tend to lead to an expectation that theories, ideas, and practices will immediately transfer across the Atlantic. When it is found that they do not, the reaction is to abandon them as "foreign" and irrelevant. A more fruitful approach might be to look for ways of adaptation.

The rest of this chapter elaborates on some of these possible differences and similarities between American and European cultures and their implications for the transfer of ideas.

I. DIFFERENCES, SIMILARITIES, AND IMPLICATIONS

A. Different Social Science Traditions (Europe—Cognitive and Psychoanalytic; American—Behavioral and Humanist)

Much American social science is based, either on behaviorism or the humanist school. In Europe, the dominant influences are the psychoanalytic schools (particularly in southern Europe), and an empirical but cognitivist approach, owing much to the gestalt school (Cooper, 1979). Thus both the two main American orientations are viewed with suspicion in Europe—the humanist theories because they cannot be subjected to scientific analysis and experimental testing, and the behaviorist theories because, although scientific, they are seen as oversimplistic and do not take internal cognitive processes into account. It is significant that theories of American origin that have achieved wide acceptance in Europe are essentially either psychoanalytic in origin (e.g., transactional analysis—Berne, 1961) or cognitivist (e.g., personal construct theory—Kelly, 1971) in approach. The theories of some humanists (most notably Maslow, 1964, Herzberg, 1966, and McGregor, 1960) were popular for a time in organizational circles. These, again, were close to the philosophical European tradition but were always, generally, unpopular with academics because of their lack of scientific testability. They have now broadly fallen out of favor to be replaced by "utility" and expectancy theories of motivation, which, although of North American origin, are much more in the European tradition (Cooper & Robertson, 1986).

B. Differences in Managerial Models (Europe—Cognitively Complex; America—Action-Oriented and Behaviorist)

The differences in the social sciences, discussed before, have their parallel in the models that managers carry in their heads in the two cultures, about both management and the world in general. This difference is neatly (if satirically) illustrated by Bertrand Russell (1927) in a comment on the differences between the gestalt and behaviorist schools of psychology:

> Animals studied by Americans rush about frantically, with an incredible display of hustle and pep, and at last achieve the desired result by chance. Animals observed by Germans sit still and think, and at last evolve the solution out of their inner consciousness.

In a similar way, European managers seem to prefer complex cognitive models of behavior in organizations. This seems to be based on an assumption that behavior is complex and therefore requires complex explanations. American managers seem to prefer direct, simpler, action-based philosophies. This distinction emerges very clearly in two studies of successful organizations. Peters and Waterman (1982) make the point that one characteristic of successful American companies is a preference for "keeping things simple." This point does not emerge from a similar study of British companies (Goldsmith & Clutterbuck, 1984). It is this difference that account for the success of books such as *The One Minute Manager* (Blanchard & Johnson, 1983) in the United States but that are viewed with suspicion in Europe. Although based on psychological principles, it appears too simple and slick to the European. This is compounded by the fact that the psychological principles are basically behaviorist and humanist.

C. Belief in the Notion of Human Complexity (Europe—Human Complexity; America—Rational Man)

There are major differences in assumptions regarding human behavior between Europe and the United States. In the United Kingdom and Europe, the underlying assumptions about human motivation are that humans are relatively complex. A human being is partly rational and does have economic motives, but he or she has complex interacting social and self-actualizing needs. This extends to understanding European organizational behavior through systems theory. These theories take the view that an organization can be viewed as an *open system*. All living things, all organizations, even countries or indeed the world, can be seen in this way. All open systems also have characteristics in common. These include inputs from the environment, outputs to the environment, conversion processes within the system, and feedback and control mechanisms. The work of people such as Woodward (1965), Miller and Rice (1967), and Burns and Stalker (1961), all from the United Kingdom, drew attention to the complex interaction between technology, the system of the organization, and individual behavior.

Much of the American assumptions on human motivation highlight the relatively simple relationships, for example, between leadership style and the performance of work groups (e.g., Likert, 1961) or the less complex characteristics of jobs (e.g., Hackman & Oldham, 1976), or what makes Japanese companies successful (Ouchi, 1981), and so forth. The American managerial world of practice and the academic world of scholarship are replete with examples of simplex theory and concepts of what motivates the human animal, many of which can be bought as paperbacks or can be seen on the American talk show.

D. Belief in Tradition (Europe—Tradition Is Valued and Change Regarded with Suspicion; America—Change Seen as Positive)

In Europe, there is a long cultural tradition stretching back well over 2,000 years. This tends to create a value in favor of stability and a belief that if something has lasted over time it must be good. America is a much younger country, proud of the pioneering spirit of the early settlers, many of whom came from persecuted and/or underprivileged minorities in Europe, and who had, therefore, an incentive to forget their origins. This has developed values where change is seen as positive, and anything more than a few years old is likely to be "out of date." There tends, consequently, to be (in Europe) a suspicion of anything new, even of European origin, and something from somewhere as different and "unconventional" as America, is even more suspect (Mant, 1981). This view is heightened by the very large flow of ideas and theories which emanate from the United States, which are then seen as a sequence of fashions or fads.

E. Suspicion of Things Foreign (Europe—Conservative and Strongly Influenced by Own Culture; America—Many Cultural Influences)

This is really an extension of the preceding point about tradition. There is in Europe a suspicion of anything foreign. This includes anything from, even, another European country. This was, of course, strong in the United Kingdom, although it has perhaps been slightly modified in recent years by the formation of the European Economic Community. In any event, there is still resistance to American ideas, simply because they are American and not local. It is not unusual to hear managers on management development programs in the United Kingdom complaining about "yet another North American input," and demanding to know why there are so few native theories. One factor in this may be the sheer volume of material coming from the United States, giving Europeans the feeling of being swamped, particularly as this is also paralleled in entertainment and other cultural imports (Cooper & Makin, 1984). Interestingly, this prejudice against items of foreign origin has been largely eroded in relation to manufactured goods, particularly those from Japan. But despite Japanese success, there is still a strong feeling in Europe that we have nothing useful to learn about their management methods because Japanese methods would be inappropriate here.

F. Suspicion of Experts (Europe—Value on Wide Education and Cultured Background, "Gifted Amateur"; America—Value on Technical Expertise and "Self-Made Man")

There is in Europe still a tendency to believe in the stereotype of the ideal manager or administrator as a classically educated and widely cultured person, who, because of his or her breadth of knowledge and general understanding of how the world works, will be able to cope with any situation—the "gifted amateur" tradition (Pugh, 1984). Even where this person is not seen as the ideal manager, he or she still has an appeal as an ideal sort of person to be. This valuing of a broad classical education runs parallel with a suspicion of anyone trained in what is seen as a narrow specialization. This is all right for dealing with mundane technical things, but not for the really complex issues of life. Thus if even the older professional and technical backgrounds are not too highly valued, there is very little chance that a relatively young and imprecise specialization such as the behavioral sciences is going to be taken very seriously. We cannot, after all, point to even a long tradition of useful application.

G. Political Orientation versus Openness (Europe—Political Values; America—More Open Values)

Probably deriving from the cultural history discussed before, there is, in Europe, a strong orientation towards political (with a small p) ways of getting things done. Decisions are made and implemented by subtle influences through a network of contacts, both at national and organizational levels. Although this, obviously, also does happen in America, there is a much more conscious value toward openness, as shown, for example, by the laws in the United States of America concerning openness of government information. In Europe, much government and company information is kept secret, much of it quite unnecessarily. This is part of the political culture. Europeans are usually proud of their political skills and tend to see Americans as naive because of a tendency to take things at face value. In the same way, much American organizational writing, certainly from the 1950s to the 1970s, tended to extol the virtues of "openness" and "trust," as a way of improving organizational performance (Child, 1985). These theories were at one time enthusiastically taken up in Europe (particularly the United Kingdom) by management trainers and OD consultants (Pugh, 1984). They have had remarkably little impact on the actual management style of European organizations, largely because they are inconsistent with the basic political culture.

H. Class Structure (Europe—Strong Class Structure [Particularly United Kingdom]; America—More Classless)

Many writers have drawn attention to the class differences that still exist in England and to some extent elsewhere in Europe. Managers and shop-floor workers often have very different social, cultural, and educational backgrounds, to an extent that frequently makes communication between the two groups quite difficult. This is an important part of European industrial relations problems. In the United Kingdom particularly, there is an assumption of an essential conflict of interest between workers and management. This comes very strongly from the trade unions, who often see their role as to extract the maximum concessions while giving minimal ground in return. This also is very much a matter of history, stemming from relationships created during the Industrial Revolution. The result is an industrial relations system based very firmly on conflict and bargaining. American humanist ideals of openness and trust developed in a more classless (but not necessarily egalitarian) society are, again, inappropriate.

I. Economic Situation (Europe—Pessimistic; America—Optimistic)

It is interesting that the height of activity in the United Kingdom, in the attempted application of humanist theories, was in the 1960s when the economy was still reasonable buoyant and there was still an air of optimism. With the declining economy there has been a definite return to more traditional styles of management, both nationally and in organizations. This may be coincidence, but is, more probably, a reversion to traditional approaches as things get difficult. It may be that more authoritarian and political styles are appropriate in difficult economic situations.

J. Management Education (Europe—Institutional; America—Stimulus-Response)

Differences between the American and European approaches to the organizational sciences can also be seen, in terms of Mant's (1981) characterization, in their orientations to management education:

> If I was forced to characterize the European vs. American approaches to management education, I would say that the European tends to veer towards the institutional and the American towards a stimulus/response behavioral model. Europeans have learned, the hard way, about the frailties of mankind and have tended to pay attention therefore to the institutions by which affairs of men are regulated. Americans are more inclined to place trust in the limitless possibilities of the human being and especially his capacity to adapt and improve his behavior directly, given encouragement, reward, and training.

The apparent failure of American organizational sciences in Europe, therefore, is not due to any proven ineffectiveness of the concepts or theory, but to the significant cultural differences between Europe and North America. It is important, albeit essential, that these concepts and perspectives are adapted to meet the needs of organizational life and management education in different contexts. If we do not, we may find ourselves depleted of the educational foundations stones necessary to translate theory and practice into effective management education. Indeed, we might find ourselves offering the following type of management education experience, which was recently humorously characterized in the *Financial Times* (Cooper & Makin, 1984, p. 7):

> Good morning gentlemen, welcome to the X management education establishment. You will have noted, perhaps with relief, the absence of faculty or curriculum. This is a regular feature of this programme and a closely-guarded secret of its alumni, present and past. If you should require any inducement to keep this secret you may be influenced by the 500 pounds in crisp ten-pound notes which is to be found in a brown envelope in your bedroom. This represents half the fee paid by your employers and approximated expenditure that would otherwise have been incurred with respect to teaching staff salaries and related costs. In the meantime, meals and other services will be provided and the bar will remain open at normal opening times. You will have discovered that your colleagues are drawn from similar organizations to your own and contain amongst them a wealth of practical experience in all manner of managerial roles. There is also a first-rate library at your disposal. How you decide to pass these six weeks is your own managerial decision; we trust you will enjoy it and find it beneficial. Thank you.

II. CONCLUSION

This chapter has considered a number of possible differences between Europe and the United States that may account for some of the resistance to American management theories. It is argued that this resistance stems from significant cultural differences, most of which are related to Europe's long history and tradition. Admittedly, much of this is, necessarily, highly speculative. A further factor may be that when, for 2,000 years, you have seen yourself as part of the most dominant continent, from which all important thinking has been initiated and which has had far-reaching effects on the rest of the world, it requires a large readjustment to accept influence from elsewhere. This is not, of course, to say that there would not be value in accepting such ideas. The reverse is, undoubtedly, true, but the ideas have to be tested for appropriateness and absorbed slowly into the local culture.

III. REFERENCES

Berne, E. (1961). *Transactional analysis and psychotherapy*. New York: Grove.
Berne, E. (1964). *Games people play*. New York: Grove.
Blanchard, K., & Johnson, S. (1983). *The one minute manager*. London: Willow.
Burns, T., & Stalker, G. M. (1961). *The management of innovation*. London: Tavistock.
Child, J. (1985). *Organizations*. London: Harper & Row.
Cooper, C. L. (1979). *Learning from others in groups*. London: Associated Business Press.
Cooper, C. L., & Makin, P. (1984). *Psychology for managers*. London: Macmillan and BPS.
Cooper, C. L., & Robertson, I. T. (1986). *International review of industrial and organizational psychology: 1986*. London: Wiley.
Goldsmith, W., & Clutterbuck, D. (1984). *The winning streak*. London: Weidenfeld & Nicholson.
Greiner, L. E. (1977). Reflections on O.D. American style. In C. L. Cooper (Ed.), *Organizational development in the UK and the USA: A joint evaluation* (pp. 65–83). London: Macmillan.
Hackman, J. R., & Oldham, F. R. (1976). Motivation through the design of work: Test of a theory. *Organizational Behavior and Human Performance, 16,* 250–279.
Haire, M., Ghiselli, E. E., & Porter, C. W. (1966). *Managerial thinking: An international study*. New York: Wiley.
Herzberg, F. (1966). *Work and the nature of man*. Cleveland, OH: The World Publishing Co.
Kelley, H. H. (1971). *Attribution in social interaction*. New York: General Learning.
Likert, R. (1961). *New patterns of management*. New York: McGraw-Hill.
Mant, A. (1981). Developing effective managers for the future. In C. L. Cooper (Ed.), *Developing managers for the 1980's* (pp. 79–88). London: Macmillan.
Maslow, A. H. (1964). *Motivation and personality*. New York: Harper & Row.
McGregor, D. M. (1960). *The human side of enterprise*. New York: McGraw-Hill.
Miller, E. J., & Rice, A. K. (1967). *Systems of organization*. London: Tavistock.
Ouchi, W. G. (1981). *Theory Z: How American business can meet the Japanese challenge*. Reading, MA: Addison-Wesley.
Peters, T. J., & Waterman, R. H. (1982). *In search of excellence*. New York: Harper & Row.
Pugh, D. (1984). *Organization theory*. London: Penguin.
Russell, B. (1927). *Philosophy*. New York: Norton.
Steele, F. (1976). Is organizational development work possible in the UK culture? *Journal of European Training, 5*(3), 105–110.
Woodward, J. (1965). *Industrial organization: Theory and practice*. London: Oxford University Press.

4

The Failure of Management Techniques in Central Planning Economies

Wiktor Askanas

This chapter examines the causes underlying economic failure in communist countries. Special consideration is given to the role of the application of Western management techniques in these centrally planned economies.

I. SYSTEMS MANAGEMENT TECHNIQUES AND THEIR LIMITATIONS

Like the weather, the lack of efficiency in central planning economies (CPE) is a subject everyone talks about but about which no one can do anything. It is a problem that provokes profound questions about the nature of the system, the future direction of the economies involved, and the structure of the most basic political and economic organizations. For the researcher, it has become a topic of more than practical and everyday relevance. More than anything else, it is the mundane routines and the policies that direct the day-to-day activities of individuals (particularly managers) in CPEs that explain why things work the way they

Wiktor Askanas • Faculty of Administration, University of New Brunswick, Fredericton, New Brunswick E3B 5A3, Canada.

do. If we can get at the way in which these minutiae determine an organization's ability to create and carry out strategy (i.e., learn how to evaluate corporate culture), we can also learn much about how not to manage. A number of research has been undertaken in this area. Unfortunately, because of the multiplicity of approaches and researchers' unwillingness to examine anything but very limited aspects of the problem, it is virtually impossible to use the existing literature to determine trends. Very few authors have tried to look at the topic in terms of an evolving system in the context of modern industrial economies. Also, few attempt to differentiate between broad classes of variables that shape the relationships such as those of ideology, structure, and process at both macro- and microlevels. A number of these gaps in the existing literature are the focal points of this chapter. Presented herein is a reconstruction of the conclusion from research conducted between 1975 and 1980 (see, e.g., Askanas, 1978a,b,c). This research consisted mainly of interviews with managers of state-owned enterprises in Poland, Czechoslovakia, and Hungary as well as the analysis of secondary data from the USSR and Cuba.

The intention here is not to rewrite the theory of bureaucracy but to explore some widely held perceptions about the internal functioning of organizations operating under the CPE doctrine in a comprehensive study. The objective is to provide a conceptual and theoretical framework to make possible clearer comparisons, and, at least partially, a synthesis of analytic perspectives. This is done by specifically examining managerial problems in state-owned-and-operated economic institutions. These problems relate to the application in the institutions of a set of techniques and processes developed in and for Western postindustrial nations and revolve around: (1) why specific techniques have been chosen, and (2) why they are maintained. In essence, one has to accept an epistemological assumption underlying all rational choice model that actors in a system are purposeful decision-makers (Scammon, 1972). They act with a singular purpose and possess the ability to maximize the achievement of goals derived from this purpose. In other words, the rational player will choose the alternative that will lead to the outcome he or she most desires.

In order to understand the consequences of this decision process, it is necessary to describe both CPE and "free-enterprise"-style bureaucracies. The central planning model is built on four governing principles. These are:

1. Impersonal rules—which largely define, often in great detail, each person's organizational task and position and specify how each member of society should behave (Richta, 1973).

2. Centralization—which places an almost impassable distance between those who decide and those affected by the decision (Staniszkis, 1984).
3. Stratification—which locks individuals into homogeneous groups that are separated from one another by an ideological set of rules (Morawski, 1976).
4. Parallel power—which emerges around unforeseen zones of relationship uncertainty and, which as a result, are uncodified and unregulated (Kaminski, 1976).

Mutually supporting and reinforcing one another for decades, these characteristics perpetuate themselves through a series of vicious circles (Crozier, 1964). At times, key actors within the system recognize them for what they are—Kafka's circuits:

> Kafka's Circuits are organizational or procedural traps for individuals. The victim repeatedly finds himself struggling to attain some important but ambiguous objective. This very objective seems to disappear as person becomes trapped in endless sub-systems of irrelevant tasks. Means and ends shift back and forth, become transformed into each other with no end to this process. (Singer, 1980, p. 22)

It is obvious that such a self-perpetuating system will sooner or later dry out its own resources and steer into economic or social crises. To avoid total collapse of the system, there are periodical actions taken in areas that have the greatest potential for improving efficiency, namely: (a) the process of decentralization, (b) the process of restructuring organizations and system, and (c) the process of computerization. These areas are traditionally well developed in postindustrial societies. Their development, however, is due to a totally different philosophy of management. An examination of the development of the bureaucracy in North American organizations (United States and Canada) gives us a better grasp of this philosophy. From studies conducted by Gouldner (1954) and Selznick (1957), one may read that American management process involves interaction, confrontation, and, what is most important, communication. In such an environment, there is a tendency to increase in behavior that could be regard as excessively cautious and analytical. As William James once said, "For American managers what is familiar seems rational" (James, 1956, p. 5). As a result, ambiguity for the manager is viewed as an affront (Gimpl & Dackin, 1980) and precludes him or her from making choices in a right way. American managers are taught that they must decide not choose, implying that control of the facts and variables is possible. The stability of the system depends on the continuing existence of common modes of interpretation and understanding. This subsequently determines perception of reality and reaction to it. Thus, it guides managerial choices among objectives and means of action (Parsons, 1951). After this description of differences between two types of bureaucracies, it is possible to analyze the CPE system in terms of concrete actions and their consequences.

An examination of curricula, texts, and other materials indicates that CPE countries are trying to follow, and eventually implement, some major ideas on managerial practice from well-established Western theories. The vocabularies of managers and politicians are full of terms taken from organizational behavior and organizational literature (Askanas, 1978a). Closer scrutiny reveals that the meanings imputed to these terms are very different from those originally intended. Democracy means dictatorship of the working class. Decentralization means a centralized democracy, and economic objectives are the tasks defined in the central plan. Built on these different interpretations of Western (organizational) concepts, the sociopolitical reality in organizations leads to management practices that are, in fact, the inverses of the original ideas. Table 4.1 presents some pairs of theoretical techniques and their inverses.

Under the concept of equifinality, as described by Osigweh (see Chapter 1), there is nothing wrong with replacing one set of techniques with another. It is a very logical alternative in a situation when the replacement set better fits the system's reality. In this case, the replacement leads to the inverse of the concept, and the intended result of greater efficiency becomes a source of dysfunction. To explain why this happens, it is necessary to discuss in detail some of these inverses and their consequences.

Table 4.1. Western Management Techniques and Their CPE Inverses

In theory, management by	In practice, management by
1. Objectives (Humble, 1965)	1. Lack of goal consciousness
2. Result (standardization of output) (Mintzberg, 1979)	2. Lack of recognition for results
3. Initiative (Child, 1984)	3. Prestige and informal authority
4. Dynamic development and growth (Tichy, 1983)	4. Overformalization
5. Adaptation (Pfeffer & Salancik, 1978)	5. Idealization of reality
6. Future orientation (Ansoff, 1984)	6. Traditionalism
7. Trust (Morgan, 1983)	7. Mistrust
8. Delegation of authority (Drucker, 1966)	8. Control
9. Competence (Peters & Waterman, 1982)	9. Obsession with position & title
10. Competition (Porter, 1985)	10. Negative competition

A. Process of Decentralization

The dogma of CPE countries traditionally demands an authoritarian and bureaucratic approach to planning and controlling. As a consequence, the process of defining strategy, objectives, and goals moves from the top of the organization downward. This top-down approach (as a power-structure maintainer) has been a powerful management technique for more than half a century. This is simply because of the rigid control and an intentionally constructed "economy of shortage" (Kornai, 1980). The approach is a very powerful one that, nevertheless, results in both inefficient use of resources and a combination of subordinate resentment and social rejection of higher management's objectives. The mechanics of these inefficiencies are very simple. Upper level management is perceived as attempting to manipulate lower levels by setting unrealistically high objectives. In reponse, lower level employees try to hide their true capacities from top management. The employees attempt to find their lowest acceptable level of output. It is usually politicians who declare that, to effectively manage other people's work, it is necessary to distinctly realize the task that requires accomplishment. So, whenever these countries initiate organizational reform, decentralization is declared to be the main priority. What is not declared is the specific philosophy attached to the process of decentralization. This philosophy states that it is responsibility *without* authority that is allocated to the lower levels. As a direct result of this, the systems in question are more centralized than ever. This is true in spite of innumerable reforms that have been undertaken. The idea of decentralization has become, in this sense, a political cliché at the level of the state. Even under the assumption that this is not the case, at the level of organizational culture, there are at least three other phenomena that occur to effectively block any attempt to decentralize the system: (1) the phenomenon of management by mistrust; (2) the phenomenon of negative composition; and (3) the phenomenon of autonomization of the control.

1. Mistrust

This phenomenon manifests itself in an overformalization of the controlled aspects of organizational behavior. There is no room for initiative. One of the major goals of decentralization is to create an atmosphere conducive to the undertaking of independent searches. Such searches seek the best ways to achieve particular objectives. The chance of taking up such a search grows when the manager feels that he or she is in a position of trust. This occurs only when interference with the ability to choose among the available methods of completing the tasks and achieving the goals is minimized. Under conditions of overformalization, whereby the appraisal of performance is based on the compliance with rules, the perception of mistrust is commonplace. Such statements as "If they manage me this way, and by such means [i.e., rules], then I must not be trustworthy" or "How can I trust my associates if they do not trust me?" indicate the level of trust being perceived by managers. Thinking in these terms is extremely common in CPE countries. The social rule of rational confidence has been supplanted by the countersystem rule of general mistrust. Offices do not trust citizens, and vice versa; managers do not trust subordinates, and subordinates do not trust managers (Kiezun, 1980). Systems management techniques based on decentralization cannot be efficiently implemented with the social mechanism malfunctioning in this way. As a result, what happens is this: When an individual is promoted to a managerial position, that individual assumes that he or she is in a position of trust. Upon discovering that this is not the case, the individual begins to assume the same attitude, eventually becoming a cynical system operator. This is the beginning of a pretense that produces a "fool's paradise." A common Polish saying that explains this is: "They are pretending to pay us for the jobs we are pretending to do."

2. Negative Competition

The second phenomenon may be characterized by the following example. In the "fight" for success in the organization or in political life, the persons involved prove not that they are better than their environment but that the environment is worse than they are. In an environment that can be characterized this way, self-defense requires that every action be surrounded by buffers of different kinds. These buffers protect the manager against attacks from others—for example, obtaining permission in advance from superiors for any actions taken, giving all decisions an artificial ideological basis, or building a network of informal lobby groups within the organization. In other words, a sequence of nonactions that act as safeguards. Such safeguards require both time and energy but do not advance the organization in the direction of its goals. The result is the development of a self-perpetuating series of Kafka-circuitlike political mazes. The effects of these mazes have a definite internal impact. As a consequence, the advancement of the organization is retarded. These mazes have no effect on the external appearance of the organizations. One of their internal effects is to cause managers to avoid both risk taking and any expression of their aspirations. Clearly, the best way to advance through the ranks of CPE systems is to avoid acting. By doing nothing, managers protect their position. By necessity, then, the manager's concern ceases to be with the advancement of the organization. Rather, to survive, all efforts are devoted to keeping out of trouble. According to one manager, "To be safe in this system, move slowly. To be really safe, do not move at all." Considering the weight to be attached to comments of this nature, it is important to remember the following. In Western societies, what is not forbidden is allowed. In CPEs, however, what is not expressly allowed is forbidden. This rule is so contradictory to the spirit of decentralization and self-government, whose basic features are structural transparency and a bias toward action, that it by itself excludes any possibility of implementing the techniques that are connected with it.

3. Autonomization of Control

All central planning states are host to a tremendous number of institutions designed to control others. Essentially, these structures are parallel and constantly overlap. Inevitably, this results in a scenario in which the control structure exists virtually for its own sake (Goscinski, 1981). That which was to constitute the means of realizing the goal—more effective management—becomes the goal itself. As a result, there exists only a mechanical linkage between the discovery of errors and the application of sanctions. It can be seen, then, that under these circumstances, the ostensible purpose of the controlling process is not to ensure that the organization moves in the proper direction. Rather, it is to ensure that the individuals currently holding positions at the upper levels can continue to move in the proper direction. Conversely, the effect on managers at the lower levels is to be constantly threatened by them, and consequently they are forced to concern themselves only with following rules and fighting decentralization. Therefore, one may state that the autonomization of control, observed in practice, leads to the loss of the system's ability to track errors and learn. From the foregoing, it should be apparent that under the CPE concept, true decentralization will never occur.

B. Process of Restructuralization

An analysis of the contents of CPE systems indicates an inability to change. This relates to both the system as a whole and to the changes in goals realized by particular organizations in different periods. A few examples of this are: products being produced, despite a lack of demand; technological obsolescence resulting from repeatedly purchasing the same technologies; and the structural rigidity of governmental institutions. In the past 25 years, CPEs (all Warsaw Pact countries: Poland, USSR, Czechoslovakia, Hungary, Bulgaria, East Germany and Cuba) have undertaken 74 attempts at reform. With the possible exception of Hungary, none of these has had any observable positive economic effect. This is the most telling indicator of the lack of restructuring potential within the systems being discussed. The reason probably lies in each change resulting in a replacement of some structures with others. This in turn involves the exchange of people between organizations, the disappearance of some organizations, and the creation of new structural solutions. These change patterns are not in line with the rigid hierarchical structure and synonymity of official subordinations represented by Marxist states. Restructuralization faces two fundamental barriers in practice. These are management by obsession with position and title and management by structural overformalization.

1. Obsession with Position and Title

This phenomenon relates to seeking prestige about the post one holds, as opposed to the work one does. The obsession with prestige created by position and title has two sources: economic stratification and social stratification. The first relates to position in the sense that the more prestigious the post, the greater the number of formal and informal privileges. The second is the result of unjustified social advancement from lower to upper classes by virtue of (not necessarily real) political commitments.

As a result, the implementation of any new structure is almost impossible. Only through crises and their resulting social upheaval (e.g., the death of a leader) are changes in the power structure effected. The scope of the ensuing structural changes is most likely relatively limited as it would impact only a very narrow elite. The incumbents, to maintain the support of the bureaucracy, must freeze the system despite rising to power by promising change. This state of affairs is further entrenched in that positions inside the CPE states are traditionally tenured.

2. Structural Overformalization

The second, and no less important, limitation to restructuralization is evident in hiring and firing practices and in the procedures for confirming organizational changes. These two elements are so overformalized and politicized that dynamic control within their framework is practically impossible.

C. Process of Computerization

Computerizing management information systems is the most popular technique applied under CPE conditions. The computer becomes a type of panacea. As there are extensive bibliographies available on the subject, there is no need for a lengthy discussion of the contents of these systems. The intention here is to indicate specific limitations in the process of computerization.

Prior to examining specific problems resulting from computerization, it is valuable to note the following. Despite 20 years experience with the application of electronic computing techniques to the process of management, it is difficult to find any truly successful implementations. For the purposes of this chapter, an implementation is recognized as successful only if the EDP (electronic data processing) system assumed any of the basic intraorganizational functions. Early in the history of computer applications, failures of all types could be ascribed to inexperience. Many of the original problems still plague the industry in CPE countries, although the pioneer period has long since ended. There are at least four possible reasons for this: (1) management by lack of goal consciousness, (2) management by lack of recognition for results, (3) management by traditionalism, and (4) management by prestige and informal authority. Each of these elements will be analyzed individually (Askanas, 1974, 1978a,b).

1. Lack of Goal Consciousness

It should be apparent that, in the majority of institutions, a specific style of management based on an autocratic-centralistic understanding of the manager's functions has developed. This affects all levels of management. Nevertheless, the impact is strongest at the middle levels of any structure. This phenomenon is manifested by the inclusion (within directives whose ostensible purpose is only to define which tasks will be undertaken by whom) of detailed instructions concerning the manner in which the tasks will be completed. In the process of management, then, answers to two questions (what? and how?) are sought. Unfortunately, the most critical question (what for?) is never even asked. As a consequence, managers not only lose the responsibility for deciding how to approach a problem but have no idea why the problem exists. The effect of this is that managers become more concerned with completing the assigned task than with achieving any specific result.

This, of course, is the most general barrier. It causes the employee to feel like an organizational automaton, whose freedom of choice reduces to the choice between joining or not joining any given organization. In the process of computerization, this barrier results in the implementation of EDP systems whose real usefulness in the process of management is insignificant. This is the result of the fact that its task is not to perform any defined activity (or group of activities) but to produce information, as such. This information does not posess any explicit destination. Also, the purposes it serves ought to be formulated every time, by the people who use it. At the same time, the implementation of the EDP system imposes a variety of new procedures on the employees. The fulfillment of these new procedures is sometimes very arduous. Furthermore, as there is no rational explanation for the existence of these new procedures, there is no apparent purpose for them. In this situation, supplementary goals and beliefs appear at the executive level. These goals are, as a rule, of a negative nature. In the case of computerization, the conviction that this process will intensify intraorganizational control is one such negatively rooted belief. As a consequence of this type of misunderstanding, actions occur. These actions are against the misinterpreted goals of the innovation and not the innovation itself.

2. Lack of Recognition for Results

The second barrier to improving the efficiency of organizations is a system of management by lack of recognition for results at the level in the organization that realized a given task. In every case, the responsibility for producing results is on the level at which the work is to be done, whereas credit is given to the levels above. All information relating to the results is phrased so that every higher level can either take all the credit for a piece of work or show that it was an important contributor to it. Intermediate levels of management, therefore, see EDP systems as a menace because of the ability of these systems to keep track of the locations of all contributions and results. This ability destroys their delicately networked information editing system. Given this, it is no wonder that the middle managing staff have the most negative attitude toward computer systems. Thus, a conflict occurs that is very difficult to rectify. To survive, it is necessary to improve the managerial system. Unfortunately, the result of such a process is contradictory to the desires of the group with the greatest power in the system. Practical experience proves there is no solution to this conflict. As a result of the conflict, none of the CPEs will really profit from the process of computerization, regardless of the size of the expenditure.

3. Traditionalism

The greatest danger to modern organizations in CPE states is the experience people gain within them. At some point, this experience stops working as a dynamic model of reality. Rather than continuing to learn, they begin to treat their experience as a data base facsimile. The data base contains the answers to all the problems they encounter. Over time, responses are learned to many specific sets of circumstances. In the future, the symptoms of actual events will be tailored to the "parameters" of known circumstances. Some facts will be ignored, and excessive weight will be placed on others. Furthermore, past experiences become a part of the official ideological language. As a result, there are a limited number of alternative approaches that exist in the official language. Gradually, this problem becomes more severe because the number of choices is always shrinking. Essentially, this represents an inability to learn and an excessive reliance on behavior patterns established to cope with vastly different needs. Many organizations have suffered huge losses only because management was unable to recognize that traditional modes of responses were incorrect under the new circumstances.

When EDP systems are involved, management by traditionalism is manifest in attempts to transfer organizational procedures tested in the past onto the computer. This limits the contents of the system to elements that are insignificant from the point of view of management processes. Referring to tradition also involves the danger of becoming "entangled in one's own incantations." That is, once there is a set precedent, management by tradition requires that the position be defended regardless of environmental changes. In the organization's design, the acceptance of such a point of view leads to a spiral. Today's problems are incorrectly matched with yesterday's methods which have already been proven inefficient. After a period of time the organization returns to its original state, reinitiating the cycle.

4. Prestige and Informal Authority

This is the last, but not the least, essential barrier. It is manifest in an ongoing search for informal allies and lobbiers whose only use may be to provide an advantage in very ordinary situations. The existence of these alliances releases, in the managing staff, an inclination to enter as many informal relationships as possible. The goal of the staff is to create for themselves the ability to arrange both official and private matters. Pursuant to the implementation of computer procedures, the managing staff has more access to information (through the computer system). Nevertheless, it finds playing the game by the existing rules much more difficult. The fight for informal power means objecting to any novelties able to destroy the long-standing and precisely constructed network of informal bonds.

II. CONCLUSION

The problem that has been examined here is not so much the content of the original techniques being developed by different schools of management thought and their fit to the CPE doctrine, but the consequences of ideological influence on the understanding and implementation of the techniques. The argument was that empirical reality proves that interpretations of techniques vary from the content and intention of the original ideas. They vary sufficiently to justify saying that, upon implementation of the techniques, their content is almost always the inverse of the original idea. Managers in CPE countries are unaware that the conceptions and views they are trying to apply cannot be effectively applied within the framework of their social system.

To an external observer, the material presented herein should dismiss the idea that it is possible to raise CPEs to a higher level of internal effectiveness within the existing culture. An externalization of the prevailing management system is social disintegration that paralyzes human ingenuity and initiative. Diagramatically this can be presented as shown in Table 4.2.

The functioning of no organization can be faultless. Nevertheless, it is dangerously utopian to suggest that the potential for efficiency exists in a system that hides, through its managerial processes, such a large supply of human resources. Such a system must desire to change its ideological priorities. Without such a change, CPE states will never gain the ability to learn anything positive. Instead, they will continue to develop effective control systems to protect the status quo in power relations.

Although it may sound paradoxical, it is true that in a system with so many distorting phenomena, only the usage of the previously described dysfunctional techniques allows managers to survive in their positions. From this point of view, their behavior is rational. When there is universal use of this type of rationality within a system, the road leads

Table 4.2. Corporate Culture Matrix

	Relationships		
Tasks	Statewide focus of attention	Corporatewide focus of attention	Peer focus of attention
Innovating	Traditionalism	Pretentiousness	Do nothing
Decision making	Overformalization	Lack of goal consciousness	Compliance with rules
Communicating	Language of ideology	Distrust	Control
Organizing	Idealization of reality	Centralization	Ad hoc achievements
Monitoring	Formal control	Rules	Selfishness
Appraising and rewarding	Prestige and informal authority	Obsession with position and title	Negative competition

inevitably to economic crises and social upheaval. This irrationality indicates that the injection of capital into these states and of new technologies will not prevent social and economic tension.

The objective of this chapter was to identify sources of the problem (why organizational science techniques fail in CPEs), and so, name the phenomena that must be taken into consideration in future search for solutions. As a result of the limitations on the subject matter, it may appear that the systems have had no economic or social successes. This is obviously untrue. Nevertheless, it is true that the price paid for the seemingly uniformed or poorly adapted use of Western organizational sciences was unnecessarily high. The goal was to break down the game played in these countries (namely that what goes unnamed does not exist—hence the prevailing ideology that no such problem exists) by showing the limitations and sources of dysfunction. This occurs simply because we have to realize that no kindly law of nature will save us from the fruits of our ignorance.

III. REFERENCES

Ansoff, J. (1984). *Implanting strategic management*. Toronto: Prentice-Hall.
Askanas, W. (1974). *The impact of technology and R&D on organizational culture*. Warsaw: Polish Academy of Science.
Askanas, W. (1978a). The language of leaders. *Organizational Review, 35*, 127–135.
Askanas, W. (1978b). *Spontaneous techniques of management*. Warsaw: Polish Society of Organizational Management.
Askanas, W. (1978c). The obstacle to system management. Warsaw, *Wektory, 11*, 47–62.
Child, J. (1984). *Organization*. London: Butler.

Crozier, M. (1964). *The bureaucratic phenomenon*. Chicago: University of Chicago.

Drucker, P. (1966). *The concept of corporation*. New York: John Day

Gimpl, M., & Dakin, S. (1980). *Management and magic*. Australia: University of Canterbury.

Goscinski, J. (1981). *Projektowanie organizac ji*. Warszawa: PWN.

Gouldner, A. (1954). *Patterns of industrial bureaucracy*. New York: Free Press.

Humble, J. (1965). *Improving management performance*. London: Management Publications.

James, W. (1956). *Sentiment of rationality*. New York: Dove.

Kaminski, A. (1976). *Organizac je a struktura klasowo—warstwowa*. Warszawa: PWN.

Kiezun, W. (1980). *Patologie organizac ji*. Warszawa: PWN.

Kornai, J. (1980). *The economy of shortage*. Amsterdam: North-Holland.

Mintzberg, N. (1979). *The structuring of organizations*. New York: Prentice-Hall.

Morawski, W. (1976). *Organizac je: Socjologia struktur, procesow, rol*. Warszawa: PWN.

Morgan, G. (1983). *Beyond method*. Beverley Hills, CA: Sage.

Parsons, T. (1951). *The social system*. New York: Free Press.

Peters, T., & Waterman Jr., R. H. (1982). *In search of excellence*. New York: Harper & Row.

Pfeffer, J., & Salancik, G. (1978). *The external control of the organizations*. New York: Harper & Row.

Porter, M. (1985). *Competitive advantage*. New York: Free Press.

Richta, R. (1973). *Cywilizacja na rozdrozu*. Warszawa: PWE.

Scammon, R. (1972). *The real majority*. Berkeley, CA: Berkeley Publication Corporation.

Selznick, P. (1957). *Leadership in administration*. New York: Harper & Row.

Singer, B. (1980, September/October). Crazy systems. *Social Policy, 2*(4), 25–37.

Staniszkis, J. (1984). *Poland's self-limiting revolution*. Princeton: Princeton University Press.

Tichy, N. (1983). *Managing strategic change*. New York: Wiley.

5

Union–Management Participation in Corporate Decision-Making

A Comparative Analysis of Codetermination in West Germany and the United States

Rolf E. Rogers and William Aussieker

Organizational effectiveness and the international competitiveness of U.S. firms have been related to different types of human resources strategies (Ferris, Schellenberg, & Zammuto, 1984; Snow & Miles, 1984; Odiorne, 1984). Labor relations and the union–management relationship have been largely ignored in the discussion on human resources strategies, but the need for change in U.S. union–management relations toward more cooperation and union or employee participation in corporate decision-making (codetermination) is supposedly suggested by the effectiveness of Japanese management techniques and other human resources strategies of successful U.S. multinationals (Ouchi, 1981; Peters & Waterman, 1982). Whereas some emphasize the "hard skills" of organizational learning and not soft skills or human resources strategies of Japanese management (Nonoka & Johansson, 1985), recent research shows more cooperation and codetermination in U.S. industrial relations (Capelli, 1983; Freedman & Fulmer, 1982; Kas-

Rolf E. Rogers • Department of Management, California Polytechnic State University, San Luis Obispo, California 93407 and Department of Management, University of Hawaii, Honolulu, Hawaii 96844.   William Aussieker • Department of Management, California Polytechnic State University, San Luis Obispo, California 93407.

salow, 1984), and in one quite recent study, a strong relationship between the union–management relationship and organizational effectiveness (Katz, Kochan, & Weber, 1985).

Research evidence on employee participation, union concessions, employee ownership, quality of working life, and other aspects of union–management cooperation and codetermination are quite prevalent in both the management and industrial relations literature. There is considerable research on the integration of organizational behavior and industrial relations concepts (e.g., Brett & Hammer, 1982), but less research exists on the integration of organizational and industrial relations theory. Comparative research is particularly limited on cross-cultural studies that examine environment and organization variables as well as differences in human resources management strategies and union–management relationships and in particular union–management cooperation and union participation in corporation decision making. This chapter offers a model of union–management relationships that includes environmental and organizational variables that are associated with different types of union–management relationships or human resources strategies.

I. CONCEPTUAL FRAMEWORK

A conceptual framework for comparative analysis of union–management relationships could include, at the very least, alternative organizational designs (Miles, 1980), and industrial relations systems (Dunlop, 1958; Kochan, 1980). These alternative conceptualizations imply that organizational structure, process, or strategy are influenced by a specific set of contextual or environmental factors. Figure 5.1 compares organization theory and industrial relations conceptual frameworks for comparative analysis of union–management relationships.

The two conceptual frameworks in Figure 5.1 have basically the same contextual or environmental variables to explain differences in either organizational structure and process or the union–management relationship. The industrial relations systems framework is a general systems theory that is applicable to different levels of analysis, including the nation-state, industry, firm, or organization. Although effectiveness is clearly the outcome of the organization framework, the focus of the industrial relations system is on the bargaining process, structure, and outcomes. However, a recent specification (Kochan, 1980) includes goal attainment as an outcome of the industrial relations system, and organizational survival or growth is also the assumed goal of the actors in the industrial relations system.

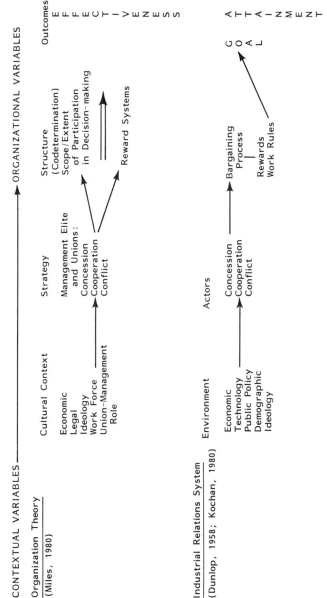

Figure 5.1. Comparison of organization theory and industrial relations conceptual frameworks for comparative analysis of union–management relationships.

Both frameworks are somewhat static and only implicitly consider organizational or human resources strategy. In terms of union–management relationship, the strategic choices appear to relate to concession, conflict, or cooperation in the bargaining on reward systems and work rules. The scope and extent of union participation in decision making (codetermination) is an aspect of organizational structure but certainly reflects a strategic choice by both the union and management that is independent, theoretically, of the bargaining process. Both the types of union–management relationship and union participation in decision making are aspects of human resources management strategy that are linked to either product–market strategy (Snow & Miles, 1984) or environmental decline (Ferris, Schellenberg, & Zammuto, 1984).

Evidence suggests similar human resources strategies of union–management cooperation and specifically codetermination in both United States and West German union–management relations (Bain, 1983; Gordon, 1985). This chapter reviews these codetermination experiences to illustrate the model of human resources strategy and union–management relationships that includes environment and organization variables in Figure 5.1.

Though limited to two data points, a comparison of both U.S. and West German union–management relationships is useful because of the absence of state ownership in similar heavily unionized industries (Monsen & Walters, 1983) and the existence of a legally structured labor relations system since post–World War II. Most importantly, the bargaining structure in both the United States and West Germany consists of industry and companywide negotiations on wages, hours, and working conditions by national trade unions affiliated with a federation of unions. Extensive employee rights are also established by statutory provisions, and employer violation of these rights may be appealed to the courts. Strikes are usually conducted by unions in collective bargaining, and unlike the company-oriented Japanese unions, U.S. and West German unions represent employees with more than one employer. On this point, the literature often ignores that unions also pursue a strategy that may vary from cooperation and concession to conflict and wage demands that put an employer out of business in a specific industry. Last, a West German comparison is of interest because the West German economy was the model of performance in the 1970s, and much of the post–World War II success was attributed to codetermination and other aspects of industrial democracy (Gordon, 1985). A West German comparison thus examines codetermination in less favorable economic conditions (Bain, 1983), and as a by-product, partially offsets the disproportionate amount of cross-cultural studies that focus on Japanese organizational success. We begin our analysis with the West German experience.

II. *MITBESTIMMUNG*

The public policy issue associated with the West German union movement has been parity codetermination, that is, equal union and management representation in decision making (Geitner & Pulte, 1979). As practiced, *Mitbestimmung* is not a homogenous concept and varies from equal representation of management, employees, and unions in the decision-making process on all issues at the supervisory board level, the highest level in West German corporations, to employee representation on committees to resolve issues at the plant level.

Figure 5.2 represents the scope and degree of union and employee participation in decision making as well as an estimate of the number of employees covered by different types of codetermination.

Full codetermination has always been a political-social issue. It was the major objective of the German labor movement in 1920 (Schregle, 1978), and full codetermination is viewed as instrumental with industrial and political democracy. This is because worker rights were obtained through legislative acts that were abolished during the Nazi regime. Historically, works councils and trade unions were dissolved by the National Socialist Party when it gained government control in 1933, and after World War II, codetermination based on earlier models was instituted in the iron, coal, and steel industries that had been placed under Allied trustee administration.

The full, limited and works council types of codetermination are required by different legislative acts. The return to private ownership of industries under trustee administration coincided with the Codetermination Act of 1951 and gave employees equal representation on the supervisory boards in the iron, steel, and coal industries. In 1952, the Works Constitution Act provided for works councils, work assemblies, and economic committees and also gave employees the right to appoint one-third of the members to the supervisory boards of firms with more than 2,000 employees, and in effect, extended codetermination to the auto and chemical industries.

The provisions in the 1952 law were amended in a revised Works Constitution Act in 1971. This act results in a compromise of the DGB (German Federation of Trade Unions) pursuit of full or parity codetermination that had become an "incessant source of embarrassment to the

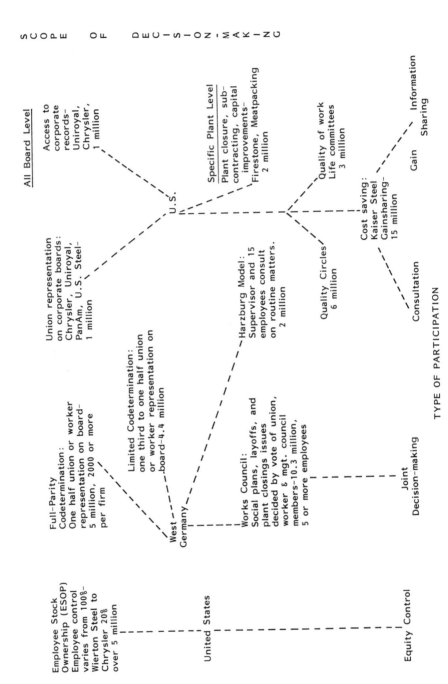

Figure 5.2. Types of union participation in decision making.

two coalition parties" in West Germany (Cullingford, 1977). When the DGB bill for parity determination in all industries was introduced in parliament, it was sent to a commission studying the steel and coal industries. The commission recognized that "management's job is to manage," but employees should participate in decision making, and the commission's views are reflected in the Works Constitution Act of 1971. This act extended the works council to all organizations with more than five employees and emphasized the workers' sense of belonging and mutual trust of unions and management. The DGB was disappointed with the absence of parity provisions, but the law gave unions and workers representation on employment issues such as plant closing and layoffs. Another provision of the 1971 act established a conciliation board that resolved disputes of the works councils by the vote of employee, employer, and neutral parties on the board.

After 5 years of extensive debate between the DGB and the Confederation of German Employers (BDA), the 1976 Codetermination Act applied to all firms with more than 2,000 employees and established that employees and unions will hold 50% of all supervisory board seats. At least one of the employee seats is held by an "executive" who is expected to vote with the stockholders' representatives. The employee representatives may or may not be union representatives, but the union is allowed a minimum number of seats. The method of election is prescribed in the act, and different proportions of union, employee, professional, and managerial employees are found on different supervisory boards.

Although the extent of employee and union interest and actual participation in decision making varies considerably between boards, the 1976 Act has clearly allowed employees greater representation in corporate decision making and a procedure for resolving disputes. Supposedly by reducing conflict, unions could cooperate with management to achieve mutual goals, but union activity has increased with the works councils. In 1977, the BDA unsuccessfully appealed to the constitutional courts to declare the 1976 act unconstitutional. (Cullingford, 1977).

A. Effectiveness

The success of the DGB in gaining greater representation on supervisory boards has led to employer concern that "shareholders and directors of business would not be even partners with the unions, but thoroughly dominated and controlled by them" (Vogl, 1973, p. 57). There is no evidence that the worker representation in steel, coal, or iron companies has caused the firms to be less efficient. Delays in decision making are offset by the knowledge that union disputes will not significantly affect projects because of the constraints on strikes and the West German collective bargaining process. However, there were strikes in the printing and steel industries in 1984.

In West Germany, collective bargaining takes place at the industry level for a region or the entire republic. Wages, hours, and working conditions are mostly negotiated by trade unions within the DGB and employers' organizations, for example, BDA. The Works Constitution Act of 1952 explicitly states that agreements between works councils and management must not deal with wage or other matters normally included in collective bargaining agreements (Schregle, 1978). Extensive employee rights are also established by statutory provisions, and employer violation of these rights may be appealed to the labor courts. Strikes may only be conducted by unions in collective bargaining, but any dispute is settled by the conciliation board. Disputes on the interpretation of a collective bargaining agreement are resolved by the labor courts that investigate the complaint and determine whether the collective agreement has been violated by the employer (Cullingford, 1977).

B. The Harzburg Model

At the individual firm level, the Harzburg model illustrates codetermination in day-to-day operations (Bernthal, 1978). In the Harzburg model, rationality and classical line-staff structure are mixed with worker participation by consultation on routine matters. The chain of command and job descriptions for each employee define responsibility, and employees are allowed to choose the method of implementation. Supervisors observe and obtain information on worker completion of tasks. Handbooks explicitly define duties, responsibilities, and authority.

In this model, individual consultation is preferred to group consultation, and extensive procedures dictate the conduct of group meetings. The group consists of the supervisor and no more than 15 subordinates. The meeting is held before or after working hours, and each meeting has a fixed agenda. At the meeting, a semicircle is formed with the supervisor in the middle to solicit questions and suggestions made by the workers. At the close of the meeting, the supervisor summarizes the discussion and reviews proposals. There is no voting, and the supervisor's decision is announced later in a brief meeting. The topics of the group meetings include work procedures and not objectives, and workers are excluded from participation in decisions made by superiors as specified by the chain of command and management job descriptions or responsibility.

III. UNION OR EMPLOYEE PARTICIPATION

The legal structure of codetermination established union represen- tation in corporate decision making, but the union claim of significant employee representation is questionable. The DGB leaders were aware of the apathy of the rank and file by the small turnout for the 1970 rallies for codetermination (Cullingford, 1977). German worker attitudes to- ward codetermination show little concern and mostly indifference, but very high satisfaction with the works council. The status differentiation of the working class establishes a level of perceived rights, and parity codetermination is not consistent with the perceived rights of workers that equates property rights as stronger than worker rights to owner- ship. Participation in meetings by the rank and file indicates a low level of interest. Surveys indicate attendance averages between 10% and 15% (Willey, 1979), and worker participation is limited to only official func- tions. (In worker interviews, one of the authors, Rolf E. Rogers, was struck by the lack of knowledge of the rank and file about codetermina- tion both in general and specific aspects of worker representation within their organization.)

Another indication of the indifference of workers toward codeter- mination is that 10 million workers have not formed works councils though allowed by law. Virtually all the workers are in small organiza- tions and are nonunion (Gordon, 1985).

Codetermination has influenced internal union structure. Full-time works council members are associated with the unions, and the works council is strongly influenced by the union decision making. The union has been most influential on limitations on plant closure, location, and layoff decisions. The legislative requirements on codetermination have been responsible for some multinationals to either not locate operations in West Germany or to change the legal form of the organization to avoid codetermination as much as possible (Gordon, 1985). Other than the obvious increase in union influence on management and the deci- sion-making process, research to date is inconclusive on whether co- determination is positively or negatively related to either productivity or organizational effectiveness (Pejovich, 1978).

A democratic-socialist ideology, beliefs in strong centralized gov- ernment, and the desires of unions for a fundamental change in the distribution of power in favor of the unions (Kuhne, 1976) are possible sociocultural explanations for the West German codetermination experience. A lingering worker–management class stratification and the beliefs that participation increases productivity and strong unions preserve democratic institutions (pluralism) have probably a more direct relationship with West German codetermination. As part of the prevailing class orientation of workers, workers defer to managers on traditional managerial decisions, but managers recognize the need for workers to have unions represent worker interests through collective bargaining. The historical association of high unemployment and weak or abolished unions with Nazism has produced a social policy that seeks to reduce employment and strengthen unions. Much of the impact of both works council and codetermination has also been to limit the ability of management to reduce employment, and other legislation makes layoffs more costly by raising the amount and duration of unemployment benefits (Gordon, 1985).

IV. U.S. CODETERMINATION

Incidents of union–management participation in corporate decision making and union–management cooperation have long been regarded as examples of creative collective bargaining and definitely as unique in U.S. union–management relations (Healy, 1965). Technological change provided the basis for joint union–management programs in the 1950s and 1960s. Training of technologically displaced employees, sharing of cost savings and profits, incentives for productivity, and joint union–management committees were the types of reported examples of union–management cooperation (Healy, 1965). The 1970s were a decade of significant change in the U.S. labor force but showed little evidence of new types of union–management cooperation. One notable exception was the Experimental Negotiating Agreement (ENA) between the United Steel Workers of America (USWA) and the Steel Industry Employer Negotiating Committee—the nine largest U.S.-integrated steel manufacturers. The ENA required arbitration of disputed issues in contract negotiation and gave a no-strike payment to steelworkers covered by the agreement (Somers, 1980).

In contrast, the 1980s have been characterized by slight labor force changes but by major changes in U.S. union–management relations. A deterioration of pattern bargaining, negotiation of plant closings, concession bargaining, union participation in corporate decision making, and employee ownership characterize the major changes and incidents of codetermination in U.S. union–management relations. According to Woodworth (1982), union concessions on wages or benefits have gained management concessions on union participation in corporate decision making, but union participation is not automatically a *quid pro quo* for concessions on employee compensation. For example, USWA negotiated an agreement with the steel employer negotiating committee for a 9% reduction in steelworker compensation and no contract provisions for union participation in corporate decision making. However, individual company and plant negotiation by the USWA focused on further union cost concessions and also employee ownership (Wierton Steel) and membership on corporate boards (U.S. Steel). The most publicized example of union concession, representation on corporate boards, was the United Automobile Workers (UAW)–Chrysler Corporation agreement that resulted in 25% reductions in employee compensation, UAW president membership on the Chrysler board, and union ownership of 10% of Chrysler stock.

Incidents of codetermination are still relatively infrequent, but approximately 30 incidents in U.S. union–management relations from 1980 to 1984 have been classified into different categories in Figure 5.2. (The plan, company or division, and union have been noted for reference.) The concession bargaining-codetermination settlements are not restricted to the domestic auto and steel industries. The United Rubber Workers (URW) negotiated agreements that specified substantial reduction in wages and benefits in exchange for worker sharing of corporate profits and union participation on corporate boards. Experiments with lifetime employment, advance notice on plant closing, and financial disclosure are part of agreements in the auto and rubber industries. Union or worker representation on the board of directors and union–management committees are incidents of codetermination in many different industries.

Employee stock ownership ranges from 100% control to minority interest. Of the different types of codetermination, employee stock ownership covers more employees in the United States, except for quality circles, quality of work life committees, or gainsharing plans that have a limited scope of decision making. Stock ownership has been negotiated by the union, but ESOP may be established without union support. Union employee stock ownership plans (ESOPs) exist primarily in retail, electronics, and airline industries (Woodworth, 1983). The popularity of ESOPs is most likely linked to a significant tax advantage, that is, the cost of the ESOP may be deducted as an expense from operating income.

Several incidents of codetermination have clearly been associated with bankruptcy or threat of bankruptcy, and, at the very least, the incidents have occurred among corporations in financial difficulty and in markets with low-cost foreign or domestic competition. Wage concession, union–management committees, lifetime employment, and restrictions on plant closings or layoffs also characterize the settlements that resulted in codetermination.

To adapt to low-cost competition, management clearly desired significant reductions in wages and benefits to lower costs but seldom desired changes in union participation. In a 1981–1982 survey of U.S. bargaining patterns, Fulmer found that half of the *Fortune 500* firms were engaged in negotiations and agreements with union concessions in the area of wages, benefits, and work rules. None of the companies was willing to grant union participation on the board of directors or union involvement in corporate planning. About 10% of the companies were willing to grant profit sharing, share financial information, or consult on plant closing, and more than half were willing to allow greater flexibility in employee assignment and scheduling (Fulmer, 1982).

The survey results indicate a prevailing belief of U.S. management in union concession without participation. However, union participation and other forms of codetermination have accompanied concessions in a few companies. These companies face similar environmental conditions, including low-cost foreign competition in primary product markets, mature production technology, and massive operating losses.

A. Effectiveness

Assessing the effectiveness of codetermination is more difficult. Companies in the lumber and meatpacking industries, where employees gained control through employee stock ownership plans, showed better operating results after employee ownership. At least six auto and rubber companies have experienced substantial improvement after codetermination. However, the effect of codetermination must be moderated with the better business conditions of 1982–1985. Casual analysis of the airline, steel, and meatpacking industries show companies in steel and meatpacking with equally dismal operating results after codetermination. Some companies in all three industries are declaring bankruptcy, avoiding the provisions of union agreements, and unilaterally cutting wages and benefits without any form of codetermination.

Ironically, the longest experiment with a form of codetermination in the steel industry is the Kaiser Steel–USWA Long Range Sharing Plan, and Kaiser Steel closed its steel manufacturing facility in 1983. Two tentative agreements that included employment security in exchange for wage and benefit concessions were not approved by the USWA. Efforts to save jobs at Kaiser Steel also included an ESOP that was also rejected by international officers of the USWA. At the present time, a nonunion steel fabricator uses a portion of the former Kaiser Steel plant, and the Kaiser Steel assets have been purchased by an outside group.

V. SUMMARY AND CONCLUSIONS

In the United States, the results of our analysis indicate that union–management cooperation and codetermination are relatively infrequent. Analysis of 30 incidents of codetermination, from both Woodworth and our review of the industrial relations literature, show that companies were faced with similar environmental conditions and effectiveness, including low-cost competition in primary product markets, mature production technology, and massive operating losses.

In Germany, there is little question that action between the unions, government, and individual enterprises has been a successful venture since the early 1960s. However, the German economy and society is now facing changes that would force the modification or substantial change of the current system. Some experts believe that the growth in the size and power of the unions will limit managerial efficiency and increase the gap between union representatives and the rank and file. Potential problem areas affect social, economic, and political institutions.

Some concerns have been expressed regarding the tendency of unions to become too closely involved with the political process. The Social Democrats are generally viewed as supporting union goals and effecting union gains through the legislative process. It is apparent from the number of laws governing rights, procedures, and other labor issues that most union gains have come through government–union interaction rather than through an enterprise–union relationship.

The power granted by relevant legislation affects the management of the individual firm and influences the freedom of decision making based on ownership. The entrepreneur's ability to make urgent decisions is reduced as a result of union-interest consultation. The continuing reduction in the number of foreign-built subsidiary operations is viewed as another result of the loss in control to unions. The financial stability of German firms is being weakened by the absence of foreign capital investments.

Unions will not permit their influence to decline even if the firm is merged or acquired. If a partner company is not willing to accept the codetermination system, the union will block the merger, with support from the labor court. As a result, Germany will have less foreign investment because of the loss of capital control, and multinationals may find that they have too little capital for massive expansion if they are subject to German law.

VI. REFERENCES

Bain, T. (1983, Winter). Employment readjustments in West Germany. *Columbia Journal of World Business, XVIII*(4), 75–91.
Bernthal, W. F. (1978, January). Matching German culture and management style: A book review essay. *Academy of Management Review, 3*(1), 75–91.
Brett, J. M., & Hammer, T. (1982). Organizational behavior and industrial relations. *Industrial relations research in the 1970's: Review and appraisal.* Madison, WI: Industrial Relations Research Association.
Capelli, P. G. (1983). Concession bargaining in the national economy. *Industrial Relations Research Association Proceedings, 297–305.*
Cullingford, E. M. C. (1977). *Trade unions in West Germany,* Boulder: Westview Press.
Dunlop, J. T. (1958). *Industrial relations system.* New York: Holt-Dryden.
Ferris, G. R., Schellenberg, D. A., & Zammuto, R. F. (1984, Winter). Human resource management strategies in declining industries. *Human Resource Management, 23*(4), 381–394.
Freedman, A., & Fulmer, W. F. (1982, March/April). Last rites for pattern bargaining. *Harvard Business Review, 60*(2), 30–48.
Fulmer, W. E. (1982). Labor-management relationships in the 1980's: Revolution or evolution. *Industrial Relations Research Association Proceedings, 397–402.*
Geitner, D., & Pulte, P. (1979). *Mitbestimmungs recht.* Munchen: Heyne Verlag.
Gordon, M. A. (1985, Winter). Equity participation by employees: The growing debate in West Germany. *Industrial Relations, 24*(1), 113–129.
Hallet, G. (1978). *The social economy of West Germany.* London: The Macmillan Press Limited.
Healy, J. J. (1965). *Creative collective bargaining.* Englewood Cliffs, NJ: Prentice-Hall.
Kassalow, E. (1984). The crisis in the world steel industry: Union-management responses in four countries. *Industrial Relations Research Association Proceedings, 341–351.*
Katz, H. C., Kochan, T. A., & Weber, M. R. (1985, September). Assessing the effects of industrial relations systems and efforts to improve the quality of working life on organizational effectiveness. *Academy of Management Review, 28*(3), 501–526.
Kochan, T. A. (1980). *Collective bargaining and industrial relations.* Homewood, IL: Richard D. Irwin.
Kuhne, R. J. (1976, Summer). Co-determination: A statutory re-structuring of the organization. *Columbia Journal of World Business, XI*(2), 17–25.
Miles, R. H. (1980). *Macro organizational behavior.* Santa Monica, CA: Goodyear.
Miles, R. E., & Snow, C. C. (1978). *Organizational strategy, structure, and process.* New York: McGraw-Hill.
Mitchell, D. J. B. (1984). International convergence with U.S. wage levels. *Industrial Relations Research Association Proceedings, 76–84.*

Monsen, J. R., & Walters, K. D. (1983). *Nationalized cmpanies.* New York: McGraw-Hill Book Company.

Nonoka, I., & Johansson, J. (1985). Japanese management: What about the 'hard' skills? *Academy of Management Review, 10*(2), 181–191.

Odiorne, G. S. (1984). *Strategic management of human resources.* San Francisco: Jossey-Bass.

Ouchi, W. G. (1981). *Theory Z: How American business can meet the Japanese challenge.* Reading, MA: Addison-Wesley.

Pejovich, Svetozar (Ed.). (1978). *The codetermination movement in the West.* Lexington, MA: Lexington Books.

Peters, T. J., & Waterman, R. H., Jr. (1982). *In search of excellence: Lessons from America's best-run companies.* New York: Harper & Row.

Schregle, J. (1978, January-February). Co-determination in the Federal Republic of Germany. *International Labor Review, 117*(1), 81–98.

Snow, C. C., & Miles, R. E. (1984, Summer). Designing strategic human resources management systems. *Organizational Dynamics, 13*(1), 36–52.

Somers, G. G. (Ed.). (1980). *Collective bargaining: Contemporary American experience.* Madison, WI: Industrial Relations research Association.

Van de Vall, M. (1980). *Labor organizations.* London: Cambridge University Press.

Vogl, F. (1973). *German business after the economic miracle.* New York: Halsted Press.

Willey, R. (1979). *Democracy in the West German trade unions.* Beverly Hills: Sage Publications.

Woodworth, W. (1982). Concession bargaining: What's in it for unions? *Industrial Relations Research Association Proceedings*, 419–424.

6

Convergence or Divergence of Strategic Decision Processes among 10 Nations

Richard C. Hoffman and W. Harvey Hegarty

The growth of strategic management practice and theory among industrialized countries has increased dramatically in recent years. Much of what we know about strategic management practices in use is based on studies of organizations located primarily in the United States. Moreover, studies conducted in other nations (e.g., Channon, 1973; Ghertman, 1976) have been based primarily on American theories of strategic management. The implicit assumption of these latter studies is that concepts of strategic management are transferable to other nations. Thus far, various compelling arguments opposing this view have been offered in the preceding chapters of this book by Adler, Doktor, and Redding (Chapter 2), Askanas (Chapter 4), Cooper and Cox (Chapter 3), and Osigweh (Chapter 1). Cultural, economic, or political conditions provide substantial barriers to knowledge transfer among cultures or nations. In this chapter we adopt the view espoused by Lammers (1976) that the issue concerning the relevance of management theories across national cultures is one subject to empirical investigation.

Richard C. Hoffman • College of Business and Economics, University of Delaware, Newark, Delaware 19716.   **W. Harvey Hegarty** • Graduate School of Business, Indiana University, Bloomington, Indiana 47405.

I. NATIONAL CULTURE AS A DIMENSION OF ORGANIZATIONAL CONTEXT

The debate of the relevance of organization and management theories among national cultures is embedded in the convergent-divergent paradigm of comparative management. The convergent view (e.g., Webber, 1969) contends that the forces of industrialization tend to minimize cultural or national differences in work organizations. Technology makes the same demands on managers and organizations wherever it is applied. The divergent view contends that differences in culture, natural resources, and pace of industrialization tend to magnify national differences in organization structures and processes (see also Adler, Doktor, & Redding, Chapter 2; Osigweh, Chapter 1). The empirical research to date is inconsistent in its support of either of these views. Some of the data suggest that differences in organization and management occur among groups or clusters of nations having similar geographic and cultural characteristics (Ronen & Shenkar, 1985). Supporters of the convergent view hold that knowledge about management and organizations is transferable, at least, among nations having similar levels of industrialization. Supporters of the divergent view do not see many opportunities for knowledge transfer.

An implicit assumption in the comparative management paradigm is that nation/culture represents the major contingency accounting for differences in management and organization. This view ignores other salient features of an organization's context as defined by the broader contingency paradigm of the organization sciences. According to this latter paradigm, contingencies represent the broad characteristics of an organization's context (or setting in which it develops) that are believed to affect its structure and managerial processes. The Aston studies conducted in Britain (Pugh, Hickson, Hinings, & Turner, 1969) have identified the following as key dimensions of an organization's context or setting: history or origin, ownership, size, technology, location, and dependence. Environmental uncertainty (e.g., Duncan, 1972) and existing strategy (e.g., Hambrick, 1981) have also been shown to be key contextual dimensions causing variations in organization and management. Within this paradigm, nation/culture becomes one of the many dimensions that can account for observed differences in management and organization. Thus, in order to demonstrate whether a theory is transferable to another nation/ culture, one should determine both of the following: (1) that nation/culture causes a variation in the phenomenon and (2) that nation/culture is a relatively more important contextual variable accounting for differences in the phenomenon. Most comparative research has focused on the first criterion and drawn conclusions about convergence or divergence solely on that basis. By ignoring the second criterion, one may exaggerate the importance of nation/culture in accounting for observed differences in organizational phenomenon. This can lead one to conclude that either a theory is or is not transferable, an all-or-none decision. By viewing nation/culture as a dimension of organizational context and determining its relative importance as a dimension, one may conclude that a theory is transferable to another national culture but with modifications. This approach has been attempted in a couple of the comparative studies in strategic management that are discussed subsequently.

II. COMPARATIVE RESEARCH IN STRATEGIC MANAGEMENT

Virtually all of the comparative research on national differences in managerial practice has been conducted in the areas of organization behavior, development, and theory. The dearth of comparative research in strategic management is understandable because it has emerged as a subfield of organization science only in the past decade. Strategic management is concerned with top management behavior and processes in developing organizational strategy and in determining the efficacy of these strategies for coping with organizational environments. The field has developed out of necessity, for managers have been faced with the need to adapt increasingly complex organizations to rapidly changing environments (Schendel & Hofer, 1979). Top managers in all nations have few theories to draw on to guide them in fulfilling their responsibilities. Thus, there is a considerable need for comparative studies in this new field.

In recent years, a few studies have focused on national differences in top management processes. Gouy (1978) found minor differences in the content and techniques used in making strategic decisions among firms located in France, Germany, and the United Kingdom. Most of the differences were later explained by other aspects of organizational context such as size, business environment, and existing strategy. The process of scanning the environment for external information and its perceived impact on strategic decisions were found to be quite similar for both U.S. and European executives (O'Connell & Zimmerman, 1979). In another study, Horovitz (1980) found that British and German firms used more formal strategic planning than French firms. However, the control practices were similar in all three nations; the firms all emphasized operating verus strategic control. Finally, Heller and Wilpert (1981)

examined the extent of participation by top-level managers and their
immediate subordinates in nonstrategic decisions. The sample was composed of 800 management dyads from seven Western European nations
and Israel. The authors concluded that "our results show only limited
influence of nation on decision making behaviors" (1981, pp. 146–147).
Participation in decision-making varied more by the type of decision and
the environmental uncertainty faced by the top managers.

These studies suggest that strategic decision and planning processes do vary among nations having similar levels of industrialization;
however, other factors in the organization's context appear to account
for more differences than does nation. This view is consistent with some
previous findings in comparative management research (e.g., Haire,
Ghiselli, & Porter, 1966; Hickson & McMillan, 1981). Thus, these findings suggest that one should incorporate other elements in an organization's context when investigating for national/cultural differences.

The purpose of this study is to explore the validity of an emerging
theory of strategic decision influence processes across several national
cultures. This will be conducted by evaluating the importance of *nation*
relative to other dimensions of organizational context in accounting for
observed differences in the process. To our knowledge, this is the first
study to simultaneously evaluate the relative importance of nation versus other dimensions of context on strategic decision-making. Gouy
(1978) investigated the effects of nation separately from other dimensions of context; whereas Heller and Wilpert (1981) did evaluate the
relative importance of nation versus other elements of context for nonstrategic decisions. We now turn our attention to a brief description of
the strategic management theory that is the focus of our investigation.

III. STRATEGIC DECISION-INFLUENCE PROCESSES

Strategic decisions seek to align the organization with its environment. Such decisions include the choice of environment (product/ markets) as well as choices internal to the organization such as technology
and structure (Miles & Snow, 1978). Research on strategic decision processes has been based on one of two paradigms. The rational/analytic
paradigm (e.g., Steiner, 1979) focuses on formal planning systems. The
sociopolitical paradigm is based on the notion that organizational decisions are made in a social context characterized by uncertainty (e.g.,
Quinn, 1980). Recent studies both in the United States (e.g., Jemison,
1981) and in Europe (e.g., Bachrach & Aiken, 1976), based on the so-

ciopolitical model, have examined managerial influence processes affecting strategic decisions.

In these studies, influence is synonymous with power and is defined as the ability to affect the outcome of strategic decisions. Organization theorists have argued (e.g., Hickson, Hinings, Lee, Schneck, & Pennings, 1971) that intraorganizational power or influence accrues to those who are able to cope with uncertainties either within or outside of the organization. Support for this view has been found in organizations located in several nations: France (Crozier, 1964), Canada (Hinings, Hickson, Pennings & Schneck 1974), and the United States (Jemison, 1981). These scholars suggest that the subunit or department is the relevant unit of analysis for examining such power relationships because the top manager's decision influence is not easily separated from his or her role as a department head. Factors posing uncertainty for strategic decision-makers are some of the key dimensions of organizational context. Because strategic decisions represent choices about matters external and internal to the firm, we conceptualize the organizational context as having external and internal dimensions. Relevant external dimensions that have been found to cause variations in strategic decision processes include nation (Gouy, 1978), uncertainty about the task environment (Miles & Snow, 1978), and industry (Hambrick, 1981). Internal features of context include characteristics of the organization itself such as technology or size and characteristics of subunits or departments within the organization such as expertise and resources (Jemison, 1981).

Top managers and their departments may gain influence either because they are well situated or because they engage in certain decision activities (Hickson et al., 1971) to cope with uncertainty. Based on previous work by policy scientists (e.g., Allison, 1971), two departmental characteristics were selected as indicators of how well situated the department might be to influence strategic decisions. The two characteristics include the department's functional orientation (internal/external), reflecting both formal position authority and expertise as a basis of influence, and the department's resource base as represented by its size.

A review of the literature revealed two types of strategic decision activities that often enable managers to cope with uncertainty. Hambrick (1981) has demonstrated the importance of environmental scanning as a source of decision influence. Organizational theorists stress the importance of the use of planning/control procedures to cope with uncertainties (Cyert & March, 1963) and to gain influence on strategic decisions (Mazzolini, 1979).

Thus, the model under investigation suggests that influence on strategic decisions is a function of decision-maker characteristics and activities that enable them to cope with uncertainties both within and external to the organization.

Two research questions have been developed to investigate the validity of this model in several nations. National, rather than cultural, differences are examined here because there are inherent difficulties in measuring culture (Ronen & Shenkar, 1985) and because national variations have been observed in strategic management practices as noted previously.

1. Is nation relatively more important than other external or internal dimensions of organizational context in accounting for most of the differences observed in strategic decision activities?

This research question recognizes the importance of discretion or action exercised by decision makers in developing their firm's strategy (e.g., Miles & Snow, 1978). It also recognizes that nation is but one dimension of organizational context.

2. Does the pattern of the sources of influence on strategic decisions differ across nations when controlling for other dimensions of organizational context?

This question more directly examines the validity of the overall model of decision influence in different national contexts. The results of this exploratory investigation will provide tentative conclusions concerning the transferability of the model of strategic decision influence to other nations either in whole or in part.

IV. RESEARCH DESIGN

A field study employing a mailed questionnaire was conducted to gather cross-sectional data from top-management teams of an international sample of business firms.

A. Sample and Data Collection

A total of 505 top managers from 135 manufacturing business units located in 10 Western industrialized nations provided data for this study. The nations and the number of firms and managers $(f-m)$ sampled in each were as follows: Denmark (5–20), Finland (6–20), France (11–40), Germany (14–53), Netherlands (15–57), Norway (7–27), Sweden (13–47), Switzerland (18–68), United Kingdom (17–66), and the

United States (29–107). The firms were identified using Dun and Bradstreet's *Principal International Businesses* (1980b) and *Million Dollar Directory* (1980a). A business unit is either an independent or dependent (division or subsidiary of a larger firm) firm engaged in one line of business as indicated by its 4-digit SIC (standard industrial classification) code. This insured that the firm's top-management team was concerned with strategic decision making for the same business environment.

An average of four top managers in each firm completed a close-ended questionnaire in which they were asked to provide information concerning their department's involvement in strategic decision-making activities as well as their perception of their firm's business environment. The questionnaire was available in English, French, or German. The translation verification procedures are described elsewhere (Hoffman & Hegarty, 1983). Two follow-ups were used to encourage responses. The usable response rate was 85%. The managers appear to have sufficient experience to provide the data requested. They reported having an average amount of influence over all of their firm's strategic decisions and had spent an average of 5 years in their present position and 14.5 years with their firm.

B. Variables and Measures

The variables include both questionnaire as well as descriptive sample data and fall into two groups: external and internal aspects of organizational context and strategic decision activities and processes.

1. External and Internal Context

The external context was assessed along three different dimensions. *Nation* is a categorical variable indicating the country in which the sample organization is located. *Industry* is another categorical variable. Because all of the firms sampled are in manufacturing, two categories were developed representing producers of durable and nondurable products. These were classified using standard industrial classifications (U.S. Department of Commerce, 1984). *Perceived environmental uncertainty* is a subjective measure of the lack of information, general uncertainty, and inability to predict the reactions of certain elements in the firm's task environment (e.g., suppliers, customers, competitors). Duncan's (1972) scale was employed as modified by Bourgeois (1985).

The internal context assessed includes one organizational and two departmental characteristics. *Dependence* indicates whether the sample firm was an independent firm or a subsidiary of a larger firm. *Functional orientation* refers to the generalized functional responsibilities of the participating managers. These were determined by self-reports and through interviews with the CEO: (1) *External* functional orientation includes general management, marketing, product management, and research and design; and (2) *internal* functional orientation includes office administration, engineering, finance, personnel, and production. *Departmental size* refers to the total number of people employed in the department as reported by the department head.

2. Strategic Decision Activities and Processes

Three broad strategic decision activities and processes were assessed via a questionnaire employing 5-point, Likert-type scales. *Environmental scanning* is the acquisition of information by departments on external trends and events in their firm's task environment. Hambrick's (1981) scale as modified by Farh, Hoffman, and Hegarty (1984) was used to measure this variable. This scale measures the scanning of four types of trends: (1) market, (2) efficiency (of processing and delivery of products), (3) administrative (organization structure and process), and (4) regulatory (government).

Planning and control procedures refer to the use of standard operating procedures to regulate departmental activities. A shortened form of Khandwalla's (1977) control and information system scale was used to assess these activities. Factor analysis revealed the use of three types of procedures: (1) planning, (2) control, and (3) specific goals.

Influence on strategic decisions refers to the extent to which top managers influence the outcome of key decisions made to adapt the firm to its environment. The scale consisted of a list of 13 strategic decisions. A multirater format similar to that used by Jemison (1981) was used to assess a department's influence on strategic decisions.

C. Data Analysis

The analysis of the effects of organization context on the decision activities of scanning and the use of planning/control procedures was conducted using univariate analysis of covariance. To supplement the analysis, an estimated omega (w^2) was calculated for each significant effect.

Regression analysis was used to investigate the validity of the model of decision influence across all nations. The dependent variable was a subunit's average influence on all 13 strategic decisions. The predictor variables included the departmental characteristics and strategic decision activities described before. Tests were conducted to determine whether the beta weights and intercepts of the decision influence model for each nation were significantly different. The level of significance for all statistical analyses was $p \leq .05$.

V. FINDINGS

A. External versus Internal Organizational Context and Strategic Decision Activities

The analyses of the first research question reveals that nation is not relatively more important than the other contextual variables in accounting for differences in the strategic decision activities investigated. In general, external and internal dimensions of organizational context each explained approximately the same amount of total variance in all seven strategic decision activities investigated as revealed in Table 6.1. The relative importance of external versus internal context varies with specific decision activities. The external context accounted for more differences in the scanning of regulatory and efficiency trends and in the use of long-term planning. The internal context accounted for more differences in the scanning of market and administrative trends as well as the use of specific goals and control procedures.

Nation and industry each accounted for differences in three of the seven decision activities, and in each case, nation explained more of the variance than did industry. By far, the most important external dimension was the managers' perceptions of the uncertainty in their firms' task environment (PEU). PEU accounted for some of the differences observed in all seven decision activities, and it was the most important dimension of external context.

National differences accounted for differences in the scanning of regulatory trends and the use of planning and control procedures. Moreover, nation was the most important dimension of external context accounting for differences in control procedures; whereas PEU was more important than nation in accounting for differences in regulatory scanning and planning. Subsequent analyses revealed that managers from the United Kingdom, Switzerland, and Norway scan regulations less than managers from most of the other nations in the sample. The findings for the Swiss managers are understandable as they have fewer business regulations as compared to other nations in the sample. Managers from both the United Kingdom and Norway scan regulations less

Table 6.1. External versus Internal Contextual Effects on Strategic Decision Activities[a]

	External context			Internal context		
	Nation	Industry	Perceived environmental uncertainty	Dependence	Department size	Functional orientation
Scanning of:						
Market trends	—	—	4%	—	—	8%
Regulatory trends	2%	1%	8%	—	—	—
Efficiency trends	—	1%	3%	—	3%	—
Administrative trends	—	—	1%	—	—	2%
Planning/control						
Goals	—	—	3%	—	5%	—
Planning	2%	—	6%	—	3%	—
Control	5%	—	2%	—	9%	1%

[a]Percentage = proportion of variance accounted for.

than managers from Denmark and Sweden among other nations. This suggests that, even among nations with extensive government involvement in the economy, there is variation in the scanning of government regulations.

West German managers use more planning procedures than managers of all of the other nations sampled except the Swiss and Norwegians. The Swiss reported the use of significantly more planning than the Swedish managers who reported the least use of planning of all of the nations sampled. The extensive use of departmental planning activities by the Germans and Swiss seems to indicate that they adhere more closely to the Weberian notion of bureaucratic procedures to reduce internal uncertainty. Managers from France, Germany, Switzerland, and Norway make significantly more use of control procedures than managers from United Kingdom, the Netherlands, Denmark, and the United States. The findings for Germany and Switzerland seem to confirm previous results for planning procedures and the smooth-running Germanic bureaucracies (Horovitz, 1980). The hierarchial nature of French managers and their need for control (Granick, 1972) also seems to be supported by these findings. The extensive use of control procedures by Norwegian managers indicates that all Scandinavian managers do not share the same managerial styles as previous studies seem to suggest (e.g., Ronen & Shenkar, 1985).

The results revealed *industry* to be the weakest external dimension of context in explaining differences in strategic decision activities. Durable goods producers reported greater scanning of efficiency trends, less scanning of regulatory trends, and less use of specific goals than producers of nondurable goods. Producers of durable goods, such as machinery and metal products, depend on economies of scale; consequently, information regarding improved efficiency is important for maintaining lower cost operations. Many of the nondurable goods producers in the sample are food processors and pharmaceutical firms whose products are quite heavily regulated in each nation. This probably accounts for their greater interest in regulatory trends. These regulations may also be a reason why nondurable goods producers are more apt than durable goods producers to use specific task goals to insure compliance.

As noted previously, managerial perceptions concerning the uncertainty in their firm's task environment (e.g., suppliers, customers, competitors) were the most important dimension of the external context for explaining differences in strategic decision activities. Managers facing uncertain environments scan fewer trends in all four sectors and used goals, planning, and control procedures to a lesser degree than those facing more certain environments. The results for scanning and planning are contrary to prevailing U.S. normative theory in strategic management that suggests a positive relationship between environmental uncertainty and strategic behavior (e.g., Miles & Snow, 1978). The negative relationship between environmental uncertainty and the use of operational control procedures and specific task goals are consistent with organization theory that suggests an increased use of formal procedures and standardized activities occurring in relatively stable environments (e.g., Burns & Stalker, 1961; Duncan, 1973). The negative relationship between environmental uncertainty and scanning and planning may reflect the reality of uncertain environments. They are difficult to plan for; thus firms place less emphasis on these activities. Another possible explanation stems from Miles and Snow's (1978) findings that the predicted relationship between environmental uncertainty is stronger in some manufacturing industries than in others. Given the wide range of industries represented, it was not possible to identify whether this, in fact, was the case for this sample.

Differences in internal organization context accounted for almost half of the variation explained in the strategic decision activities investigated. The two dimensions relating to the manager's departmental characteristics, size, and functional orientation accounted for all of the internal differences in strategic decision activities. Organizational dependence did not account for any differences in decision activities (see Table 6.1). Differences in internal organization context were more important than differences in external context in accounting for variations in scanning of market and administrative trends and in the use of goals and control procedures. The importance of internal context to the latter three activities is understandable because they are concerned with either information or processes relevant to the internal functioning of the organization.

Department size was by far the most important internal characteristic both in terms of the number of activities it affected and in the amount of variance explained. Department size accounted for differences in scanning of efficiency trends. Because production departments were almost three times larger than the average department in the sample (622 versus 216), the effect of size probably reflects cost-conscious production departments that are constantly seeking new ways to improve their efficiency. Department size also accounted for most of the organizational differences in the use of goals, planning, and control procedures. As departments increase in size, the need to set specific goals, plan, and control their activities increases (Khandwalla, 1977). This is supported by the positive correlation of size with each of these procedures ($r = .24, .20,$ and $.32$).

A department's functional orientation accounted for differences in the scanning of market and administrative trends (see Table 6.1). Externally oriented departments (e.g., marketing, product management) scan market trends more and administrative trends less than internally oriented (e.g., production, finance) departments. This finding suggests that departments scan information most relevant to their own function rather than maintaining an overall strategic outlook. This result is consistent with the findings of Hambrick (1981) among U.S. organizations. Internally oriented departments reported the use of more control procedures than externally oriented departments. These departments are the primary developers and users of control procedures. For example, finance and accounting departments develop the cost information for budgets. Production departments use budgets to control their costs and quality.

Overall, the results reveal that the external context is more important than the internal context in explaining differences in environmental scanning and long-term planning and is equally as important as the internal context in explaining differences in the use of goals and control procedures. These results are consistent with prevailing strategic management theory that suggests externally oriented organizational activities are primarily affected by environmental factors; whereas internally oriented activities are primarily affected by organizational contingencies (e.g., Hambrick, 1981; Miles & Snow, 1978).

Although the external context explained some of the differences in all seven activities, the effect of national differences was minimal. First, dimensions of the internal context explained most of the variance in four of the seven activities examined. Second, in those three cases where the external context was a more important source of variation, uncertainty of the task environment was two to four times more important than nation in accounting for the differences observed. Finally, even in the one case (use of control procedures) where nation was the most important external dimension, the internal context explained twice as much of the variance in control than did nation. Thus, based on the results of this exploratory study, nation is a relevant dimension in the organization's external context, but its importance in accounting for variation in strategic decision activities is considerably less than other dimensions of context.

B. Strategic Decision-Influence Process

Previously, a generalized model of the decision influence process was described and is summarized in the following equation:

Influence on
strategic decisions $= f$ (externally oriented characteristics and
                                activities; internally oriented characteristics and
                                activities)

The second research question was posed to test whether this model is transferable to other nations. In order to test the validity of the model, regression equations of decision influence were developed using two subunit characteristics size (resources) and functional orientation as well as the seven strategic decision activities of the previous analysis as predictor variables. Industry and environmental uncertainty were controlled for in the analysis. In the full test model, there were 10 sets of predictors—one set for each sample. In the restricted model, the nations were represented by dummy variables along with the 7 predictor variables. The regular model consisted of an equation with all 9 predictors and no variables pertaining to nation. To test validity, one first tests if the regression lines are parallel (test for common beta weights). If the lines are parallel, then one tests for differences among their intercepts (Kerlinger & Pedhazur, 1973).

The results of the analysis suggests that the model of decision influence, as depicted, is valid across the 10 national samples. The results, comparing the full test model to the restricted one, revealed that the beta weights for each national sample were not significantly different ($F = .30$, df 98, 386). In other words, the predictive ability of the 9 subunit characteristics and activities on decision influence is not significantly different across the 10 nations. Having established that the decision influence model has validity across the national samples, one can test whether knowledge of the nationality of the sample adds significantly to the prediction of decision influence beyond that explained by the predictor variables. This amounts to testing whether one regression line can be best fitted to the data (test for differences of intercepts). The results, comparing the restricted to the regular model, revealed that there were no differences among the intercepts ($F = .91$, df 9, 495). Thus, one regression line can be best fitted to the data, and nation does not moderate the relationship between decision influence and the predictor variables of the model. Similar analyses were conducted for each of the predictor variables with the same results.

Thus, we conclude that the model of decision influence is valid across all of the sample nations. Table 6.2 depicts the results of the regular model for the total sample. Departmental characteristics were the most important determinants of decision influence with the functional orientation being relatively more important than size of human

Table 6.2. Sources of Influence
on Strategic Decisions Relevant to All 10
National Samples ($N = 505$)[a]

Departmental characteristics[b]
  + Functional orientation[b,c]
  + Size of human resources[b]
Planning and control[b]
  + Specific goals[b]
  + Controls[b]
  + Planning
Scanning environmental trends[b]
  − Administrative[b]
  + Efficiency
  + Regulatory
  + Market

[a]Sources of influence listed in descending rank order
based on proportion of variance accounted for.
[b]Denotes a significant relationship.
[c](+)denotes positive relationship; (−)denotes negative relationship.

resources. The use of planning and control procedures were the second most important determinants of influence. The use of specific goals and controls rather than planning are the more important sources of influence in this set. Environmental scanning explained relatively little influence on strategic decisions. The only significant relationship was negative; those subunits who tended to scan administrative trends reported less influence on strategic decisions. This is contrary to Hambrick's (1981) results. One reason for the difference is that a larger proportion of the strategic decisions investigated here dealt with internal rather than environmental choices.

VI. SUMMARY AND CONCLUSIONS

The answer to our first research question is that nation is not the dominant contingency affecting strategic decision activities of scanning and planning. Although not dominant, some national differences were found among strategic decision activities. Many of these national differences were consistent with other studies. The contextual dimensions closest to the strategic activity seem to explain most of the observed differences rather than the more remote national dimension.

The answer to our second research question is that the model of strategic decision influence process (as a function of internal and external sources of influence) is valid among the 10 nations sampled. Moreover, neither industry, PEU, nor dependence had a significant effect on subunit decision influence; only departmental characteristics and activities explained variation in decision influence as suggested by the model. This suggests that the model is generalizable to a variety of organizational contexts.

The results of both research questions lend support for convergence among the national samples concerning certain strategic management practices contrary to the arguments made in the two preceding chapters of this book for the organization sciences in general. There are a couple reasons why the forces for convergence might be greater than those for divergence in this study. First, the influence model is based on American theories of intraorganizational power that have been further developed by European scholars (Crozier, 1964; Hickson *et al.,* 1971). The strategic decision processes investigated represent work-related activities that are most likely to be affected by the similarities of the technologies (Webber, 1969) that span the industrialized nations in the sample.

This study reveals the importance of including other dimensions of organizational context when evaluating national/cultural differences among organizational phenomena. Had we used nation as our only contingency variable, we would have found national differences for scanning and planning and overstated the case for divergence among the sample nations. The existence of other contextual variables in the research design permitted us to evaluate just how important nation was in accounting for variations in selected strategic decision processes. This places nation more appropriately in the broad contingency paradigm of the organization sciences. Furthermore, we can conclude, with respect to the concepts examined here, that they are largely transferable. Prior to transfer, some modifications to the concepts are necessary because of the existence of some national differences. This supports the view presented in Chapter 3 by Cooper and Cox that a useful approach for transferring concepts and practices abroad is to look for ways of adaptation. Cooper and Cox contend that where American organization science has failed in Europe is often due to the belief that it is immediately transferable.

Some implications can be drawn from this study for strategic management. The greater evidence for convergence corroborates the findings of the other comparative strategic management studies described earlier. All of these studies have used similar samples. This seems to suggest that complex firms facing changing environments in Western industrialized nations find strategic management practices equally appealing or perhaps their only viable alternative for coping with the dilemmas they face. Another possible reason for an apparent convergence between Europe and the United States concerning strategic management practices may lie in the characteristics of the field itself. European organization science like strategic management is characterized by: (1) a macro- or structural perspective; (2) a focus on the organization as a whole and its interface with the environment; and (3) the use of a contingency or some other nonuniversalistic framework (Kassem, 1976). These similarities may render American strategic management theory more intuitively appealing to Europeans.

Some caution is warranted before we hastily export strategic management theories abroad. The field is new, and many of the theories are either untested or have weak empirical support. For example, the strategic decision influence model as operationalized in this study explained only 28% of the variance in departmental influence on strategic decisions. This suggests that considerably more work is needed in identifying salient sources of influence and in operationalizing these concepts. Just proving a model might be transferable to other nations does not mean that it is worth transferring in its present state. Comparative management theorists would also agree that more work is needed in determining just what aspect of the contextual dimension we call location is important for distinguishing variations in organizations. Distinctions between locations have been made on the basis of technology (e.g., Webber, 1969), political boundaries (e.g., Granick, 1972), and culture (e.g., Ronen & Shenkar, 1985). Technology may be too broad and national boundaries too narrow to develop sufficient variation for a global measure of location. Furthermore, if both forces of convergence and divergence appear to be present concerning a given organizational phenomenon, one might, as Lamers (1976) suggests, want to view nation/culture as a moderator rather than an independent variable. In this way, one can examine whether nation/culture strengthens or weakens the relationship between other dimensions of context and organization processes. This approach might be useful to determine the modifications needed prior to transferring a theory abroad.

Our pragmatic American culture leads us to conclude that it is up to us as organization scientists to empirically demonstrate whether convergence or divergence among nations/cultures exists for each of our theories. In conducting this study, it has become increasingly apparent that successful transfer of organization sciences to other locations depends not only on *what* is transferred but also *how* the transfer is accomplished. Regarding the transfer process, we offer three recommendations. First, prior to transfer, a theory should have demonstrated explanatory power in a given national/cultural setting. Secondly, it must be established that convergence between two or more nations/cultures exists. This should be accomplished by incorporating other dimensions of organizational context besides location in the assessment. Finally, the timing of the transfer is important to its receptivity. The theory should address problems currently facing organizations in the target nation. What we are suggesting is the need for the development of a useful theory of knowledge transfer. Such a theory could be based on prevailing views of organizational change. The success of any change, such as the introduction of a new theory to a nation/culture, is dependent not only on the relevance of the content of the change (e.g., theory) but also on the process by which the change is accomplished (transferred).

VII. REFERENCES

Allison, G. T. (1971). *Essence of decision: Explaining the Cuban missle crisis.* Boston: Little, Brown.

Bachrach, S. B., & Aiken, M. (1976). Structural and process constraints on influence in organizations: A level-specific analysis. *Administrative Science Quarterly, 21,* 623–642.

Bougeois, L. J. (1985). Strategic goals, perceived uncertainty, and economic performance in volatile environments. *Academy of Management Journal, 28,* 548–573.

Burns, T., & Stalker, G. M. (1961). *The management of innovation.* London: Tavistock.

Channon, D. F. (1973). *The strategy and structure of British enterprise.* Boston: Harvard University.

Crozier, M. (1964). *The bureaucratic phenomenon.* Chicago: University of Chicago Press.

Cyert, R. M., & March, J. G. (1963). *A behavioral theory of the firm.* Englewood Cliffs, NJ: Prentice-Hall.

Dalton, D. R., & Kesner, I. E. (1987). Composition and CEO duality in boards of directors: An international perspective. *Journal of International Business Studies, 18,* 33–42.

Dun & Bradstreet. (1980a). *Million dollar directory.* New York: Dun & Bradstreet.

Dun & Bradstreet. (1980b). *Principal international businesses.* New York: Dun & Bradstreet International.

Duncan, R. B. (1972). The characteristics of organizational environments and perceived environmental uncertainty. *Administrative Science Quarterly, 17,* 313–327.

Duncan, R. B. (1973). Multiple decision-making structures in adapting to environmental uncertainty: The impact on organizational effectiveness. *Human Relations, 26,* 273–291.

Farh, J. L., Hoffman, R. C., & Hegarty, W. H. (1984). Assessing environmental scanning at the subunit level: A multitrait-multimethod analysis. *Decision Sciences, 15,* 197–220.

Ghertman, M. (1976). The strategy formulation process of the foreign subsidiary of a french multinational corporation. *International Studies of Management and Organization, VI,* 27–53.

Gouy, M. (1978). Strategic decision making in large European firms. *Long Range Planning, 14,* 41–48.

Granick, D. (1972). *Industrial management in four developed countries: France, Britain, United States and Russia.* Cambridge, MA: M.I.T. Press.

Haire, M., Ghiselli, E. E., & Porter, L. W. (1966). *Management thinking: An international study*. New York: Wiley.

Hambrick, D. C. (1981). Environment, strategy, and power within top management teams. *Administrative Science Quarterly, 26*, 253–276.

Heller, F. A., & Wilpert, B. (1981). *Competence and power in managerial decision-making: A study of senior levels of organization in eight countries*. New York: Wiley.

Hickson, D. J., & McMillan, C. J. (1981). *Organization and nation: The Aston Programme IV*. Westmead, Hampshire, England: Gower.

Hickson, D. J., Hinings, C. B., Lee, C. A., Schneck, R. E., & Pennings, J. N. (1971). A strategic contingencies' theory of intraorganizational power. *Administrative Science Quarterly, 16*, 216–229.

Hinings, C. R., Hickson, D. J., Pennings, J. N., & Schneck, R. E. (1974). Structural conditions of intraorganizational power. *Administrative Science Quarterly, 19*, 22–44.

Hoffman, R. C., & Hegarty, W. H. (1983). A model for development of a data collection instrument. *Proceedings of the Annual Meeting of the Academy of Management*. Dallas, Texas.

Horovitz, J. (1980). *Top management control in europe*. London: Macmillan.

Jemison, D. B. (1981). Organizational versus environmental sources of influence in strategic decision making. *Strategic Management Journal, 2*, 77–89.

Kerlinger, F. N., & Pedhazur, E. J. (1973). *Multiple regression in behavioral research*. New York: Holt, Rinehart & Winston.

Kassem, M. S. (1976). Introduction: European versus American organization theories. In G. Hofstede & M. S. Kassem (Eds.), *European contributions to organization theory* (pp. 1–17). Amsterdam: Van Gorcum.

Khandwalla, P. (1977). *The design of organizations*. New York: Harcourt Brace Jovanovich.

Lammers, C. J. (1976). Towards the internationalization of the organization sciences. In G. Hofstede & M. S. Kassem (Eds.), *European contributions to organization theory* (pp. 25–42). Amsterdam: Van Gorcum.

Mazzolini, R. (1979). *Government controlled enterprises: International strategic and policy decisions*. New York: John Wiley & Sons.

Miles, R. E., & Snow, C. C. (1978). *Organizational strategy, structure, and process*. New York: McGraw-Hill.

Norburn, D. (1987). Corporate leaders in Britain and America: A cross-national analysis. *Journal of International Business Studies, 18*, 15–32.

O'Connell, J., & Zimmerman, J. W. (1979). Scanning the international environment. *California Management Review, 22*, 15–23.

Pugh, D., Hickson, D., Hinings, C., & Turner, C. (1969). The context of organization structures. *Administrative Science Quarterly, 14*, 91–114.

Quinn, J. B. (1980). *Strategies for change: Logical incrementalism*. Homewood, IL: Richard D. Irwin.

Ronen, S., & Shenkar, O. (1985). Clustering countries on attitudinal dimensions: A review and synthesis. *Academy of Management Review, 10*, 435–454.

Schendel, D. E., & Hofer, C. W. (Eds.). (1979). *Strategic management: A new view of business policy and planning*. Boston: Little, Brown.

Steiner, G. A. (1979). *Strategic planning*. New York: Free Press.

U.S. Department of Commerce, Bureau of Census. (1984). *Statistical Abstract of the United States—1984*, 104th ed. Washington, DC.: U.S. Government Printing Office.

Webber, R. A. (1969). Convergence or divergence? *Columbia Journal of World Business, IV*, 75–83.

III
INSIGHTS AND PERSPECTIVES
FROM ASIA

7

The Diffusion of American Organizational Theory in Postwar Japan

Schon L. Beechler and Vladimir Pucik

Since the late 1970s, the poor economic performance of Western industrialized nations, contrasted with Japan's advances in the international arena, has led to a keen interest in Japanese management techniques by practitioners and academics alike. American authors have not failed to highlight the fact that some of the management practices attributed to the Japanese actually originated in the United States. The assumption among many Americans is that, although the quality and cost of our products may not be competitive, we are still "No. 1" in the battle of the intellects, and the Japanese merely copy and adapt our ideas. However, as a few authors have pointed out (Cole, 1985; Hall & Leidecker, 1981), the Japanese transformation of imported ideas concerning management contributes a new quality to theories of organization and cannot be dismissed as mere imitation.

Although the impact of Japanese "intellectual borrowing" from the West and from the United States in particular may be subject to different interpretations, there is no doubt that a significant transfer of ideas has

Schon L. Beechler and Vladimir Pucik • School of Business Administration, The University of Michigan, Ann Arbor, Michigan, 48109.

taken place. Less well-known is the manner in which American organizational theories were disseminated in Japan. This chapter reviews the flows of ideas about management and organizations between the United States and Japan, focusing on the differences in diffusion patterns over time and across different classes of adopters.

Neither the transfer of management concepts across cultures nor the related diffusion processes occur in a vacuum. Relatively stable factors, such as the cultural distance between countries (Hofstede, 1980), play an important role in determining the effectiveness of "idea exports" across national boundaries. In addition, we propose that more dynamic factors, such as changes in relative economic power and the particular actors involved in the exchange, exert a powerful influence on the speed, scope, and direction of the diffusion process. We will attempt to show in this chapter how the characteristics of the diffusion process of American organizational theories (AOT) in Japan have changed with transformations of the relative socioeconomic conditions in the two countries, with changes of economic priorities on micro- and macrolevels, as well as with changes in interests and needs of the American organizational theory (AOT) adopters.

I. DIFFUSION STAGES

We divide the postwar exchange of ideas on management and organizational practices between Japan and the United States into five stages (Table 7.1). Each stage is characterized by the emergence of a distinct approach to American organizational theory and management by two key classes of adopters—academics and practicing managers.

During Stage 1, which began in the early postwar years and lasted until the mid-1960s, American organizational theory and management practices were accepted as new theology on nearly unconditional terms by both Japanese academic and management communities. In Stage 2, which began in the mid-1960s, pioneers in the academic profession pushed to supplement the armchair theorizing, then dominant in the Japanese social sciences, with empirical analyses based on conceptual models developed in the West. At the same time, many practitioners continued to look to the United States for answers to specific organizational problems, but now with a more critical attitude.

The emergence of Japan as a new economic superpower in the early 1970s (Stage 3) was accompanied by a revival of "Japan-is-unique" theories that implicitly, and often explicitly, rejected the validity of empirical research based on Western analytical concepts. Beginning in the

Table 7.1. Diffusion of American Organizational Theories in Japan

Stage	Adopters	
	Academics	Managers
Stage 1 AOT as a new theology (1945–)	Value system: Using AOT as a counter-weight to Marxism and traditionalist ideology	Professionalism: Implementing scientific management tools in industry
Stage 2 AOT as an empirical guide (1965–)	Research application: AOT as framework for research in Japanese organizations	Pragmatic adaption: Application of "soft" and "hard" concepts from AOT in industry
Stage 3 Rejection of AOT: Culturalist rollback (1970–)	Methodological rejection: Inapplicability of AOT to "unique" Japan	Reexamination of the past: Focus on the "superior" attributes of Japanese firms
Stage 4 New directions in AOT (1975–)	Analytical tool: Using AOT in empirically validated theory building	Pragmatic universalism: Using experiences of American firms as examples to learn from
Stage 5 Integration of Japanese management concepts and AOT (1981–)	Collaborative efforts: Research joint ventures and comparative studies	Reverse imports: Exporting Japanese practices to Japanese firms overseas

mid-1970s, however, resistance to unidimensional positions of culturalism led to Stage 4, characterized by pragmatic approaches to the transfer of management techniques both to and from Japan and by an increased use of rigorous research methodologies. Finally, Stage 5 of the diffusion process began to emerge in the early 1980s with the export of managerial techniques from Japan, supplemented by an increase in collaborative ventures between American and Japanese researchers drawing on an integrated methodological framework.

Although the beginning of each new diffusion stage can be identified with relative precision, the transition between stages was gradual. Paradigms that dominated an earlier diffusion stage often continued to exist concurrently as new paradigms developed. It is also important to recognize that a number of scholars associated with the process of AOT diffusion in Japan shifted their paradigmatic positions over time. In such cases, the classification of their individual contribution into one of the diffusion stages characterizes their thinking at the time. In addition, the references cited in the discussion of each stage are meant to be representative, not exhaustive.

A. Stage 1: The New Theology

At the end of World War II, the modernization of Japan as a whole became one of the major concerns of Japanese intellectuals and writers. The Japanese embarked on a path of reindustrialization by seeking out the best business minds in the Western world. Not only in organizational science, but in all the social sciences, Western, and especially American, concepts and values were perceived for several years after the war as a "new revelation" that should replace the discredited Japanese creeds of the recent past. The primary concern of Japanese social scientists was with finding and dismantling premodern, semifeudalistic elements remaining in the social structure, social relations, and social consciousness (Ishikawa, 1982). In the area of management, Western concepts were also intended to serve as a counterweight to the diffusion of Marxist ideas that were ideologically unacceptable to most managers, as well as to the American occupational authorities, who played an active intermediary role in the diffusion process.

Because foreign travel was nearly impossible under the government-controlled economy during the early postwar years, American management principles were first disseminated in postwar Japan through domestic training programs sponsored by the occupation authorities (Takamiya, 1983). This effort was supported by the strong legacy of the "scientific management" boom that occurred during the 1920s in Japan. A number of executives who were in charge of the reconstruction of Japanese industry had received an early training based on Western manuals and techniques. This background in "scientific management" among many managers and executives made it easier to assimilate the newly arrived concepts of management, particularly in the area of quality control.

The first quality control (QC) seminars in Japan were conducted by a representative from the Allied General Headquarters in 1949 and were followed by seminars given by W. Edwards Deming in 1950 and J. M. Juran in 1954. The QC technology introduced by Deming and Juran, although eventually modified substantially by the Japanese, played a large role in modernizing Japanese management. The Japanese also imported American management control systems on a mass scale during this period. For example, Ono Toyoaki, an executive with a major company and later a management scholar, translated the *Management Guide* of Standard Oil and introduced it to a large number of Japanese firms (Ono, 1972). Western management ideas also entered Japan freely in tandem with technological assistance from American firms to their Japanese partners.

The most influential Western management theorist of this period was Peter Drucker, whose major works were translated into Japanese and were widely read by Japanese managers. Drucker himself was a frequent visitor and seminar speaker in Japan. The Japan Productivity Center, established in 1955, was a major actor in the diffusion of AOT during this period, inviting many other American management experts to visit Japan. Numerous missions to the United States were also sponsored by the center, furthering management transfer and significantly enhancing the professionalism of Japanese management (Takamiya, 1983).

The diffusion of AOT among academics was less direct than among practitioners. Until about 1960, Japanese organizational theory was dominated by two competing Marxist interpretations of the development of Japanese capitalism (Shimada, 1983). The prevailing view was that Japanese capitalism was semifeudal and immature. From this perspective, all of the conspicuous labor practices such as the emergence of enterprise unions, lifetime commitment within a closed enterprise community, and the length-of-service reward system were seen as evidence that Japanese capitalism was backward. Western management practices were seen as "progressive" but not necessarily desirable in the long run.

Among the non-Marxist groups, the history of managerial sciences after World War II can be characterized as a process of "naive" inclination to American views (Ishikawa, 1982, p. 11). Interest in the realities of Japanese management was low, an attitude reflecting traditional Japanese academism that had long been absorbed with adopting Western theories without taking into consideration their applicability to local conditions.

B. Stage 2: Empirical Guide

A new trend, again spearheaded primarily by practitioners, began to emerge in the early 1960s. AOT ideas, especially those concerning leadership, management style, management information systems, and organizational design, continued to be assimilated directly, with important modifications that reflected local conditions. For example, Sony launched a drive to convert its "mechanistic" organization into an "organic" one, based on ideas drawn from the work of Rensis Likert and from managerial concepts developed by the company's founders (Kobayashi, 1970). During this period, a number of firms also began to experiment with Western job enlargement and job enrichment techniques that, coupled with quality control techniques introduced earlier, led to the now-famous "quality control circles." Organizational innovations such as the introduction of management information systems (MIS) were also rapidly disseminated among Japanese firms. For example, Nippon Telegraph and Telephone used the examples of AT&T and Westinghouse as models for the introduction of their own organization development and management information systems (Takahashi, 1970).

The impact of AOT on Japanese organizational theory also shifted. A small minority of those in academia began to use AOT concepts to enhance the methodological quality and empirical foundations of organizational research in Japan. However, their work was often better known abroad than at home, mainly through their personal links to foreign scholars. Several of the empirical studies conducted in this stage were products of early cooperative efforts among Japanese and American scholars. For example, Whitehill and Takezawa (1968) used research methods in social psychology in their questionnaire survey of workers' perceptions and attitudes in a comparative analysis of the United States and Japan.

Among those promoting empirically driven methodologies of social analysis, Kazuo Koike played a key role. He investigated Japanese internal labor markets and their impact on the career development of various groups of employees (e.g., Koike, 1978, 1983a,b). However, it gradually became evident that Koike's analytical approach clashed with some emerging trends in the Japanese social sciences that questioned the applicability of Western methodology to the analysis of Japanese organizations, and he and his colleagues came under increasing attack.

On the theoretical side, some organizational theorists began to trace the origins of popular management practices back to social relations in Japan's largely agrarian preindustrial society. Others invoked the research efforts of such Western scholars as Benedict (1946) and Abegglen (1958) to legitimize their views. Abegglen's book, describing the results of his field survey of a small number of large Japanese plants, was especially useful in this regard because, in explaining Japanese industrial relations, it emphasized the rule of anthropological and cultural legacies. A number of Abegglen's propositions were rebutted, for example, by Taira (1970), who pointed out that Japan's development was by no means unique and embedded in its culture but could be fully explained by neoclassical economic theory. Nevertheless, as we point out later, changes in the economic environment were seen as giving additional support to the culturalist positions, and the arguments of Abegglen's critics did not make much headway outside of a small group of scholars.

A significant number of studies that were relatively atheoretical in nature were also conducted during this time. Researchers such as Masumi Tsuda, Taishiro Shirai, Mikio Sumiya, Ichiro Nakayama, Noamichi Funahashi, Kazuo Okochi, and others gathered a large amount of information on topics ranging from the structure of the labor market and personnel administration to decision making and technological change. They analyzed the structure and operation of various institutions inductively, providing data that contributed greatly to general knowledge in the field. These descriptive studies also provided much fuel for later debates concerning the applicability of AOT to Japanese management.

C. Stage 3: Culturalist Rollback

As research on Japan blossomed, criticism of existing organization theories based on concepts imported from the West continued to increase. This development was partially a function of theoretical weaknesses embedded in the mechanistic transfer of ideas across cultural boundaries. However, the key factor supporting the revisionist thinking was the change in the economic and social status of Japan from a devastated, war-torn country to a major international competitor. As Japan's economic successes spurred increased confidence in indigenous management policies, a number of Japanese scholars began to promote the view that Japanese management and organizational practices promoted, rather than hindered, Japan's economic growth. Japanese business leaders also became increasingly convinced that their management practices were valuable assets rather than deterrents to the international competitiveness of their firms (Shimada, 1983).

Theories focusing on supposedly "unique" features of Japanese society emerged in all areas of the social sciences. Given the dominance of organizations in contemporary Japanese social life, this *nihonjinron* boom could not bypass the field of organizational science. Although specific constructs were often newly minted, many were, by and large, derivatives from nationalist management theories that had prospered until Japan's World War II defeat (e.g., Fujihara, 1936). As a result, organizational theory in Japan during the 1970s came to be dominated by a methodological culturalism that emphasized the organizational impact of "unique" characteristics of the Japanese, such as "groupism" or "dependence." The culturalist approach was reinforced by the apparent failure of AOT to prevent the decline of American economic competitiveness. From a very pragmatic viewpoint, the Japanese asked, "If it doesn't work over there, why use it here?" A new consensus began to form, asserting that Japanese organizations have not only unique, but also superior qualities.

This pattern of alternating wholesale adoption of Western ideas with their nearly complete rejection has a long history in Japan. The holistic view of Japanese society as a unique entity, resurrected during the culturalist rollback by Japanese organizational theorists, can be traced back to the idea of *wakon kansai* (Chinese learning with Japanese spirit) in the eighteenth century (Mouer & Sugimoto, 1983).

As noted by Hazama (1971), the assumption was that the behavioral characteristics of the group and the individual were incomprehensible to people outside of Japan who were socialized under a system of well-developed individualism. "Uniqueness" was the basic paradigm, leaving nothing else to prove, and thus, no empirical research was deemed necessary. Iwata (1977, 1978), for example, asserted that psychological traits are peculiar to each society and determine the particular pattern of management. Thus, he insisted that AOT does not have universal validity and that the uniqueness of the Japanese management system cannot be revealed through comparative qualitative analyses. At the same time, Kumon (1981) argued for the need for both a culturalist approach and an environmental (qualitative) approach. Because of the particular psychology of the Japanese, Kumon maintained that it is not possible to formulate a general theory, either by deductive or inductive methods.

Tsuda (1976, 1977), although adopting a number of the culturalist propositions, criticized this psychological approach to the Japanese style of management and proposed to explain its formation and existence from the way of life in Japanese society as a whole. Tsuda emphasized that the Japanese company makes up for the lack of a local communal life system by playing the role of such a system itself. It is this characteristic that makes Japanese management unique.

D. Stage 4: New Directions

Since the late 1970s, however, it became quite obvious that the dominance of the culturalist paradigm in Japanese organizational theory was weakening. This does not imply a renewed worship of AOT, but a more balanced integration of Western and Japanese concepts. The slowing down of the rapid economic growth after the oil crisis of 1973 led many to reexamine the validity of claims concerning Japan's superiority in management.

Urabe (1978) presented one of the earliest critiques of theories of the Japanese style of management, criticizing both American and Japanese scholars who:

> . . . tend to ascribe characteristics of Japanese-style management to Japan's traditional culture and society or to Japanese psychological traits without

paying due attention to the technological and economic factors that precondition Japanese-style management. Consequently, their observations often turn out to be one-sided or lead to simple-minded generalities. (pp. 33–34)

Ishikawa (1982) also concluded that the methodological nationalism of the culturalists had led to an oversimplification of the native pecularities in Japan.

To address these criticisms, Japanese theorists began to formulate more sophisticated theories and research methodologies. For example, Okamoto (1981) presented an evaluation of the development of Japanese business through an analysis of empirical observations on management in postwar Japan. Paralleling recent developments in Western organizational theory, he focused on managerial strategy and the economic environment. He saw the rise of "traditional" Japanese management practices, such as lifetime employment, as a rational response to various environmental contingencies facing Japanese firms.

Empirical research, which until the late 1970s had been conducted by only a few academics, received a boost from a new generation of researchers who, because of their mainly Western training, are quite comfortable with analytical tools popular in contemporary AOT. The ability to engage in rigorous empirical research provides this generation with an opportunity to outflank the culture-bound traditionalists.

A number of scholars used rigorous quantitative analyses to examine the relationship between reducing working time and labor productivity. In addition, Kashiwagi (1982) used statistical analysis to explain the success and failure of T-group and encounter-group training methods in Japan. Kono (1982) performed a large-scale quantitative analysis on the product diversification strategies of Japanese companies from 1962 to 1978. Using path analysis, Shinohara (1980) characterized the corporate strategy creation process in Japan, and Uchino (1981) analyzed interorganizational relations by focusing on interlocking directorates.

Generalized theoretical frameworks were used by both Hanada (1980) and Kido (1980) in their analyses of the organizational commitment of Japanese employees, and Wakabayashi (1979) examined managerial career development in a department store chain by utilizing Graen's (1976) theoretical framework. In addition, international collaborative research, such as Mannari and Marsh's (1980) replication of studies by Woodward (1965), Blau (1968), and the Aston group, although still infrequent, was part of the trend toward empirically validated theory building.

During this same period, practitioners continued to examine AOT and related managerial practices in order to apply them, with necessary modifications, to their own organizations. A clear example of the assimilation of AOT ideas in Japanese business can be found in organizational changes at Toshiba (Taku, 1981). Faced with tumbling business conditions after the first oil crisis in the early 1970s, Toshiba analyzed the organization of General Electric, which utilized the strategic business unit (SBU) and product portfolio management (PPM) concepts and adopted them with modifications for their organization in 1976.

Similar changes occurred in other large Japanese firms. For example, Hitachi, which introduced a full product division structure in the 1960s, decentralized profit center responsibilities after studying the experiences of American firms (Okamoto, 1981). In the late 1970s, following trends emerging among Western multinational corporations, Matsushita Electric abolished the separation of domestic product departments and their international division, and created global product divisions (Ono, 1979).

E. Stage 5: Integration

Internationalization of business in both the United States and Japan has presented a new testing ground for organizational theory. Substantial cross-national research in various countries has added to the body of knowledge, providing researchers with a wealth of comparative data. A more informed and sophisticated approach has emerged that focuses not only on the differences or the similarities in the social relations in organizations of various countries but contends that the truth lies somewhere in between the previous extreme approaches (Yamada, 1980). Urabe (1978), for example, does not deny that there are differences between Japan and the West in terms of their social relations and management systems but notes that each has its own strengths and weaknesses. Both Urabe (1978) and Yamada (1980) emphasize that Japanese style-management is dynamic and continues to adapt to its environment.

The push for integration of Japanese management concepts with AOT was abetted by calls from practitioners for universal frameworks to help export Japanese practices to Japanese affiliates abroad as the internationalization of the Japanese economy continued to progress. Managers knew from experience that a number of "unique" Japanese practices were transferable; what they needed was a more thorough way of organizing how to go about it. A number of Japanese theorists responded by examining management in overseas Japanese firms in order to determine which aspects were transferable to foreign countries.

Such studies have been conducted by, among others, Ishida (1981), Kobayashi (1982), Hanada (1981, 1982), Takamiya (1981), and Yoshihara (1983). In more general terms, Kono (1982) emphasized the fit between the corporation and the environment in discussing whether Japanese management philosophy can be exported. He argued that some characteristics of Japanese management had their origins in Japanese tradition but that others were the result of rational judgment and adjustment to environmental circumstances.

An increased interest in Japanese organizations by American researchers, coupled with an increased appreciation for empirical research, have also led to a number of collaborative research efforts. Most of these collaborative works focus on comparative research. Among them, the work of Lincoln, Hanada, and Olson (1981) examined the commitment of employees in Japanese-owned firms in California. Howard, Shudo, and Umeshima (1983) examined the motivation and values among Japanese and American managers, and Naoi and Schooler (1985) compared occupational conditions of workers in both countries. Some collaborative studies, however, have focused only on Japanese organizations but have used concepts derived from AOT. For example, Nonaka and Johansson (1985) examined characteristics of Japanese organizations from an information-processing and environmental scanning perspective, and Kono (1982) used the concept of "fit" between an organization and its environment in his paper discussing whether Japanese management philosophy can be exported.

A growing number of Japanese scholars have not only integrated AOT in their studies but have also modified and expanded theories developed in Japan and the West to arrive at a more general, less ethnocentric, culture-bound explanation of various aspects of organizational behavior. For example, Misumi (1985) presents research on the performance–maintenance (PM) theory of leadership. The concepts of PM leadership theory are derived from existing concepts about basic group processes postulated in the social sciences in the United States, but PM leadership theory is distinguished from other leadership research outside Japan by its incorporation of Japan's cultural and historical context (Misumi & Peterson, 1985, p. 203).

Kagono et al. (1981) gathered data on a large number of American and Japanese companies, focusing on strategic adaptation to the environment. The point of departure for their study was the environmental adaptation theory, which the authors see as an expansion of the classic works of Burns and Stalker, Woodward, Lawrence and Lorsch, and Galbraith. They have enlarged upon theories developed in a Western context, attempting to devise an analytical framework of increased comparative applicability and validity.

As more and more organizations internationalize and are exposed to different management practices, the exchange and application of multicultural management concepts and values will intensify, at least in some areas. In addition, the growth of Japanese investment in the United States, coupled with a transfer of technology and management practices that reverses the trend experienced in Japan two and three decades ago, brings with it a heightened awareness of Japanese organizational concepts. An increasing number of these concepts have begun to appear in American periodicals in articles authored by Japanese, a trend that is expected to continue. The number of Americans who are able to cross the language barrier and obtain direct access to current Japanese theoretical developments is also growing.

II. CONCLUSION

In our analysis of diffusion patterns of American organizational theories in Japan, we have attempted to show that factors other than cultural distance may influence the process of diffusion of organizational theories across national boundaries. In particular, we focused on the relative economic power of the sender and recipient countries (the United States and Japan). We also illustrated how theoreticians in academia and practicing managers differed in their approaches to the process of diffusion. The resulting picture is one of great dynamism as the appeal of AOT in Japan oscillated considerably over time.

Throughout the postwar period, the transferability of American concepts of management to Japan was clearly associated with the fundamentals of the economic relationship between Japan and the United States. When the United States dominated, acceptance of American "hardware" technology was accompanied by broad and rapid diffusion of American management "software." However, when the relative economic power began to change, so did the scope and intensity of the diffusion process. Ultimately, the future roles of sender and recipient may be reversed in accord with the changed economic fortunes of the two countries.

At the same time, the diffusion of AOT in Japan has been influenced by differences between the frequent methodological extremism of the theoreticians and the pragmatism of the practitioners, with the latter serving as transfer agents or gatekeepers as well as moderators of swings in the diffusion process. In particular, the gatekeeping role played by Japanese managers deserves attention. On numerous occasions, the capacity of Japanese organizations to scan culturally alien environments, to discover and to experiment with potentially useful ideas, and to rapidly internalize those ideas that have passed the test was substantially larger than the capacity of their Western counterparts to learn within their own cultural milieu.

The recent trend toward cross-pollination of organizational theories and management practices in the two countries also has important implications for American researchers. For example, "transplant" organizations (Japanese-owned firms in the United States) provide challenging opportunities for testing the cross-cultural applicability of existing organizational theories taken for granted within a unicultural environment. This active approach not only enhances opportunities for information sharing, the exchange of ideas, and collaborative efforts between scholars in Japan and in the United States, but also supports the long-overdue internationalization of the American social sciences. Japanese experience shows that "looking out," although not without its pitfalls, is nevertheless eminently worthwhile.

ACKNOWLEDGMENTS

This chapter draws upon research previously reported in *Sociology and Social Research*, 71(1), 1986, pp. 20–26. The authors would like to gratefully acknowledge the research assistance of Kiyohiko Ito and the helpful comments of Professors Robert Cole and Mitsuyo Hanada.

III. REFERENCES

Abegglen, J. (1958). *The Japanese factory: Aspects of its social organization.* Glencoe, IL: The Free Press.

Benedict, R. (1946). *The chrysanthemum and the sword.* Boston: Houghton Mifflin.

Blau, P. (1968, January). The hierarchy of authority in organizations. *American Journal of Sociology, 73,* 453–467.

Cole, R. E. (1985, December). The macropolitics of organizational change: A comparative analysis of the spread of small-group activities. *Administrative Science Quarterly,* 560–586.

Fujihara, G. (1936). *The spirit of Japanese industry.* The Hokuseido Press.

Graen, G. B. (1976). Role-making processes within complex organizations. In M. D. Dunnette (Ed.), *Handbook of industrial and organizational psychology* (pp. 1201–1246). Chicago: Rand McNally.

Hall, J., & Liedecker, J. (1981, Winter). Is Japanese management anything new? A comparison of Japanese-style management with U.S. participative models. *Human Resource Management,* 14–21.

Hanada, M. (1980, January). Nihonteki Keiei niokeru jyugyoin no kizoku ishiki: genjitsu to kenkyu suijun no hazamade. *Kenkyujo Kiho, 5,* 2–3.

Hanada, M. (1981). *Shokuba niokeru ningenkankei no kokusai hikaku.* Tokyo: Ningen Noryoku Kaihatsu Center.

Hanada, M. (1982). *Gaikokuseiki chishiki rodosha no katsuyo no jittai: uchigawa karano kokusaika.* Tokyo: Ningen Noryoku Kaihatsu Center.

Hazama, H. (1971). Nihonteki keiei no tokushitsu. In H. Hazama (Ed.), *Nihonteki keiei, shudanshugi no kozai* (pp. 9–74). Tokyo: Nihon Keizai Shimbun Sha.

Hazama, H. (1979, October). Comment [on Fruin, 1979]. *Organizational Science, 13*(3), 66–67. In Japanese.

Hofstede, G. (1980). *Culture's consequences.* Beverly Hills: Sage Publications.

Howard, A., Shudo, K., & Umeshima, M. (1983). Motivation and values among Japanese and American managers. *Personnel Psychology, 36,* 883–893.

Imaizumi, M. (1984, Spring). Past and present status of quality management in Japan. *Management Japan, 17*(1), 18–22.

Ishida, H. (1981, Fall). Human resources management in overseas Japanese firms. *Japanese Economic Studies, X*(1), 53–81.

Ishikawa, A. (1982). A survey of studies in the Japanese style of management. *Economic and Industrial Democracy, 3,* 1–15.

Iwata, R. (1977). *Nihonteki keiei no hensei genri.* Tokyo: Bunshindo.

Iwata, R. (1978). *Gendai Nihon no keiei fudo.* Tokyo: Nihonkeizai Shinbunsha.

Kagono, T., Nonaka, I., Sakaibara, K., & Okumura, A. (1981, July). Strategies and structures of U.S. and Japanese firms: An empirical analysis. *Organizational Science, 15*(2), 11–34. In Japanese.

Kashiwagi, S. (1982). The measurement of the efficiency of the encounter-group method. *Organizational Science, 16*(2), 54–63. In Japanese.

Kido, Y. (1980, August). A study of organizational commitment in Japanese Companies. *Mita Business Review, 23*(3), 132–151. In Japanese.

Kobayashi, N. (1982). The present and future of Japanese multinational enterprise: A comparative analysis of Japanese and U.S.-European multinational management. *International Studies Management and Organization, XII*(1), 38–58.

Kobayashi, S. (1970, November/December). The creative organization—A Japanese experiment. *Personnel,* 8–17.

Koike, K. (1978). Japan's industrial relations: Characteristics and problems. *Japanese Economic Studies, VXII*(1), 42–90.

Koike, K. (1978). Japan's industrial relations: Characteristics and problems. *Japanese Economic Studies, VII*(1), 42–90.

Koike, K. (1983a). Internal labor markets: Workers in large firms. In T. Shirai (Ed.), *Contemporary industrial relations in Japan* (pp. 29–61). Madison: University of Wisconsin Press.

Koike, K. (1983b). Workers in small firms and women in industry. In T. Shirai (Ed.), *Contemporary industrial relations in Japan* (pp. 89–115). Madison: University of Wisconsin Press.

Kono, T. (1982). Japanese management philosophy: Can it be exported? *Long Range Planning, 15*(3), 90–102.

Kumon, S. (1981). Nihonteki Keiei no tokushitsu towa nanika. In *Nihon shakai no tokushitsu* (pp. 99–126). Tokyo: Nihonkeizai Kenkyu Center.

Lincoln, J., Hanada, M., & Olson, J. (1981, March). Cultural orientations and individual reactions to organizations. *Administrative Science Quarterly,* 93–114.

Mannari, H., & Marsh, R. (1980, December). Organizational structure of Japanese factories: A test of technological implication theory. *Organizational Science, 14*(4), 61–75. In Japanese.

Misumi, J. (1985). *The behavioral science of leadership.* Ann Arbor: University of Michigan Press.

Misumi, J., & Peterson, M. (1985). The performance-maintenance theory of leadership: Review of a Japanese research program. *Administrative Science Quarterly, 30,* 198–223.

Mouer, R., & Sugimoto, Y. (1983). Internationalization as an ideology in Japanese society. In H. Mannari, & H. Befu (Eds.), *The challenge of Japan's internationalization: Organization and culture* (pp. 267–297). Tokyo: Kwansei Gakuin University and Kodansha International.

Naoi, A., & Schooler, C. (1985). Occupational conditions and psychological functioning in Japan. *American Journal of Sociology, 90*(4), 729–749.

Nonaka, I. (1984, Autumn). A comparison of management in American, Japanese and European firms (II). *Management Japan, 17*(2), 20–37.

Nonaka, I., & Johansson, J. (1985). Japanese management: What about the 'hard' skills? *Academy of Management Review, 10*(2), 181–191.

Nonaka, I., & Okumura, A. (1984, Spring). A comparison of management in American, Japanese, and European firms (I). *Management Japan, 17*(1), 23–40.

Okamoto, Y. (1981, Fall). Nihon Kigyo no grand strategy. *Chuo Koron Kikan Keiei Mondai,* 277–306.

Okuda, K. (1971a). Managerial evolution in Japan [I] 1911–1925. *Management Japan, 5*(3), 13–19.

Okuda, K. (1971b). Managerial evolution in Japan [II] 1926–1945. *Management Japan, 6*(4), 16–23.

Ono, T. (1972). A personal survey of the modernization of business administration in Japan. *Management Japan, 6*(1), 20–27.

Ono, T. (1979). *Organizational strategies of Japanese firms.* Tokyo: Managemento sha. In Japanese.

Pucik, V., Beechler, S., & Ito, K. (1986). American organizational theory in Japan: Western concepts, Japanese spirit. *Sociology and Social Research, 71*(1), 20–26.

Shimada, H. (1983). Japanese industrial relations—A new general model? A survey of the English-language literature. In T. Shirai (Ed.), *Contemporary industrial relations in Japan* (pp. 3–28). Madison: University of Wisconsin Press.

Shinohara, M. (1980). Empirical study of corporate strategy in Japan: Environment-top management strategy. *Mita Business Review, 23*(4), 86–103. In Japanese.

Taira, K. (1970). *Economic development and the labor market in Japan.* New York: Columbia University Press.

Takahashi, T. (1970). Management information system: A critical appraisal. *Management Japan, 4*(1), 18–23.

Takamiya, M. (1981, Summer). Japanese multinationals in Europe: Internal operations and their public policy implications. *Columbia Journal of World Business,* 5–16.

Takamiya, S. (1983). Development of Japanese management. *Management Japan, 16*(1), 10–18.

Taku, Y. (1981, July). Strategic business organization. *Organizational Science, 15*(2), 35–48. In Japanese.

Tsuda, M. (1976). *Nihonteki keiei no yogo.* Tokyo: Toyokeizai Shinposha.

Tsuda, M. (1977). *Nihonteki keiei no ronri.* Tokyo: Chuo Keizaisha.

Uchino, T. (1981, December). On the measurement of interorganizational relations: Focusing on interlocking directorates. *Organizational Science, 15*(4), 53–63. In Japanese.

Urabe, K. (1978, October). Nihonteki keieiron hihan, *Kokumin Keizai Zasshi, 138,* 1–18.

Wakabayashi, M. (1979). *Management career progress in a Japanese organization.* Ann Arbor: UMI Press.

Whitehill, A., & Takezawa, S. (1968). *The other worker.* Honolulu: East-West Center Press.

Woodward. J. (1965). *Industrial organizations: Theory and practice.* Oxford: Oxford University Press.

Yamada, M. (1980). Beikoku ni miru Nihon-teki keiei. In T. Shishido & the Nikko Research Center (Eds.), *Nihon kigyo in USA* (pp. 104–131). Tokyo: Tokyo Keizai Shimpo Sha.

Yoshihara, H. (1983, September). Cumulative type of management—Japanese management abroad. *Kokumin Keizai Zasshi, 148*(3), 119–138. In Japanese.

8

Rational Man Theory in American and Japanese Performance Control

Jeremiah J. Sullivan, Teruhiko Suzuki,
and Yasumasa Kondo

The essence of an organization is people working together to produce goods and services in order to attain the organization's ends. Organizational science has focused on this process in a number of ways through several disciplines. Organizational behavior mostly examines the individual in terms of external influences on his or her thoughts and behavior in the workplace. Human resource management studies often center on the performance control process, which is made up of managers monitoring the actions of workers, attributing a level of responsibility to each worker for the performance output of the relevant work unit, and adjusting pay and bonuses accordingly. Some research questions that have emerged from these disciplinary studies are: How much monitoring do managers do? How well do managers make attributions? What is the relationship between monitoring, attributions, and rewards?

We have been conducting research on these questions for several years in American and Japanese organizations. Our goal is to identify similarities and differences between American and Japanese managers regarding their attitudes and beliefs about the performance control pro-

Jeremiah J. Sullivan • Department of Marketing and International Business, Graduate School of Business Administration, University of Washington, Seattle, Washington 98195.   Teruhiko Suzuki and Yasumasa Kondo • Department of Commerce, Doshisha University, Kyoto, Japan.

cess. Specifically, we first wanted to learn how rational each national group is in its performance attributions, that is, the extent to which responsibility judgments are grounded in evidence and free of bias. In America, a long line of research in cognitive and social psychology has identified the tendency of American managers to overweight individual effort and ability in performance attributions in comparison with attributions to the situation or to luck. Would Japanese managers tend to exhibit the same "fundamental attribution error"?

Our second goal was to learn the implicit (emic) theories of performance control held by American and Japanese managers. Do both hold the same theory, and is that theory the same as the textbook theory (etic) of performance control?

The two experiments described in this chapter yielded results that suggest: (1) that both American and Japanese tend to make the fundamental attribution error; (2) that both appear to hold the same theory of performance control; and (3) that this theory, the "rational man model," is the same as that which guides many researchers in organizational science in studies of individual behavior in organizations. An additional finding was that American and Japanese managers do have differing culture-bound ideas about what the function of work groups should be. Thus they are similar in their approach to managing people but different in their ideas about managing groups.

I. EXPERIMENT 1

A. The Fundamental Attribution Error (FAE)

This study investigated the existence of the fundamental attribution error in both American and Japanese performance attribution settings. The object of the study was to test competing theoretical explanations for its occurrence. These were: (1) the availability explanation, which focuses on cognitive flaws and biases in human information processing; and (2) the culture explanation, which focuses on culture-bound beliefs and values regarding responsibility for an individual's behavior.

B. Attribution Theory

Attribution theory attempts to describe the cognitive activities of persons as they make inferences and judgments about the causes of behavior that they either observe or in which they engage (Heider, 1958). Knowledge of systematic ways in which people make attributions can lead researchers to an increased understanding of human thought processes and to predictions about human responses to certain kinds of acts.

Of particular interest to attribution researchers has been the attempt to explain why persons attribute the causes of their own or other persons' behaviors to forces internal or external to them (Kelley & Michela, 1980). Is an act caused by an *internal* disposition characterized by ability or effort? Or is an act the result of *external* forces such as the environment or perhaps randomness? An understanding of how persons employ such categories or attributions (internal vs. external) reveals how people cognitively organize the world they perceive about them and hints at their attitudes and responses to the world (Frieze, Bar-Tal, & Carroll, 1980).

Attributions, particularly of the internal-external variety, play a part in the performance evaluations superiors make about subordinates in organizations (Mitchell, Green, & Wood, 1981). These attributions are cognitive elements that combine with organizational norms and policies to produce responses in the form of performance appraisals, promotions, rewards, punishments, and the like. If superiors are systematically biased in their attributions, they may be systematically biased in their responses. Indeed, it seems that superiors do tend to overattribute performance to internal dispositions, even when the evidence seems to indicate that an attribution to external circumstances is appropriate. This overattribution to internal disposition has been called the "fundamental attribution error" (Nisbett & Ross, 1980).

According to recent summaries of attribution research, the fundamental attribution error, although not occurring in every situation, context, or event, nevertheless is pervasive (Kahneman, Slovic, & Tversky, 1982). Most of the research has been conducted employing student subjects in contrived situations. Among a number of explanations for the phenomenon, one has emerged for which strong empirical support exists. The availability explanation hypothesizes that information about internal effort or ability is more salient to observers of behavior than is information about external situational phenomena. Consequently, internal information will be more available in an observer's memory for attributional purposes.

C. The Availability Hypothesis

Information that is salient becomes easily available for retrieval when it is stored in memory and can influence attributions more than can nonsalient information. Observers of others' behaviors are believed to find evidence of internal causes for the behaviors more salient than external causes. The evidence for internal causes becomes more available in observers' memories, and they tend to make internal attributions. In terms of superiors' attributions of a subordinate's performance, the superior finds that the evidence for the subordinate's effort or ability as causes of performance is more striking or vivid and easier to conceptualize than is evidence for situational or random causes. The evidence of internal and external causes is stored in memory, but the vivid internal evidence is more easily retrieved and thus is weighted more heavily in making an attribution. The result is the tendency of superiors to see effort and ability as the key causes of performance, regardless of the situation.

If observers have been found to commit the FAE and to overattribute to internal causes, *actors* have been found sometimes to overattribute to situations. Researchers have theorized that it is difficult for actors to observe themselves as they act. The evidence of their effort or ability, therefore, will not be as vivid as will evidence for situational causes. Situational evidence will be more available in memory (Monson & Snyder, 1977). Subordinates will see their behavior as mostly situationally caused—just the opposite explanation that superiors give to subordinate performance.

What are the consequences of the FAE on the part of superiors in terms of performance attributions, appraisals, and rewards? We can envision a common occurrence in organizations in which able, hardworking employees who do poorly on tasks because of the tasks' difficulty or because of bad luck will be labeled as lacking in effort or ability. Their evaluations for the period of the tasks will be poor, and limited organizational rewards will flow to them. Over time, these employees will learn that good performance evaluations (based on attributions of high competence and hard work as the causes of good performance) are more likely to occur when tasks are easy than when they are hard. These employees will seek out relatively easy work in the organization rather than challenging tasks.

No organization can tolerate such a state of affairs for long, and so management would somehow want superiors to stop committing the FAE. If salience and availability are the source of the error, management would want superiors to become more attentive to and to think more about situational causes for performance. In fact, this strategy is followed in many organizations simply by having superiors and subordinates sit down together to review the employee's performance during a given period. Because the subordinate will have many situational explanations for his or her activities, the superior will become attentive to situational evidence. Presumably, the superior will then have salient information about both internal *and external* causes of performance easily available in memory. He or she will then avoid the FAE and make a balanced assessment of the employee's performance. The superior–subordinate meeting, therefore, corrects the fundamental attribution error, if the FAE is due to salience and availability difficulties.

D. The Culture Hypothesis

So far we have been dealing with the conventional wisdom about what causes the FAE and how to cope with it. However, a second explanation assumes the existence in people's minds of experience-based and culturally determined cognitive structures—called schemata—that provide rules and guidelines for processing incoming information (Fiske & Linville, 1980). These cultural schemata can be the source of the FAE rather than the easy availability of salient information in memory.

In American culture, each person has an inventory of schemata that have been learned throughout his or her life. These schemata—many of which are almost identical across large numbers of Americans—tell the individual how to think about and how to evaluate what he or she attends to (Taylor, 1982). One schema says that the individual rather than the situation is responsible for his or her acts. American history tells Americans this, and American institutions are constructed to embody this cultural belief. Many Americans thus carry in their minds an intuitive processing rule that says, "If you observe another's or even your own behavior, you generally should attribute the cause of that behavior to effort or ability."

In virtually all contexts, then, both American employees and their superiors can be expected to make internal attributions.

In terms of subordinate performance, the cultural schema theory predicts that both superiors and subordinates will generally overattribute performance to effort/ability rather than to situation/luck. One could raise the objection at this point that scores of research studies have found evidence that availability of salient information is the cause of the FAE. However, it may be that most of these studies involved pallid and noninvolving settings that did not allow cultural values to come into play. Without any reason to employ a cultural schema, subjects in these experiments were influenced to make the FAE by easily available information.

Clearly, availability does explain the FAE in many settings. Our point here, however, is that in American organizations where American culture is pervasive—especially regarding performance appraisal—the cultural schema directing internal attributions may dominate the impact of availability and may be the major cause of the FAE. If so, then the corrective strategies devised by management to overcome the FAE— superior–subordinate meetings—will have only minimal success. Making situational information salient and available to superiors through superior exposure to subordinate explanations during an interview in an American organization will not work because *both* parties will be making the FAE.

The solution to the problem posed by the culture-bound fundamental attribution error is not interviews, although these are useful in dampening the potential difficulties posed by availability. Of more significance are efforts to get managers to understand their culture and how its values become embodied in cognitive schemata that often can be quite powerful in influencing their behavior. An ongoing program of such training can help managers to correct the fundamental attribution error and to assess the causes of an employee's performance in terms of evidence rather than schemata.

E. Research Design

Our research objective was to test two theories of the fundamental attribution error, availability and culture, in cross-cultural experimental settings. If the FAE is a human information-processing flaw (availability), then it should occur across cultures, and the error should be associated with differential retrieval of person and situation information from memory. If the FAE is the result of a cultural value in America, then it should not occur in a cultural setting where culture-bound cognitive schemata regarding individual responsibility are weak or nonexistent. Japan was chosen as the appropriate comparison culture for the study. A number of researchers and theorists have noted the dominance of groups in Japanese social life and the merging of the individual into his or her group (Lebra, 1976; Nakane, 1972; Rohlen, 1974). One could expect that most Japanese would attribute observed behavior to group–situation influence rather than to effort–ability influence. Thus the FAE, if it is a culture-bound American phenomenon only, should not occur in Japan.

Experimental designs testing the FAE must investigate *two* versions of the phenomenon. Harvey, Town, and Yarkin (1981) note that the FAE can be either a bias or an error. An error is an inconsistency between a hypothesis (such as an attribution) and evidence. In an experiment, the error would occur when subjects were given strong evidence for situational causes of behavior and weak evidence for person-related causes and yet still made a person attribution. A bias is a tendency to prefer a given cognition over its alternatives. Bias occurs when evidence for person or situational causes of behavior are equally probative and yet subjects still make a person-related attribution.

Accordingly, the experiment consisted of a 2 (strong-weak evidence for person responsibility) × 2 (strong-weak evidence for group responsibility) factorial design. A scenario was constructed describing an employee's failure to carry out a task. Evidence was presented for both internal and external causes of the failure. Then attributions were requested from subjects. After several minutes of distractor activity (to eliminate information from short-term memory), subjects were given a memory test to investigate the availability issue.

F. Method

1. Subjects

The experiment was conducted with Japanese and American college students and then replicated with Japanese and American managers. Replication with a more experienced group allowed us to examine the effect of organizational learning and experience, if any, on attributions. Table 8.1 describes the subject groups. Yet all groups had had experience in directing subordinates. The American managers represented approximately 50 different organizations in the banking, manufacturing,

Table 8.1. Comparison of Japanese and American Samples

	Japanese	Americans
Students (mean scores)	($n = 81$)	($n = 43$)
Age	21.5	23.7
Education	12.2	15.0
F/T experience (months)	0.0	24.3
P/T experience (months)	9.2	33.4
Leadership experience (months)	2.3	14.0
Number of subordinates (maximum)	2.9	5.0
Managers (mean scores)	($n = 63$)	($n = 51$)
Age	35.7	39.0
Education	12.4	15.6
F/T experience (months)	156.6	175.0
P/T experience (months)	7.2	29.7
Leadership experience (months)	41.2	63.3
Number of subordinates (maximum)	15.4	30.8

and services industries. The Japanese managers came from these industries and also from college administration. The experiment was administered to students during scheduled classes and to managers (United States) during seminars and during work hours (Japan).

The English version of the test instrument was translated into Japanese by one of the Japanese authors. It was then translated back into English by an American. The two versions were compared, and some minor changes to the Japanese version were made.

2. Procedure

Subjects were asked to take part in a study of supervisory style. A case was presented to them, and they were asked to put themselves in the position of the supervisor in the case. They then were given 2 minutes to read the scenario. Exposure was controlled so that differential exposure would not bias the results of the memory test.

The scenario described a young male employee given a common American or Japanese name. Information was given on his job tenure, education, and work group. An incident was described in which the employee was to meet a client for dinner. The employee failed to meet the client. The supervisor then tried to collect information useful in helping him decide why the employee failed at his task. Two types of evidence were presented: (1) about the employee's past behavior, and (2) about his relationship with his work group. Three pieces of information were presented for each type of evidence so that subjects read six pieces of evidence. An attempt was made to create types of evidence with relatively equal probative value by employing Kelley's attribution model (Kelley, 1973). Kelley theorizes that people make attributions based on three kinds of evidence, which he calls distinctiveness, consistency, and consensus. In the scenario, subjects read about the person-related evidence in these terms. For example, the strong/weak person-related evidence was described as follows: consistency evidence, "Paul has (has not) frequently failed to meet clients for dinner in the past"; distinctiveness, "Paul has (has not) frequently failed to get his other jobs done in the past"; consensus, "Other employees in your section rarely (frequently) have failed to meet clients for dinner after work."

The group-related evidence was as follows: consistency evidence, "The group makes many (few) demands on Paul's time"; distinctiveness, "Paul's membership in this work group has (has not) had much influence on his work performance during the past year"; consensus, "The whole group sometimes meets after work to enjoy each other's company and to discuss important work. Last night, when Paul was supposed to dine with the client, the group in fact did (did not) meet."

After reading the scenario, subjects were asked to fill out the 7-point likely-unlikely scales relating to effort, situation, ability, and luck attributions. The effort (internal) and situational (external) scores served as the dependent measures. The other attribution measures were collected to allow subjects to express their beliefs regarding these other causes on separate scales rather than on the dependent measure scales. In this way the effort scale, for example, was measuring an effort attribution instead of an effort plus an ability attribution. The effort scale followed the statement, "How likely is the employee's lack of effort as an explanation for his performance?" The scales were anchored at *very unlikely* (1) and *very likely* (7). The midpoint was "don't know."

Subjects were given approximately 90 seconds to fill out the scales and then to report their age, education, and experience. This reporting was designed to wash out short-term memory. After this, subjects were given 90 seconds to fill out a 10-item memory test consisting of five person-related items and five situation-related items. The test instruments were then collected and the subjects debriefed.

G. Results

Table 8.2 presents the effort and situation mean attribution scores for the various subject and treatment groups and for the person and situation memory tests. The boxed data represent significant differences based on two-tailed *t*-tests within each treatment cell.

The results are virtually identical for the two American samples. No indication of either attribution bias or error was detected. The significant differences noted in the attributions are what one would expect if subjects were processing the scenario evidence in an unbiased, error-free, rational manner. For example, when evidence for the group as the cause of the employee's failure was strong and person evidence weak, the American subjects saw a situation attribution as more likely than a person attribution. Because no error or bias existed in the American sample, differential availability was not an issue, and with two unexplained exceptions, no overall differences in memorability of the two types of evidence was noted.

The Japanese subjects exhibited both the fundamental attribution error and bias. Moreover, the recall tests indicate a tendency for greater recall of person information to be associated with biased or error-prone person attributions. In the four instances in which the Japanese subjects

Table 8.2. Attribution and Recall Mean Scores for Treatment Groups[a]

Evidence for person responsibilty	Evidence for situation (group) responsibilty	Effort attribution	Situation attribution	Bias/ error	Person recall (correct answers)	Situation recall (correct answers)
		U.S. students				
Low	Low	3.82	3.18		3.27	3.45
Low	High	2.82	4.18		3.45	3.18
High	Low	5.55	3.09		3.18	4.00
High	High	3.90	4.50		3.80	3.20
		U.S. managers				
Low	Low	4.00	3.09		3.54	3.07
Low	High	2.92	4.62		3.15	2.85
High	Low	5.57	3.14		3.60	3.13
High	High	4.21	4.53		3.60	2.93
		Japanese students				
Low	Low	5.17	2.93	Bias	4.63	4.00
Low	High	4.78	5.11		4.06	3.67
High	Low	5.58	2.63		4.32	4.26
High	High	5.79	4.64	Bias	3.86	3.64
		Japanese managers				
Low	Low	4.47	3.33		3.47	3.53
Low	High	5.09	3.65	Error	3.26	3.21
High	Low	5.53	3.27		3.27	3.40
High	High	6.10	4.00	Bias	3.80	3.20
Grand means		4.80	3.67		3.67	3.71

[a]Italic means are significantly different at $p < .05$.

showed evidence of the fundamental attribution error, person recall was significantly greater in one instance and in the right direction in the other three (see Table 8.2).

The results suggest an information-processing rather than a cultural explanation for the fundamental attribution error. If the FAE were only the result of an American cultural value, we would not expect it to occur in Japan, especially in light of Japanese emphasis on group and situational influences on individuals.

H. Discussion

This study offers support for the theories of psychologists who offer human information processing flaws as explanations for the fundamental attribution error. But in doing so, it compels a reexamination of culture-bound theories of Japanese organizational behavior. The Japanese subjects were remarkably prone to make the fundamental attribution error, contrary to the implicit expectations of cultural theorists such as Nakane and Lebra, among many others. Regardless of the evidence presented, they tended to blame the employee for failing to meet the client. For the Japanese participants in the experiment, an employee's poor work performance is his own responsibility and cannot be attributed to the influence of his group. Failure cannot be excused. The person is always held to be responsible.

Although American participants in this study did not commit the FAE, strong evidence exists for its frequent occurrence in American settings. Given the current findings of a Japanese tendency to commit the error—a tendency occurring across age and organizational experience levels—it may be that American and Japanese managers are not so different as some researchers have claimed. Both groups appear to underweight the situational (group influence) determinants of an employee's behavior. Consequently, both groups are likely to make biased judgments in the performance appraisal process. Americans, who have generally recognized the existence of such biases, have developed the employer–employee meeting as a way of countering attribution and judgment errors. Japanese managers generally do not hold such meetings. Perhaps they should.

In sum, then, the experiment showed that the fundamental attribution error occurs in a non-American organizational setting. Evidence was presented that indicates that the FAE is caused by information processing flaws rather than cultural values.

II. EXPERIMENT 2

A. The Performance Control Process

Are there differences in the way Japanese and American managers make sense of and give meaning to performance control processes? This experiment sought to identify the theories of the performance control process held by American and Japanese managers and to compare them with those developed by social scientists observing both cultures.

Theories developed by social scientists observing behavior are referred to as *etic*, whereas those held by participants are called *emic* (Pike, 1967). The adequacy of etic research depends on its ability to generate fruitful explanations of sociocultural differences and similarities, whereas the value of emic research is based on the identification of the categories and rules actually held by participants and used to guide thinking and actions.

According to Marvin Harris in his influential book, *Cultural Materialism*:

> Those research strategies that confine themselves exclusively to emics or exclusively to etics do not meet the general criteria for an aim-oriented social science as effectively as those which embrace both points of view. (Harris, 1980, p. 34)

Much of the theorizing about Japanese and American approaches to managing the performance control process is etic in nature and somewhat normative in tone (Ouchi, 1981). In our research, we attempted to identify the theories of performance control held by Japanese and American managers, to compare them to each other, and to compare them to the etic theories of social science. Our goal was to enrich etic studies and keep them in touch with emic formulations.

According to researchers, individuals in organizations often have their own held theories of relationships between different variables and performance (Staw, 1975). These theories are likely to influence managerial perceptions and judgments about an individual's and his or her work group's performance, especially when empirical evidence is lacking (DeNisi & Pritchard, 1978). In our research, based as it was on managerial reactions to a scenario containing limited information, we expected that participants' internal beliefs and theories of performance control would play an important part in their evaluations. We sought to identify those beliefs and theories.

B. Group versus Individual Focus

Individual performance in a work group can be viewed as the result of both (1) the individual's influence on himself or herself and (2) the group influence. In Western culture, performance theories tend to focus on the individual and his or her evaluators acting in a rational manner (Staw, 1980). For the individual, this means that information in the environment is processed so as to determine levels of effort to achieve personal goals of reward or satisfaction. For the manager, it means that information about the individual is collected and used to determine rewards and monitoring as a part of a performance control process leading to the attainment of organizational goals.

In some Asian cultures, the focus tends to be on the group as the fundamental work unit in the organization. In Japan, the individual is said to merge himself or herself into the work group, subsuming his identity within that of the group. Our research examined the extent to which Japanese managers actually do view the individual as subsumed within the group. In general, moreover, we sought to identify similarities and differences in Japanese and American managers' theories of individual influence on person performance and in their theories of work group functioning.

1. Etic Theories of the Performance Control Process

Explanations of Japanese and American management generally involve discussions of the process of controlling individuals within work groups to achieve optimum performance. What is the nature of this control process? To begin with, the functioning of any organization depends on the establishment of social order, which in turn depends on the control of behavior. To control behavior, social and performance norms emerge or are promulgated, and a process is followed of (1) monitoring individual actions for compliance with norms, (2) assigning a degree of responsibility for actions and outcomes, and (3) assigning rewards or punishments accordingly for conditioning or motivational purposes. Thus the orderly functioning of an organization depends on how managers go about monitoring performance, attributing responsibility, and awarding sanctions (Shaw & Iwawaki, 1972).

2. Social Group Model

At the same time this process of individual behavior control is occurring, a related process of group functioning is also underway. In all cultures, groups serve multiple purposes (including behavior control), such as sharing of risk, sharing information, developing consensus and trust, and handling complex tasks. However, some theorists have noted that Japanese culture can be distinguished from other cultures to the extent that it values the merging of the individual behavior control process with group functioning. Indeed, the individual is said to become submerged in the work group so that the control process becomes one of monitoring group (not individual) behavior, assigning responsibility to groups, and awarding sanctions to groups. A group member, then, should usually receive the same monitoring as the group, be assigned the same responsibility as his or her group for performance, and be given the same level of rewards or punishment as the group. This theory of performance control in groups is supposedly unique to Japan and has been referred to as Japanese "groupism" or the social model of Japanese group processes (Befu, 1980). In the theory, the work group, not the individual, is the primary functional work unit of the organization. Worker behavior in groups is focused on creating harmony and a communal spirit. The result will be social order, which will form the basis for productivity and organizational success. A recent articulation of the social group theory is Ouchi's theory Z.

3. Rational Man Theory

As Befu notes, the social group theory of performance control may be more of a prescription for, rather than a description of, Japanese groupism, and alternative theories of group and person functioning may apply. An individual-focused, "etic" explanation of performance control, common in Western culture, comes from microeconomic theory, sometimes called the rational man theory. This theory, focused on individuals rather than groups, proposes that all humans are need satisfying, purposeful, goal-oriented, and utility maximizing. In terms of managing, supervisors should offer appropriate rewards to workers in exchange for productive performance. If the exchange is to be successful, the reward must take into account the needs of workers and the quality/quantity of their performance. To establish a performance evaluation, a process of individual rather than group monitoring is followed; responsibility is individual-based, and so are sanctions. Thus the evaluation of an individual's performance can be quite different from that of his or her group, depending on the extent to which the group influenced and took part in the individual's performance. The group is not a community nor the fundamental work unit; it is simply a convenient management tool emerging out of the organization's bureaucratic structure.

4. Reduction of Ambiguity/Uncertainty

Neither the social model nor the rational man theory have received much empirical testing in cross-cultural research. One approach to performance control has focused on the reduction of ambiguity and uncertainty as important culture-bound influences on individual behavior in organizations (Hofstede, 1980). Hofstede notes that entities that offer uncertainty reduction in a culture where members are uncomfortable with uncertainty will be highly valued. His research showed that Japan is such a culture and the United States is not.

It may be that work groups in Japan are viewed by managers as something more than tools for building communal values and behavior, as the social model would have it. In addition, they may serve as an uncertainty-reducing mechanism. In groups, employees share and integrate information to a degree not possible if they work alone. Over time, groups may become associated with managerial perceptions of consistency and predictability in the organization. Thus individual inputs may be deemed responsible for unpredictable, unexpected performance, whereas group influence may become associated with predictable, expected person performance.

We have then three etic perspectives on performance control: the social model, with its focus on groups; the rational man theory, which concerns itself with individuals; and uncertainty avoidance, which compares individuals to groups. The independent variables in this study were derived from the key types of information needed to assess performance control under the various perspectives: information on group and individual influence or individual performance, information on the nature of the performance, and whether the performance was expected or unexpected.

C. Hypotheses

If the social model is an important component of the theory of performance control held by Japanese managers, we hypothesized that the Japanese individual would be merged into the group much more so than the American in terms of perceived responsibility for his or her performance, assigned rewards, and future monitoring. Nor would the perceived level of the group's influence have any effect on control evaluations—if the person becomes one with the group, there ought not to be any consideration of degrees of oneness in assigning responsibility, rewards, and monitoring.

If rational man theory is influential, then we hypothesized sharp distinctions being made regarding managerial perceptions about the contribution to an individual's performance by himself and the group. These distinctions would be based on information about the level of group influence. In addition, we hypothesized differences in individual rewards and monitoring based upon information about responsibility for performance and about the nature of the performance (successful or unsuccessful).

Finally, if the Japanese are more intolerant of ambiguity and uncertainty than the Americans, then we hypothesized that they would exhibit a stronger interest in the impact of expectations on their performance control evaluations. An expectation is a prediction about the future that reduces present uncertainty. If expectations/predictions are not met, their failure would be of concern to people intolerant of uncertainty. Specifically, we expected information than an outcome was unexpected (in comparison with expected) to lead to an increase in person responsibility, a decrease in person rewards, and an increase in future monitoring. The rationale for this is the presumed managerial perception that only the foibles of individual workers, which can never be fully predicted or controlled, could be responsible for an unexpected outcome. Rewards and monitoring would be adjusted accordingly.

D. Research Design

The research question and the need to test all of the theoretical perspectives required an experimental design with independent variables of performance (good/bad), interaction of the individual with the group (high/low), and predictability of the performance (expected/unexpected). The perceived (by Japanese and American managers) impact of these variables on the performance control process was measured by dependent variables reflecting attributions, rewards, and future monitoring.

Based on a pilot study, we constructed a realistic scenario describing a performance control process with which managers in the study most likely would be familiar. Information was provided on the level of group influence on an individual's performance (high-low), the nature of the performance (successful-unsuccessful), and whether or not the group manager expected the outcome. We asked subjects to role-play the manager and to evaluate both the individual and the group in terms of responsibility and the need for future monitoring. We also asked them to allocate shares of a bonus to the individual and the group based on the performance.

E. Method

1. Subjects

From a comprehensive mailing list of senior managers in the Seattle area, 250 names were chosen at random from the entire range of standard industrial classifications. These were contacted by mail and asked to participate. Of them, 100 responded, for a response rate of 40%. Similar groups were approached in person in the Kyoto, Japan area. All of this group, 266, participated. Table 8.3 describes both American and Japanese managers. The classifications had to be slightly modified from the standard industrial classification (SIC) approach to accommodate Japanese categorizations.

The American and Japanese subjects were quite similar, with some minor exceptions. A greater proportion of the Japanese sample came from banking, and the Japanese sample was younger. However, postex-

Table 8.3. Comparison of American and Japanese Managers in the Study

	Americans (n = 100)	Japanese (n = 266)
Business		
Agriculture, mining, construction	15.2%	2.4%
Manufacturing	15.2	11.9
Transportation, communications	11.1	2.4
Trade	19.2	15.0
Banking, credit, insurance	11.1	41.1
Business services	9.1	6.3
Health, legal, educational	13.1	11.9
Many different businesses	6.0	9.0
Total	100.0%	100.0%
Perceived business environment		
Growing markets, strong competition	47.5%	44.1%
Growing markets, weak competition	4.0	1.4
Stable markets, strong competition	45.5	43.2
Stable markets, weak competition	3.0	11.3
Total	100.0%	100.0%
Sex	All male	All male
Age	50.1	37.1

periment analysis revealed no relationship between the dependent measures and any of the sample characteristics (business background, perceived environment, age).

2. Procedure

Each manager was asked to read the following description of a work situation and to imagine himself in the position of the manager. In the scenario, the manipulation of information about the independent variables is noted.

Group influence (high/low)

During the last 3 months, David Johnson (Japanese name), an employee in the 10 person work group that you manage, undertook an important task assignment that required him to work (*in close coordination with his work group in a highly interdependent manner*) (*alone, independent of his work group.*) During the task, he (*frequently*) *(hardly ever)* communicated with his group. He *(was)* *(was not)* highly influenced by the group's attitudes and advice.

Based on your prior experience as a manager, you expect that an important task assignment of this kind usually will be done *(well)* *(poorly)*. The work *(almost never)* *(almost always)* has to be redone.

Manager's expectation (expected performance/ unexpected performance)

When David Johnson(Japanese name) finished the task, you evaluated the results.

Performance (successful performance/ unsuccessful performance)

(As you expected) *(Unexpectedly)* the results were *(good)* *(bad)*. The task *(will not)* *(will)* have to be redone.

Eight versions of the scenario were developed, corresponding to the 2 (influence) × 2 (expectation) × 2 (performance) factorial design.

After reading the scenario, the managers were asked to respond to a series of questions that probed their vision of the performance control process. On 5-point responsible/not responsible scales, they first listed the responsibility of the work group and of the individual for the performance outcome. Next, they were told that they had $1,000 (or 1,000,000 yen) to allocate to individuals in the 10-person group as rewards for individual performance during the 3-month period described. They were asked to list the amount given to the individual described in the scenario and the average amount given to the group. Finally, they were asked to respond on 5-point scales to the question, "How closely will you monitor the group's (David Johnson's) work in the future?" The dependent measures consisted of: (1) group attribution and person attribution measures, (2) the group average share of the bonus and the person's share (both expressed on a ratio scale of 0 to 1,000 to allow for cross-cultural comparison), and (3) the perceived future monitoring of the group and of the person. These three sets of measures reveal the degree to which the individual is merged in the group in the performance control process, which can be described in terms of assignment of responsibility for performance, allocation of awards, and monitoring assessments.

3. Translation

To develop equivalent English and Japanese versions of the questionnaire, a blind Japanese translation of the English version was made by a Japanese person and then translated blind back to English by an American. The translation was compared with the original English. After a series of discussions between the American and Japanese translators, the two versions were deemed equivalent.

F. Results

A multivariate analysis of variance revealed the following results for group and person responses. Table 8.4 lists main effects. In terms of the *group*, both American and Japanese managers saw the group as more responsible for person performance and less in need of future monitor-

Table 8.4. Response Means for MANOVA Main Effects

Independent variable	F	P	Means	
	Group			
Nationality (United States/Japan)				
Group responsibility	25.65	.001	United States = 2.57	Japan = 3.38
Group monitoring	9.07	.003	United States = 3.56	Japan = 3.88
Group influence (high/low)				
Group responsibility	23.49	.001	High = 3.43	Low = 2.84
Group monitoring	8.11	.005	High = 3.73	Low = 3.90
Performance (successful-unsuccessful)				
Group responsibility	13.05	.001	Successful = 3.37 Unsuccessful = 2.92	
	Person			
Nationality (United States/Japan)				
Person responsibility	8.24	.004	United States = 4.23	Japan = 3.92
Person reward	6.19	.013	United States = 173.73	Japan = 136.63
Group influence (high/low)				
Person responsibility	8.09	.005	High = 3.89	Low = 4.15
Performance (successful/unsuccessful)				
Person reward	31.00	.001	Successful = 180.36 Unsuccessful = 107.73	
Person monitoring	27.38	.001	Successful = 3.56 Unsuccessful = 4.09	
Expectations (expected performance/unexpected performance)				
Person responsibility	5.31	.020	Expected = 3.89	Unexpected = 4.11

ing when its influence was high. In addition, both rewarded the group more when person performance was successful. The managers differed over group responsibility for performance. Japanese saw the group as more responsible and more in need of future monitoring than the Americans did.

Regarding *person* evaluations, both sets of managers saw the person as more responsible for his performance when the group influence was low. Both rewarded the person more and monitored him less when his performance was successful. And both saw the person as more responsible for unexpected than for expected performance. The managers differed in that the Americans saw the person as more responsible and worthy of reward than the Japanese did.

Both Japanese and American managers tended to see person re-

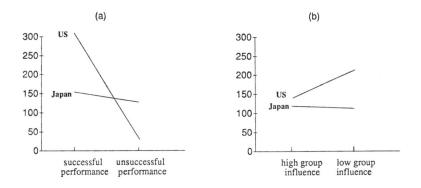

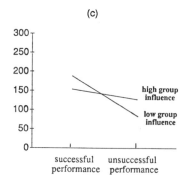

Figure 8.1. MANOVA interaction effects: Person reward.

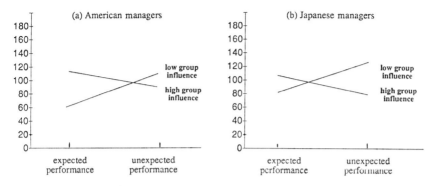

Figure 8.2. Interaction effects: Group reward.

sponsibility as greater than group responsibility. This evidence of bias replicated the results of Experiment 1.

Figure 8.1 describes two-way interaction effects, all of which focused on person rewards. In Figure 8.1(a), the Japanese managers gave smaller person rewards than the Americans for successful performance (one-way ANOVA, $F = 36.8$, $df = 1,185$, $p = .001$) and greater rewards for unsuccessful performance ($F = 30.5$, $df = 1,160$, $p = .001$). In 8.1(b), the Americans gave greater rewards than the Japanese when the influence of the group was low ($F = 6.7$, $df = 1,154$, $p = .01$). In the minds of American managers, then, the successful person *working alone* can expect to receive a high share of rewards. For the Japanese, the successful person *working in a group* can expect a high share of rewards.

In Figure 8.1(c) both sets of managers rewarded the unsuccessful performer more when group influence was high than when it was low ($F = 5.5$, $df = 1,160$, $p = .02$).

Figure 8.2 describes the only three-way interaction, which focused on reward to the group. The American managers gave greater (but not significantly greater) rewards to the influential group rather than the noninfluential group when person performance was as *expected* ($F = 0.9$, $df = 1,45$, $p = .35$). The Japanese gave greater rewards to the influential group when person performance was *unexpected* ($F = 2.99$, $df = 1,126$, $p = .08$).

G. Discussion

The results clearly do not support the social model as a theory of performance control held by Japanese or American managers. As Table 8.4 suggests, both the American and Japanese managers saw responsibility for individual and for group performance as influenced by the amount of interacting the person does with the group (a replication of the experiment with American and Japanese college students generated the same findings). In the social model, the individual would be simply merged with the group, and the level of person–group interaction would not be an issue. This careful attention to information on influential input to performance is more in accord with the rational man theory—the etic theory of Western social science.

In addition, both sets of managers tended to want to monitor the future work of the individual more after poor performance than after good performance. Once again, this information-based focus on the individual is more in accord with rational man theory.

The social model would predict a uniform distribution of rewards within the group. Clearly this was not the case for the American managers. However, a comparison of the allocations of the Americans and the Japanese revealed some interesting differences. The Americans, in accord with rational man theory, gave greater rewards to the individual for successful rather than for unsuccessful performance and when group influence on performance was low rather than high. The Japanese, however, gave the same rewards regardless of the performance outcome, and they gave a greater reward to the individual who had been influenced by his group than they did to the isolated performer ($F = 4.99$, $df = 1,251$, $p = .02$). Japanese appear to see the reward allocation as an incentive to get individuals to interact with their work groups. Regardless of their level of performance, they will get more by choosing to become part of the group.

We can see here a weak version of the social model at work. The Japanese managers do not hold a theory of performance control in which the group is the fundamental work unit and the individual is submerged within it. Instead, they want the individual to choose to interact with his or her group and will use a bonus allocation to persuade him or her that there is much to gain and nothing to lose.

Why do Japanese managers want the individual to work more closely with his or her group? Clearly, both American and Japanese managers in the study believed that groups help facilitate performance and should be rewarded accordingly. The Japanese, however, saw the group as more important in the facilitation process than the Americans did. Consequently, they view the individual as less responsible and less worthy of reward than do the Americans. Moreover, the Japanese appear to have a different theory of work group functioning than Americans do.

We can get a sense of these differing theories by examining Figure 8.2. It shows the three-way interaction effect for rewards to the group revealed by the analysis. For the American managers, the focus is on expected performance. When a person performs as expected, the influential group gets a greater bonus than does the noninfluential group. Thus the influential group is associated with and rewarded for person performance coming out as expected. Influential groups, then, facilitate expected performance by members. What the American managers may believe is that functioning groups, in which members are interacting with each other, help guarantee that members do assigned and thus expected work. In this sense, the Americans have a theory of work group functioning focused on *risk reduction*. The probability of unexpected and unpleasant outcomes is reduced by a well functioning group.

For the Japanese managers, Figure 8.2 reveals just the opposite. Here the focus is on the unexpected. The influential, functioning group is associated with and rewarded for unexpected person performance. Influential groups facilitate unexpected performance by individual members. We can speculate that where Americans see unexpected person performance as negative and provide incentives to groups to try to avoid it, the Japanese see unexpected individual performance as often positive and try to persuade groups to foster it. The Japanese managers believe that groups are *productivity enhancers* that bring out more from workers than one would ordinarily expect. Here is the reason why the Japanese in this study created incentives for individuals to take part in group functioning.

The strong version of the social model, then, cannot be supported as a description of the theory of performance control held by Japanese managers. The individual is not merged into the group. Indeed, he or she is managed much more in accord with rational man theory in which information on his or her degree of responsibility for performance is assessed and combined with information on performance outcomes. This information then is used to assign rewards and to determine the level of future monitoring. Both American and Japanese managers seemed quite similar in this regard. Where they differed is in their theory of the function of work groups. The Americans saw groups as risk-reducing entities useful in avoiding unexpectedly bad worker performance. The Japanese saw groups as productivity enhancers useful in fostering unexpectedly good worker performance. This positive focus of the Japanese managers fits in nicely with what we call the weak version of the social model.

In comparison with the Americans, the Japanese managers did not show a stronger propensity to be influenced in their evaluations by the expectedness or unexpectedness of the outcome, a finding that Hofstede's claim of their greater intolerance of ambiguity would have led us to expect. However the pallid nature of the scenario may not have engaged much cognitive effort on their part, and the test of Hofstede's finding may not have been a fair one. Be that as it may, *both* sets of managers did see the person as more responsible for his or her unexpected than his or her expected performance. This finding tentatively suggests that in both cultures, individuals, as opposed to groups or to randomness, are seen as likely to have caused unexpected outcomes. Clearly more research is needed on this point and on the supposed greater Japanese intolerance of ambiguity.

In sum, the results of the study suggest that both Americans and Japanese managers hold a rational man theory of managing individual performance in organizations. However, their theory of work group functioning appears to be different. The American managers view work groups as risk-reducing tools in performance control. The Japanese view them in a more positive light as performance-enhancing entities.

Regarding etic theories, the social model, at least in its strong version articulated as Ouchi's Japanese theory Z, may play little part in the emic perspectives of Japanese managers. They, and the American managers, appear to hold a theory of individual performance control similar to that described in rational man theory. *Homo economicus* appears to be a useful conceptualization for Japanese and American managers just as much as it is for Japanese and American social scientists.

III. CONCLUSION

Our research suggests that American and Japanese managers both approach performance control mostly in the way that microeconomic theory says that rational decision makers do. Indeed, the Japanese seem even more rational in their skilled use of incentives to induce employees to cooperate with their work groups. And when they violate rational man theory, they both do it in the same way, by ignoring evidence and overweighting individual responsibility for performance.

There are two ways to approach cross-cultural organizational research involving Westerners and Japanese. In the first, the researcher assumes that fundamental differences in values, beliefs, and behavior will exist because of different historical and cultural influences. In the second, the assumption is that the functions and goals of managers in organizations are similar and thus their behaviors will be similar. Moreover, because human nature is a powerful influence, then both sets of managers ought to exhibit similar foibles (e.g., the fundamental attribution error). The results of our experiments suggest that the second approach is more appropriate as a starting point. However, it should not be an ending point. Cultural and historical influences are powerful mediating and moderating factors and ought to be taken into account. The rational man theory describes the emic approach of managers to performance control, as we have shown, and thus is a good candidate for an etic theory of performance control as it actually takes place. Nevertheless, a large body of research indicates that culture is an important differentiator of American and Japanese organizational behavior. It cannot be ignored. Our only claim is that American and Japanese managers initiate the performance control process with the same rational perspective, marred somewhat by the same quasi-rational foibles.

IV. REFERENCES

DeNisi, A., & Pritchard, R. D. (1978). Implicit theories of performance as artifacts in survey research: A replication and extension. *Organizational Behavior and Human Performance, 21*, 358–366.

Fiske, S. T., & Linville, P. W. (1980). What does the schema concept buy us? *Personality and Social Psychology Bulletin, 6*, 543–557.

Frieze, I. H., Bar-Tal, D., & Carroll, J. S. (1980). *New approaches to social problems.* San Francisco: Jossey-Bass.

Harris, M. (1980). *Cultural materialism.* New York: Vintage.

Harvey, J., Town, J., & Yarkin, K. (1981). How fundamental is the "fundamental attribution error"? *Journal of Personality and Social Psychology, 40*, 346–349.

Heider, F. (1958). *The psychology of interpersonal relations.* New York: Wiley.

Hofstede, G. (1980). *Culture's consequences: International differences in work-related values.* Beverly Hills, CA: Sage.

Kahneman, D., Slovic, P., & Tversky, A. (1982). *Judgment under uncertainty: Heuristics and biases.* Cambridge: Cambridge University Press.

Kelley, H. H. (1973). The process of casual attribution. *American psychologist, 28*, 107–128.

Kelley, H. H., & Michela, J. L. (1980). Attribution theory and research. *Annual Review of Psychology, 31*, 457–501.

Lebra, T. (1976). *Japanese patterns of behavior.* Honolulu: University Press of Hawaii.

Mitchell, T. R., Green, S. G., & Wood, R. E. (1981). An attribution model of leadership and the poor performing subordinate: Development and validation. *Research in Organizational Behavior, 3*, 197–234.

Monson, T., & Snyder, M. (1977). Actors, observers, and the attribution process. *Journal of Experimental Social Psychology, 13*, 89–111.

Nakane, C. (1972). *Japanese society.* Berkeley: University of California Press.

Nisbett, R., & Ross, L. (1980). *Human inference: Strategies and shortcomings of social judgment.* Englewood Cliffs, NJ: Prentice-Hall.

Ouchi, W. C. (1981). *Theory Z: How American business can meet the Japanese challenge.* Reading, MA: Addison-Wesley.

Pike, K. L. (1967). *Language in relation to an unified theory of the structure of human behavior.* The Hague: Mouton.

Rohlen, T. (1974). *For harmony and strength: Japanese white collar organization in anthropological perspective.* Berkeley: University of California Press.

Shaw, M. E., & Iwawaki, S. (1972). Attribution of responsibility by Japanese and Americans as a function of age. *Journal of Cross Cultural Psychology, 3,* 71–81.

Staw, B. M. (1975). Attribution of the 'cases' of performance: A general alternative interpretation of cross-sectional research on organizations. *Organizational Behavior and Human Performance, 13,* 414–432.

Taylor, S. E. (1982). The availability bias in social perception. In K. Kahneman, P. Slovic, & A. Tversky (Eds.), *Judgment under uncertainty* (pp. 190–200). Cambridge: Cambridge University Press.

9

Chinese Enterprise Management

Rosalie L. Tung

In order to analyze and understand management practices and organizational processes in a planned economy like that of the People's Republic of China (PRC), it is necessary to examine the impact of broad societal-environmental variables (such as the economic, sociopolitical, and cultural systems) as constraints on the operations of industrial enterprises. This chapter will first examine the impact that each of these societal-environmental variables has on business and management systems. It will then discuss various aspects of enterprise management in China. The following points should be borne in mind when reading the industrial practices discussed herein:

First, despite the fact that China is currently more willing to provide information on the operations and performance of industrial enterprises to foreign researchers, particularly bilingual scholars, it is still very difficult to gather data using rigorous methodologies. This may prove disappointing from the viewpoint of the academician.

Second, China is a planned socialist economy. The state prescribes the overall policies and guidelines that industry should follow in the operation and management of its enterprises across different industries, both large and small. These policies ensure a certain degree of uniformity in the types of procedures used for organizing the productive forces within organizations.

Third, in striving toward the goals of the Four Modernizations

Rosalie L. Tung • School of Business Administration, University of Wisconsin-Milwaukee, Milwaukee, Wisconsin 53201.

(which search for economic development through progress in agriculture, industry, science and technology, and military defense), China is actively seeking to restructure its industrial enterprises and to learn modern management techniques from abroad so as to increase overall efficiency and effectiveness. The practices reported here represent the latest in vogue in the country, but they are subject to change.

Fourth, given space limitations here, the treatment of the various topics can only be superficial and does not purport to be comprehensive. For a more comprehensive discussion of the economic system and sociopolitical systems, see Tung (1982).

I. ECONOMIC SYSTEM

The year 1949 marked the end of the civil war in China and the establishment of the People's Republic. The same year also witnessed the beginning of the socialist reconstruction of the country—a colossal task that involved rebuilding it from the ruins of economic and technological stagnation, massive social disorientation, runaway inflation, and political chaos brought about by almost a century of imperialist exploitation, external wars, and internal strife.

The new government acted swiftly to embark on a series of national economic policies and plans that were known as the Rehabilitation Years (1949–1952) and the First 5-Year Plan (1953–1957). Policies adopted during the Rehabilitation Years brought encouraging results. Within 18 months of liberation, inflation was curbed. Prices of essential commodities, such as grain, salt, cooking oil, fuel, and cloth, were controlled. The First 5-Year Plan marked the movement toward collectivization of both the urban and rural means of production. Control was established over private banking and businesses. By 1956, the nationalization of all private enterprises in the country was completed.

A. Central Planning

Because China is a planned socialist economy, all economic activities and undertakings are subject to a centrally developed and administered plan. Formerly, the state set production goals and targets for the enterprises, allocated resources and raw materials to them, laid down broad policies and guidelines to be followed in their operations and management, and distributed or marketed their output. With 400,000 industrial enterprises operating in the economy, and literally hundreds of thousands of products being manufactured, it has become virtually impossible for the state to devise a plan comprehensive enough to encompass all minute details and yet flexible enough to accommodate all contingencies. This practice has often led to the following problems: bottlenecks in operations; the production of certain commodities that had no immediate market, whereas other products that were in demand were produced in insufficient quantities; excessive delays in decision making; and a spirit of unhealthy complacency among certain managers and workers in the industrial enterprises because state-owned enterprises were not treated as independent accounting units and hence were not responsible for their own profit and loss. In addition, the concept of marketing was foreign to the Chinese industrial scene until very recently.

With the Four Modernizations effort, the government recognized the limitations inherent in the past economic structure and was determined to rectify the situation. Recent changes in the economic system include the following:

1. *Decentralization of authority*. This allows some industrial enterprises greater autonomy with respect to decision making, planning, and handling of financial matters. A select group of enterprises were designated as experimental units. These were allowed the following rights: to retain a portion of the profit after the payment of taxes; to use their own funds to expand existing production facilities; to draw up subsidiary production plans after fulfilling the state plan; to market products manufactured by the factory that the state did not purchase; to export their products and to retain a portion of the foreign exchange thus earned. This foreign exchange could, in turn, be used for the import of foreign technology, equipment, and raw materials; to distribute bonuses at the enterprise's own discretion, within the guidelines stipulated by the state; and to impose penalties on workers, factory directors, and party secretaries who, through negligence, incurred severe economic losses for the state. In Shanghai, the most advanced city in China, the stock market is making a comeback, albeit on a very limited scale.

2. *Simplification of the administrative organizations*. In the past, excessive administrative levels were necessary to some extent because of the elaborate mechanisms whereby the state assigned, allocated, and distributed all the means of production. With the granting of greater autonomy to the individual enterprise, many of these administrative organs could be eliminated and the number of cadres at all levels reduced.

3. *Use of economic means*. In the past, China relied primarily on administrative means to manage the country's economy. Since 1979, however, more emphasis has been given to the law of value and the role of the market. "Free" markets have been allowed to operate, on a limited scale, in the cities and villages. The government argues that the market

mechanism will not replace central planning but will supplement the latter and play a subordinated role.

Besides the introduction of the market mechanism, Xue Muqiao, a leading Chinese economist, advocated the adoption of the following economic measures: (a) the imposition of taxes to regulate the production of various categories of commodities; (b) the use of price policy to regulate the production of certain categories of commodities; and (c) the granting of loans at reduced interest rates and priority in the allocation of resources and raw materials to those enterprises and industries that the government seeks to develop. In addition, the state is actively promoting the use of the contract system between various sectors of the economy.

B. Types of Ownership

Chinese industrial enterprises are of two main types: state- and collectively owned enterprises. The 1978 Constitution permitted the establishment of individually owned enterprises. In the past, state-owned enterprises were considered superior and hence were emphasized. The Chinese government now states that the superiority of an ownership system is neither judged nor measured by the extent of public ownership but in terms of economic results. The government contends that these three types of economy should be allowed to coexist because each plays a different role in the national economy and each supplements the others. For the development of large, modern industries, the establishment of state-owned enterprises may be most appropriate. In the countryside, however, collective ownership may be more appropriate. Also, collectively owned enterprises can be established with minimal capital investment and can provide an important source of employment for the huge Chinese population. In addition, because of their smaller size, such enterprises are usually more flexible. Consequently, they may be more adept at revamping their complete product lines within a relatively short period of time to meet changing market needs. Individual enterprises, on the other hand, can play an important role in the retail trade and service sectors, areas that were previously neglected in the national economy.

C. The Four Modernizations

In August 1977, China embarked on the Four Modernizations program, which seeks development and progress in the fields of science and technology, industry, agriculture, and military defense. Through this effort, the country hopes to raise the per capita income of its people to $1,000 (U.S.) by the year 2000.

To attain this goal, widespread reforms have been adopted in the political and economic arenas since 1978. Some of these changes have included resuming diplomatic relations with capitalist countries, permitting foreign firms to engage in joint-venture investments (including wholly owned subsidiaries in special cases) in China to develop the country's industries and natural resources, and engaging in technical and cultural exchanges with other countries. Many policies and practices that were denounced as capitalist during the Cultural Revolution (1966–1976) have now been reinstated. Examples are the use of material incentives, the establishment of collectively owned enterprises, emphasis on the individual's technical expertise and innovation through the reinstitution of entrance exams to universities, and the use of technical competence as an important criterion for recruitment and promotion to managerial and technical positions.

II. SOCIOPOLITICAL SYSTEMS

In China, political considerations have a pervasive influence on all aspects of society. Political and economic considerations, for instance, are often inextricably interwined. Consequently, in order to comprehend fully the complexities of Chinese industrial society, it is imperative to examine China's political system and the role played by the Chinese Communist Party in influencing various aspects of Chinese society, including the operations and management of industrial enterprises.

The philosophy guiding the administration of China, as prescribed in the 1978 constitution, is primarily threefold: proletarian dictatorship, democratic centralism, and socialist democracy. Each of these principles is explained briefly:

1. *Proletarian dictatorship* means that the working class will exercise leadership over the state through the Chinese Communist Party (CCP). The CCP is the leading political party in the country. Party branches and party committees are set up in factories, schools, neighborhoods, and detachments of the People's Liberation Army.

The leading organs in most enterprises consist of a party committee and a working committee. Each party committee is headed by a party secretary. The working committee is headed by the factory director and is made up of deputy directors and responsible technical and administrative cadres. In the past, the working committee was under the leadership of the party committee. Changes are now underway to separate the party committee from the administrative organization in an enterprise. It has been proposed that the party committee should engage in political and ideological work and should no longer assume administrative duties, whereas the working committee under the leadership of the factory director should be responsible for the operations and management of the enterprise. However, the party committee will continue to play a supervisory role to ensure that party policies and state laws are adhered to and that production targets set forth in the state plan are fulfilled.

2. *Democratic centralism* means allowing democracy, on the one hand, and centralizing authority, on the other, to ensure unity and enforce discipline among China's 1 billion people. The party has prescribed the authority relationships that should prevail among the various elements of society:

> The individual is subordinate to the organization; the minority is subordinate to the majority; the lower level is subordinate to the higher level; and the entire Party is subordinate to the Central Committee. (*Eleventh National Congress*, 1977, p. 104)

3. *Socialist democracy* ensures that all citizens except those who have committed crimes against the state (such as murder, rape, other serious criminal offenses, or counterrevolutionary activities) are guaranteed certain fundamental rights, such as the right to participate in the country's administration, the right to work and take adequate rest, and the right to education.

In 1977, the country's leaders declared that the primary mission of the party, and of the country as a whole, for the last quarter of the twentieth century is no longer that of class struggle but rather socialist modernization.

III. THE CULTURAL SYSTEM

It is impossible to describe all the rich cultural traditions that have shaped China over the millennia. Rather, the focus here is to analyze China along the four cultural dimensions hypothesized by Geert Hofstede, namely power distance, uncertainty avoidance, individualism, and masculinity. Detailed justifications for analyzing countries based on Hofstede's (1980) dimensions have been provided elsewhere in this book (see, e.g., Sekaran and Snodgrass, Chapter 13). In examining China along each of these dimensions, it is important to bear in mind the following three points:

First, Hofstede uses Taiwan and Hong Kong as being archetypical of the Chinese culture. One can question the validity of Hofstede's findings among the Hong Kong and Taiwan samples of HERMES corporation. The questionnaire was administered in English in these two samples. Although the respondents were presumably fluent in English, research has shown that native and nonnative speakers of English can interpret the same message differently. Even among samples of native speakers of English, for example, Americans and British, similar words may carry quite different connotations between the two groups.

Second, the cultural milieu shaping the mentality and behavior of the Chinese in the PRC is a unique blend of socialism mixed with Confucianism. The vast majority of Chinese on the mainland have been raised under this blend of Marxism–Leninism–Maoism. The average age in China is 26, with approximately 65% of the population under 30 years of age. Thus, the majority of the country's population has been raised and indoctrinated with this Maoist ideology.

Third, given the very different socioeconomic and political systems among the PRC, Hong Kong, and Taiwan, it would be erroneous to generalize from the findings of Hong Kong and Taiwan to that of the PRC (see also the study by Dunphy & Shi, Chapter 10, in this book). Because no empirical study has been published to date on the PRC using Hofstede's conceptual framework, aside from the empirical data presented in Chapter 10 by Dexter Dunphy and Jeanette Shi, I can only hypothesize along these four dimensions.

A. Power Distance

Hofstede found that Hong Kong and Taiwan scored higher on the power distance index as compared to the United States. In the PRC, I would expect it to be substantially lower for several reasons: One, China is deemed to be a classless society. Two, there is less disparity in income distribution among the masses. There is a mere 10-fold difference in income between the highest and the lowest paid persons in the country. Three, the country encourages worker participation in management and management participation in physical labor. This is elaborated upon subsequently. Four, in recent years, the CCP has criticized the special privileges enjoyed by some of its cadres. Reforms have been implemented to do away with such abuses of power.

B. Uncertainty Avoidance

Hofstede found that Hong Kong Chinese exhibited a low uncertainty avoidance, whereas Taiwan Chinese scored high along this dimension. In the PRC, I would expect a low uncertainty avoidance for several reasons: One, political upheavals have plagued the country since its establishment in 1949. As such, the people have acquired a certain tolerance for such vicissitudes in life. Two, like many of its Asian counterparts, the Chinese possess a very long-term orientation toward planning. When projecting 10, 20, or even 50 years into the future, it is inevitable that ambiguities and uncertainties will abound. Three, because China is a centrally planned economy, the people know that the state will provide. Once hired, there is virtually no layoff of workers. The state pays a generous retirement benefit including funeral costs. Thus, much of the uncertainty about the future is eliminated.

C. Individualism

Both the Hong Kong and Taiwan samples scored low on Hofstede's individualism dimension. In China, I would expect a similar situation because of the following reasons: One, the tenets of socialism call for communal sharing. The CCP preaches that the interests of the individual should be subjugated to that of the state. Two, Chinese culture emphasizes that one's identity is derived from the family or the village to which one belongs. Under communism, the concept of family was broadened to that of the nation-state. Thus, individualism as stressed in the United States, is alien to the Chinese mentality.

D. Masculinity

Both the Hong Kong and Taiwan samples scored high on Hofstede's masculinity dimension. In China, I see a mixed picture because it scores high on some of the masculinity norms and low on others. For example, people orientation is strong in the PRC. Until very recently, material possessions were frowned upon. Furthermore, male domination is deemphasized in the PRC. Men and women enjoy the same pay for the same work. Women are elected or appointed to high-level positions in factories and ministries, although the number of women in senior administrative positions is less than that of men. This latter situation stems from the fact that prior to 1949, higher education for women was discouraged. Consequently, among the older generation, the sample from which most senior administrators are drawn, there are comparatively fewer qualified women. Perhaps, the most outstanding demonstration of this equality between the sexes is the fact that women now retain their maiden name after marriage and children (particularly the second born in the family) can adopt the mother's surname. The PRC scores low on these masculinity norms but high on others, such as the emphasis on work and achievement. Article 10 of the 1978 constitution dictates that "he who does not work, neither shall he eat" and that "work is an honorable duty for every citizen able to work." All able-bodied persons in China have to work in order to earn their means of livelihood. As noted earlier, the achievement motive is emphasized in China.

IV. ENTERPRISE MANAGEMENT SYSTEMS

This section focuses on business and management practices unique to China.

A. Recruitment of Workers

Since 1956, China has adopted a system whereby the state labor department in the various towns and cities assumes responsibility for the recruitment and placement of all workers and staff members in state-owned enterprises. Under this system, workers have the right to refuse a job assignment. However, this would mean that their names would once again be placed into the common pool of people applying for jobs, and it might take some time before another suitable opening came along. This, coupled with the fact that those "waiting for employment" (a euphemism for unemployment) amounts to approximately 25% of the industrial work force, mean that most people accept the jobs assigned to them by the state.

In 1979, the state introduced, on a trial basis, the method of recruiting workers in the various trades and professions through examination. This policy is conducive to industrial growth because it ensures that workers employed in a particular enterprise would possess the minimal qualifications for performing the job satisfactorily. Collectively owned enterprises and private operators are free to recruit their workers from neighboring communities and elsewhere.

B. Promotion to Managerial Level

In the past, managerial personnel were appointed or selected from among those workers who were considered both "red" (i.e., politically sound) and "expert" (i.e., technically competent).

With the current emphasis on technical competence and leadership abilities as two important qualifications for managerial positions, experimental reforms in the cadre system are underway. These include the recruitment of managerial personnel through examinations, the election of cadres by secret ballots, the holding of opinion pools once every 6 months to check and appraise the performance of elected cadres, the demotion of cadres who are technically incompetent, and the provision of continuing education to cadres. Training programs for cadres generally emphasize the development of business and management skills, which are recognized as weak links in the nation's economic work.

C. Role of Factory Director

The current attempts to separate the party committee from the working committee were discussed earlier. The discussion here will focus on the relationships between the leader and the led. Although leadership abilities are now emphasized more than ever before, factory directors and cadres are reminded constantly that they should not alienate themselves from their subordinates. The ideal management–labor relationship in a Chinese enterprise is one of peaceful cooperation. The aim is not for one group to dominate the other but for both parties to learn from each other and carry out the responsibilities and duties assigned to each.

D. Worker Participation in Management

The degree of worker participation in management affairs has oscillated with periods of thought reform. In the post-Mao era, the principal vehicle through which workers take part in management is the Congress of Workers and Staff that has been established in all the advanced factories. At each annual congress, the factory's leading members report on their work over the past year, listen to criticisms and suggestions from the representatives, and adopt resolutions on various matters. An inspection group is elected to check on the implementation of the resolutions adopted once every 3 months. Representatives to the congress are elected directly by the workers and staff. All workers and staff have the right to vote and stand for election, provided they meet the following qualifications: (1) are politically and ideologically sound; (2) do well in production, fulfill assignments, and abide by rules and regulations; (3) have close ties with the workers; and (4) are good at collecting the workers' opinions and relaying fully the spirit of the resolutions adopted.

When the congress is not in session, the representatives are divided into several groups on the basis of workshops, sections, or offices. Each group elects one member to the inspection group of the congress. This group checks on the implementation of the resolutions adopted by the congress every quarter; reports to the party committee, the cadres, or the workers and staff respectively on problems it has discovered; criticizes those who have not met their quotas; and recommends ways and means of solving outstanding problems. The trade union attached to each enterprise is a working body of the congress and directs the work of the inspection group.

In addition to the congress of workers and staff members, the party requires that party committee members, the factory director, and the deputy directors go among the workers as frequently as possible to keep themselves abreast of actual conditions on the shop floor. Meetings between leading cadres and workers are scheduled regularly, so that any problem encountered in production can be brought up for discussion before the party committee and the working committee. In addition, workers sit on other administrative and technical committees of the enterprise.

E. Trade Unions

Chinese trade unions are mass organizations of the working class, formed on a voluntary basis under the leadership of the CCP. Trade unions are organized according to trades and geographical locations. Each factory, school, or hospital has a union.

Although the constitution provides for the right to strike, strikes and walkouts are very rare because enterprises are either state- or collectively owned. In the trade unions, the spirit of cooperation between workers and management is emphasized. This notion is rather foreign to the Western world, where the trade union is basically looked upon by the workers as a citadel from whence they can bargain with management from a position of strength.

The activities performed by the trade unions in China are primarily fourfold:

1. They serve as a link between the party and the masses. On the one hand, the trade unions frequently transmit the workers'

opinions and needs to the party to provide a basis for the latter to formulate or readjust its principles and policies. On the other hand, the trade unions educate the workers to understand and properly implement the party's policies.

2. They serve as a communist school. The trade unions conduct ideological, cultural, and technical education programs among the workers, such as how to run spare-time schools, cultural palaces, and recreational halls, and launch socialist emulation campaigns.

3. They serve as the pillar of state power. Trade unions organize workers to fulfill state production plans, educate them to observe the constitution, laws, and policies of the state, and recommend outstanding workers to leading posts at various levels of the party.

4. They promote the welfare of the workers. The trade unions also run workers' sanatoriums and help workers to solve problems, for example, by building houses with funds provided by factories and by rehabilitating workers that have committed mistakes in the past.

In short, the function of the trade union is primarily to promote cooperation between labor and management, foster enthusiasm for work, and boost morale among the workers.

F. Motivational Devices

Daniel Katz and Robert L. Kahn in their book *The Social Psychology of Organizations* (1978) identify three basic types of motivational pattern: rule enforcement, external rewards, and internalized motivation. The motivational devices used in Chinese industrial enterprises can be analyzed according to these three basic motivational patterns.

1. Rule Enforcement

As compared to their Western counterparts, Chinese industrial personnel (both managers and workers) are given very exact and detailed prescriptions of what is expected of them as members of a factory, workshop, or work unit. China is a planned socialist economy. Besides setting production targets, allocating raw materials, marketing, and purchasing for the enterprises, the state also prescribes the overall policies and guidelines that industries should follow in its enterprises. The principles, policies, and guidelines adhered to in the current operation of

Chinese industrial enterprises include the Plan on Readjustment, Restructuring, Consolidation, and Improvement of China's economy.

Under readjustment, conscientious efforts are made to bring about relatively good coordination in the development of agriculture and light and heavy industries and to maintain a proper ratio between consumption and accumulation.

Under restructuring, the earnings of an enterprise and the income of its workers will be commensurate with their contributions to the state. Absolute egalitarianism should be eliminated because it tends to breed conplacency among workers. In addition, overlapping and inefficient administrative organs will be eliminated, and greater powers will be granted to the local authorities in planning, capital construction, finance, materials, and foreign trade.

The principle of consolidation calls for the establishment of a system of clearly defined responsibility for everyone in the enterprise; the establishment of a system of specialization of labor and coordination of economic activities across different enterprises to achieve greater economies of scale in production; consolidation of badly managed enterprises through reorganization and mergers; and establishment of rules and regulations to govern all aspects of factory operations and to ensure the strict implementation of these rules and regulations.

The principle of improvement calls for upgrading the existing levels of production, technology, and management. Practices recommended in this regard include the organization of socialist labor emulation drives that are discussed subsequently; the raising of vocational skills of cadres and workers through education; the learning of science, technology, and management techniques from foreign countries; and the development of foreign trade so as to generate sufficient funds for importing foreign technology and equipment.

2. External Rewards

The constitution prescribes two types of incentives to motivate workers to heighten their performance. The state "applies the policy of combining moral encouragement with material reward, with the stress on the former" (*Constitution of the People's Republic of China*: Article 10).

The principal forms of material incentives used are wages, subsidies, and bonuses. China's wage policy is governed by two basic principles. On the one hand, it is opposed to wide wage spread. On the other hand, it is opposed to absolute egalitarianism. In state-owned enterprises, the wages of workers are governed by the eight-grade wage system, differentiated according to variations in skill. Wages are fairly uniform across enterprises in different types of industries and across different parts of the country.

The current system dictates that bonuses should not exceed two months of the workers' annual wage and that they should be tied to individual performance. In addition to wages and bonuses, the workers are provided generous benefits for sickness, injury, disability, maternity, retirement, and death.

3. Internalized Motivation

In China, internalized motivation is almost synonymous with moral encouragement. Moral encouragement involves the principle of "fight self," that is, the individual must seek to emulate the ideal communist man—one who is prepared to sacrifice his or her own self-interest for the general welfare and progress of all others and of the state. It also involves the application of the principle of "from each according to his ability," whereby every worker should do his or her very best, regardless of wage. The principal means of moral encouragement used are socialist labor emulation drives, commendations as pacesetters, and political indoctrination.

(a) Socialist Emulation Drive. In China, certain factories, work units, and individuals periodically are designated as advanced factories, units, or workers to be upheld as models for emulation by others. Socialist emulation drives are designed to serve two major purposes: one, to develop friendly competition between factories, workshops, and individuals so that they will surpass past performance records and set new highs; two, to help the less advanced units and workers catch up with the work of the more advanced. The latter notion is foreign to U.S. enterprises. In China, the aim of such campaigns is to develop a spirit of cooperation to enable the more advanced units and individuals to help the less productive ones improve on their past performance. In enterprises throughout the country, one comes across colorful charts drawn on blackboards or huge posters, complete with statistics, indicating the targets set for and the results attained in the emulation campaigns between workshops, groups, or individuals. Little red flags, cut out of paper, are pinned next to the winner's name. The practice of publicizing the productivity rates of each worker generates a lot of peer pressure among the less productive workers to improve performance.

(b) Commendations as Pacesetters at National Meetings. The outstanding achievements of certain advanced workers and work units are publicized nationally via radio, television, and newspapers so that workers and units from other parts of the country can seek to emulate, learn from, and catch up with these advanced units and individuals. In addition, there are national conventions where the most illustrious workers are praised and commended by leading party officials as pacesetters.

(c) *Political Indoctrination.* China's leaders recognize that material incentives and moral encouragement by themselves may not work unless they are accompanied by effective political indoctrination. At each factory, the party committee and the trade union organize weekly political discussion sessions for the workers. At present, workers at most factories are discussing and studying how they can make their own contributions toward realizing the goals of the Four Modernizations.

4. Discussion

The material incentives in vogue in Chinese enterprises are essentially similar to those in capitalist economies, that is, in return for their contribution to the organization to the organization's goals, the employees earn the means of livelihood.

The nonmaterial incentives used in China are somewhat foreign to the Western mentality. Because many observers of the Chinese industrial scene are amazed to see how nonmaterial incentives can serve as a motivating device, I would like to postulate some reasons or factors that contribute to the relative success of moral encouragement in Chinese industrial society:

One, in accordance with Maslow's theory of the hierarchy of human needs, once the basic physiological needs of the worker have been satisfied, he or she seeks to attain higher needs. In China, the basic physiological needs of all workers are taken care of by the state—social insurance benefits for workers cover sickness, retirement, disability, death, and the like. Consequently, the workers aspire to fulfill their higher level needs. Of course, it can be argued that the living standard of the Chinese worker is still far below that of his or her Western counterpart. Nevertheless, Factors 2 and 3 outlined next, coupled with the fact that the workers' lot has improved substantially (as compared to pre-1949 China), should be taken into consideration in evaluating the needs of a Chinese worker.

Two, although the amount of consumer goods available to the Chinese has increased over the past 2 years, they are still very limited compared to Western standards. Even though the Chinese are currently willing to spend more on clothing and other so-called luxury items, they are still very cautious about such purchases lest they be criticized by their colleagues. In China, if an individual flaunts his or her wealth, he or she can easily fall victim to the following situations: "red-eye disease," that is, subject of jealousy, or "white-eye disease," that is, target of ostracization. In China, criticism by one's peers, subordinates, and superiors exerts considerable pressure on an individual to fall in line.

Three, the CCP carries out very effective indoctrination and mass education campaigns to ensure that the people will conform to the party's policies and guidelines.

G. Reprimands

Chinese enterprises use two primary means for dealing with individuals who have deviated from the work and performance standards prescribed by the state and the enterprise. One is through patient talks, criticisms, and political indoctrination. The other involves more drastic measures such as economic sanctions, demotion, or dismissal from the job altogether. Each of these two mechanisms is discussed briefly next.

1. Patient Talks, Criticisms, Political Indoctrination

At the quarterly meetings of the Congress of Workers and Staff, the representative reports on the implementation of resolutions passed at the congress. Those who have performed well are commended, whereas those who have erred are criticized. The purpose of such criticism is not to tarnish a person's reputation nor to breed ill feelings among fellow workers but merely to help those who have erred to see what is wrong, what needs to be done, and how they can change for the better. This technique of criticism reminds one of the T-group sessions in the West. Criticism is often combined with patient talks and political indoctrination.

2. Demotion, Dismissal, and Imposition of Economic Sanctions

Cadres who do not perform up to standard are demoted. Economic sanctions are imposed upon those who fail to fulfill their quotas. Dismissal is seldom used at present because most enterprises still adhere to the "iron rice bowl" practice or system of lifetime employment. The government is trying to eliminate this system because it tends to breed complacency among some workers. However, it is very difficult to eliminate this practice.

V. CONCLUSION

This chapter has provided a brief overview of Chinese business and management practices and how they are influenced by broad societal-environmental variables. It is apparent that the Chinese are anxious to learn new management techniques from abroad to improve the overall efficiency of their enterprises. Consequently, in the years ahead, new practices and procedures will be adopted. However, it would be erroneous to assume that China will transplant Western management techniques in their entirety and apply them indiscriminately to Chinese factories. Even in espousing the socialist principles of Marxism–Leninism, the Chinese did a sort of preliminary screening and "sinicized" Marxism–Leninism somewhat in its eastward movement before its principles were implemented. China's leaders are aware of the tremendous differences, both cultural and economic, that exist between socialist China and the Western capitalist nations. Time and again, they have emphasized that China should only adopt those practices and procedures that are suited to the peculiar conditions of the country.

Throughout the course of history, the Chinese have proven themselves to be a very pragmatic people with an uncanny instinct for survival, who are ready and willing to change and follow the times. This attribute, above all else, may account for the fact that the country has been able to survive for thousands of years despite the civil wars that took place within the country between the changing imperial dynasties; foreign domination by the Monguls and Manchus during the Yuan and Ching dynasties, respectively; and a semicolonial status for almost a century and a half under the Western imperialist powers. Time and again, the Chinese have proved that they were able to "rise from the ashes," so to speak and rebuild the country anew. After the latest debacle of the Cultural Revolution (1966–1976), which brought the country to the verge of political, economic, and social collapse, China has recovered sufficiently to show rising productivity in various sectors of the economy. It is this Chinese ability to survive in the face of tremendous adversity and, more remarkable yet, to recover from these havocs and disasters, that has intrigued and fascinated Western observers for so long. Many of these fine qualities and attributes are kept alive today in the organization and running of Chinese industrial enterprises. They make for interesting study on the part of researchers who are interested in the principles of organizational theory and behavior. When the Chinese indicate a desire to learn advanced management techniques from the West, they are chiefly interested in things like cost accounting, quality control, cost-benefit analytic techniques, forecasting, how to accommodate the role of market factors in the drafting of production and purchasing plans, and how to raise worker productivity. It does not mean an abandonment of the principles and practices that have served the country well over the past decades.

Although many of the principles and techniques currently in vogue in China may not be applicable to the United States, given the tremendous cultural, political, and economic differences between them, it would benefit both practitioners and academicians to be aware of the differences and similarities. Such information would be particularly useful to practitioners who have business dealings with the Chinese. It is imperative for these practitioners to be aware of the country's organizational practices and principles if they expect to reap the full benefits of such business relationships.

Knowledge of the similarities and differences in various aspects of organizational functioning and processes, such as leader–member relations and motivational practices in the two countries, could help theorists and researchers in comparative management, organizational theory, and organizational behavior to better understand how broad environmental variables, such as ideology and socioeconomic variables, can influence the functioning of organizations and their effectiveness. Comparisons of similarities and differences would enable researchers to have a better comprehension of the antecedents and outcomes of certain organizational practices or variables and the dynamics of the relationships between various organizational variables. Such knowledge could prove invaluable in the development of principles of organizational theory and organizational behavior and could contribute to the development of better frameworks or models of comparative management, which is very important to the advancement of theory and knowledge in international business.

VI. REFERENCES

Constitution of the People's Republic of China. (1978). Beijing: Foreign Languages Press.
Eleventh National Congress of the CCP documents. (1977). Beijing: Foreign Languages Press.
Hofstede, G. (1980). Culture's consequences. Beverly Hills, CA: Sage.
Katz, D., & Kahn, R. L. (1978). The social psychology of organizations. New York: Wiley.
Tung, R. L. (1982). Chinese industrial society after Mao. Lexington, MA: Lexington.

10

A Comparison of Enterprise Management in Japan and the People's Republic of China

Dexter Dunphy and Jeannette Shi

I. THE SIGNIFICANCE OF JAPAN AND CHINA FOR MANAGEMENT THEORY

Japanese enterprises have attracted much scholarly and popular attention in recent years. Japanese management, in particular, has been seen as a test case for the possibility that there may be other management philosophies as effective as, or more effective than U.S. management philosophy, particularly when managing in non–U.S. cultural contexts. More broadly still, Japanese management practices have been seen as a challenge, not just to U.S. management theories, but to Western management philosophy as a whole. It is this management philosophy that has dominated most management schools throughout the world since their inception.

Much of the scholarly and popular debate has centered around the extent to which Japanese management methods are distinctive, and, if distinctive, whether they are culture-bound or "exportable" (Dunphy, 1987).

Japan's economic rise has also delivered a major challenge to the

Dexter Dunphy and Jeannette Shi • Australian Graduate School of Management, University of New South Wales, Kensington, New South Wales, Australia 2033.

prevailing convergence theory of national economic development. Convergence theory postulated that Anglo-American management philosophy was the sole philosophy that would "fit" technologically advanced economies. The theory argued that other cultural "designs" for the enterprise, and other culturally variant management styles, would eventually be replaced with the Anglo-American versions as part of the modernization process. The fact that the Japanese persistently manage (in Japan) in their own distinctive way has led to some reexamination of the theory.

China, however, has been the neglected Asian giant in management literature. Standard texts ignore China, despite the fact that China has a long managerial tradition and, since the revolution, has been the stage for the world's largest and most fundamental experiments in managerial change. China continues to experiment on a vast scale today. For example, one program in which the senior author has consulted is a management development program for 200,000 middle managers in the Chinese health system. Of course, the PRC will be of increasing significance in international trade as Deng's "open door policy" and the "four modernizations" continue. But management in the PRC is relatively unresearched, although there is more published material available in English than is immediately obvious (Dunphy & Shi, 1986).

However, the PRC has theoretical as well as practical significance. Management theory has been dominated by Anglo-American experience and is arguably ethnocentric. One of the most important contributions to creating a truly cross-cultural comparative management theory was Geert Hofstede's (1980a) monumental international HERMES survey of 1966. Hofstede's studies provide strong evidence for the existence of "cultural clusters," that is, groups of nations with similar work-related values, based on common ethnic and linguistic traditions. Studies such as this provide powerful evidence that most existing management texts are teaching managerial principles that may apply only to Anglo-American work forces, rather than to the work forces of other cultural clusters.

A major omission from Hofstede's research, and other similar surveys which followed, is data from the PRC. Hofstede, himself, was clearly frustrated by this for, throughout the book, he tries to make inferences about the PRC from data collected from nonmainland Chinese states, such as Taiwan and Hong Kong, and from other sources. These have, however, the status of thoughtful speculations. In particular, Hofstede was concerned to establish whether there was one or more Asian cultural clusters. He never fully resolved this. In a brief paragraph toward the end of the book he suggests that there are two cultural clusters in Asia: Japan—"a more developed Asian country" and "a secondary cluster of less developed Asian countries—Hong Kong, Singapore and Taiwan" (Hofstede, 1980a, pp. 335–336). But the position of the PRC in relation to these countries was not established, and one is left to presume that, being less developed, it would eventually appear somewhere in the secondary cluster.

Other management theorists have suggested, however, that there is one "East Asian" cultural cluster with many common characteristics, notably a relatively high and sustained economic growth rate in the 1960s and 1970s. In particular, Roy Hofheinz and Kent E. Calder (1982), S. Gordon Redding and George Hicks (1983), and Hicks and Redding (n.d.) have argued this viewpoint very strongly. They have, however, no "hard" data on values. Hofheinz and Calder argue, nevertheless, that these nations have in common values of respect for hierarchy, predictability, and flexibility (1982, p. 250). Redding sees values such as these as arising out of a common Confucian heritage (Redding & Hicks, 1983; Hicks & Redding, n.d.).

So we are left with the following questions:

1. Is there a single East Asian or "Confucianist" cultural cluster or are there more cultural clusters in East Asia? Stated another way: Are there or are there not, common values held by the work forces of the various East Asian nations?

2. If there is more than one Asian cluster, as Hofstede argues, where is China placed? Hofstede sees Japan as a "cluster" in itself, that is, as having a unique and distinctive set of values, related to, but distinguishable from, other less developed Asian cultures.

3. Do cultural clusters develop distinctive approaches to enterprise management? Stated in another way: Do work forces with different value systems lead managers to create different enterprise "designs" and to manage differently?

This chapter attempts to answer these theoretical questions. The information sources used are of two kinds. First, to answer questions 1 and 2, we draw on three recent unpublished studies (by other authors) of several small samples of PRC managers. We will give details of these studies later. Second, we attempt to answer the third question by reviewing a range of secondary evidence on the operation of enterprises in Japan and China. This evidence consists of two extensive and comprehensive annotated bibliographies (and the corresponding library collections) prepared by us and colleagues. These bibliographies cover English language publications on the enterprise and its management in

Japan and China respectively (Dunphy & Stening, 1984; Dunphy & Shi, 1986). They represent the most up-to-date and comprehensive resource of English language works on the subject and they are the source of our discussion of enterprise and management characteristics in the two countries.

II. IS THERE A SINGLE EAST-ASIAN CULTURAL CLUSTER?

Hofstede's data does show powerful evidence for a distinctive East Asian cluster. Two of his factors in combination neatly discriminate between *all* East Asian countries in his sample and all Anglo-American and northern European countries. The two key value indexes are "power distance" and "individualism/collectivism." As Figure 10.1 shows, all East Asian countries fall into the quadrant that is characterized by high power distance and collectivism, whereas all Western countries fall into the diagonally opposite quadrant of small power distance and individualism. Thus, these two dimensions together are sufficient to provide an elegant discrimination between East and West. (Note that the southern European countries, Spain, France, Belgium, and Italy, are in a third quadrant, that is, of high power distance and individualism.) Japan is distinctive, however in being in the "eastern" quadrant but closest in value terms to the West.

However, as we have noted, Hofstede's sample contained no PRC representatives. Three recent but unpublished studies provide some first small samples of PRC managers that are indicative of where the PRC is placed on these value dimensions.

The first study is by Lim Eng Chong, John P. Cragin, and Steven A. Scherling (1983). This study administered a Chinese version of Hofstede's questionnaire to 150 upper-middle-level managers in the China National Machinery and Equipment Import and Export Corporation (CMEC). The managers were surveyed while in attendance at a management program at the Chinese University of Hong Kong.

The second study is by Tse-leung "George" Lai and Yip-wai "Constant" Lam (1986). Their sample was of 91 managers, 44 from Beijing and 47 from Wuhan, who were participants in a basic management course taken in these cities. The third study is by Philip H. Birnbaum and Gilbert Y. Y. Wong (1985). The Birnbaum and Wong samples were 49 managers from the PRC (and 49 "matched" managers from Hong Kong). The PRC sample were participants in an executive program held in Guangdong Province.

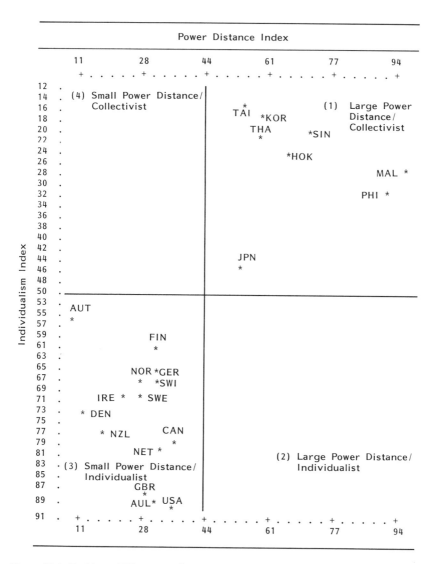

Figure 10.1. Position of Western and East Asian nations on the power distance and individualism scales.

Table 10.1 shows the results of these studies on the Hofstede dimensions of power distance and individualism. (Note that the first study of Chong *et al.* also quotes Lai and Lam's data before it was published elsewhere and that the average score from all PRC data on these dimensions is taken from Chong *et al.*) Figure 10.2 adds the PRC data to the results presented for other countries in Figure 10.1, allowing a comparison of the PRC with those countries.

What is clear is that there is considerable variability for the PRC in results on these two dimensions. There are two possible explanations of this. One is that the variability is due to the severely limited numbers in these "convenience" samples of a huge potential population of PRC managers. The other is that there is, as might be expected, considerable variability in a nation as large and culturally heterogeneous as China. Birnbaum and Wong's sample was drawn from Guangdong managers, and it is possible that they represent a subculture distinctively different (and perhaps more traditional in value terms) than those drawn from Beijing and the CMEC organization. Nevertheless, as expected, the variant scores and central tendency place the PRC much more in the "Eastern" quadrant of high power distance and high collectivism than in the "Western" quadrant of small power distance and individualism.

Overall, these studies indicate that PRC managers are closer to Japan than to other East Asian countries on the two vital dimensions that distinguish East Asia from the West. (The exception is the extreme score on collectivism from the Birnbaum and Wong study). Therefore, Japan does not appear to be a unique cluster in itself but is closely associated with the PRC. East Asian work forces can be seen as having a common commitment to these two fundamental values; so to this extent, there is

Table 10.1. Results of Three Studies of Values of PRC Managers

Study	Power distance	Individualism
1. Chong, Cragin, and Scherling (1983) CMEC managers[a]	55	57
2. Lai and Lam (1986)[b]		
(a) Beijing managers	33	13
(b) Wuhan managers	77	40
Total: Studies 1 and 2[c]	55	45
3. Birnbaum and Wong (1985)[d]		
Guangdong managers	55.7	−3.3

[a]See Chong, Cragin, and Scherling, 1983, Table III, p. 9.
[b]See Lai and Lam, 1986, Part II, Tables 18 and 20, pp. 35, 37.
[c]See Chong, Cragin, and Scherling, 1983, Table III, p. 9.
[d]See Birnbaum and Wong, 1985, Table 3, p. 26.

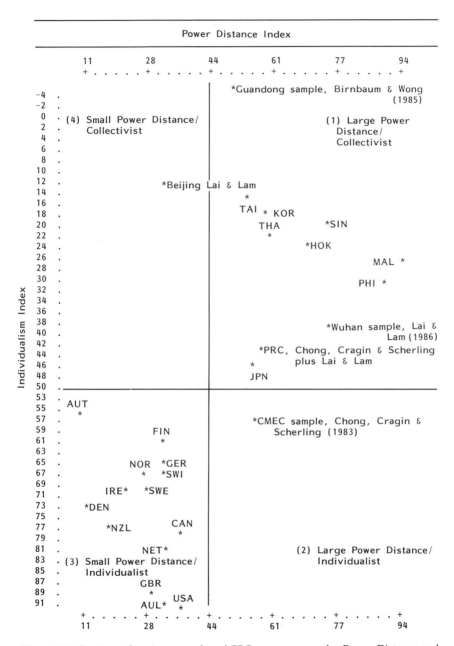

Figure 10.2. Position of various samples of PRC managers on the Power Distance and Individualism scales.

an East Asian cultural cluster. Japan and the PRC are similar, however, in that they stand midway between the East and the West, particularly the Western democracies of the United States, Great Britain, and Australia. Japan and the PRC are still, for the most part, East Asian but nevertheless strategically midway between the values of the two cultural worlds. It seems likely that this would give them both a distinct advantage in dealing with East and West.

We can be fairly confident, therefore, in comparing Japan and the PRC that their managers share some common value orientations around these key concepts.

We may break off here to speculate about why PRC managers, on the average, express less support for power distance than their overseas Chinese counterparts. One might expect the overseas Chinese to be less respectful of authority, less hierarchical because of their greater contact with the more egalitarian West. Ironically, it may well have been the anti-Western Maoist attacks on established authority in China's period of revolutionary fervor that effected a major change in this value area and brought China closer to the Western values her leaders despised. A high level of economic exchange with the West does not seem to have had the same effect for other East Asian nations whose dominant elites migrated from China, or whose antecedents did. Thus, cultural contact does not necessarily produce cultural similarity. To the contrary, these expatriated Chinese seem to have clung strongly to the traditional values of Chinese culture.

So far, we have examined values that Japan and the PRC share, though to a lesser degree, with other East Asian cultures. There is, however, another value Japan and the PRC have in common, but that is *not* shared by other East Asian cultures. Hofstede's study shows Japan to be high on "uncertainty avoidance." The studies mentioned before also show PRC managers (from various samples) to be high on uncertainty avoidance. Several other East Asian countries such as Singapore and Hong Kong are not. Uncertainty avoidance stresses a search for creating a sense of security by attempting to reduce uncertainty. At the organizational level, it leads, for example, to the use of systematic planning strategies, and these countries emphasize planning of this kind. It also leads to a concentration on managerial control techniques, such as operations research. Not surprisingly, the Japanese have combined group methods closely with operations research (OR) techniques in their widely used "quality circle" approach and other techniques that reduce uncertainty in production, such as the "kanban" technique. The Chinese have also emphasized such techniques, originally deriving them from the Russians but more recently from the Japanese.

Uncertainty avoidance also leads to the use of bureaucratic rules.

Enterprises in both countries are characterized by use of extensive written rules, regulations, and procedures (Azumi & McMillan, 1975; Lingnan University Research Institute, 1982).

III. DIFFERENCES IN VALUES BETWEEN JAPAN AND CHINA

Japan and the PRC show remarkable similarity on some value dimensions, but they occupy divergent positions on others. In Hofstede's study, Japan has the highest score of all nations on "masculinity" (95%)—other East Asian countries are, in descending order, Hong Kong (51), Singapore (48), Taiwan (45), and Thailand (34). Chong, Cragin, and Scherling's paper (quoted before) also shows a dramatic contrast between Japan and China on this value. Their samples show the PRC to be the most "feminine" of all countries. Similarly, Birnbaum and Wong found that "masculinity" was the most significant factor in discriminating between their samples of Hong Kong and PRC managers, with Hong Kong managers expressing more "masculine" values. Lai and Lam's study also shows the PRC managers as extremely feminine. All samples but their Wuhan samples are lower than all other countries, and the Wuhan sample is lower than all but four Nordic countries (Lai & Lam, 1986, p. 39).

Thus, we have evidence that the most powerful value discrimination between Japan and the PRC is the masculinity–femininity dimension. Of all national groups surveyed, the Japanese respondents express the most support for "masculine" values, and the PRC respondents express very strong or the strongest support for "feminine" values. (Hofstede's characterization of these two factors as "masculinity" and "femininity" is unfortunate because it perpetuates sex role stereotyping. The terms *tough-minded* and *tender-minded* would be preferable. However, the terms are now standard in the literature).

We shall now examine some implications of these value similarities and differences between Japan and the PRC for the management of the enterprise in these two countries.

IV. SOME IMPLICATIONS

A. Societal Objectives

Before examining the relationship of social values to enterprise characteristics, let us look just at the economic objectives of those two countries. Both countries took as their central economic objectives the industrialization and modernization of their economies and the creation of strong military power. Japan took on these objectives at the time of the Meiji Restoration in the 1880s, whereas China set out firmly on the same road much later, after the party came to power in 1949. We need to keep in mind China's later start on the modernization path.

However, the two countries have pursued these objectives in different ways. China at first tried to emulate the Russian model but later in 1956 broke away from it. At this time, China turned inward and tried to develop an indigenous model. Part of this process involved virtual international economic isolation, at a time when Japan was vigorously pursuing international markets.

After the death of Mao and the downfall of the "gang of four" in 1976, China made a major economic reorientation with the four modernizations program (see Tung, 1982; Chapter 9) and the progressive reorganization of the seaboard economy toward international trade. However, China is still only laying the base for large-scale international trade. By contrast in Japan, even relatively small firms are able to trade successfully overseas through availing themselves of the services of large trading companies, the "soga shosha."

China's leaders faced, and still face, a much larger and more complex set of problems than Japan's leaders. China's population in 1982 was 1,008,170,000 people as against Japan's 118,450,000. Moreover, China's population consists of extremely diverse cultural groups speaking many different languages and dialects. At the time of the revolution, the country was devastated, the people impoverished, starving, and disorganized (a "sheet of loose sand," Sun Yat-sen called them). Consequently, the Communist Party's priority was on achieving national unity and political control. The political continued to dominate the economic at least until 1978. Although Japan was also devastated after World War II, she had already modernized the economy by this time, achieved national unity, and had a relatively homogeneous population.

The means to political unification and modernization in China was the development of state and collective ownership of the means of production, combined with a high degree of central planning. Government policy in China, as in Japan, was to concentrate initial investment in the development of heavy industry. But in China, this policy led to major catastrophes in economic development against which the enterprise was relatively powerless to act as it was captive to the state. It is this issue of the relationship of the enterprise to the state that we take up next.

1. Power Distance

In order to understand the impact of the "power distance" value on management, we need to look at the position of the enterprise in the total power structure of society. Countries with high "power distance" stress the psychological difference between superiors and subordinates and create strong hierarchies that emphasize the relative power of those at the top (Hofstede, 1980b).

The chief center of power in a society is normally the state. In high "power-distance" nations, we would expect the state to be invested with a high degree of power, vis-à-vis the enterprise, and to use this power. Hofheinz and Calder (1982) refer to the important economic planning and guidance role played by the state in East Asian countries. Both Japan and the PRC do have strong state direction, as one would expect in societies that are relatively high on power distance. Historically, national governments in both countries have had similar aims of creating modern powerful industrial states (Chen, 1978; Rapp, 1977; Tsunoyama, 1978; Watson, 1978). However, the means used to achieve this have differed.

The Japanese system can be referred to as "guided free enterprise." A consistent national economic policy is developed through political debate and negotiations between government bureaucrats and management of the large companies that comprise the core of the Japanese economy. Japanese economic policy has evolved through a far-sighted but pragmatic appreciation of local and international market forces. Coordination occurs through a range of policies, structures and formal and informal communication channels.

In the early stages of industrialization in Japan, the Meiji government set up capital intensive enterprises in key industry areas and actively regulated private business activities. Later, the government divested itself of the enterprises it had founded, handing them over to private ownership. The result was a much more flexible system, with more play for entrepreneurial activity. This policy also led to the private sector viewing the state as supportive of private enterprise.

To strengthen Japan's international competitive capacity, the Japanese government played a major role in the Industrial Rationalization Movement in Japan. A thorough rationalization and elimination of surplus enterprises was achieved by government intervention. Japan's policies have evolved in a consistent way under the direction of highly selected bureaucrats in key government departments such as the Ministry of Trade and Industry. These bureaucrats have provided continuity and accumulating expertise, thus earning the respect and cooperation of managers in most enterprises.

In the PRC, from the time of the revolution, ideology has tended to dominate economic expediency. The state initially founded major industrial enterprises but rather than handing these over to the private sector, it progressively nationalized private sector enterprises until all enter-

prises of significance were state-owned and state-controlled. By expro-
priating private enterprises and controlling them centrally, the PRC
failed to develop independent, innovative entrepreneurs. In Japan, the
relative "loose coupling" of enterprises with the state encouraged the
emergence of such entrepreneurs, particularly in the interwar years,
where they created great progress in some of Japan's leading industries
such as automobiles and aircraft.

Historically, industrial management policies in the PRC lacked continuity and were subjected to reversals as the prevailing ideology
changed (Richman, 1971). The state assumed the major decision-making
role for enterprises, setting minimal production targets, allocating raw
materials, specifying markets, and purchasing a fixed percentage of the
enterprise's output (Tung, 1982). In China, there have been major savings in government policy relating to the autonomy of the enterprise.
The initial system was highly centralized to 1958, then relatively decentralized but still handicapped by bureaucratic rigidities, ambiguities
and disagreements (Cocke & Robinson, 1981; Eckstein, 1977; Lardy,
1975; Richman, 1971). Later, it was recentralized. These swings led to
confusion at the enterprise level.

Only in the late 1970s was a significant policy change adopted that
established a consistent set of economic goals. The "four modernizations" policy initiated a restructuring and rationalization of the economy
similar to that undertaken in Japan years earlier. It also loosened the
state's direct control over major decisions affecting the enterprise's operations. There had been some movement in this direction earlier, but the
reforms of 1978 were thorough, far-reaching, and vigorously pursued
(Laaksonen, 1984).

So, in both countries, we see the state playing an important and
powerful role in relation to the enterprises. Basic economic development
policies had some similarities, but the state in Japan played a guidance
role that provided consistent policies and strong support for private
sector enterprise. In China, by contrast, the state assumed centralized
control of most enterprises and strong ideological swings led to inconsistency in economic development policies until the late 1970s.

Other values than power distance have played an important role in
defining these differences in emphasis. Central to the Japanese value
system has been the concept of "harmony" (wa), derived originally from
Chinese Confucianism. This value has been consistently reinforced by
the state and by enterprise managers in Japan and has contributed to the
Japanese emphasis on resolving differences and achieving consensus on
economic policies. The Communist Party in China attacked Confucianist
values and replaced the value of harmony with that of "struggle." This

value reinforced ideological conflicts, particularly under Mao, and led to the pendulum swings in ideological policy that confused and frustrated managers of enterprises in the PRC.

Management philosophy in both countries has, however, consistently stressed the importance of human factors in the enterprise. Strong emphasis has been placed on human resource planning and management, emphasizing in particular the importance of capturing the "hearts and minds" of the work force. Ideology in Japan, however, is strongly differentiated at the enterprise level, with attempts being made to mold the "Mitsui Man" or the "Toyota Man." In China, the "model worker" has been defined by the state rather than the enterprise, and workers have not been differentiated on an enterprise basis. Thus, both countries try to socialize workers into a "clanlike" entity, but the collective focus is different in the two countries.

The somewhat different relationship of the enterprise to the state in the two countries leads to corresponding differences in enterprise goals. Japanese firms emphasize enterprise growth (particularly in market share), high productivity, product innovation, and work-force stability and commitment. This stands in some contrast to the Western emphasis on short-term profit maximization (Kagono et al., 1980).

In the PRC, the major enterprise goal until the late 1970s was simply to fulfill production quotas set by the state and to provide stable employment for the work force (Pyle, 1981). Thus, detailed state policy setting in China virtually eliminated economic competition between enterprises. Since 1978, however, there has been a progressive move to establish the "responsibility" system in enterprises. This reflects a shift of power to the enterprise, designed to increase labor productivity and profits. Enterprises still have state quotas to fulfill but firms are increasingly encouraged to market the rest of their production on the open market. Thus, we see a convergence of control practices in the two countries. Both countries seem to be opting to maintain a powerful role for the state in central planning with an autonomy for enterprises within state guidelines that provide incentives at enterprise level for increasing productivity and profitability. Such a resolution of the control issue reflects a value on power distance that is considerably higher than in the West, but somewhat lower than the more centrally controlled regimes of some other East Asian countries.

A similar "medium-high" power distance resolution can also be seen at the enterprise level itself. Traditional Japanese management practices reflected high power distance. However, a significant modification of these practices has occurred in the post–World War II period. Under General McArthur, the Allied occupation regime instituted various democratic reforms designed to modify traditional Japanese attitudes to authority. Apart from instituting democratic political reforms, other reforms were instituted at the enterprise level. These included removing over 1,000 of the most senior executives in war-related industries and fostering trade unionism. Subsequently, the Japanese themselves adopted extensively many of the participative practices recommended by U.S. proponents of the "human relations school." Over a period of 40 years, therefore, there has been a significant shift away from "shogunlike" management practices to a system that still emphasizes the status of management but that combines status hierarchy with a series of formal and informal participative practices.

In China, the Russian model of management emphasized the authority of the enterprise director, and this was consistent with traditional attitudes to authority. However, the party stressed its authority and the authority of the cadres that represented the party at the local enterprise level. It also preached an egalitarianism that emphasized the importance of worker participation. Although the actual power of these potentially conflicting power centers has varied dramatically from one period to another, the trend has been to modify central control at the enterprise level but to retain authority in the hands of the enterprise director. The enterprise director is, however, responsible to the state (which appoints him) and to the party and the Workers Representative Congress (who review his performance). Although this is structurally a different system from the Japanese, it represents a similar emphasis on maintaining the authority of the chief executive but tempering it by stressing participative practices.

2. Collectivism

The collectivism value is very evident in enterprise organization in both countries. It is evident first in what we in the West would refer to as "paternalistic" practices but that are more properly seen as extended family or clan practices designed to create a sense of loyalty in employees.

Both societies offer lifetime employment to some or most employees. In Japan, it is permanent employees in large corporations who are accorded job security throughout their working career (to an average age of 57 years). Many of these same companies also provide housing and a wide range of other benefits. However, employees with these benefits represent only about 30% of the work force (Fletcher, 1984).

In the PRC, the vast majority of workers have their needs for housing, health, and education taken care of by the enterprise. Until recently, permanent workers could not be fired, and dismissal is still most uncommon. However, in both the PRC and Japan, there exist categories of temporary or support staff who receive lower wages and are entitled to fewer benefits. Published figures on the proportion of nonpermanent staff in Chinese enterprises are not available, but the proportion appears to be substantially less than in Japan. Unlike Japan, there is no mandatory retirement age. In the PRC recently, however, strong persuasion has been exercised on large numbers of older senior executives to retire, and no new managers may now be appointed who are over 45 years of age (Ma Hong, personal communication, 1985).

These practices strongly reinforce the "clanlike" character of enterprises in both countries. However, the differences in practice have significantly different consequences. The extreme competition for places in the elite organizations in Japan allows for highly selective entry on educational criteria and the creation of a highly selected meritocracy. In China, universal benefits have created decreased initiative. *The iron rice bowl* is the term used in the PRC to indicate (usually with some distaste) the prevailing system where wages and benefits derive from membership in the enterprise rather than from effort or output.

Collectivism can be seen to be expressed also in the extensive use of groups in the workplace in both Japan and China. In Japan, enterprises are organized into work units where evaluation is based on group performance and group loyalty is emphasized. Quality-control circles are an example of this. In PRC enterprises, groups have been used since the revolution to create conformity and commitment to the party line, and to promote self-criticism, discussion, and study. They have also been used to ensure quality control, safety, and maintenance.

The group-oriented character of enterprise operations also affects decision-making in enterprises in the two countries. In Japanese enterprises, the decision-making process is characterized by the much publicized *ringi seido* (joint decision-making system). It consists of a lengthy process of first discussing the parameters of a problem and then widespread discussion of options among those directly affected. This continues until a satisfactory solution has been negotiated that all are willing to support. Then senior management formalizes the decision. Thus, worker participation is a basic principle of the Japanese decision-making system.

Worker participation in decision-making has been a much debated issue in the PRC and, historically, the extent of worker participation and the forms have varied dramatically at the enterprise level. At the time of the Cultural Revolution, workers seized direct control of many enterprises, deposing managers. However, the current prevailing form of worker participation in China gives workers the right to elect members of the workers congress in each enterprise, which meets annually to review managerial policy and performance. The workers congress also has the power to discuss, examine, and propose production targets and plans and the power to decide enterprise policies on labor protection and welfare. Enterprise "directors" (CEOs) are not elected by the work force (as in Yugoslavia) but rather appointed by the state, although in some cases the workers congress does have the right to nominate. Although shop-floor participative practices vary widely, it is clear that there is a prevailing climate encouraging grass roots participation in setting goals, standards, and procedures.

Both Japan and the PRC, therefore, have strong patterns of worker participation. However, although participation modifies power distance, it does not typically reduce it to levels commensurate with Western values. Participation is combined with respect for authority.

Collectivism as a value is also expressed in the pattern of trade unionism. Both countries have developed forms of enterprise unionism as against craft or trade unionism (Fletcher, 1984). In both countries, the trade unions extend the collective welfarism of the enterprise.

However, in the PRC, the role of the trade union is relatively restricted to a welfare and morale-boosting role (Tung, 1982). Unions in China are the "working organ" of the workers congress and are not allowed to engage in wage pushes or to organize strikes. Japanese unions are active in this wider role. The result is that Japanese unions have successfully and consistently raised the real incomes of employees in profitable enterprises and industries, thus linking profitability and employee welfare. In China, until recently, wages were centrally controlled, and there was no link between enterprise profitability and returns to employees. Hence, motivation to increase enterprise efficiency and profitability was often low.

Enterprises in both countries supplement regular wages with a range of other incentives such as bonuses, sickness and other benefits, housing or housing subsidies. They also use methods of moral encouragement and forms of public social recognition (Alston, 1982; Tung, 1982). However, Japanese enterprise managers organized early to develop expertise and lock it into the enterprise through the "lifetime employment" system. Large companies developed personnel systems that select for high educational attainment and then consistently reward the development of expertise.

The Chinese revolutionary values, by contrast, were ambivalent about expertise. Throughout the history of the PRC, there has been a continual debate about the relative importance of "red" versus "expert." At the time of the revolution, most revolutionary leaders were political cadres of largely peasant backgrounds with little or no technical expertise or training. Experts, by contrast, were mostly products of and supporters of the previous establishment and therefore, politically suspect. This suspicion of experts was compounded by the strong egalitarianism of the party members. Mao himself consistently downgraded expertise and unleashed the Red Guards to persecute experts in the Cultural Revolution. Consequently, there were no consistent incentives for expertise to be developed and maintained. This "ultraleftism" is now seen as a mistake, but meanwhile it will take time to develop high levels of technical expertise in key areas where it is lacking.

We argue, therefore, that the combination of relatively high power distance and collectivism in East Asia supports a preparedness on the part of nationals of these countries to support a high level of state direction and control of the economy, which can be seen in all East Asian countries. We would also argue that it supports a distinctive style of management that is authoritative, but nonindividualistic. In other words, shared and linked conceptions of the nature of the collectivity and of authority support congruent roles for state and enterprise management. This does not imply, however, that there is no conflict over the *distribution* of power between state and enterprise in those countries. To the contrary, in both countries, there has been, and continues to be, a tug-of-war over what should be controlled by government and what by the enterprise. However, compared to the West, there is ideological (value) agreement that the state should have relatively more power than Western ideology suggests is appropriate (i.e., high power distance), and this is also reflected in relatively greater control given enterprise managers within the enterprise in East Asian countries. Similarly, the high collectivism scores suggest support for a stronger emphasis on collective needs (rather than on individual freedom) than is common in the West. This is reflected at the national level in more centralized state planning and, at the enterprise level, in a range of human resource (personnel and industrial relations) policies that are designed to bind the fate of the individual to the fate of the enterprise much more closely than is acceptable in the West.

What we have shown here, however, is that, for most managers sampled in Japan and the PRC, both "power distance" and "collectivism" are *relatively* low compared to most other East Asian nationals. It seems likely that what we have in East Asia is an East Asian cluster whose distinctive values originally arose out of the social realities of rice-growing empires—in particular, the need for the collective effort needed to grow rice and the marked authority required to organize the resources needed for large-scale irrigation projects and their defense. This value system has been supported by a strong family socialization process emphasizing authority acting in the interests of the extended family—again "power distance" and "collectivism." The same values have been supported by the powerful, prevailing traditions of Buddhism and Confucianism.

We would argue that China and Japan's values on these two key dimensions were congruent with those of other East Asian countries but that both "power distance" and "collectivism" have been tempered by severe social events that first disrupted and then reduced the hold of these traditional values. In Japan, the loss of World War II and the "democratic" reforms of the occupation were the critical events. In China, the revolution that overthrew the monarchy and also imposed "democratic" reforms was the critical event. These, however, are only conjectures, as no longitudinal studies of values are available.

B. Value Differences

We have shown that Japan and China have extraordinarily high scores on "masculinity" and "femininity," respectively. What do these differences mean in practice? According to Hofstede, the clearest differences are as follows: "Masculinity" is accompanied by high scores on the importance of advancement, earnings, competition, and assertive patterns of behaviors. Work is more central to life in "masculine" countries. Masculine countries have fewer women in professional and technical jobs. Femininity, by contrast, is accompanied by high scores on the importance of interpersonal relationships, rendering service, cooperation, and physical conditions with a generally nurturing pattern of behavior. Work is less central to life in these countries, and people are more concerned with life satisfaction than with job satisfaction.

All these aspects are clearly related to differences between the PRC and Japanese society and their component organizations. Japan has a very high level of sex role differentiation. Competition for advancement in the education system is extreme by international standards, and competition for entry into the elite companies also extreme. However, within the enterprise, open competition is strongly discouraged, and an ethic of harmony (*wa*) is promoted. *Between* enterprises there is, however, an extremely high level of competition.

The PRC, by contrast has relatively low sex-role differentiation since the revolution. Women are to be found in all occupations and professions and at all levels of the society. Even significant differences in dress between the sexes has been discouraged. The revolution introduced a strong ethic of equality between the sexes. In addition, great stress was placed on job security and working conditions with the result being the creation of the "iron rice bowl" that the current Chinese leadership sees as dampening work motivation. Only recently has some limited competition between enterprises been permitted.

Interestingly, Hofstede's results show "need for achievement" to be highly related to high scores on "masculinity" and "uncertainty avoidance"; (Hofstede, 1980a, p. 170), and the studies by Birnbaum and Wong (1985), Chong, Cragin, and Scherling (1983), and Lai and Lam (1986) all show PRC managers to be high on uncertainty and avoidance. As we have noted, all three studies also show the PRC managers' views to be negatively associated with "masculinity."

Thus, the PRC managers share with Japanese managers a common concern for security, but this does not have the tough-minded, assertive (masculine) characteristics, present in the Japanese value system, that lead to high need for achievement in Japan. Further, we would argue that some major differences between enterprise operation in China and Japan can be related to this feminine/masculine value dichotomy.

Both countries have devoted strong attention to developing systematic enterprise personnel policies. Both sets of policies stress security of tenure (as described before). However, in China, a range of aspects relating to social security have been pursued for their own sake, as communist or socialist ideals, whereas in Japan, they have been systematically linked to rewards for achievement.

V. CONCLUSION

What we see emerging in East Asia is a modern technological state built to a different model than the Western. Although China and Japan have moved closer to the West than other East Asian states on the relevant value dimensions, these represent only a modified Eastern value set, not a convergence to Western values. The new East Asian high technology superstate combines support for authoritative control with a strong emphasis on collective welfare. Japan and China share a very similar position on these critical values. Their East Asian position arises out of a common long-term historical heritage. Their current close value compatibility arises out of very different historical experiences since World War II. Although these experiences were dissimilar, nevertheless they may have had a similar impact in tempering "power distance" and "collectivism."

What we suggest, therefore, is that China and Japan represent a subset within the East Asian cultural cluster. There is some evidence that they are converging with each other, both in a value sense and in a structural sense, as enterprise in the PRC is encouraged to become increasingly autonomous and export-oriented. However, while the countries diverge on "masculine" versus "feminine" values, it can be expected that Japanese enterprises will continue to compete more strongly and work will be more central in the lives of employees in that country.

China's different national characteristics will, however, continue to support significant differences in operations at the enterprise level. The geographical and population size of China and its cultural variety and diversity mean that the imperative of maintaining political unity will always dominate economic planning. The key question for the current Chinese leaders is how much autonomy can be granted the enterprise without creating centrifugal forces that endanger national unity. Chinese leaders realize that historically China has only remained unified under strong, paternalistic centralized control. Enterprise autonomy will therefore always be subject to stronger political controls in China than in Japan.

What is the significance of the new East Asian nations and their relative economic success? We suggest speculatively that the first phase of the Industrial Revolution demanded individualistic competitiveness and low power distance. The Protestant European countries had values that supported this, as Max Weber and other comparative social scientists and historians pointed out. However, we argue that the current (second) phase of the Industrial Revolution demands collective competitiveness and national industrial policies that can most readily be instituted in countries with strong respect for national leadership. Similarly, this pattern must be repeated at the enterprise level with authoritative decisions by a respected managerial leadership, matched with collective commitment to the enterprise by its work force. Japan fits this pattern. What China has lacked until recently in this regard is the opportunity to develop enough enterprise managers, entrepreneurs, and experts who can provide the leadership and know-how to modernize the nation. It remains to be seen whether the current pursuit of the "four modernizations," combined with increasing enterprise autonomy, will provide the managerial and professional elites necessary to move China's masses to trade off elements of security for achievement.

VI. REFERENCES

Alston, J. P. (1982). Awarding bonuses the Japanese way. *Business Horizons, 25*(5), 46–50.

Azumi, K., & McMillan, C. J. (1975). Culture and organization structure: A comparison of Japanese and British organizations. *International Studies of Management and Organization, 5*(1), 35–47.

Birnbaum, P. H., & Wong, G. Y. Y. (1985). *Cultural values of managers in the People's Republic of China and Hong Kong.* Unpublished paper presented at the American Academy of Management Meetings, San Diego.

Chen, N. R. (1978). Economic modernization in post-Mao China: Policies, problems and prospects. In U.S.A. Congress, Joint Economic Committee, *Chinese economy post-Mao* (pp. 165–203). Washington, DC: U.S. Government Printing Office.

Chong, L. E., Cragin, J. P., & Scherling, S. A. (1983). *Manager work-related values in a Chinese corporation.* Unpublished paper. Hong Kong: Chinese University of Hong Kong. Also presented to the Academy of International Business, 1983 Annual Meeting, San Francisco.

Cocke, E. C., & Robinson, A. J. (1981). For a new management recipe, China samples a Western menu. *Asian Business, 17*(5), 72–75.

Dunphy, D. C. (1987). Convergence and divergence—A temporal review of the literature on the Japanese enterprise and its management. *Academy of Management Review, 12,* 445–459.

Dunphy, D. C., & Shi, J. (1986). *Management and the enterprise in the People's Republic of China: An annotated bibliography.* Informal publication. Sydney, Australia: Australian Graduate School of Management, University of New South Wales.

Dunphy, D. C., & Stening, B. W. (1984). *Japanese organization behaviour and management: An annotated bibliography.* Hong Kong: Asian Research Service.

Eckstein, A. (1977). *China's economic revolution.* Cambridge, MA: Cambridge University Press.

Fletcher, M. D. (1984). Chinese industrial policy and reforms—Preliminary comparisons with Japan. *Australian Journal of Chinese Affairs, 11,* 121–130.

Hicks, G. L., & Redding, S. G. (n.d.). *Uncovering the sources of East Asian growth.* Unpublished and undated paper. Hong Kong: Department of Management, University of Hong Kong.

Hofheinz, R., & Calder, K. E. (1982). *The East-Asia edge.* New York: Basic Books.

Hofstede, G. (1980a). *Culture's consequences: International differences in work-related values.* Beverly Hills, CA: Sage.

Hofstede, G. (1980b, Summer). Motivation, leadership and organization: Do American theories apply abroad? *Organizational Dynamics, 46,* 42–63.

Hofstede, G. (August, 1985). *Cultural differences in teaching and learning.* Unpublished paper presented at the Colloquium on Selected Issues in International Business, Honolulu, Hawaii.

Kagono, T., et al. (1980). Mechanistic vs. organic management systems: A comparative study of adaptive patterns of U.S. and Japanese firms. *Kobe Annual Reports, 115*–139.

Laaksonen, O. J. (1984). The management and power structure of Chinese enterprises during and after the Cultural Revolution: With empirical data comparing Chinese and European enterprises. *Organization Studies, 5*(1), 1–21.

Lai, Tze-leung (George), & Lam, Yip-wai (Constant). (1986). A study on work-related values of managers in the People's Republic of China (Parts I, II, and III). *The Hong Kong Manager* (Dec.–Jan. 1986), 23–41; (Feb.–Mar. 1986), 91–51; (Apr.–May. 1986), 7–17.

Lardy, N. R. (1975). Economic planning in the People's Republic of China: Central-provincial fiscal relations. In U.S.A. Congress, Joint Economic Committee, *China: A reassessment of the economy* (pp. 94–115). Washington, DC: U.S. Government Printing Office.

Lingnan University Research Institute. (1982). Principles of management in a socialist economy. *International Studies of Management and Organization, 12*(2), 20–44.

Pyle, T. H. (1981). Reforming Chinese management: The P.R.C. is testing a number of strategies and considering some bold new moves. *China Business Review, 8*(3), 7–19.

Rapp, W. V. (1977). Japan—Its industrial policies and corporate behavior. *Columbia Journal of World Business, 12*(1), 38–48.

Redding, S. G., & Hicks, G. L. (1983, February). *Culture causation and Chinese management.* Unpublished paper. Hong Kong: University of Hong Kong.

Richman, B. M. (1971). Ideology and management: The Chinese oscillate. *Columbia Journal of World Business, 6*, 23–33.

Tsunoyama, S. (1978). Government and business: An introductory essay. In International conference on Business History, Fuji Education Center *Government and business: Proceedings of the Fifth Fuji Conference* (pp. 1–18). Tokyo: University of Tokyo Press.

Tung, R. L. (1982). *Chinese industrial society after Mao.* Lexington, MA: Lexington.

Watson, A. (1978). Industrial management—Experiments in mass participation. In W. O. Brugger (Ed.). *China: The impact of the cultural revolution* (pp. 171–202). London: Croom Helm.

IV
OTHER SPECIFIC INSIGHTS
AND PERSPECTIVES

Contradictions between Brazilian and U.S. Organizations
Implications for Organizational Theory

Kim S. Cameron, Myung Un Kim, and Sarah J. Freeman

I. INTRODUCTION

Conceptions of excellence, the quality of work life, value patterns, power relationships, stress factors, and so on have been found to differ among cultures throughout the world. The manner in which individuals perceive their own realities differs significantly among different cultures as individuals process cognitive cues in culturally homogeneous ways (Haire, Ghiselli, & Porter 1963; Hofstede, 1984). Similarly, the organizational behaviors arising from these unique cultural perspectives may also differ in important ways in different countries, and the theories of organizational functioning that arise from observation of that behavior may, therefore, reflect cultural bias.

As American businesses have found themselves losing ground in international competition, we have seen increasing interest in the management practices of other cultures. American practitioners and scholars alike are eager to learn about Japanese management in particular; the success of books on Japan (e.g., Pascale & Athos, 1981; Ouchi, 1981) and the vast numbers of articles in management and trade journals touting

Kim S. Cameron, Myung Un Kim, and Sarah J. Freeman • Graduate School of Business Administration, University of Michigan, Ann Arbor, Michigan 48109.

the excellence of Japanese management systems attest to this interest. Additionally, as the introductory essay by Osigweh (Chapter 1) documents, there is a growing trend toward the internationalization of American corporate activities, seen both in direct investment and in joint ventures overseas. However, despite the increasingly globalized interests and practice of American firms, there remains a dearth of research interest in, and understanding of, cross-cultural differences in organizational practices (Adler, 1983). To stay abreast of the major issues arising from the globalization of American business, organizational scientists should increase their investigation of cross-cultural organizational dynamics. They must begin to determine if organizational theories and skills developed in and for a particular country are culture-bound or if they can be applied across national and cultural boundaries.

Scientific theories often take on a quasi-religious and symbolic nature that results in their acceptance and promulgation in inappropriate circumstances. In particular, Adler *et al.* (Chapter 2) and Osigweh (Chapter 1) have elaborately noted in this volume that organizational theories and perspectives developed in the United States have frequently been advocated as being almost universally appropriate in other cultures when it is not at all clear that this is true. As Hofstede pointed out, for example:

> Western ethnocentrism has become too evidently untenable. Countries trying to transfer Western ideas wholesale have been in trouble. Countries translating them in a way consistent with their own cultural traditions are now outperforming the West. . . . It is time to bid farewell to ethnocentrism in social science theories. (1984, p. 397)

Theories of organizational behavior that describe and prescribe functioning in U.S. organizations may be much less appropriate in other cultures, even when technological and economic variables are similar.

The focus of this investigation is characterized by the same two objectives that typify most cross-cultural organizational research: (1) to examine the applicability of management principles across settings and (2) to study the manifestations of unique organization phenomena in different cultures (Triandis, Malpas, & Davidson, 1973). However, unlike many previously published studies of cross-cultural phenomena, this investigation was not initially designed as a scientific inquiry. It was only during the process of discovering cross-cultural differences related to organizational functioning and observing some apparent aberrations from organizational theory that systematic analysis was imposed on the data-collection activities.

This study began when one of the authors (Cameron) visited Brazil as part of a Fulbright Distinguished Scholar Program in 1984. One purpose of the visit was to identify possible joint research projects or inter-institutional linkages between American and Brazilian colleges and universities. Visits were made to institutions in Puerto Alegro, Rio de Janeiro, Salvador, Natal, Brasilia, and Belo Horizonte. In addition, meetings were held with individuals in three federal agencies or offices dealing with higher education, and a conference on higher education issues was convened in Gramado, attended by representatives from institutions throughout Brazil.

The information on which this chapter is based came from those activities, particularly from interviews held with faculty members and university administrators on campuses and with agency heads and federal employees in the government. No attempt was made to be comprehensive or even thoroughly representative of the U.S. or Brazilian systems of higher education. In fact, it is acknowledged that the information uncovered may be biased or partial. However, because some of it was so surprising and contrary to expectations, questions were asked of several people to try to confirm or refute initial impressions. In general, all information was verified with more than one source.

The primary outcome of these interviews and interactions was surprise about the seeming discrepancies between actual practice in Brazilian institutions of higher education and theoretical prescriptions developed in the United States. What organizational theory predicts to be effective in the United States seems to be contradicted by the organization and operation of Brazilian colleges and universities. This chapter both describes those surprising contradictions and makes an attempt to explain them.

The chapter begins with some brief background on the cultural environment of Brazil. We then identify a few obvious similarities between the higher education systems of Brazil and the United States particularly when comparing an average Brazilian university with an average U.S. university. Next, we describe 10 apparent contradictions between the functioning of Brazilian institutions and well-known organizational theories in the United States. Finally, we conclude by explaining and integrating several of these contradiciions.

II. BRAZILIAN CONTEXT

Brazil occupies nearly half of South America and has nearly half its population. Abounding in natural resources, Brazil has played a role in Latin America that is often compared to that of the United States prior to World War II. Brazil is becoming the heart of economic development for

the region. Some of the distinctive features that are likely to affect institutions of higher education are as follows.

A. Political Conditions

Following its independence from Portugal in 1811, Brazil was ruled
by two successive emperors; this period lasted until 1889. During both
the Colonial and the Empire periods, the political structure tended to be
highly centralized. The first Brazilian republic was launched in 1891 as a
federation of 20 states. Tightly organized political sectors emerged in
each state, and mutually beneficial relationships between rural bosses
and state political leaders were established. The constitutional decentralization created by the republic often failed to be realized in practice. For example, it was common practice for rural bosses to produce
bloc votes in any election in return for which they were guaranteed their
share of the power monopoly (Skidmore & Smith, 1984).

The military has a history of intervention in Brazilian politics, beginning with the fall of the last empire (Flynn, 1978). From the time of the
1964 coup d'etat until the civilian government took over in March 1985,
the country was governed by generals along with coalitions of military
officers, technocrat administrators, and old-line politicians. The military
influence remains strong today. Many social and government institutions have characteristics that are associated with the military, such as
an emphasis on conformity, hierarchical structure, and strict status
differentiation.

B. Economic Conditions

In the past, Brazil's economy was based largely on agricultural production. However, during the 1970s coffee was surpassed by manufactured goods as Brazil's leading export, and this trend has continued with
greater industrialization.

Economic difficulties have plagued Brazil, although there was a
period of rapid growth from 1968 to 1974. An extraordinarily high inflation rate (e.g., 233% in 1985), labor strikes, world recession, severe
unemployment (as much as 40%) and the Third World's highest foreign
debt have served to dampen economic development, as the government
struggles to build an infrastructure and industrialize the agricultural
economy. These have also exacerbated economic inequalities within Brazilian society. Socioeconomically, Brazil is a two-tiered society with a
thin middle-class layer. In addition, nonrational mechanisms such as
side payments and a large, secondary "black market" economy have

become important for both public resource allocations and personnel selection.

Facing falling agricultural exports during the Great Depression, the Brazilian government invited a number of foreign investors into its domestic industry, hoping to obtain access to modern technologies that could not be as quickly developed internally. Many of Brazil's larger firms are foreign-owned, especially by British and American companies. These foreign capitalists maintain strong bonds with the country's powerful political leaders (Evans, 1979). However, strong feelings of nationalism coupled with what the military government saw as the requirements of national security limited foreign investment in many industrial sectors. In 1984, nearly 500 of the largest firms were state-owned, with former and active generals occupying positions of top management. The country's huge foreign debt is sometimes ascribed to the mismanagement of these state-owned firms (*Business Week,* June 1985, p. 51).

C. Demographic Conditions

Brazil is a multiracial society. The importation of slaves to work the large coffee and sugar plantations during Colonial times, coupled with European immigration and the indigenous Indian population, added a strong ethnic dimension to Brazilian society and influenced value systems and customs. Unlike the situation in the United States, racial identity is not governed by a rigid descent rule, and more than a dozen racial categories may be recognized, each grading into the next (Harris, 1964). In fact, individuals in the same family may be considered to be of different races, and there is intermarriage and social mobility across racial lines. Although racial discrimination and stratification may appear to be substantially less than in the United States, race is strongly correlated with social status (Degler, 1971). However, "race" may change with social mobility. Brazilians say "money whitens," meaning that the richer or more successful a dark individual becomes, the lighter will be the racial category to which he is assigned by others.

D. Social Conditions

Prior to the military regime, Brazil had a democratic constitution, influenced by the American legal system. However, implementation in general was guided by patron–client relationships rather than by the letter of the law. Persons of power and status protected less powerful persons by granting favors in return for labor, goods, loyalty, and political alliance (Hall, 1977). Patrons were thus able to monopolize political power, wealth, education, and communication with the central government (Stein & Stein, 1970).

This system originated with the agricultural plantations that were economically, politically, and geographically distant from the centralized government. In consequence, family background and personal links with powerful figures, rather than individual competence, have been important determinants of social mobility and benefits. Mutual benefits rather than legal regulations play a critical role in making decisions (Hall, 1977; Skidmore & Smith, 1984).

E. Religious Homogeneity

Roman Catholicism has been the national religion of Brazil since the Portuguese invasion, and more than 90% of the population is Roman Catholic. Catholicism is, compared to Protestantism, generally considered to be more hierarchical and authoritarian, placing greater emphasis on conformity, and reinforcing the patron–client relationship typical of the political system (Hall, 1977).

F. Summary

The Brazilian attributes described before may have had a decisive influence on the genesis and formation of Brazilian social systems, including institutions of higher education. The themes of centralization, formalization, dualism, and dichotomization emerge from the cultural context of Brazil. Political, social, and economic power are centralized, and these power relationships tend to be formalized. However, daily intercourse takes place along dual systems—the formally prescribed system may bear little resemblance to the informal system by which transactions are actually accomplished and decisions are made. Detailed, rational rules and procedures are circumvented via acknowledged rule-breaking processes, side payments, and informally structured relationships. Dichotomization is evidenced in the distinctions between rich and poor, patron and client, superior and subordinate.

III. SIMILARITIES BETWEEN BRAZILIAN AND U.S. INSTITUTIONS

Before discussing incongruencies between Brazilian and U.S. institutions of higher education, it is useful to point out some obvious similarities. Consistent with the proposition that technology constrains organizational form (Hickson, Pugh, & Phesey, 1969; Thompson, 1967), both systems are characterized by several formal consistencies. To help make those similarities clear, however, it is necessary to describe briefly the overall higher education system in Brazil.

At the time of the study, 891 institutions of higher education existed in Brazil. Of this group, 819 were known as "invisible" schools, characterized by a large percentage of part-time instructors, few terminal degree holders on the faculty, a relatively narrow range of programs offered, low enrollments, and no federal support. The remaining group consisted of federal institutions, universities, and a few "isolated" (i.e., private) schools that had achieved much higher status in the country as institutions of higher education. These were characterized by full-time faculty, research emphasis, and a broad array of programmatic offerings. Whereas invisible schools comprise about 92% of the total number of institutions in Brazil, they had only about 35% of the enrollments. Approximately 65% of student enrollments were associated with the latter, more prestigious schools.

Examples of some obvious similarities between this system and that found in the U.S. are as follows:

1. *Similar spectrum of organization types.* Both the Brazilian and U.S. systems include institutions that are either publicly or privately funded. Public institutions are almost all federally funded in Brazil, however, whereas in the United States they are almost all state funded. Public institutions are larger on average than private institutions in both countries. In addition, a similar set of degrees is offered across both systems so that distinctions such as those made by the Carnegie Commission in the United States—for example, liberal arts, comprehensive, major doctoral institutions—are also typical of Brazilian institutions.

2. *Two major communities.* Cameron (1987) suggested that each institution in the United States is characterized by two different "communities": the campus community and the disciplinary community. The campus community consists of activities such as teaching, student services, and administration, activities that occur within the boundaries of the institution itself. The disciplinary community consists of activities such as publication, obtaining research grants, and collegial interactions that may occur outside the boundaries of the institution. The success of the campus community is assessed by *effectiveness* measurements: The success of the disciplinary community is assessed by *quality* measurements. Similar to U.S. institutions, these two communities also typify Brazilian institutions. Both systems function to serve students' interests as well as the interests of the scholarly and professional constituencies.

3. *Loosely coupled systems.* The educational organizations of both countries lack tight internal coordination. In particular, instructional activity is decoupled from organizational control and structure. Although the university administration tends to exert relatively tight control of specific areas—students, faculty, and curriculum selection—the formal structure is nonintrusive regarding how teaching and research activities are actually carried out (March & Olsen, 1976; Weick, 1976). The formal structure of the universities is more concerned with overseeing the institution's ceremonial or ritual functions (Meyer & Rowan, 1978).

IV. SURPRISES REGARDING BRAZILIAN HIGHER EDUCATION AND CULTURE

The preceding characteristics constitute major similarities between the Brazilian and U.S. systems of higher education, and these would seem to uphold the cross-cultural application of organizational theory and practice. These consistencies make even more surprising the discovery of apparent contradictions between Brazilian practice and U.S. organizational theory. Those surprises are outlined briefly and are compared to popular prescriptions of generally accepted organizational theories.

At the outset of this discussion, it should be pointed out that the Brazilian higher education system is generally considered to be the best in Latin America. The effectiveness and quality of Brazilian colleges and universities was unquestioned among the individuals interviewed. This implies that whatever contradictions exist between theory and practice do not seem to negatively affect overall institutional performance.

1. *Few financial incentives for excellence exist.* It was surprising to note that all faculty members are paid at the same rate throughout Brazil, provided they are at the same position level. Promotions from level to level within major faculty ranks are automatic every 2 years, regardless of academic achievement in terms of publications, teaching evaluations, or peer group assessment. Formal evaluations occur when faculty are promoted to a different rank (e.g., full professor), but levels within ranks—which determine salary level—are reached automatically.

This practice appears to contradict the predictions of expectancy theory (Vroom, 1964), probably the most commonly accepted theory of motivation in the U.S. According to expectancy theory, when no connection exists between the effort expended, the likelihood of successful performance, and valued outcomes (e.g., pay and promotion), motivation will be zero.

Of course, other valued outcomes and rewards may be present for faculty and administrators in Brazilian institutions, and the theory may still hold. On the other hand, pay and promotion rewards lie at the center of the motivation system in most U.S. institutions—especially for the campus community—and it would be difficult to imagine the presence of high motivation if pay and promotion of faculty members were removed as rewards. Mitchell (1974) concluded that most tests of expectancy theory have been culturally biased, and this observation of Brazilian university functioning suggests that its tenets may not be universal.

2. *Norms do not exist to govern work and productivity.* It is not clear how much time or effort should be expended by university faculty members or what output level is acceptable. There is wide divergence in faculty member behavior. At the time of the study, there was an enormous inflation rate in Brazil (over 220% annually) that led the International Monetary Fund to impose strict guidelines on any pay increases given to federal employees. Faculty members at public institutions (all of whom are federal employees), therefore, could not receive pay increases equal to the amount of inflation. Consequently, purchasing power of faculty salaries had fallen in 1984 to about 30% of what it had been 5 years earlier. Under these circumstances, it was not unusual for faculty members to obtain appointments in more than one institution—that is, to hold at least two full-time jobs. As a result, it became common for some faculty to appear only in the classroom, to take no additional assignments, and to be unavailable for departmental or school business. Both those who held other appointments and those who did not engaged in this behavior. At the same time, other faculty members worked 50 to 60 hour weeks, took their departmental and committee assignments seriously, conducted research, and performed other institutional support roles. No norms—or rewards—existed, however, to determine the extent to which this variance in behavior was appropriate.

This circumstance appears contradictory to the prescriptions of equity theory (Adams, 1965) and role theory (Biddle & Thomas, 1966). In simplistic terms, equity theory indicates that to be motivated to perform, individuals must perceive a congruence between their contributions and their rewards. That ratio must also be perceived as consistent with comparable others' ratios of contributions to rewards. Neither condition exists in Brazilian higher education. There is neither a consistent match between the effort and performance of faculty members and the rewards they receive (assuming salary and promotion as rewards) nor between one person's contribution–reward ratio and another person's. Motivation would be expected to be low but apparently is not.

Role theory research has suggested that a strong link exists between role clarity—the presence of norms and rules to clarify expectations of work—and performance. When lack of clarity exists or when ambiguity exists regarding expectations and rewards, dysfunctional consequences result (e.g., stress, turnover, dissatisfaction). No evidence exists that these consequences are any more prevalent in Brazilian institutions, however, than in U.S. institutions.

3. *The curriculum and base budgets of all federal universities are uniform.* Regardless of the geographical locale or size of the federal institution, curriculum and base budgets are standard throughout the country. This means that regardless of the unique needs of a particular city or region to prepare students for certain occupations or regardless of the special economic or social circumstances that may exist, institutions are highly standardized. Particularistic needs are not generally considered in the overall system.

This standardization seems to contradict both structural contingency theories (Lawrence & Lorsch, 1969) and strategic constituencies models of organizational effectiveness (Cameron, 1986; Zammuto, 1982). Structural contingency theories argue that the design of an effective organization depends on various contextual factors. Contingency theories predict that the goodness of fit between organization structures and the three major contingencies of size, technology, and environment will determine organizational effectiveness. Yet despite high variety in the size and environments of individual Brazilian institutions, technology (curriculum) and structure appear to be standard.

Similarly, one important approach to organizational effectiveness, called the strategic constituencies approach, defines effectiveness as the extent to which an institution at least minimally satisfies strategic constituencies. This means that to be successful, organizations must provide goods and services to both internal and external stakeholders. In the case of Brazilian colleges and universities, however, standardized curricula and budgets seem to contradict this need for responsiveness to multiple and varying demands. Institutional functioning occurs with little apparent regard for differences in constituencies.

Because Brazilian institutions of higher education seem to function effectively within these budget and curriculum policies, there must be other factors at work. Not only must we avoid applying structural contingency theories and multiple constituency approaches wholesale, but we must seek the specific factors that do lead to a satisfactory fit with the environment. A broader search for appropriate definitions of adaptiveness and "fit" may be an important agenda for organizational researchers.

4. *The federal government is heavily involved in both the professional disci-*

pline side of the university and the campus administration side of the university. As implied in 3, the discretion of local faculty and administrators is severely limited. In American universities, loose linkages with higher-level state and federal agencies are deemed essential to a high level of organizational effectiveness. Loose coupling is a hallmark of most U.S. educational institutions (Weick, 1976). Some of the functions served by loose coupling include the buffering of the core technology (i.e., faculty teaching) from external intervention, the preservation of academic freedom, the fostering of innovative and unconstrained research, the insulation of certain subunits from the problems or difficulties of other subunits, and the social control of widely dispersed personnel. Each of these functions is assumed to foster educational excellence in U.S. higher education. The centralized control of Brazilian universities, however, seems to contradict common assumptions about the value of loose coupling in educational institutions.

5. *Most administrators are elected.* Whereas department chair positions in many U.S. colleges and universities are elected by participating faculty, most administrative positions are elected in Brazilian institutions—from president to dean and department head. This creates the need for campaigning, side payments, and conservatism on the part of would-be administrators. High degrees of risk taking and entrepreneurship are frequently inhibited under such conditions because there is a need to nurture powerful coalition support and to avoid visible mistakes. The values of academic freedom may be threatened by the need to preserve position through political rather than through traditional scholarly means.

This practice exists because there is a distrust of authority figures throughout the Brazilian higher education system as well as through much of society. The election of administrators introduces political factors into what is usually regarded as a nonpolitical human service organization. The connection of candidates with political figures is usually regarded as the most important determinant of administrator selection.

The elective process for most administrative offices seems to contradict traditional assumptions about the value of loose coupling in knowledge-based institutions and the value of loose coupling for fostering scholarly activity. Much of the work on innovation and new venture creation in organizations suggests that separation and autonomy best foster these outcomes (MacMillan, 1985). The production of good scholarship is generally viewed as being associated with independence and academic freedom (Cameron, 1986). However, in political systems such as Brazilian institutions, many couplings must be tight because of the elective process: Compromise and campaigning would seem to inhibit academic work. Again, however, Brazilian institutions seem to operate in contradiction to these theoretical prescriptions.

6. *Universities are characterized by mandated turbulence.* Not only are most administrators elected in Brazilian institutions, but the terms of office are relatively short. Presidents serve only 4 years, deans serve 3 years, and department heads serve 2 years. Turnover is required by strictly limited terms for these administrative positions. If the purpose of the limited terms of administrative positions were to rotate jobs and provide a variety of experience for administrators, this seems to be a reasonable practice. However, the manifest reason for the imposed tenure cutoff is to limit the power and authority of individual administrators. Basic distrust of administrative power and centralization, stemming from a history of dictatorial rule in Brazil's political system, has led to conditions characterized by continual turbulence in administrative positions. Little long-term planning, lack of continuity of policies, and a tendency to wait out rather than resolve conflicts with personnel are all likely consequences of such turbulence.

This limited power and instability of top administrative teams is at variance with the practices mandated by contingency theories of organization design (Lawrence & Lorsch, 1969). Particularly under conditions of decline and turbulence, a stable administrative team should be necessary to carry out the core technology of educational organizations, teaching and research. However, in Brazilian colleges and universities, there appears to be a poor fit between organizational structures and their technology and environment. This, in turn, should result in organizational ineffectiveness. Yet again, Brazilian institutions of higher education appear to be functioning reasonably effectively.

7. *Only a few elite institutions receive the majority of federal grants and benefits.* Federal agencies (e.g., Coordenacao de Aperfeicoamento de Pessoal de Nivel Superior) evaluate the performance or quality of each institution each year. Unless the institution is evaluated highly, no federal benefits (e.g., operating expenses and self-improvement funds, *not* just research grants) are given. The evaluators themselves are almost always from a select group of institutions that are always evaluated highly. For the majority of Brazilian institutions, there is no chance for improvement. The higher the quality or perceived quality of the university, the more supportive the federal grant system. This practice serves to broaden the gap between good and poor performers, so that inevitable inequality prevails.

This practice of ignoring underfunded, lower quality units in a system seems to violate common strategic planning wisdom. That is, when units whose survival is vital to the overall system are not provided needed resources (as is the case with the 819 invisible institutions plus many other federal and private institutions that are always evaluated poorly), the system itself is severely weakened by the eventual demise of the unfunded units. Yet somehow these institutions, receiving neither federal grants and support nor public credibility, continue to survive and attract students, and they still constitute the large majority of institutions in Brazil.

In addition, the practice of selectively rewarding quality is as much a violation of the norms of justice and equity in the United States as it is a violation of the prescriptions of organizational theory. From the American criteria of distributive justice, the exclusive allocation of federal resources to elite universities is unjust: Representatives of the nonelite universities believe that they contribute as much to Brazilian society as do the elite institutions, albeit in different ways. A distribution is just when the relations between inputs and outputs are perceived as equal for all participants (Leventhal, 1976). This clearly is not the case in Brazil, yet no serious interorganizational conflict seems to occur. Martin's (1981) theory of relative deprivation is therefore violated by this practice. According to Martin, an unjust distribution of critical resources should result in conflict between the elite and the deprived, yet such a predicted outcome is not generally observed in Brazil.

8. *Political pull, nepotism, or graft is the most common explanation for the receipt of benefits.* Both inside and outside the university, research grants, professional development opportunities, and so on are seen as products of informal, marginally ethical payoffs or political connections. Although political connections are a universal source of power, this extreme case may reflect the conditions of Brazilian society. In Brazil, political rather than rational explanations are generally more persuasive in understanding the distribution of public resources. This tendency may have increased since the generals took power in the coup of 1964. If political pull, nepotism, and graft came to be regarded as the most effective means for getting things done, university members are simply part of this trend. The Brazilian characteristics of dualism and dichotomization intensify the significance of political and nonrational factors in decision making. What is noteworthy is that the Brazilian higher education system seems to be functioning effectively, despite these practices that are dysfunctional in terms of U.S. theories of distributive and procedural justice.

9. *No accountability is maintained for the receipt of federal financial benefits.* There is no monitoring of research grants, professional leaves, or the receipt of other federal benefits. No knowledge exists of what benefit Brazil gets from the monies expended. The federal agencies controlling

universities appear to be more interested in the maximum display of their power and control over resources than in auditing the effectiveness of their distributions. To some degree, there is always difficulty in evaluating the outcomes of educational grants and benefits: The criteria are inherently ambiguous, and the outcomes are difficult to measure. However, the absence of formal, even ritual, procedures for checking the coupling between inputs and outputs is noticeable in Brazilian institutions of higher education.

The absence of accountability for federal funds may encourage universities to concentrate on how to obtain as many federal benefits as possible, rather than on how to effectively utilize the resources received. If Brazilian universities operate effectively without any monitoring system, this contradicts U.S. theories of goal accomplishment and motivation. Locke (1968, 1978) and Locke *et al.* (1981) identified accountability for goal accomplishment as a critical factor in predicting successful performance. When individuals did not have to account for their performance, they performed less well than those who were assessed and held accountable. Similarly, the lack of assessment, monitoring, and accountability associated with the distribution of resources by federal agencies in Brazil would suggest widespread waste and ineffective performance. Although there is no evidence to indicate what really is the case in Brazil, the practice clearly contradicts the prescriptions of U.S. organizational theory.

10. *In most universities, less qualified, and even unqualified, faculty members determine the promotion to full professor of those with higher degrees.* Faculty members reach the level of full professor only by passing an examination constructed by peers who, in most cases, do not have PhDs. In many universities, those without doctorates have the responsibility of testing PhD holders on their expertise, although the PhD knows far better than the examiners what the examination should contain. This results partly from a shortage of full professors holding PhDs in Brazilian universities.

This practice also seems to be at variance with U.S. motivation theories that would predict faculty members' dissatisfaction with the promotion system and decreased commitment to organizational objectives (Adams, 1965). Equity theories of motivation clearly associate motivation and performance with perceptions of fairness and equality. This promotion system, however, is seen by midlevel PhD holders as arbitrary and neither fair nor equitable. At the same time, however, the system is not challenged or changed, and promotion continues to be reliant on practices that contradict U.S. theories of effective organizational functioning.

A. Summary

These ten characteristics of Brazilian universities can be classified into three main themes: centralization of structures, formalization of structures, and political processes in decision making. The undeviating reward and promotion systems, the strictly limited terms of administrative positions, uniform curriculum and base budget, and the exam for promotion to full professor are all examples of the formalized structure of Brazilian universities. The importance of political factors is revealed in the election of administrators, the use of political connections and side payments for federal grants, and, implicitly, in the exclusive receipt of federal benefits by a few elite institutions. The Brazilian system of higher education is also heavily centralized: Decisions about the two major functions of the university, administration and professional disciplines, are usually made by the federal government.

Contradictions to U.S. organizational theory generally fall into three main categories as well. First, several of the attributes of Brazilian institutions contradict commonly accepted theories of motivation. In particular, expectancy theory, equity theory, and goal theories appear not to be predictive of successful performance in Brazilian colleges and universities. Contradictions to those three theories are rampant (see characteristics 1, 2, 7, 9, and 10). Similarly, contingency theories of organization design, including prescriptions for loose/tight coupling, seem to be contradicted by Brazilian institutional practices (see characteristics 3, 4, 5, and 6). Inappropriately, tight coupling is present in some instances, whereas in others insufficient accountability and monitoring occur. Finally, prescriptions resulting from distributive justice theories are also contradicted by the centralized, yet political and seemingly arbitrary functioning of the governance structure (see characteristics 3, 4, 7, and 8). Resource allocation and gatekeeping functions appear to violate principles of justice and equity commonly accepted in most U.S. organizations.

It should be noted that the themes and issues emerging from our observation of Brazilian universities are consistent with the cultural characteristics identified previously in the chapter. The dominance of political criteria in decision making can be inferred from the combination of all four cultural aspects—centralization, formalization, dichotomization, and dualism. These make it likely that members of the Brazilian education system will rely on political factors as the most efficient mechanism for getting things done.

With the previously mentioned attributes in mind, American scholars, armed with their predictive principles of organization design, might be tempted to assume that most Brazilian universities are in trouble. We do not know exactly how effectively the Brazilian universities characterized by these attributes meet the demands of their multiple constituencies (e.g., students, faculty members, administrators, and society). But given the fact that most Brazilian universities have survived over a long period of time without serious challenge and have contributed to national development (Lawlor, 1985), U.S. theories of organization seem to fail to apply in Brazil, at least in the predictive sense. Social systems have vocabularies of effective functioning that do not always survive translation.

But we must use caution in assessing the lack of fit of U.S. organizational theories in Brazil as well as in their application. What appear to be anomalies may in fact be perfectly reasonable systems, consistent with many principles of organizational functioning, once culturally contingent factors are considered. For example, it has been pointed out that Brazilian practices relating to pay, promotion, and the distribution of federal benefits seem to violate commonly accepted theories of motivation. However, it is possible that outcomes other than pay and promotion, unobserved but nonetheless valued, are acting as sufficient motivators for Brazilian faculty. A general expectancy theory may apply, but we are using culturally biased and subjective outcomes to test it (Mitchell, 1974). The incentives used may be different than those we are accustomed to measuring.

Goal theory need not be contradicted if we consider the Brazilian tendency to base important decisions on political criteria rather than on academic output. Alternative goals, such as conforming to strong social norms regarding professional work, may be in operation. Although these goals are not specific in nature, they may serve to motivate hard work on the part of the faculty. In fact, the second distinctive attribute discussed before follows logically from the first. Brazilian universities could be unable to enforce specific norms of productivity because these would be incongruent with the uniform and automatic reward schedules used.

The practice of basing promotions to full professor on an exam, often constructed by less qualified faculty members, is consistent with the formalized systems that exist throughout Brazil. These overt aspects of the system, along with the uncontrollable nature of a shortage of PhD holders, may lead to widespread acceptance of the practice. The dissatisfiers that operate in the United States are not necessarily relevant in Brazil.

Likewise, practices that seem to violate the prescriptions of structural contingency theories may be appropriate when the cultural environment is also considered. Centralized control was found to be a property of many Brazilian systems throughout the country's history. If tight, centralized control does not work against the effectiveness of Brazilian universities, then the fit between technology and organizational structure predicted by contingency theories seems to be moderated by Brazilian cultural variables. It might be the case that centralized control is more effective in a turbulent, often unstable environment.

The Brazilian systems of mandated turbulence and elected administrators also fit well with Brazilian formalization, centralization and dualism. Although elected administrators are relatively powerless, the business of the university may be carried on by other, nonelected administrators and subordinates and by systems outside the elected administration. These practices encourage the development of written rules and enable central agencies to exert more control over universities. However, delineated, rational rules may coexist with implicitly acknowledged rule-breaking procedures. The cultural fit of organizational structures may alleviate, or even make irrelevant, any dysfunctional effects of the structural misfit with noncultural contingencies.

We should also use caution in applying U.S. theories of procedural and distributive justice. The theories themselves may be applicable, whereas the definitions of justice are more culture-specific. Justice criteria vary with social characteristics (Sampson 1980), and the Brazilian concept of distributive justice is likely to be different than that found in the United States. The previously noted dichotomies in Brazil may provide one explanation. Allocations are made, not on the basis of need, but according to maximum mutual interest, which will be served best by offering grants to the category of elites. Social and political power in Brazil are most effectively increased via favorable relationships with powerful others. If the dichotomization of Brazilian society is accepted implicitly, then institutions that are excluded from federal grants and benefits may accept this practice without serious resistance.

The procedural elements of a decision affect the degree of justice perceived in the decision (Tibaut & Walker, 1975). Although the Brazilian distribution system may violate American ideas of procedural justice, it may be considered acceptable in Brazil. If the system is accepted and functions without serious challenge, then perhaps Brazilians operate under a different, independent definition of justice. Using this definition, the use of political criteria in the allocation of valued resources is deemed acceptable. In sum, definitions of distributive and procedural justice in Brazil may be different from those of the United States simply because they originated in different social and justice systems (Hall, 1977).

V. EXPLANATION BASED ON HOFSTEDE'S BRAZIL

Further understanding of the nature of these surprising characteristics of Brazilian institutions comes from Hofstede (1980a). Although
it has limitations, many reviewers and critics agree that Hofstede's study
of attitudes, perceptions, and preferences about work in 40 countries is a
solid and comprehensive study of the relationship between culture and
organizational phenomena (Child & Tayeb, 1982; Jaeger, 1986; Sorge,
1983). Although there are certainly differences between the members of
the IBM Brazil branch and those of Brazil's higher education system,
what IBM's employees possess as Brazilians, we assume, is shared by
those in universities. Hofstede's data on Brazil and the United States
were utilized as supplementary data in our analysis. This was done with
some caution, considering that admittedly, we do now know the extent
to which Brazilian culture has changed since Hofstede's data were collected in 1972. However, there is a great deal of evidence that cultural
patterns change very slowly. It is therefore unlikely that our interview
data were gathered in a cultural context that was significantly different
from what Hofstede found 12 years earlier.

According to Hofstede (1980a), *power distance* represents the extent
to which unequally distributed power is accepted in organizations. Citizens of a country with a high score on this dimension tend to feel
comfortable with strong leadership. *Uncertainty avoidance* refers to the
extent to which people try to avoid uncertain conditions. High uncertainty avoidance is associated with tendencies to seek career stability
and establish formal rules and with intolerance of deviant behavior.
Innovative thinking is regarded as inefficient. "Individualism" scores
express the degree of self-interest seeking. Individualistic people are
expected to place more emphasis on their own gains than on collective
goals. *Masculinity* measures the extent to which individuals value material wealth and being assertive over interpersonal relations. People with
high masculinity scores are likely to be workaholics and to achieve goals
such as money and status.

As can be seen in Table 11.1, Brazil scores above average and higher
than the United States on power distance (Brazil 60, United States 40,
Mean 51) and uncertainty avoidance (Brazil 76, United States 46, Mean
64). Brazil scores below average and lower than the United States on
individualism (Brazil 38, U.S. 91, Mean 51) and masculinity (Brazil 49,
U.S. 62, Mean 51). Based on these scores, Brazilians are expected to
prefer strong, autocratic leadership, security over uncertainty, and conservatism over innovativeness. They are expected to deemphasize self-
interest and to value interpersonal relations over individual achieve-

Table 11.1. Comparison between Brazil and the United States
on Hofstede's Four Value Dimensions[a]

Value dimensions	Rank (actual score)		Mean (median)	Range
	United States	Brazil		
Power distance	26 (40)	7 (69)	51 (56)	11–94
Uncertainty avoidance	32 (46)	16 (76)	64 (62)	8–112
Individualism	1 (91)	25 (38)	51 (50)	12–91
Masculinity	13 (62)	23 (49)	51 (53)	5–95

[a]Based on Hofstede (1980a).

ment. The three themes identified here are well connected with these value scores.

Because the preferred control system in a culture depends on those who are being led (Ouchi & Jaeger, 1978), it can be inferred from the previously listed scores that, relative to the people of the United States, Brazilians desire more dominant leadership and are likely to endorse a more centralized organization structure. The heavy involvement of the federal government in university activities, for example, reflects this tendency. Brazilians would also be expected to favor more autocratic, less participative leadership styles than would be tolerated in the United States.

In addition, persons in a culture with a high power distance score are expected to tolerate inequality and the illegitimate use of power (Hofstede, 1980b). This trend is manifested in the significance of political criteria in resource allocations made by Brazilian federal agencies and in the exclusive distribution of benefits to a few elite universities.

Uncertainty avoidance relates to a need for written rules and regulations (Hofstede, 1980a; Pfeffer, 1981). The risk aversion of Brazilians may lead them to establish more formalized systems, for example, uniform salary levels, automatic promotion systems, standardized curriculum, and nonprioritized budget allocation. In countries with high uncertainty avoidance, a large number of new policies tend to be initiated by legislation rather than by local experiment (Jaeger, 1986). Therefore, government-guided organizational change, rather than initiatives undertaken at individual institutions, is more pervasive in Brazil.

The principles of expectancy theory, which emphasize the individual's expectation of a return or consequence for every act, may work best in cultures with high scores on individualism. In the United States, with its extremely high score, this theory may explain individual moti-

222   Kim S. Cameron *et al.*

vation. It might be less helpful in Brazil, where tight links between the contributions given and the incentives received (March & Simon, 1958) are not sought so vigorously. It is also plausible that a high degree of collectivism allows Brazilians to tolerate and adapt efficiently to a centralized and formalized system as well as to institutionally imposed practices that appear, to American eyes, unjust.

VI. DISCUSSION

We have noted several differences between practices in the higher education systems of Brazil and the United States. Following the predictions of U.S. organizational theories, many of these practices would seem to be dysfunctional and to limit the effectiveness of Brazilian universities. Some of these practices seem to refute the applicability of expectancy and goal theories of motivation, contingency theories of organization design, and theories of distributive justice, particularly if cultural factors are ignored.

Yet the Brazilian higher education system seems to be effective. The system and the individual institutions within it continue to operate along the lines spelled out here with few or no serious challenges in evidence. A population ecology view of effectiveness is taken here; we are assuming that if the institutions in question are surviving and operate without serious challenge to their existence, then they are effective within their context.

This leaves several factors to be addressed. First, the addition of cultural considerations would seem to enhance the applicability of many organizational theories developed in the United States. In some cases, the theories themselves may survive more or less intact, but the variables within them need to be redefined. For example, the pay and promotion practices of the Brazilian higher education system would be expected to act as demotivators if one assumes, as is often done in the United States, that pay or promotion opportunities are primary motivators and should function as rewards for a given level of output. However, if we allow the prominence of other incentives, for example, professional status, esteem from one's peers, or the opportunity to do interesting research, the pay and promotion systems need not be dysfunctional. Furthermore, these systems may be well accepted by organization members due to other factors in the Brazilian context, particularly the emphasis on formalization and centralized control.

Many Brazilian practices seem to violate structural contingency theories. Federal control of budgets, curriculum, professional disciplines, and university administration ignore the more localized requirements of individual universities. This system tightens outside linkages, where the core technology of education seems to require loose coupling between the institution and outside agencies. The relatively short tenure of administrative teams makes them less able to confront the challenges and turbulence facing each university as well as creating a new, internal source of turbulence. However, centralized control may be appropriate for the turbulent environment that exists throughout Brazil. Distrust of local authority figures may well serve the purposes of federal-level administrators, particularly if a primary purpose is to consolidate power. This system may also be well accepted because formalization and centralization are seen throughout the Brazilian environment and because the presence of parallel formal and informal systems allows each institution to function effectively despite oversight and intrusion from the federal level.

Theories of procedural and distributive justice developed in the United States are violated in a system that reinforces the positions of elites by relying on political pull and side payments to determine the receipt of federal financial and professional benefits. This virtually ensures that only elite insitutions and their members will receive benefits. But these theories rely on perceptions of justice rather than on some objective standard. If the system is well accepted by the members of both elite and nonelite Brazilian institutions, then a different perception of what is just is likely to be in operation. In addition, this system is congruent with the dichotomization and dualism that exist elsewhere in Brazil. Even if the system is not accepted as inherently just, it may function effectively simply because organization members see it as immutable, as a reflection of how society in general is known to operate.

Another issue to be addressed is the definition of effectiveness. From the population ecology perspective, the higher education systems in both Brazil and the United States operate effectively. That is, they are surviving within their environments and are therefore effective. However, we should acknowledge the probability that the criteria for effectiveness within each system are likely to differ on both the institutional and the individual levels. Using the strategic constituencies approach to effectiveness, for example, points out important differences between the two systems' perspectives.

The purpose of the Brazilian system of higher education may be, at least partly, to reinforce the position of those elites that seem to benefit most from it. It may also serve as another avenue for the consolidation of power in the hands of the central agencies and prominent political figures. The production of quality teaching and research and academic excellence may be only secondary criteria in judging the effectiveness of an institution or of the system as a whole. And because each institution

depends on the patronage of centralized authorities and political figures, it behooves them to consider the purposes of these entities in their
own operations and practices.

Likewise, individual faculty members may be judged primarily on
the strength of their political connections and their ability to exploit
them rather than on the, often more nebulous, criterion of academic
excellence. If the ability to pull in federal benefits is paramount to survival, and yet there is no investigation of the return received in exchange
for those benefits, it makes sense for political considerations to take
precedence over research production or teaching excellence. If the formal system pays all faculty at the same rate, within a given level, but an
informal system based on political pull and graft allows more expansive
benefits, then emphasis will be given to the informal system.

Political criteria and machinations are certainly not absent in the
American system of higher education. In particular, institutions dependent on the largesse of federal and state governments must be sure to
meet their requirements in the production of qualified students and
research or the application of knowledge. Conflicting coalitions often
demand a voice in how universities will operate. Individual organization
members acknowledge that political and power considerations enter
into many kinds of decisions. However, this is much more obvious in
Brazil and is seen as the central way of operating rather than as an
ancillary consideration. The dual systems in Brazil are much more
pronounced.

No value judgments are implied here. We are simply saying that the
effectiveness of each system ought to be evaluated according to its own
criteria. Whether or not these are valid criteria is a separate issue. In the
case of Brazil, the primary purpose of the higher education system may
be to reinforce existing power and benefit relationships. Centralized
control may be perfectly appropriate to maintain the overall system in a
highly turbulent environment, although it may not allow each institution to maximize production, productivity, or its own interests within its
microenvironment. A system depending heavily on political pull and
graft may be considered acceptable, and even efficient, within a society
that relies heavily on often cumbersome formal procedures alongside an
informal expediting system.

VII. IMPLICATIONS

As discussed before, the basic frameworks of many organization
theories developed in the United States seem to apply to the Brazilian

system of higher education, but the specific variables and relationships within those frameworks may not. Brazilians operating within this system exert efforts in accordance with their expectations of the link between efforts and outcomes. Their own perceptions of justice are important to the acceptance of the distribution of resources and of the procedures for determining the distribution. They consider the contingencies of technology along with environmental characteristics to structure their organizations efficiently. However, the "made-in-America" links among the elements of theories may not be applicable to organizations existing in different cultures. It may be that a given concept underlying organizational theory exists across cultures, but the value attached to that concept changes significantly from one culture to another.

Understanding this limitation is particularly important when using organizational theories for prescriptive purposes. Wholesale application of U.S. organization theory, intact, to the Brazilian context is likely to be ineffective at best, and damaging at worst, unless the cultural aspects underlying the processes addressed are also considered. Organizational systems arise from many factors, including technology, economic system, or even climate (Child, 1981). But they are also partially manifestations of the culture within which they exist; this cannot be overlooked when seeking to apply the product of U.S. organizational research abroad, even if the theories are being used as a framework for investigation. Underlying assumptions must be investigated to determine modifications needed in the framework, or if the framework is appropriate at all.

VIII. CONCLUSION

The research discussed in this chapter was not undertaken with any *a priori* hypotheses about the applicability of organizational theories developed and accepted in the United States, nor did the researchers have strong prior expectations about what kinds of practices would be found in Brazil. The purpose of the investigation was simply to develop an understanding of the Brazilian higher education system so that potential synergies could be fostered. In his naiveté, Cameron had no *a priori* expectation that contradictions and inconsistencies would be encountered. Hence the surprise at the differences that were observed.

These differences are interesting, in that they lead us to question the universal applicability of theories developed on the basis of how organizations in the United States are designed and function. Because the Brazilian higher education system is functioning, and without serious challenge, it has been labeled *effective* in its environment. Given this, the apparent violation of many well-accepted theories of organizational functioning and design calls into question their utility in cross-cultural investigations. Although the basic theory may be valid, the assumptions underlying specific relationships and linkages may not be. The Brazilian system is operating according to its own definition of effectiveness.

ACKNOWLEDGMENTS

The senior author would like to extend special thanks to the Fulbright commission for financial support through the Distinguished Scholar Program. He also gratefully acknowledges the financial support of the Graduate School of Business, University of Michigan.

IX. REFERENCES

Adams, J. S. (1965). Inequity in social exchange. In L. Berkowitz (Ed.), *Advances in experimental psychology* (pp. 100–235). New York: Academic.

Adler, N. J. (1983c). Cross-cultural management research: The ostrich and the trend. *Academy of management review, 8,* 226–232.

Biddle, B. J., & Thomas, E. J. (1966). *Role theory: Concepts and research.* New York: Wiley.

Business Week (June, 1985). "Now It's All up to Brazil's Young Turks," pp. 51–54.

Cameron, K. S. (1986). Effectiveness as paradox: Consensus and conflict in conceptions of organizational effectiveness. *Management Science, 32,* pp. 539–553.

Cameron, K. S. (1987). Effectiveness and quality in higher education. In M. W. Peterson & L. A. Mets (Eds.), *Governance, management and leadership* (pp. 222–242). San Francisco: Jossey-Bass.

Child, J. (1981). Culture, contingency and capitalism in the cross-national study of organizations. *Research in Organizational Behavior, 3,* 303–356.

Child, J., & Tayeb, M. (1982). Theoretical perspectives in cross-national organizational research. *International Studies of Management and Organizations, 12*(4), 23–70.

Degler, K. (1971). *Neither black nor white: Slavery and race relations in Brazil and the United States.* New York: Macmillan.

Evans, P. (1979). *Dependent development: The alliance of multinational, state and local capital in Brazil.* Princeton, NJ: Princeton University Press.

Flynn, P. (1978). *Brazil: A political analysis.* Boulder, CO: Westview.

Haire, M., Ghiselli, E. E., & Porter, L. W. (1963). Cultural patterns in the role of the manager. *Industrial Relations, 2,* 95–117.

Hall, A. (1977). Patron-client relations: Concepts and terms. In S. W. Schmidt, J. C. Scott, C. Lande, & L. Guasti (Eds.), *Friends, followers and factions* (pp. 510–512). Berkeley, CA: University of California Press.

Harris, M. (1964). *Patterns of race in the Americas.* New York: W. W. Norton.

Hickson, D. J., Pugh, D. S., & Phesey, D. C. (1969). Operations, technology and organization structure. An empirical reappraisal. *Administrative Science Quarterly, 14*, 378–397.

Hofstede, G. (1980a, Summer). Motivation, leadership and organizations. Do American theories apply abroad? *Organizational Dynamics*, 42–63.

Hofstede, G. (1980b). *Culture's consequences. International differences in work-related values.* Beverly Hills, CA: Sage.

Hofstede, G. (1984). The cultural relativity of the quality of life concept. *Academy of Management Review, 9*, 389–398.

Jaeger, A. M. (1986). Organization development and national culture. Where's the fit? *Academy of Management Review, 11*, 178–190.

Lawlor, H. (1985). Education and national development in Brazil. In Brock, C., & Lawlor, H. (Eds.), *Education in Latin America* (pp. 130–145). Dover, NH: Croom Helm.

Lawrence, P. R., & Lorsch, J. W. (1969). *Organization and environment.* Homewood, IL: Irwin.

Leventhal, G. S. (1976). The distribution of rewards and resources in groups and organizations. In L. Berkowitz & E. Walster (Eds.), *Advances in experimental social psychology, 9*, 92–133.

Locke, E. A. (1968). Toward a theory of task motivation and incentives. *Organizational Behavior and Human Performance, 3*, 157–189.

Locke, E. A. (1978). The ubiquity of goal setting theories of and approach to employee motivation. *Academy of Management Review, 3*, 594–601.

Locke, E. A., Shaw, K. N., Saari, L. M., & Latham, G. P. (1981). Goal setting and task performance: 1969–1980. *Psychological Bulletin, 95*, 125–152.

MacMillan, I. C. (1985). Progress in research on corporate venturing. New York University: Center for Entrepreneurial Studies.

March, J. G., & Olsen, J. P. (1976). *Ambiguity and choice in organizations.* Bergen, Norway: Universitetsforlaget.

March, J. G., & Simon, H. A. (1958). *Organizations.* New York: Wiley.

Martin, J. (1981). Relative deprivation: A theory of distributive justice for an era of shrinking resources. *Research in Organizational Behavior, 3*, 53–107.

Meyer, J. W., & Rowan, B. (1978). The structure of educational organizations. In M. Meyer (Ed.), *Environments and organizations.* San Francisco: Jossey-Bass.

Mitchell, T. R. (1974). Expectancy models of job satisfaction, occupational preference, and effort. A theoretical, methodological, and empirical appraisal. *Psychological Bulletin, 81*, 1053–1070.

Ouchi, W. G. (1981). *Theory Z: How American business can meet the Japanese Challenge.* Reading, MA: Addison-Wesley.

Ouchi, W. G., & Jaeger, A. M. (1978). Type Z organizations: Stability in the midst of mobility. *Academy of Management Review, 3*, 305–314.

Pascale, R. T., & Athos, A. G. (1981). *The art of Japanese management.* New York: Warner.

Pfeffer, J. (1981). *Power in organizations.* Marshfield, MA: Pitman.

Sampson, E. E. (1980). Justice and social character. In G. Mikila (Ed.), *Justice and social interaction* (pp. 285–313). New York: Springer-Verlag.

Skidmore, T. E., & Smith, P. H. (1984). *Modern Latin America.* New York: Oxford University Press.

Sorge, A. (1983b). Culture's consequences: International differences in work-related values. *Administrative Science Quarterly, 28*, 625–629.

Stein, S. J., & Stein, B. H. (1970). *The colonial heritage of Latin America.* New York: Oxford University Press.

Thompson, J. D. (1967). *Organizations in action*. New York: McGraw-Hill.

Tibaut, J., & Walker, L. (1975). *Procedural justice: A psychological analysis*. Hillsdale, NJ: Erlbaum.

Triandis, H. C., Malpas, R. S., & Davidson, A. R. (1973). Psychology and culture. *Annual Review of Psychology, 24*, 355–374.

Vroom, V. (1964). *Work and motivation*. New York: Wiley.

Weick, K. E. (1976). Educational organizations as loosely coupled systems. *Administrative Science Quarterly, 21*, 1–19.

Zammuto, R. F. (1982). *Assessing organizational effectiveness*. Albany, NY: State University of New York-Albany Press.

12

The Influence of Societal Culture on Corporate Culture, Business Strategy, and Performance in the International Airline Industry

Durhane Wong-Rieger and Fritz Rieger

I. INTRODUCTION

Culture is defined as the agreed upon set of values, norms, and behaviors shared by the members of a particular social group (Segall, 1979; see also Adler, Doktor, and Redding, Chapter 2). Organizations exist in at least three different types of cultures: societal, industry, and corporate. The purpose of this study is to examine the influence of these cultures on the operating strategies and policies of international airlines.

A. Societal Culture

Societal culture refers to the norms, roles, and values generally accepted by the societal members. At the organizational level, it influences the structure, work roles, processes, and operating values of the entire organization (Child, 1981; Hofstede, 1980; Maurice & Brossard, 1976). At

Durhane Wong-Rieger and Fritz Rieger • Department of Management, University of Windsor, Windsor, Ontario N9B 3P4, Canada.

the individual level, societal culture influences the cognitive processes and leadership style of key decision makers.

B. Industry Culture

Industry culture encompasses two types of norms and values. The first is the formally accepted rules and regulations as defined by industry associations or cartels. The second includes the informally shared assumptions and operating principles, that is, the "common wisdom" about how to succeed in the industry and the generally accepted managerial "recipes" about how to organize the firm under various circumstances (Grinyer & Spender, 1979). As such, it depends upon environmental factors such as availability of resources, market conditions, and available technology, and this drives organizations in the same industry toward similar functional systems and production methods. Industry culture reflects not only the values and beliefs of the current industry leaders and participants but also those of the industry's founders (Mintzberg, 1979; Stinchcombe, 1965).

This perspective does not necessarily imply that all industries will have uniform cultures. Indeed, the variability of strategic orientations within an industry has been well demonstrated (see, for example, Harrigan, 1980; Hatten, Schendel, & Cooper, 1978; Miles, 1982; Porter, 1980). However, in some industries, the range of strategic alternatives appears to be more constrained than in others. Industry culture is uniform and strong to the extent that there is consensus among the participants on issues of production and competition. It is therefore especially strong in industries where competitors collude to regulate competition and ·prices through cartellike associations such as the International Air Transport Association (IATA). Additional influences contributing to this effect are intergovernmental agreements, the tendency of the smaller, newer airlines to follow the practices established by the larger and older airlines, and the tendency of the industry to evolve "recipes" for reacting to the competitive environment. Industry culture is also strengthened by the relative homogeneity of the technological and competitive environment, which in the airline industry is defined by a highly singular technology and a limited number of suppliers.

Conversely, uniformity is lessened in the airline industry by small affiliative networks and regional influences. These influences lead to the development of localized industry cultures, determined, for instance, by intergovernment agreements, small-group cartels, maintenance-pool arrangements, and partnerships between developing and established airlines. Likewise, airlines within a particular geographic region tend to be influenced by environmental conditions such as local economic recession or growth and the development of tourism in the area.

C. Corporate Culture

Corporate culture is the sum of the values, social ideals, and beliefs that organization members come to share (Siehl & Martin, 1981). It is sometimes thought of as the social or normative glue that holds an organization together (Tichy, 1982). Conceived this way, corporate culture fulfills a variety of functions. It conveys a sense of identity for organization members, facilitates the generation of commitment to something larger than the self, enhances the stability of the social systems, and serves as a sense-making device that can guide and shape behavior (Smircich, 1983). Whereas societal and industrial cultures are conceived as the backdrop against which the corporation operates, corporate culture is often thought of as something the organization possesses, that is, a tool that can be deployed to make its strategies more effective. Those firms that have corporate cultures supportive of their strategies would tend to have a higher probability of success (Smircich, 1983).

All three types of cultures thus guide and shape organizational behavior; therefore, in order to understand an organization's strategies and policies, it is necessary to understand the relative contribution of each type of culture in that organization. Four potential patterns of cultural influence are represented in Figure 12.1. The first three all suggest nondistinct corporate cultures. Figure 12.1a portrays a situation in which the societal and industry cultures are highly similar, and the organization functions according to these norms. Organizations represented by Figure 12.1b follow industry prescriptions but not their societal norms, which are quite different. Conversely, Figure 12.1c illustrates organizations that are closely aligned with their societal cultures but distinct from the practices of the rest of the industry. Finally, Figure 12.1d depicts organizations that display unique features such as innovative leadership, technological advances, or novel market approaches that set them apart and thus define them as possessing a unique corporate culture.

D. Societal Culture Configuration Model

Fundamental to the cultural model underlying this research is Miller and Mintzberg's (1983) configuration theory. Adopting a functional perspective, they see organizations as inherently driven toward a lim-

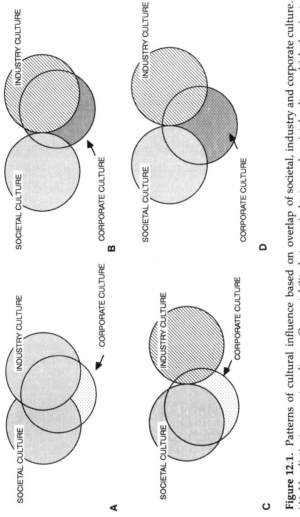

Figure 12.1. Patterns of cultural influence based on overlap of societal, industry and corporate culture. (A) Nondistinct corporate culture—Compatability between industry and societal culture which dominate corporate culture (Lufthansa). (B) Nondistinct organization culture—Societal culture different from industry culture. Industry culture dominates corporate culture (PIA, PAL). (C) Nondistinct corporate culture—Societal culture dominates corporate culture (Alitalia). (D) Unique corporate culture—Unique corporate culture due to visionary leader/founder (Thai Int'l, SIA).

ited number of viable archetypes. Thus, cultural characteristics do not operate independently but exist in logical patterns that define a limited number of cultural types; the configuration hypothesis implies that there are a limited number of viable organizational types across cultures.

An orienting framework relating societal culture and organizational characteristics was derived from the existing research literature, in particular the clustering studies of Haire, Ghiselli, and Porter (1966), Hofstede (1980), and Ronen and Shenkar (1985). These employ primarily "etic" or universalistic methods for comparing cultural influences on organizations. In addition, Rieger (1987) reviewed emically based descriptive field studies of organizations in 12 societies (Latin America, Germany, France, Turkey, Thailand, India, Nigeria, East Africa, Zambia, Great Britain, Japan, and Indonesia) in order to identify configurations and underlying cultural dimensions. The resulting framework proposed here is based on four primary societal dimensions and two secondary ones.

Power refers to the ability of the leaders to effect decisions and to control choices in the organization. To the degree that they exercise unilateral control, then their power is high. *Authority distance* refers to the degree of separation between the superior and the subordinate in the hierarchical structure. It affects the flows of information between key decision makers as well as the centralization of decision-making activities. *Group orientation* refers to the use of small groups to accomplish social or organizational goals. It affects the informal circulation of information and the support of group members for their leader, especially in interactions with other groups. Finally, *cognitive orientation* refers to the way information is processed by the key decision makers. It is characterized as either intuitive, that is, based on executive judgments of timely, qualitative information or analytic, characterized by linear and systematic analysis of quantitative information.

The two secondary variables, risk orientation and fatalism, were considered to play a lesser role in determining organizational functioning.

Although the four primary dimensions give rise to 16 possible combinations, all of the field studies could be subsumed under five configurations. This finding is consistent with the original contention that cultures form a limited number of holistic gestalts. The five configurations as they appeared in the field studies review are described next:

1. The *autocracy* (AUT) was characterized by the presence of a powerful entrepreneurial leader who made unilateral decisions based on personalistic judgments and intuition. The leader controlled all phases of the decision process.

2. The *political entourage* (PE) was typified by decision making that was negotiated among group leaders. The source of the entourage leader's strength was the support of his or her entourages.
3. The *traditional bureaucracy* (TB) corresponded to the stereotype of a marginally dysfunctional bureaucracy. Decisions were made analytically following rigidly established procedures that were occasionally superseded by powerful executives.
4. The *modern bureaucracy* (MB) corresponded to the Weberian ideal-type bureaucracy (Gerth & Mills, 1946). Decision making was almost exclusively analytic in nature and was influenced by professional experts on the staff. Two features that distinguished the MBs from the TBs were lower authority distance and a somewhat more analytic orientation.
5. The final type, the *consensus* (CON) configuration, had high group orientation and low authority distance that facilitated the sharing of decision-making responsibility throughout the organization. Decision making was holistic, combining features of analytic and intuitive modes. The CON configuration was apparently unique to the Japanese and therefore was not studied in either the preliminary field work nor in the archival analyses reported here.

II. STUDY 1—FIELD RESEARCH

To develop the preliminary framework, a series of field studies was conducted using a sample of international airlines representing the first four societal configurations. Several questions were addressed. First, to what degree do organizational structure, processes, and values reflect societal structure? Second, do the four dimensions and four configurations adequately describe the airline's structure and strategies? Third, in what ways might the framework be modified to more adequately reflect societal influences in the airline industry.

A. Method

International airlines from nine countries were classified into the four configurations, using the published data about their respective countries' norms and values. The four primary dimensions (power, authority distance, group orientation, and cognitive orientation) and two secondary dimensions (risk orientation and fatalism) were used as the basis for classification. Figure 12.2 shows the hypothetical position of each of the airline countries within the proposed cultural framework.

Data about each airline's organizational structure, operational processes, and strategic decision making were then gathered through executive interviews and unobtrusive observations of administrative ac-

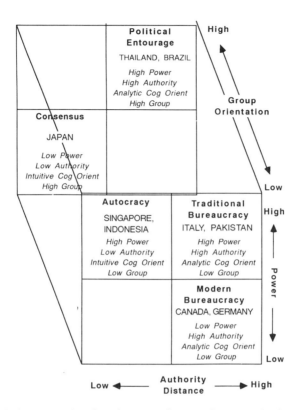

Figure 12.2. Preliminary cultural configuration framework prior to Study 1 showing theoretical placement of airlines.

tivities. In this way, the four primary dimensions were directly assessed for each airline.

B. Results and Discussion

The field data generally supported the proposed framework; however, there were a few important deviations. Most significant was the presence of transitional or hybrid organizations that exhibited characteristics of two configurations. In the case of Singapore Airlines (SIA), for example, the company's classification as an AUT accurately characterized its operations throughout the 1970s, but in the early 1980s, it began to shift toward the MB model. Alitalia (in Italy), which had been classified as a TB, appeared to take on some characteristics of an autocracy during a protracted period of organizational difficulty but was also experiencing pressures to become more of an MB.

The field data also revealed greater-than-expected differences between the two proposed MBs. Air Canada was less analytically oriented but more prone toward risk than the West German airline—Lufthansa. Although unanticipated, this finding was consistent with Hofstede's (1980) model that argued for separate Anglo and Germanic clusters based on his construct of uncertainty avoidance. Finally, there was a lack of strong evidence supporting the proposed PE configuration. High group orientation should have distinguished the two hypothetical PEs from the TB; however, they exhibited few of the expected group characteristics.

The deviations, in general, may be attributed to several factors. First, transitions in societal culture may have produced changes in the organizational culture; for example, Singapore had rapidly evolved sophisticated planning techniques at the levels of both the government and the airline. A second reason may be rooted in the interaction of industry and societal culture influences. This was noticed in the cases of Thai International and Varig in Brazil.

Finally, the field data suggested that some deviations could be attributed to two variables related to corporate culture. The first was the presence of a strong charismatic leader whose personal influence had become institutionalized. This was definitely the case at Alitalia and, to a lesser degree, at Varig (in Brazil). A second variable was extraorganizational influences, particularly the political interference by government officials, which was observed in the airlines of Pakistan and Thailand as distorting the normal cultural tendencies.

As a result of the noted discrepancies, several changes were made to the framework (Figure 12.3). The PE was abandoned, and a new configuration, the implicitly structured (IMP) organization, was proposed. Related to this, the dimension of risk orientation, which distinguished the IMP from the MB, was added, and the dimension of group orientation, which failed to discriminate the PEs, was dropped. The IMP firms were expected to exhibit higher risk and consequently greater reliance on intuitive judgment than the MBs. In terms of this sample, the IMPs included the predominantly anglophone and Scandinavian countries plus the Netherlands.

Another modification was the reclassification of some of the European airlines, such as Air France, Sabena, and Alitalia, from TBs to MBs because of certain key shifts in their societal culture and their apparent organizational structure. Alitalia, for example, appeared to have a flatter hierarchical structure and greater emphasis on technical operations than

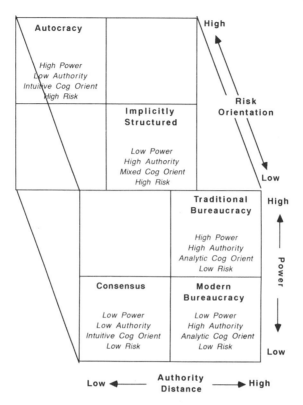

Figure 12.3. Revised cultural configuration framework reflecting abandonment of group dimension and addition of risk dimension.

would be expected for a TB. These changes were attributed to the influence of trade and technical agreements (all were members of the ATLAS maintenance pool), a concern for the technology demands of the airline industry, and the overall level of their societies' industrialization.

A final modification was made in the reclassification of some of the Latin American airlines from TBs to AUTs. On the one hand, Hofstede had categorized these as "pyramidal" structures (which roughly corresponded to the TB classification); on the other hand, the field study review suggested that Latin American organizations would be structured like AUTs (Davis 1968; Gillin, 1960). The resolution of this controversy, for the purpose of the research here, was to classify the smaller Latin American airlines as AUTs and the larger ones as TBs on the basis of the power and authority distance differences related to size.

III. STUDY 2—QUANTITATIVE ANALYSIS

The purpose of the second study was to test the influence of the three different types of culture—societal, industry, and organizational—on airline performance using archival data. To this effect, a sample of 35 international airlines representing the five cultural groupings defined in the field study was selected. (However, the data for Japan were eliminated from all of the group comparisons because it was the only airline in that cultural grouping. Moreover, because of missing data, fewer than 34 airlines are represented in some of the statistical tests. In each analysis, the actual number of degrees of freedom is indicated.) Countries were classified using the four dimensions of power distance, authority distance, analytic orientation, and risk orientation, relying on societal data drawn primarily from the work of Hofstede (1980) and Ronen and Shenkar (1985).

A. Clustering Analysis

As indicated in the field study, airlines are not perfect reflections of their societal characteristics. Thus, the first step here was to attempt to recluster the sample of airlines. This was accomplished using an organizational index that also reflected a cultural dimension, and this was the "number of administrative personnel as a percentage of total personnel." This measure indicates the amount of bureaucratization and amount of management control in an organization and was chosen as a surrogate measure for organizational structure that, as shown in the field study, varied by societal grouping. If the airlines in this sample reflected their societal values, one would expect to find clusters formed on the basis of administrative percentages to correspond to the societal groupings.

Different clusters, on the other hand, might indicate that airlines were influenced more by other factors. For example, if clustering revealed a single group, this would suggest a strong uniform industry culture. Clustering according to geographic region would suggest local environmental influences, and groups composed of airline partners would suggest the influence of formal norms.

Hierarchical clustering was performed, using an average linkage algorithm that creates clusters by computing the squared Euclidean distance between observations in two adjacent clusters. Figure 12.4 presents a tree diagram of the clusters with the average linkage distance plotted along the ordinate and the proposed societal grouping and actual percentage of administration in parentheses. The results suggested

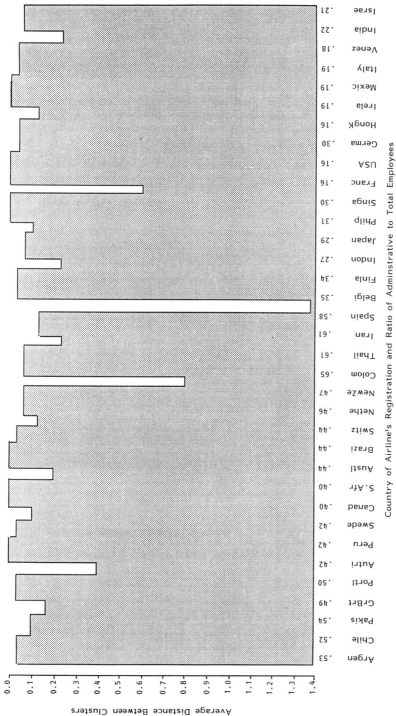

Figure 12.4. Tree diagram of societal cultures using average linkage algorithm.

two to five clusters, with the high administration TBs and IMPs toward one end and low administration MBs and AUTs toward the other. However, if the airlines were reordered according to actual administrative percentages, it is clear that the cluster comprised of Colombia, Thailand, Iran, and Spain, which had the highest percentages, would be more appropriately located at the end of the diagram next to Argentina.

The results tend to support the proposed societal groupings. The TBs and IMPs form one large cluster, with the TBs clustered toward one end and moderately distinct from the IMPs. The AUTs and MBs were located in the other large cluster; however, they could not be differentiated from one other. Only four airlines were clearly misplaced; these were Austria and Switzerland, two hypothetical MBs that appeared with the IMPs, and the United States and Ireland, two IMPs that were clustered with the AUTs and MBs. In terms of the ambiguous airlines, the clustering indicates that Venezuela and Mexico are more like AUTs than TBs. Similarly, the transitional societies, Belgium, France, and Italy, appeared more like MBs than TBs. Overall, these clusters might be interpreted as indicating the validity of societal culture as a means for clustering international airlines.

However, an alternative, although not mutually exclusive, explanation for the clustering is the impact of industry culture. From this perspective, the fact that Italy, Belgium, and France clustered with West Germany may be accounted for by their partnership in the ATLAS pool. Similarly, Scandinavia, Switzerland, and the Netherlands, which represent different societal groups, clustered together because they are all members of the KSSU maintenance pool. In sum, the results here suggest that both industry culture and societal culture may play roles in determining the percentage of administrative personnel. The next question was whether societal groupings predicted differences in other areas of the organization's operations and strategies.

B. Industry Performance Analysis

Table 12.1 presents the data for several indexes of the airline industry operations for the years 1974 and 1978 and the percentage of change between the two years. During this period, the industry was just recovering from a recession engendered in part by the fuel crisis of 1973. In many respects, this seemed to be a good period for expansion. The soaring increases in fuel costs clearly stressed the need for more economical operations. From 1973 to 1974, fuel prices had jumped from 12% to over 18% of total operating expenses. However, during this sample period from 1974 to 1978 they had leveled off considerably (only to

Table 12.1. Changes in International Airline Industry,
1974 to 1978

Index of operations	1974	1978	Percentage change
Operating expenses[a]			
Flight operations (total)	10,426	16,700	60
Crew salaries	2,845	4,756	67
Fuel	6,170	10,220	66
Sales and promotions	4,511	8,601	91
Operating profit	792	3,100	291
Passenger kilometers performed[b]			
Europe	238,080	321,270	35
Middle East	10,940	25,640	135
Asia and Pacific	75,310	125,640	67
Africa	15,340	24,050	57
North America	286,790	393,170	37
Latin America	29,990	46,590	55
Total	656,440	936,350	43

[a]Measured in millions of U.S. dollars
[b]Measured in millions of kilometers

dramatically leap again to 28% in 1980). Airlines were faced with several strategies for addressing fuel costs, the most effective of which would be the upgrading to the higher capacity, more fuel-economic widebodies. Moreover, the airlines were in a particularly good bargaining position because manufacturers were all competing to establish their new wide-bodies. The industry culture, then, could be described as favoring fleet expansion or upgrading.

Of the regional factors, economic growth was probably the most important. Development was particularly active in the Pacific Rim and Middle East regions and moderately active in Latin America. It was relatively low, however, in Europe and North America, which were already heavily industrialized. Similarly, because of the low costs, the Pacific and Latin America were becoming increasingly popular as tourist areas at the same time as Europe and North America were experiencing a decline.

C. Size, Operating Strategies, and Performance

Based on the previous framework and the results of the cluster analysis, 31 of the 35 airlines were categorized into four cultural groupings (see Table 12.2). They were also classified according to four geo-

Table 12.2. Sample Partitioned according to Societal Groups and Geographic Regions

	Societal groups		
Autocracies	Traditional bureaucracies	Modern bureaucracies	Implicit structure
Hong Kong	Argentina	Austria	Australia
India	Brazil	Belgium	Canada
Indonesia	Chile	Finland	Great Britain
Philippines	Colombia	France	Netherlands
Singapore	Iran	Germany	New Zealand
Venezuela	Mexico	Italy	South Africa
	Pakistan	Switzerland	Sweden
	Peru		
	Portugal		
	Spain		
	Thailand		

	Geographic regions		
Asia/Africa	Europe/ North America	Latin America	Pacific basin
India	Austria	Argentina	Australia
Iran	Belgium	Brazil	Hong Kong
Pakistan	Canada	Chile	Indonesia
South Africa	Finland	Colombia	New Zealand
	France	Mexico	Philippines
	Germany	Peru	Singapore
	Great Britain	Venezuela	Thailand
	Italy		
	Netherlands		
	Portugal		
	Spain		
	Sweden		
	Switzerland		

graphical regions: Pacific Rim, Asia/Africa, Latin America, and Europe/North America. The operations and performance data published by the International Civil Aviation Organization (ICAO) for the years 1974 and 1978 were examined for each of the airlines and for the industry as a whole. Analyses were performed on 21 indexes representing five areas of airline functioning: volume and size, personnel deployment, flight operation strategies, growth and diversification, and productivity. Multivariate analyses of variance (MANOVAs) were conducted for several subgroups of variables, and subsequent ANOVAs and post-hoc Student Newman-Keul tests performed for each individual measure.

1. Influence of Size

Because of the potential influence of airline size on operation and performance, five size-related variables, total assets, equipment assets, number of ton-kilometers performed, number of personnel, and operating revenues, were analyzed across societal groups and regions. As shown in Table 12.3, there were significant differences by societal grouping for four of the variables. The IMPs and the MBs were clearly much larger than the AUTs and the TBs in terms of assets, kilometers performed, and revenues. However, the differences in number of personnel were not significant. There were no significant differences by geographic region, although the European and North American airlines all tended to be somewhat larger than those in other regions. Overall, these results suggest that in interpreting the performance data, differences apparently due to societal group might also be attributable to size.

2. Personnel Deployment

The personnel in airlines may be divided into five functional divisions: pilots, cabin crew, maintenance, sales, and administration. On the one hand, because of the prescribed nature of international flight operations, it was possible that all airlines would show approximately the same proportions of personnel deployment, and this would indicate the influence of a uniform industry culture. On the other hand, as suggested by the cluster analyses, personnel deployment might also differ according to societal culture. A two-way MANOVA indicated there were significant differences across the five societal groups ($F[15,44] = 4.40$, $p < .0001$) but not across regions. Subsequent ANOVAs indicated differences existed in four divisions by societal group. As shown in Table 12.4, they differed considerably in their percentages of administrative, sales, pilot, and cabin personnel. The percentage of administration in the TBs (54.4%) was more than twice the percentage among the AUTs (23.7%), and this difference was significant according to the post-hoc comparisons. The IMPs also had a significantly lower percentage (43.7%) than did the TBs but significantly higher percentages than did the MBs (29.8%), who were not different from the AUTs.

If the non-flight-related categories (sales and administrative) are added together, however, the IMPs emerge as most similar to the MBs. These findings, then, conform to expectations, with the high authority distance/high power distance TBs having the most top-heavy admin-

Table 12.3. Measures of Airline Size according to Societal Group and Geographic Region

	Total assets (US$ millions)	Equipment assets (US$ millions)	Total volume (Ton-kms)	Operating revenue (US$ millions)	Total personnel
Group					
Autocracy	459.3	190.6	1,030.2	348.0	8,072.0
Modern bureaucracy	958.5	357.8	2,491.4	1,031.0	16,152.6
Implicit	1,225.8	510.6	3,218.2	1,140.0	20,731.4
Traditional bureaucracy	383.5	160.7	1,074.4	361.0	11,307.5
F (df)	3.67(3,26)*	3.12(3.26)*	4.04(3,27)*	3.46(3,27)*	2.07(3,30)NS
Region					
Asia/Africa	452.2	164.0	1,283.6	418.0	14,286.0
Europe/North America	1,082.5	420.5	2,969.7	11.0	20,015.5
Latin America	263.4	93.8	756.0	261.0	7,127.1
Pacific rim	555.2	273.3	1,270.1	443.0	8,647.4
F (df)	1.19(3,26)NS	0.90(3,26)NS	1.74(3,27)NS	1.37(3,27)NS	1.95(3,30)NS
Airlines					
Indonesia	585.6	389.3	862.6	320.6	6,582.0
Philippines	235.4	83.6	799.2	284.8	9,349.0
Singapore	995.7	309.5	1,950.0	667.4	10,246.0
Germany	1,617.0	669.0	4,942.0	2,096.6	29,838.0
Italy	877.6	280.0	2,656.0	1,072.0	17,604.0
Canada	1,166.6	519.4	4,587.0	1,157.0	22,468.0
Brazil	582.5	233.6	1,766.0	623.0	16,793.0
Pakistan	424.3	126.2	1,234.5	334.0	22,025.0
Thailand	314.3	214.3	775.0	221.1	6,571.0

*$p < .05$.

Table 12.4. Airline Personnel Ratios according to Societal Group and Geographic Region

	Pilots percentage	Cabin percentage	Maintenance percentage	Sales percentage	Administrative percentage
Group					
Autocracy	7.0	14.2	24.4	30.3	23.7
Modern bureaucracy	6.6	11.5	24.5	26.8	29.8
Implicit	6.6	11.6	25.9	12.2	43.7
Traditional bureaucracy	4.8	9.2	20.0	11.7	54.4
$F\,(df)$	7.49(3,30)**	3.31(3,30)*	2.89(3,30)†	8.33(3,30)***	20.5(3,30)***
Region					
Asia/Africa	4.2	8.2	27.1	15.9	44.5
Europe/North America	6.4	11.2	23.8	20.2	38.0
Latin America	6.9	11.3	20.7	18.7	42.0
Pacific Rim	5.8	13.5	23.0	20.7	36.9
$F\,(df)$	8.97(3,30)***	1.28(3,30)NS	1.69(3,30)NS	0.20(3,30)NS	0.87(3,30)NS
Airlines					
Indonesia	6.8	10.8	22.1	32.5	27.8
Philippines	5.5	8.5	27.1	28.3	30.6
Singapore	7.1	18.5	27.7	16.3	30.4
Germany	6.7	11.8	27.6	37.0	16.8
Italy	7.4	13.1	19.5	41.2	18.9
Canada	8.0	13.3	20.1	16.9	39.7
Brazil	5.7	9.1	19.7	21.2	44.3
Pakistan	2.7	5.0	24.5	13.6	54.3
Thailand	3.3	10.6	11.9	10.0	64.2

***$p < .001$; **$p < .01$; *$p < .05$; †$p < .10$.

istration and the low authority distance AUTs, the least. In between are the low power/high authority distance IMPs and MBs.

The findings were reversed for cabin personnel. The AUTs had the highest percentage of cabin crew (14.2%), and the TBs the lowest percentage (9.3%), with the IMPs and MBs intermediate and similar (11.5%). In terms of the sales division, the AUTs and MBs appeared highly sales oriented (30.3% and 26.8%, respectively) and the IMPs and TBs significantly less so (12.2% and 11.7%). Overall, the AUTs appeared to have the most aggressive customer orientation, and this fits with their societal values of service and high risk. An explanation for the TBs lack of customer emphasis is suggested by the markets and routes that they serve. Many of the TB airlines primarily transport their own people and/or promote low-cost tourism to their country rather than compete internationally. (The exceptions are Thai International and, to some extent, Varig, in Brazil). Thus, for the AUTs and TBs, societal culture provides at least a partial explanation for cabin and sales personnel deployment.

3. Diversification

Diversification and growth measures were analyzed to compare long-range strategies among the airline groups. A surrogate measure for diversification examined here was the percentage of investment in non-flight assets, for example, in hotels, restaurants, and resorts. Table 12.5 presents the average percentages of diversified investment for each of the four societal groups. The most diversified appeared to be the MBs and the least, the IMPs; however, a two-way ANOVA showed this was not a significant main effect. By region, airlines in the Pacific Rim were least diversified, whereas those in Latin America, the most. This effect was marginally significant. Overall, there seemed to be a fair amount of consensus, with three-fourths of the airlines reporting between 50% and 70% diversification, and this would suggest the existence of a strong industry norm regarding the optimal amount of diversification.

4. Growth Strategies

Three indexes of growth were analyzed: growth in capacity (number of international kilometers offered), growth in performance (total number of kilometers sold), and growth in total assets (Table 12.5). A MANOVA showed that there were significant main effects for both societal group and region ($F[9,42] = 2.47$, $p < .03$ and $F[9,42] = 3.87$, $p < .0001$, respectively).

Table 12.5. Diversification and Growth Factors according to Societal Group and Geographic Region

	Diversified assets (% nonequipment assets)	International TKM[a] (growth factor)	Total TKM (growth factor)	Assets (growth factor)
Group				
Autocracy	60	1.97	0.95	2.51
Modern bureaucracy	63	1.30	0.41	1.54
Implicit	56	1.42	0.43	1.52
Traditional bureaucracy	60	2.65	0.88	1.90
F (df)	0.48(3,26)NS	2.53(3,28)†	5.92(3,28)**	5.72(3,23)**
Region				
Asia/Africa	64	2.63	2.38	2.17
Europe/North America	62	1.38	1.36	1.43
Latin America	67	2.30	1.46	1.37
Pacific Rim	49	2.05	2.07	3.19
F (df)	2.96(3,26)†	0.63(3,28)NS	13.08(3,28)***	20.11(3,23)***
Airlines				
Indonesia	33	2.00	2.02	3.20
Philippines	64	1.96	1.77	
Singapore	69	2.72	2.72	3.00
Germany	59	1.42	1.42	1.62
Italy	68	1.18	1.16	1.13
Canada	55	1.23	1.17	0.99
Brazil	60	1.23	1.29	1.24
Pakistan	70	2.50	2.42	2.26
Thailand	32	2.55	2.55	6.68

***$p < .001$; **$p < .01$; *$p < .05$; †$p < .10$.
[a]TKM = Ton-kilometers.

The univariate *F*s for societal grouping indicated that differences in measures of total asset and overall mileage growth were significant, whereas growth in international mileage was marginally significant. On the average, the MBs and IMPs had grown the least in every respect. The AUTs, in contrast, had increased tremendously in terms of total assets, by a factor of 2.51 from 1974 to 1978 as had the TBs, who were 1.9 times larger than in 1974. The TBs and AUTs were also similar in terms of international growth, with the TBs performing at 2.65 times their 1974 level and the AUTs at 1.97. The reasons for these patterns, however, are likely related to regional factors.

Regional differences were very pronounced in terms of overall mileage and total assets. Growth in total assets was most dramatic among the Pacific Rim airlines, which had increased to three times their 1974 size in 4 years. The Asian/African group had grown to about twice their original size, whereas the European/North American and the Latin American groups showed about a 40% increase. A similar growth pattern was found in terms of miles performed, with both the Pacific Rim and the Asian/African airlines approximately doubling their mileage. Interestingly enough, there were no significant differences in growth of international mileage, primarily because the Latin American airlines had increased as much as the other two regions.

In summary, these results reflected the influence of both societal and regional factors on growth. The TBs and AUTs were the most aggressive societal groups. By region, the Pacific and Asian airlines seemed to have been building their fleets, whereas the Latin American airlines had been concentrating on developing their international routes and not upgrading fleets. As indicated previously, many of the Latin American airlines seemed to be operating older planes with relatively low seating capacity. One interpretation of these data is that the Pacific and Asian airlines were anticipating continued route expansion, whereas the Latin American airlines were simply taking advantage of their existing capabilities. This may be related to the differences in economic conditions in the two regions; the Pacific and Asian countries were undergoing intensive industrial development, whereas Latin America was experiencing a moderate economic recession.

5. Performance

Perhaps the most important aspect of organizational functioning to predict is performance. The question of interest here was whether airlines differed in their productivity and profitability on the basis of societal culture. The measure of productivity used was the total flight kilometers per employee; the two profit measures were operating profit and operating margin (profit to sales) A two-way MANOVA indicated no overall group or region effects; however, several ANOVAs were significant, although these need to be interpreted with caution.

There were significant differences by societal group for productivity, with the IMPs emerging as the best performers. The TBs had the lowest productivity ratio, seemingly because of their top-heavy bureaucratic structure, which, as discussed previously, can be related to their societal dimensions of high authority and high power distances.

The univariate differences by societal grouping for operating profit were marginally significant ($F[3,27] = 2.77$, $p<.10$), although the differences for operating margin were not ($F[3,27] = 1.90$, n.s.). As shown in Table 12.6, the IMPs earned more than twice the total profit of any other group and almost eight times as much as the lowest group, the

Table 12.6. Performance Indexes according to Societal Group
and Geographic Region

	TKM/person (millions)[a]	Operating profit (US$ millions)	Operating margin (percentage)
Group			
Autocracy	0.081	24.37	6.2
Modern bureaucracy	0.078	7.86	1.4
Implicit	0.091	60.26	5.6
Traditional bureaucracy	0.056	24.57	6.2
F (df)	10.22(3,30)***	2.77(3,27)†	1.90(3,27)NS
Region			
Asia/Africa	0.055	44.27	10.7
Europe/North America	0.078	29.66	2.3
Latin America	0.067	20.65	5.5
Pacific rim	0.087	29.55	7.0
F (df)	6.26(3,30)**	0.27(3,27)NS	2.22(3,27)NS
Airlines			
Indonesia	0.049	28.70	8.9
Philippines	0.051	4.60	1.9
Singapore	0.131	46.60	7.0
Germany	0.103	53.10	2.5
Italy	0.091	32.20	3.0
Canada	0.096	73.90	6.4
Brazil	0.065	60.40	9.7
Pakistan	0.028	38.20	11.0
Thailand	0.076	28.50	13.0

***$p < .001$; **$p < .01$; *$p < .05$; †$p < .10$.
[a]TKM = Ton-kilometers.

MBs. Interestingly enough, the most profitable and the least profitable group consisted of the airlines that were largest in size. Thus, although the amount of profit is biased by the amount of total revenues, it is clearly not the only determining factor. One possible explanation is that all the MB airlines examined here had very high operating costs, whereas the IMPs included some airlines located in less developed countries (Venezuela and Mexico, for example) with correspondingly lower costs.

Operating margin (profit returned on sales), the most frequently used index of profitability, attempts to compensate for the size bias. Even though the differences by societal grouping were not significant, the trend is worth noting. Table 12.6 suggests that the two groups with the highest operating margin, the AUTs and the TBs, were composed of the smaller airlines; however, the IMPs were almost as profitable. Overall, these findings suggest that the factors accounting for profitability differ in large and small airlines and that different strategies may be successful in each of these contexts.

In terms of regional differences, only productivity was significantly different. The best performers were the Pacific Rim airlines and the worst, the Asian/African ones. Overall, then, societal grouping seems to be a more important determinant of performance than region. The three indexes combined indicate that the IMPs are the best performers. They are the most productive, show the highest profit, and are highly profitable. As indicated in the previous analyses, they appear to take advantage of economies of scale (like the MBs) but also pursue efficient operating strategies (characteristic of the AUTs).

The TBs and the AUTs performed similarly well relative to their size, although it seems as if the reasons for success are quite different in each case. The AUTs are profitable because of their aggressive sales and promotion, whereas the TBs appear to succeed primarily because of their low costs. Finally, the MBs showed the poorest profit outcomes, which may be attributed in part to their high operating costs and, consequently, poor profitability. The following sections test some of the specific factors related to each of these performance measures.

D. Determinants of Performance

To determine potential influences on performance, a series of multiple correlation analyses were performed combining data across all the airlines. There were two purposes here. The first was to attempt to reveal operating strategies that were independent of cultural grouping. The second was to determine the non-culture-specific factors that were related to successful airline performance.

1. Correlations of Performance and Strategy

Table 12.7 presents the correlation coefficients relating performance and operating strategy variables. One group of variables that emerged might be labeled a *high utilization strategy*. The number of seats per plane is positively correlated with hours of flying time per plane and kilometers of flight per employee. It is negatively correlated with ticket pricing and diversification but positively correlated with the load factor (kilometers performed as a ratio of kilometers available). Overall, this combination suggests a strategy of concentration on flight operations, efficient usage of planes and personnel, and high volume traffic.

Examination of growth measures indicates both positive and negative relationships among the three growth measures analyzed here. Growth in total kilometers and growth in international kilometers performed were positively correlated with each other ($r^2 = .54$, $p < .01$); however, only growth in international performance was correlated with the growth in assets ($r^2 = .70$, $p < .001$). There was a significant negative relationship ($r^2 = -.49$, $p < .01$) between growth in assets and the percentage of diversified investment that suggests that airlines were expanding by increasing or upgrading their fleets rather than by diversifying into nonflight areas. This conforms to the industry culture analysis that suggested that the move to larger, more fuel-economic planes would be a preferred strategy.

There was a highly negative correlation between growth in international performance and hours of flight per long-distance plane ($r^2 = -.70$, $p < .001$). This relationship is understandable in terms of the stages of airline expansion. As was noted at Thai International and SIA, the airlines tended to upgrade their fleets first and then to increase their international routes; it was only after the routes had been firmly established that they were able to realize efficient utilization of their new planes.

Diversification as a strategy presented a very interesting pattern. As noted previously, it was negatively related to the growth in assets, indicating an overall industry tendency to avoid expanding in nonflight areas. Moreover, diversification did not appear to be a successful strategy. The return on diversified investments, which was calculated as the "ratio of nonflight revenues to nonflight assets," was negatively correlated with diversification ($r^2 = -.40$, $p < .05$). In other words, the greater an airline's investment in nonflight assets, the less profitable the investment. This relationship is examined more closely in the next section.

In summary, the multiple correlations suggest that high operating

Table 12.7. Correlations of Selected Airline Characteristics

	2	3	4	5	6	7	8	9	10	11	12	13	14	15
1. Total TKM[a]	.92***	.54**	-.12	.45***	.27	-.11	.25	-.22	.22	-.06	-.10	-.23	-.28	-.14
2. Personnel		.60***	-.04	.18	.28	-.12	.17	-.17	.10	-.03	-.10	-.15	-.24	-.14
3. Operating profit			.57**	.18	.27	-.11	.34†	.05	-.39†	-.03	-.37†	.12	-.12	-.05
4. Operating margin				-.13	.14	-.02	.25	.15	.63**	-.17	-.44*	.59**	-.02	.54**
5. Productivity					.43**	-.22	.43*	-.17	.37†	.43*	-.03	-.09	-.12	.11
6. Load factor						-.53*	.35+	.25	.14	.05	-.14	.07	-.16	.12
7. Ticket price							-.14*	-.42*	.53*	.26	-.08	-.07	-.14	-.07
8. Seats/plane								.38	-.14	-.41	-.11	.20	-.00	.28
9. Hours/plane									-.29	-.21	.00	-.06	.05	-.17
10. Hours/long distance plane										-.06	-.52*	-.59**	-.69***	-.19
11. Diversified assets											-.40*	-.18	.17	-.48*
12. Diversified revenues												-.34†	-.32	-.17
13. Growth—total TKM[a]													.54**	.70***

***p < .001; **p < .01; *p < .05; †p < .10.
[a]TKM = Ton-kilometers.

profits are related to airline size, seating capacity, and utilization of long-distance planes. The profitability, or operating margin, is correlated with high overall profit as well as growth in assets; however, it is negatively related to utilization of long-distance planes.

2. Predictors of Performance

To determine more precisely the factors related to performance, stepwise multiple regressions (MRs) using backward and forward selection were performed on three performance measures: operating profit, operating margin, and diversified profits-to-assets. Likewise, MRs were performed on two growth measures for the period 1974 to 1978: change in international kilometers performed and change in total assets. Predictor variables included dummy coding of each of the four cultural groupings and the four geographic regions represented by the sample: Europe, Latin America, Pacific, and Asia–Africa. The other variables were airline size (total kilometers performed in 1978), percentage of administrative personnel, ticket price, seats per plane, hours per plane, diversification, productivity of equipment and personnel, and amount of international traffic as a percentage of total traffic. Diversified profits-to-assets was included as a predictor for the two operating profit measures, and the growth in international performance and growth in assets as independent variables for all three performance measures. The results of the MRs for each of the five variables are presented in Table 12.8.

There were only two significant predictors of total operating profit: number of personnel and not being a modern bureaucracy. Not surprisingly, the most important determinant of overall profit is the size of the airline. The presence of the second variable, however, indicates that a combination of other factors also contribute to low profits. As noted previously, the MBs are, on the average, the second largest in size but the lowest in terms of overall operating profit. The data here suggest this finding may be attributed to both their operating strategies and their environmental conditions. As implied by the ANOVAs, their "full-fared" luxury strategy appeared least well matched to consumer demands. They were also in a poor position in terms of fleet upgrading; the MBs were all located in low-growth regions, and they tended to be large, mature airlines, which were not in an as auspicious a position to expand or upgrade as were the newer, smaller airlines.

The stepwise MR on operating margin yielded four significant predictors, two regional variables, and two performance variables. Airlines that earned the highest return on sales were, in general, those not located in Europe or North America and also those that were not headquartered in Latin America. As indicated by the r^2's, geographic location

Table 12.8. Societal, Regional, and Organizational Variables Predicting Profit and Growth

Dependent variable	Source	B	F	R²	F	R²	F
Operating margin	Intercept	.162					
	European region	-.078	15.14***	.29	7.92**		
	Latin America	-.046	3.79†	.13	3.88*		
	Diversified ROI	.085	5.26*	.09	3.20†		
	Grow capacity	-.015	3.63†	.09	3.62†	.602	6.04**
Operating profit	Intercept	44.838					
	Implicit culture	56.394	9.96**	.34	9.74**		
	Diversified ROI	-57.600	3.58†	.11	3.58†	.448	7.31**
Growth international TKM[a]	Intercept	3.242					
	Traditional bureaucratic culture	1.409	8.54**	.28	7.65**		
	Diversified ROI	-1.542	3.03†	.09	3.03†	.376	5.73*
Growth total assets	Intercept	7.899					
	Pacific region	.603	1.42ns	.40	12.57**		
	Hours/plane	.000	27.90***	.12	4.68*		
	European region	-1.655	16.94**	.14	7.08**		
	Diversified invest	-4.782	11.20**	.14	11.20**	.802	16.16**

***$p < .001$; **$p < .01$; *$p < .05$; †$p < .10$.
[a]TKM = Ton-kilometers.

accounted for 42% of the total variance in operating margin. One commonality between the two regions is the high cost of personnel, albeit for very different reasons. In Europe and North America, personnel costs are directly related to the high cost of living. For the Latin American airlines, however, it is the relatively large number of personnel that boosts costs. As was noted previously, personnel productivity (the number of kilometers performed per employee) was significantly lower in the TBs than in any of the other airlines.

The two performance factors, which accounted for a combined total of 18% of the variance, were "low return on diversification" and "low international growth." Two airlines visited during the field study help to illustrate this performance profile. Varig (in Brazil) was a mature airline successfully exploiting rather than increasing its international routes. Singapore Airlines, in contrast, appeared less profitable because of its tremendous expansion during this period. One interpretation of these results is that airlines that were not focused solely on flight operations, that is, that were concentrating on nonflight areas or on expansion were less profitable. Perhaps, as suggested by Peters and Waterman (1982), it is important for airlines to "stick to the knitting" in order to succeed. Alternatively, low profitability may be a temporary situation, and performance can be expected to improve as the new ventures mature. It is likely that both interpretations are valid, depending on the situation.

The final profit measure analyzed was diversified return on assets. As can be seen in Table 12.8, there were seven significant predictors, all except one that reflected airline strategy. The only regional predictor was "not being located in Asia or Africa"; there was no significant cultural variables. Perhaps most important was the fact that profits were negatively related to the amount of diversification, so that airlines that had the largest percentage of investment in nonflight assets also yielded the least return on their investment. Overall, the other predictors suggest that diversified profits are best among airlines that handle a large percentage of international (as opposed to within-country) traffic and that have not grown in their total assets.

The MRs on the two growth measures yielded somewhat different sets of results. In terms of growth in international kilometers performed, the only two predictors that emerged were a cultural and a regional factor. The most important predictor of an airline's international growth was its being classified as a TB. The other factor was not being located in Europe or North America. This pattern is compatible with the previous ANOVA and the MR findings that indicated that European and North American airlines were in disadvantageous positions relative to the industry culture.

The predictors of growth in assets reiterated, in part, the findings for international performance. The two most important influences were regional: location in the Pacific Rim and not being in Europe or North America. In addition, plane usage (flying hours) and diversification appeared as negative factors, so that airlines that increased the most in total assets were the least likely to invest in nonflight areas.

In summary, the analyses in this section suggest that the two most important influences on performance and growth reflect industry culture, that is, the size of the airline and geographic location. Societal culture, however, also appears as a unique source of variance for several indexes, and this finding then helps to confirm the differences among societal groups that was noted in the ANOVAs.

E. Corporate Culture

Corporate culture, which is defined as an organization's shared norms and values, is determined in part by societal and industry cultures and, in this respect, would be similar for organizations in the same societal group or region. However, it is also influenced by an organization's singular history and leadership, and in this respect would be unique. Thus, as presented in the initial model, to understand the strategies of any particular organization, it would be necessary to examine the joint influences of all three types of cultures.

There are two important dimensions of corporate culture examined in this research. The first is strength, which is manifest by the degree to which individuals identify with the organizational mission, the consensus about values and norms, and the support for the leader. Corporate cultures also vary as to their distinctiveness. It is most evident when an organization deviates from the industry or societal norms; however, an organization that is a recognized leader whose strategies are followed by its competitors would also be considered to have a distinctive culture. A primary determinant of both strength and distinctiveness is the presence of a strong leader.

The main purpose of this section is to consider the impact of common societal and industry forces, on the one hand, and idiosyncratic organizational forces, on the other, in shaping the corporate culture in the airlines visited. The following discussion is based on data drawn from the statistical analyses as well as the field visits, although it is important to note that the field data were gathered approximately 3 to 4 years after the period represented by the statistical data. One implication of the tricultural model is that organizations whose corporate culture matched their societal culture and the industry culture would function most effectively.

Four of the five airlines with the best operating margin in 1979 had been visited in the field study; these were Thai International, Garuda (in Indonesia), Pakistan International Airlines (PIA), and Varig. Also visited were the eighth and tenth best, SIA and Air Canada. In contrast, the remaining three visited, Philippines Airlines (PAL), Lufthansa, and Al-italia, had the sixth, seventh, and eighth worst operating margins. By cultural grouping, these individual rankings correspond to the group tendencies; the best performers were AUTs and TBs, and the worst included the two MBs. The only anomaly was Philippine Airlines, classi-fied as an autocracy but showing the poorest margin among the field sample.

The characteristics common to most of the top airlines were, first, a corporate strategy that matched both their regional industry culture and their societal culture and, second, a strong, innovative leader (with the exception of Air Canada). These characteristics are exemplified well by SIA, which appeared to be the prototypical autocratic and Pacific Rim airline. The SIA strategy reported as setting the industry norm for air-lines doing business in the Pacific region was much imitated by others. Thus, its corporate culture was not unique but certainly innovative and strong.

Certainly it met the criteria of having a powerful leader. Pillay had been the chief executive officer since the airline's inauguration and was recognized as a brilliant, competitive strategist. Under Pillay, SIA was one of the pioneer Pacific airlines to expand into the North American and European markets. SIA successfully exploited the image of the Ori-ental airlines as providers of "luxurious, low cost" service. As can be seen in Table 12.4, SIA had one of the highest percentages of cabin crew, second only to Cathay Pacific (Hong Kong). Overall, then, SIA's corpo-rate culture took full advantage of its environmental conditions, and its success set the industry norms for the region.

One of those who attempted to follow the SIA strategy was Thai International, a TB that was directed at the time not by a Thai but by an expatriate Dane originally with Scandinavian Airlines (SAS). As can be seen in Table 12.4, Thai maintained a prototypically bureaucratic struc-ture with over 64% of its personnel in administration and less than 14% providing direct flight services. In other respects, however, Thai seemed to be influenced more by its regional industry culture than by its societal culture. Like the other Pacific Rim carriers, Thai featured high seating configurations combined with low ticket prices. Its growth pattern was also typical of the region; it showed the highest increase in assets of all the airlines in the study (an increase by a factor of 6.68 from 1974 to 1978). Finally, like the other Oriental carriers, Thai emphasized its in-flight passenger services.

It was apparent from interviews with the key executives, however, that Thai's corporate culture had been influenced strongly by its leader. In 1978, Lumholdt was in a very strong leadership position having steer-ed the airline through a severe crisis. Thai International was pursuing a strategy of aggressive international route expansion that had two inno-vative characteristics. The first was the development of highly eco-nomical navigational routes (the "great circle" concept) that resulted in considerable time and fuel savings. The second was the establishment of North American ports in the strategic underserviced locations of Dallas and Seattle. The success of these maneuvers was directly attributable to Lumholdt's ability, first, to develop the strategies and, second, to sell them to the governing bodies. In summary, Thai's corporate culture reflected the regional industry culture and societal culture; however, like SIA, it was primarily determined by the efforts of its leader.

A notable exception to the SIA strategy was Garuda, which was led by Wiweko, the most powerful of the autocratic leaders. Wiweko, like the others, set out to capture a share of the international market. In 1978, Garuda had tripled its assets and doubled its routes over the 1974 level. Wiweko, however, was more technically and less commercially oriented than the other two leaders, and he focused on building a superior fleet. For example, it was Wiweko who developed the controversial cockpit arrangement for the new Airbus that allowed it to fly more economically over long distances. Unlike SIA and Thai, Garuda offered a "bare-bones" service that seemed to appeal primarily to the patriotic loyalty of the Indonesian traveler. Wiweko's strategies took advantage of a market niche, and their success is indicated by its very profitable operating margin. In short, Garuda's corporate culture was clearly less conforming to industry norms and reflected strongly the direction of its leader.

PIA followed close behind Indonesia in profitability. Its personnel structure, as shown in Table 12.4, very clearly fit the TB model. Like the model TB, it showed extraordinarily low productivity (miles performed per employee), and this appeared somewhat puzzling vis-à-vis its prof-itability until one recognizes the compensatory low employee salaries. In many respects, corporate culture did not appear to be highly dis-tinctive at PIA. PIA had suffered from continually changing leadership and dependence on the national government that had freely interfered with its operating policies. At the time of the field visit, Pakistan was governed under martial law, and PIA's CEO did not appear free to exercise leadership or to set independent goals.

However, the situation had been somewhat different in 1978. Under the leadership of its previous CEO, PIA had also embarked upon an expansion policy and had very successfully capitalized upon the profitable Middle East traffic. That CEO was described by employees as an autocrat who did not hesitate to use his political connections, for example, to wield deals with Boeing and other aircraft manufacturers. He was, in fact, later castigated for his independent activities. Overall, however, because of its political dependence and lack of a powerful leadership position, PIA could not be characterized as exhibiting a strong corporate culture. In the field interviews, there was markedly less commitment to the airline expressed among the middle- and lower-senior-level managers than that which had been found elsewhere.

Varig was the only Latin American airline visited, and it was different from the previous top performers in not having undergone extensive growth during the period studied. The aspects of Varig's operating policies that made it so highly successful at the time reviewed are not clear. It clearly outperformed the average TBs and Latin American airlines; yet in most respects, it closely reflected the regional and societal norms. Like other TBs, it maintained a high percentage of nonflight personnel (65% overall). As indicated in Table 12.9, the only deviation in its flight operating strategies was a very large number of flying hours per plane. Otherwise, it does not appear to have any particular advantage.

Perhaps, as suggested by the interviews, Varig was still functioning under the influence of the legendary Rubin Berta. Under his directorship, Varig had emerged as the only Latin American airline with an international reputation; Berta had carved a niche by promoting an image of elite, highly personalized service. Thus, in 1978, while Varig was officially led by Carvalho, its policies still reflected the corporate culture developed by Berta. Certainly, there was a strong sense of esprit de corps and highly shared values. However, there was also evidence of a widening split between the "old, traditional, elitist guard" and the new, efficiency oriented leaders. Like PIA, Varig's culture was undergoing change and unless strong leadership emerges, it may prove less successful in meeting new environmental challenges.

Air Canada, which had originally been classified as an MB, was, in fact, almost an archetypal IMP. It was large and efficiently run; its personnel structure included a higher-than-average percentage of administrative personnel (39.7%) but compensatory lower percentages of sales (16.9%) and maintenance (20.1%) employees. The influence of a strong

Table 12.9. Airline Operating Strategies according to Societal Group and Geographic Region

	Seats/plane	Revenues/TKM[a] (U.S. cents)	Average flying time[b] (All aircraft)	Average flying time[b] (Long-distance aircraft)
Group				
Autocracy	201	56.4	7,356	3,193
Modern bureaucracy	154	79.8	6,735	4,095
Implicit	238	58.7	3,850	3,560
Traditional bureaucracy	168	54.7	8,455	2,865
F (df)	10.22(3,30)***	2.06(3.26)NS	3.37(3,29)*	5.76(3,22)**
Region				
Asia/Africa	219	55.8	8,462	2,514
Europe/North America	172	71.0	4,384	3,726
Latin America	152	54.7	7,607	3,229
Pacific rim	237	53.5	8,823	3,314
F (df)	6.26(3,30)**	0.12(3.26)NS	3.80(3,29)*	1.15(3,22)NS
Airlines				
Indonesia	186	79.0	8,895	—
Philippines	208	46.7	16,720	—
Singapore	233	46.2	4,276	3,032
Germany	169	68.5	4,782	3,967
Italy	186	68.5	4,782	3,399
Canada	210	52.5	5,850	3,294
Brazil	132	55.4	11,617	—
Pakistan	182	57.1	6,176	2,839
Thailand	227	46.5	3,881	—

***$p < .001$; **$p < .01$; *$p < .05$.
[a]TKM = Ton-kilometers.
[b]Index proportional to the annual aircraft hours flown.

corporate culture was not evident, perhaps because of its status as a crown corporation. The CEOs historically had been appointed from other government positions and were held strictly accountable to the Ministry of Transportation. Thus, in contrast to the other top performers but in keeping with the IMP model, a strong leader was not readily identified. Rather, power appeared to be decentralized to functional directors who were encouraged to exercise their individual decision-making authority.

Like Varig (and unlike the others), Air Canada had a limited growth pattern. This could be attributed primarily to regional conditions but also, in part, to its own lack of an aggressive marketing orientation. As suggested by its relatively low ratio of sales personnel, Air Canada was not committed to increasing its inernational market share; rather, it had been mandated to provide "service to Canadians," and during this period, it was somewhat protected by the federal government from serious indigenous competition. Overall, among this group of highly profitable airlines, corporate culture as determined by a compelling organizational mission and/or strong leader was least evident in Air Canada.

Lufthansa ranked twenty-fifth among the sample in terms of its profit-to-assets ratio, and this was in line with the average performance of the MBs in this sample. Structurally and operationally, it appeared to be the quintessential MB airline, emphasizing efficiency and reliability. There are several examples of this from the statistical and field data. First, the personnel figures reveal an extraordinarily low percentage of administrative personnel (16.8%) and correspondingly large percentages of functional and technical staff (37% sales and 27.6% maintenance). Second, it was highly productive as evidenced by the kilometers-to-personnel ratio presented in Table 12.6. Third, its marketing campaign was built around the concept of "on-time" service, as indicated by its brochures and magazine ads.

Lufthansa's corporate culture clearly matched the societal culture and was typical of the region, although it was not well matched to the overall industry demands. Its operating strategy clearly did not follow the pattern of high tourist competition, route expansion, and price cutting that had proven so successful among Asian–Pacific airlines. Instead, Lufthansa was one of the leading proponents of a distinctly European strategy that catered to the business segment, combining low seating with high ticket prices. If the Oriental approach could be characterized as innovative and risky, then Lufthansa's would be conservative and establishment-oriented.

Overall, there was a high degree of consensus regarding Lufthansa's corporate culture. However, it was neither particularly distinctive nor strong, partly because there was not a very powerful leader. Run-hau, Lufthansa's CEO during this period, was very popular. He brought a strong business orientation to the airline, and under his leadership, it greatly increased its technological capabilities. However, because decision making was decentralized to a five-person board, Runhau exercised little individual power, and his personal orientation did not make a strong impact on airline strategies. Indeed, Runhau was removed in 1982 because of implications that he had overstepped his role.

Alitalia, like Italy itself, appeared to be in a state of progression from a traditional to a modern bureaucracy. At Alitalia, this was facilitated by the CEO—Nordio. His goal had been to streamline operations and to increase efficiency, and this had been achieved with a moderate degree of success. The percentage of administrative staff, for example, had been considerably reduced, so that its overall personnel ratios in 1978 were very similar to Lufthansa's. However, the strength of the corporate culture appeared rather weak, partly because it was dissimilar to the values of many of the employees and the society as a whole. Unlike the situation at Lufthansa, for example, the field visit did not indicate that other executives and staff strongly shared in Nordio's philosophy or approach.

Alitalia's culture also appeared to lack distinctiveness. As indicated in Table 12.9, it mirrored Lufthansa's seating and ticketing profiles, and it was nearly as productive (see Table 12.6). However, unlike Lufthansa, it was more of a "follower" than an innovator of these strategies. Overall, then, Nordio enjoyed considered more power than the Lufthansa CEO and had made a definite personal impact on Alitalia's corporate culture; however, the culture appeared less strong and less distinctive.

The poorest performing airline among those visited was PAL. This was surprising, given the fact that it had the advantage of being an autocracy and a Pacific carrier, two groups that had performed very well. To understand PAL, however, it is necessary to appreciate its history of domination by Western powers; the Filipino culture, more than that of any other Southeast Asian country, reflects both Asian and Western values. Moreover, PAL had had had a close relationship with Pan Am during its founding years, similar to the situation at Thai International with SAS. However, the Western influence was more evident at PAL than at Thai International, and PAL seemed to be caught between two cultures.

In some respects, PAL appeared to follow the autocratic pattern. It was superficially like SIA in its personnel structure with one critical difference: PAL had much lower percentages of pilots and cabin crews, and this seemed to effect its ability to successfully carry out its intended strategies. Also like Alitalia, PAL seemed to be an imitator rather than an innovator of strategy. This tended to reduce identity with the organization.

IV. IMPLICATIONS AND CONCLUSIONS

In this study, we raised the question of the relative importance of societal culture on organizational effectiveness in a global industry. In particular, we have suggested that organizational effectiveness is determined by a critical match among three sets of cultures: corporate culture, societal culture, and the environmental conditions, which we have labeled the industry culture. Based on the research literature, we have proposed that the essential components of an organization's corporate culture, such as its structure, decision-making processes, and strategic time frame, would tend to function most effectively when they reflect the values, beliefs, and norms of its members and the surrounding society. This proposition is similar to the position taken by Sekaran and Snodgrass (Chapter 13) whereby they define effectiveness in terms of congruence between individual and organizational goals.

However, as our studies indicated, those organizations whose corporate cultures also fit the *ideal industry culture* tended to outperform those whose corporate cultures did not. This finding has important implications for studies in comparative international management. Thus, whereas the article by Cameron, Freeman, and Kim (Chapter 11) suggested that it would be unwise to apply organizational theories without taking into consideration specific societal cultures, this research suggests that it is equally important to consider the prevailing industry culture. The latter would be defined by factors such as the age and technology of the industry, cost of raw materials, economic conditions, uniform standards and operating principles, and trade regulations and agreements. From this perspective, it is apparent that as the environmental conditions change, so does the ideal corporate culture.

There are two major sources of change in industry culture, one that has a localized influence and the other, industrywide impact. Regional variations in economic growth, for example, will dictate different industry cultures across geographic locations. On the other hand, global changes, such as an increase in oil prices, will shift the industry culture for all organizations. In either situation, an organization will need to modify its corporate culture in order to remain effective. However, we would propose that change will be inherently more difficult for a particular organization when the results of that change are counter to the societal values and norms. For example, if an organization were in a traditional, stable industry that suddenly underwent rapid economic growth because of a technological breakthrough, it may need to change its corporate culture from highly centralized and conservative to decentralized and high-risk. Organizations in government-controlled, bureaucratic societies may find it somewhat difficult to make this transition, whereas those in an autocratic, high-risk society may have a natural preference for this change.

Finally, we would suggest that the tricultural research framework proposed here has relevance for issues of international management. For example, a multinational corporation may have developed a highly successful corporate culture. A key question for the corporation is how well this culture would fit in with the values, beliefs, and customs in another locale. At the same time, however, the corporation would also need to consider the regional influences on the industry culture. We would propose that the effectiveness of the multinational will depend on the degree to which it can adapt its corporate culture to match the indigenous societal culture and the regional industry culture.

V. REFERENCES

Child, J. (1981). The cross national study of organizations. In L. L. Cummings and B. M. Straw (Eds.) *Research in organizational behavior* (Vol. 3). Greenwich, CT: JAI Press.

Davis, S. (1968). Managerial resource development in Mexico. In R. Rehder (Ed.), *Latin American management: Development and performance* (pp. 166–179). Reading, MA: Addison-Wesley.

Gerth, H., & Mills, C. W. (Eds.) (1946). *From Max Weber: Essays in sociology.* New York: Oxford University Press.

Gillin, J. (1960). The middle segments and their values. In R. Adams *et al.* (eds.), *Social change in Latin America today.* New York: Vintage.

Grinyer, P. H., & Spender, J. C. (1979). *Turnaround—Managerial recipes for strategic success.* London: Associated Business Press.

Haire, M., Ghiselli, E., & Porter, L. (1966). *Managerial thinking: An international study.* New York: Wiley.

Harrigan, K. R. (1980). *Strategies for declining businesses.* Lexington, MA: Lexington Books.

Hatten, K. J., Schendel, D. E., & Cooper, A. C. (1978). A strategic model of the U.S. brewing industry: 1952–1971. *Academy of Management Journal, 21,* 592–610.

Hofstede, G. (1980). *Culture's consequences.* Beverly Hills, CA: Sage.

Maurice, M., & Brossard, M. (1976). Is there a universal model of organization structure? *International Studies of Management and Organization, 24,* 612–629.

Miles, R. H. (1982). *Coffin nails and corporate strategies.* Englewood Cliffs, NJ: Prentice-Hall.

Miller, D., & Mintzberg, H. (1983). The case for configuration. In G. Morgan (Ed.), *Beyond method: Strategies for social research* (pp. 57–73). Beverly Hills, CA: Sage.

Mintzberg, H. (1979). *The structuring of organizations.* Englewood Cliffs, NJ: Prentice-Hall.

Peters, T. J., & Waterman, R. H. (1982). *In search of excellence: Lessons from America's best-run companies*. New York: Harper & Row.

Porter, M. E. (1980). *Competitive strategy*. New York: Free Press.

Rieger, F. (1987). *The influence of national culture on organizational structure, process and strategic decision making: A study of international airlines*. Unpublished PhD dissertation, McGill University.

Ronen, S., & Shenker, O. (1985). Clustering countries on attitudinal dimensions: A review and synthesis. *Academy of Management Review, 10*, 435–454.

Segall, M. H. (1979). *Cross-cultural psychology: Human behavior in global perspective*. Monterey, CA: Brooks/Cole.

Siehl, C., & Martin, J. (1981). *Learning organizational culture*. Graduate School of Business, Stanford University.

Smircich, L. (1983). Concepts of culture and organizational analysis. *Administrative Science Quarterly, 28*, 339–358.

Stinchcombe, A. (1965). Social structure and organizations. In J. G. March (Ed.), *Handbook of Organizations* (pp. 142–193). New York: Rand McNally.

Tichy, N. (1982). Managing change strategically: The technical political and cultural keys. *Organization Dynamics*, Autumn, 59–80.

V
CONCLUSION

13

Organizational Effectiveness and Its Attainment

A Cultural Perspective

Uma Sekaran and Coral R. Snodgrass

Organizations have been defined as purposeful systems choicefully designing their subsystems to attain organizational effectiveness (OE). With the growing complexity of modern organizations and globalization of competition, the concept of OE and how it can be achieved through appropriate motivational structures and reward systems have gained increased attention but hitherto eluded satisfactory answers. This chapter proposes that attempting a universally applicable definition of OE and a universal prescription for its attainment are nonfunctional. Instead, a meaningful, culture-specific approach to understanding and attaining OE is advocated. That is, rather than fruitlessly attempting to integrate the plethora of OE models suggested in the literature, this chapter conceptualizes a model of OE from the perspective of the cultural orientations of the members within organizations. With such a perspective, purposeful theory building can progress. The model proposed also indicates how managers operating in different parts of the world will differ both in the criteria they set to measure OE and in designing the organizational systems to attain it.

Uma Sekaran and Coral R. Snodgrass • Department of Management, College of Business and Administration, Southern Illinois University, Carbondale, Illinois 62901.

I. A BRIEF REVIEW OF ORGANIZATIONAL
EFFECTIVENESS LITERATURE

Organization theorists have defined OE in various ways, emphasizing different criteria as to what denotes OE. For instance, OE is described in terms of objectives (Georgopoulos & Tannenbaum, 1957), goals (Etzioni, 1960), efficiency (Katz & Kahn, 1966), resource acquisition (Yuchtman & Seashore, 1967), employee satisfaction (Cummings, 1977), and interdependence (Pfeffer, 1977a). As Philip B. Coulter (1979) remarks, there is little consensus on how to conceptualize, measure, or explain OE. Frank Hoy, David D. Van Fleet, and Melvin J. Yetley (1984), who examined three models of OE, found that they were not even measuring the same construct. This should not surprise us because OE models are, as rightly pointed out by Raymond F. Zammuto (1984), essentially value-based classifications of the construct (the values here being those of the researchers), and the potential number of effectiveness models that can be generated by researchers is virtually limitless. Actually, Sharon Clinebell (1984), who reviewed the OE literature for the period 1978 to 1983 found that researchers had used 10 different models during this period. She, however, remarked that, although the goal model seemed to be dominant, researchers are slowly moving away from a single model, taking a contingency approach to conceptualizing the OE dimensions in their studies (Cameron, 1981; Cunningham, 1977; Hoy et al., Yetley, 1984; Provan, 1980). Clinebell identified four criteria guiding the contingency models of OE proposed by researchers: (1) the dominant constituencies served by the organization, (2) whether the organization is private or public, (3) the environment in which the organization operates (i.e., whether stable or dynamic), and (4) the organization's life cycle. Yet there is no reason why any one frame of reference in the construction of the models should be considered more valid or valuable than the others.

Should we then abandon our efforts at conceptualizing OE? Certainly not, because OE is too useful and important a concept to be ignored or abandoned. In fact, Jeffrey Pfeffer (1977b) discussed the usefulness of the concept and the methodological barriers that exist in comparing the effectiveness of different organizations. He remarked that even though the term *effectiveness*, like the term *leadership*, is becoming a red flag that elicits visceral reactions, we cannot dispense with it but need to continue our efforts to better understand and conceptualize the concept.

We take the position that we can conceptualize OE in a meaningful way, if, instead of conceptualizing models that are based on the values of researchers, we design models based on the values of organizations and their members, thereby making the concept meaningful and useful to the organizations themselves. The issue then is, how would or could or should organizations set their own criteria for effectiveness against which they can assess their performance? When we start examining the issue from the organizations' perspective, several questions come to mind. For instance, would all industrial and business organizations subscribe to the same criteria of effectiveness? Would similar organizations—say private-sector industrial organizations facing the same kind of environment—in different parts of the world choose to attach the same weight to criteria such as profits, as opposed to such criteria as employee satisfaction? The answer is "probably not." For instance, a study conducted in 1984 by the Foundation for Organization Research that surveyed several hundred managers at various levels in the public, private, joint, and government sectors as well as professional organizations all over India found that the total sample ranked morale, team work, and job satisfaction as the most important indicators of effectiveness (Sunderarajan, 1985). Profits were not considered an important factor even by the managers in the private sector who ranked it fifth. This, of course, is not necessarily true for other cultures, such as for instance, the United States. Thus, organizations in different cultures might formulate totally different criteria for assessing OE. Realistic and meaningful research on OE can progress only when we begin to understand the operationalization of the concept from the organizations' standpoint.

Thus, much of the previous work, although enlightening and useful, has failed to bring closure to the topic of OE. As an example, Robert H. Miles (1980), following John P. Campbell (1977), listed 30 measures for the concept of OE, including such variables as absenteeism, management control, conflict, stability, value of human resources, participation and shared influence, and training and development. In another approach, Frank Friedlander and Hal Pickle (1968) discussed the several publics that need to be effectively served by organizations to achieve OE. These include the owners or shareholders, employees, customers, suppliers, creditors, the community, and the government. However, neither of these studies is able to establish a definitive rank ordering, and the question remains as to how organizations will prioritize the publics and the criteria to assess their own effectiveness. We believe such a prioritization will be in a manner that is in keeping with the organization's cultural norms and values. In other words, organizations *establish* their criteria for effectiveness based on the dominant values operating in the culture. We further believe that the key to the *achievement* of effectiveness is through the design of organizational systems that are both congruent with the organization members' cultural values and appropriate with the individuals' concept of how they want to be integrated into the organization. Thus, OE is achieved by establishing the right criteria and the appropriate structures that are congruent with the cultural norms and values of the organizations and its members.

Let us reemphasize the two points made before. One, OE is *defined* in terms of the effectiveness measures "valued" by members of a society. In other words, these cultural values operate at the macrosocietal level. Two, OE is *achieved* by industrial and business organizations when they design systems that are congruent with the organizational members' preferred cultural values operating at the microlevel. Such designing helps the integration of organizations and their members. The important points made here then are that: (1) organizations will define and pursue such achievements that the dominant culture defines as valuable (OE), but (2) they will achieve OE only to the extent that they create motivational structures that will integrate the organizational members into the system. Although this second point has not been explicitly discussed in the organizational literature, it has been discussed oftentimes in the accounting and control systems literature.

Chris Argyris (1967) and Kenneth A. Merchant (1985), among others, have stressed the importance of integrating the individuals' goals and the organizations' goals. The importance of recognizing the inextricable linkages between individuals and OE cannot be overemphasized because it is through individuals' efforts that OE is achieved. Because integration of individuals into the organization is generally thought to be achieved through what is referred to as "goal congruence" (Merchant, 1985), the problems associated with a lack of goal congruence can be devastating to the organization. Merchant points out a number of such problems and the costs thereof to the organization. Examples are employee theft (estimates are that U.S. business loses between $50 and $200 billion per year from white-collar crime), loafing, inappropriate use of sick leave, and use of drugs on the job, all of which are quite costly to the organization. Estimates are that just wasting time during work hours costs U.S. employers $125 billion (Merchant, 1985, pp. 6–7). The costs, financial and otherwise, to organizations in the United States and in other countries from several other problems associated with lack of goal congruence such as lost sales, alienated employees, dissatisfied customers, angered governmental units, and other ineffective outcomes must also be staggering. We therefore believe that any attempt to come to grips with culture-specific definitions of OE must also be explored in conjunction with culture-specific understanding of how it can be achieved. In the remainder of this chapter, we refer to what organizational members want for the organization in terms of societally valued criteria as OE and the systems that allow individuals to get what they want from the organization as *integrating systems* (IS). Organizations become truly effective only when attention is paid to both OE and IS.

II. THE CULTURAL RELATIVITY OF ORGANIZATIONAL EFFECTIVENESS

OE and IS are both concerned with what is of "value" to the organization and its individual members. Because of this concern with values, we can look at culture as an explanatory variable in defining differences in criteria for OE and IS. Culture, as we use it, is a "shared system of meanings" that revolves around value orientations in the minds of the members of the culture group (Inzerilli, 1985; see also Adler, Doktor, & Redding, Chapter 2; Wong-Rieger & Rieger, Chapter 12). Because value orientations differ from group to group (in fact, they differentiate one group from another), the valued criteria for OE and IS will be different in different cultures. Because both OE and IS criteria are seen as culture specific, by understanding the cultural variations on both dimensions, we can evolve a framework for what OE is and how it can be achieved by organizations through appropriate IS in different cultures. We can then have an understanding of OE and how it can be attained.

Very few studies have attempted large-scale empirical research on organizational variations across cultural boundaries. A past review of organizational literature on work values and attitudes by Simcha Ronen and Oded Shenkar (1985) uncovered only six studies that had examined organizational differences across more than 10 countries. Of these, one was done nearly 20 years ago by Mason Haire, Edwin E. Ghiselli, and Lyman W. Porter (1966), three were done in the 1970s (Hofstede, 1976; Ronen & Kraut, 1977; Sirota & Greenwood, 1971) and the remaining two were published in 1980 (Griffeth, Hom, Denisi, & Kirchner, 1980; Hofstede, 1980). The fact that many of the cross-cultural studies are dated is not a major concern. Although, with the passage of time, cultures do change and they vary in terms of homogeneity, they still exhibit dominant and fairly stable value orientations (Kluckhohn & Strodtbeck, 1961). However, the small number of culture units sampled in most of the studies does limit their usefulness. In fact, the Griffeth *et al.* study investigated only Western countries. Geert Hofstede's (1980) is the only large-scale, multiculture study that included over 40 countries. Thus Hofstede's work provides an appropriate base for examining culture-specific criteria for OE and IS.

There is another compelling reason for us to use Hofstede's delineation of cultural variations in organizational values as the basis for evolving models of OE. Hofstede's is the only study that taps the cultural dimensions that are most closely linked to the concepts of IS and OE that are of direct interest to this chapter. None of the other multicultural studies, including those in the international finance or accounting area, tap the dimensions that are useful in investigating the specific issues that are examined here. Another problem arises when a number of cultural differences are lumped together by researchers in order to cluster countries into smaller groups. Much of the richness of understanding the finer points in cultural variations on specific dimensions then get lost, as demonstrated by us later. For instance, Ronen and Shenkar's (1985) clustering of countries according to empirically derived criteria of work attitudes culled from several published studies does not help us to understand why countries clustered in the same group have different OE and IS criteria. To comprehend these finer nuances, one has to go back to Hofstede's finer and more comprehensive delineation of cultural dimensions. Thus, of the studies that have been published so far, only the Hofstede (1980) study measured dimensions of cultural variation that are directly relevant to our concern and detailed enough for developing culture-specific criteria of OE and IS. Thus, for reasons of the vast number of cultures investigated, specificity of organizationally relevant dimensions of cultural variations, and the appropriateness of the operationalized variables to our question at hand, we have chosen to use the work of Hofstede as the framework for our taxonomy.

Hofstede has sometimes been criticized for basing his research on a single multinational corporation (MNC) and for having relatively small sample sizes for some countries despite his overall huge sample (Goodstein, 1981; Hunt, 1981; Triandis, 1982). However, Harry C. Triandis himself, along with several others (for instance, Jaeger, 1984; Ronen & Shenkar, 1985), recognized that Hofstede's is a landmark study that controlled for industrial and organizational climate variables and hence accounts for true variations in work values due to national differences. Triandis (1982) suggested that researchers put their hypotheses to test using Hofstede's results because there is much conceptual coherence in the empirically derived cultural dimensions in Hofstede's study. Indeed, Alfred M. Jaeger (1984) and Risto Tainio and Timo Santalainen (1984) have done empirical research based on Hofstede's cultural dimensions to test the effectiveness of OD interventions and the transferability of OD programs cross-culturally. We intend using the four dimensions delineated by Hofstede that are central to determining OE and how to achieve it by designing IS.

III. HOFSTEDE'S CULTURAL DIMENSIONS: ORGANIZATIONAL EFFECTIVENESS (OE) AND INTEGRATING SYSTEMS (IS)

Hofstede (1980) empirically established, through ecological correlations, four organizationally relevant dimensions of culture, and mapped over 40 countries along these dimensions. He called these four dimensions power distance, uncertainty avoidance, masculinity–femininity and individualism–collectivism. These four dimensions provide a useful and meaningful way to theorize about which cultures will predominantly subscribe to which particular criteria of macro-OE and micro-IS. The masculinity–femininity dimension, as described later, dictates the cherished achievements that organizations in different cultures will pursue, and the other dimensions (as explained later) define the integrating mechanisms that will be most valued by the organizational members in terms of what they want from the organization.

The theory proposed by us, then, is that organizations will be "effective" only when there is an alignment or "fit" among: (1) the cultural context in which the organization is embedded, (2) the criteria that the organization sets for OE, and (3) the IS systems it uses. If either the OE criteria established or IS, or both are out of synch with the culture, then OE is compromised. In other words, the outcomes for the organization will not be satisfying, and the organization will not be "effective" if the organization is not pursuing achievements that the dominant culture defines as valuable in terms of the masculinity–femininity dimension, or if its integrating systems are not such as are valued by the organizational members who function within an organizational cultural context in terms of the other three dimensions and the individualism–collectivism dimension in particular.

A. Masculinity–Femininity

Masculinity highlights the importance that people in a country generally attach to such tangible job-related aspects as monetary earnings, advancement, recognition, and so on—aspects usually associated with the male role. Femininity, on the other hand, highlights importance that people in some cultures attach to more intangible job-related aspects such as cooperation, empathy, a good quality of life, and the like—

aspects usually associated with the feminine role, to which all individuals in such societies subscribe, whether they are men or women.

B. Individualism–Collectivism

Individualism basically refers to the relative importance that members of a society attach to personal time, job-related freedom, and challenge. Individualism connotes members' preferences for goal-oriented, active, and self-directed behaviors. Collectivism, on the other hand, indicates a preference for group-oriented behavior and acting in the collective capacity (in contrast to being individualistic). It also signifies some degree of dependence of members on the organization to train them and provide them with working conditions that are conducive to the accomplishments of the task at hand. Collectivism thus indicates preferences for collective or group functioning and a certain degree of passivity and dependence of members on the organization for goal direction and goal achievement.

C. Power Distance

Power distance (PD) relates to the cultural values determining how comfortable organizational members are with the way power is distributed within the system. Where the PD is large, there is a powerful group at the top hierarchical level, making decisions that are implemented without much questioning by people at the lower levels. Such a system followed by organizations would be effective in cultures where people at lower levels have a high dependency need. In culture groups with low PD, the people at various hierarchical levels operate in a consultative decision-making mode where both superiors and subordinates interact interdependently. There is no cherished and valued desire for members higher up in the hierarchy to be authoritarian or for the members at lower levels to be entirely dependent on the higher-ups in the organization.

A hierarchy with centralized, rigid decision-making powers will mesh with a culture group high on the PD dimension, and a decentralized, fluid hierarchical structure with egalitarian interactions will mesh with the low PD culture groups. Thus decision making and hierarchical structures are related to the PD dimension.

D. Uncertainty Avoidance

Uncertainty avoidance (UA) reflects the extent to which culture groups are stressed by the uncertainty of an unknown future. Cultures weak on UA have a high tolerance for ambiguity and do not feel stress at the prospect of facing uncertainty and what the future might bring to them. Cultures high on UA have a lower tolerance for ambiguity and experience high levels of stress because of an unknown and uncertain future.

In organizations embedded in a high UA culture, organizational members from top to bottom will feel compelled to "beat the unknown future." They would like to accomplish this through comprehensive long-range planning and trying to install "security cushions" such as rules, regulations, contingency modes of operation, having extensive information flow mechanisms, and the like. Their monitoring systems could become pretty complex. A need for a good deal of formalized procedures will also pervade such systems. Organizations that find themselves in a low UA culture will have a very low level of need for such structures because they are not unduly apprehensive of the uncertainties of the future. In such cultures, too many structures to ward off uncertainty might become irksome to members.

E. OE and the Masculinity–Femininity Dimension

Though the terminology *Masculinity–Femininity* may not be the most apt one to describe what Hofstede intends, we will continue to use Hofstede's labels in this chapter.

The masculinity–femininity dimension gives us an idea of what organizations in different cultures value and how they would define their effectiveness. Organizations in masculine cultures attach importance to money, performance and growth, bigness and fastness, achievement, and excellence in performance. Organizational members in feminine cultures value people orientation, quality of life and environment, service ideals, being in unison with others, and smallness and slowness (Hofstede, 1980, 1983). Thus, whereas in masculine cultures, financial criteria and growth might be indicants of OE, in feminine cultures, soft measures such as product safety, customer satisfaction, and social responsiveness in terms of clean air and healthy products might become prime factors for assessing OE. These criteria are valued for their own sake and not because they have an influence on profits.

F. Integrating Structures and the Other Three Cultural Dimensions

The individualism–collectivism dimension clearly throws light on how organizations can design IS to offer individuals what they desire from the organization. For instance, in cultures where employees value getting ahead, autonomy, and an outlet for individual initiative (individualistically oriented members), IS should be designed around promotion, increased autonomy, and exhibited creativity. Fast tracks, and individually based reward systems could well become parts of the integrating structure in such systems. Where members desire to work together harmoniously as groups and depend on the organization to provide them training, direction, and a good quality of life (collectivistic members), the IS should be designed around group work and group members's satisfaction. Group-based work and performance reward systems, good training programs, guided supervision, and facilities that enhance the working conditions within the system are some of the structures that organizations should have to ensure IS that are congruent with what members want from the system.

Because the PD dimension indicates the level of comfort or discomfort members feel with either decentralized and egalitarian decision making or centralized and authoritarian decision-making styles, organizational power has to be distributed within the hierarchy in a way that is congruent with members' preferences. In high PD cultures, if organizations initiate too much decentralization, members at the lower levels may feel acutely uncomfortable and ill-equipped to interface with their work. By contrast, maintaining a respectful distance between superior and subordinate, using formal modes of addressing male superiors as Mr. X or "sir," and superiors instructing subordinates on what to do and how to operate would make both superiors and subordinates feel comfortable and be "at ease." This will enhance the members' operating effectiveness. By contrast, in low PD cultures if organizations try to stratify their employees and centralize decision making too much, the members will feel "put down" and will not be motivated to give forth their best. In such cultures, more egalitarian practices and involving employees in participative decision-making processes will motivate them to perform well.

Likewise, the extent of planning, formalization, and installation of complex information systems in organizations is a function of the extent of UA proneness of the members in different cultures. For instance, if attention is not paid to long-range planning, formulating extensive policies and procedures, and highly systematized management information systems (MIS) in cultures high in UA, the attainment of OE might be greatly compromised. Having an excess of these in organizations weak in UA, on the other hand, will be perceived by organizational members as "too much red tape and stifling bureaucratic procedures." Being frustrated and totally dissatisfied, the members then will be reluctant to make their full and valuable contributions to the organization that would again compromise the attainment of OE.

In sum, OE will be defined by organizations in different cultures in terms that are congruent with the cultural dimensions of masculinity–

femininity, and OE will be achieved when organizations have IS that are congruent with what organizational members prefer in terms of the other three dimensions of individualism–collectivism, PD, and UA. When there is not such an alignment among the cultural dimensions, the criteria set for OE and the IS for attaining them, organizations will not be effective.

It is entirely possible that, operating within an overarching dominant value system, organizations in different industries, sectors, environments, and in different life-cycle stages—the contingency situations identified by Clinebell—within the same culture will differentially assign weights to the different components of OE. The important point to note, however, is that the criteria of OE are choices that would be made by organizations in different ways in different cultures, conforming to some critical underlying dominant cultural values that govern their environment. Within the confines of this dominant value, different types of organizations in the same country might assign different weights to different criteria.

For the sake of clarity and ease of reference, the value-based preferences on the two extreme points in the continua of the four cultural dimensions are listed in Table 13.1. Hofstede used his empirical results

Table 13.1. Dimensions of Culture and Valued Outcomes

Masculinity	**Femininity**
Monetary gains	Cooperation
Growth and bigness	Empathy
Performance and productivity	Quality of life
	Service ideals
	Social welfare
Individualism	**Collectivism**
Personal time	Training
Freedom on the job	Supportive work environment
Challenge	Goal direction
Individual responsibility	Collective responsibility
High power distance	**Low power distance**
Giving and receiving orders	Egalitarian relationships
Top-down decision making/stratification	Consultative decision making
Rigid hierarchies/stratification	Flexible hierarchies
	Participative management
High uncertainty avoidance	**Low uncertainty avoidance**
Explicit rules and regulations	Very few formalized rules and regulations
Well-defined organizational structures and procedures	Flexible organizational structures and procedures
High need for long-term planning	Low need for long-term planning
Explicit information systems	Lower need for MIS

to substantiate the cultural relativity of various concepts such as need for achievement, self-actualization, and quality of life (Hofstede, 1981, 1983). He, however, did not examine the concept of OE and its attainment in relation to the dimensions he had delineated. We have used Hofstede's empirically established cultural dimensions to conceptualize OE in terms of both what is desired for the organization from a societal level (OE) and how that can be achieved by organizations through their members by paying attention to what organizational members want from the organization and designing the right structure (IS). The one without the other does not ensure OE. Thus our theory of OE builds upon Hofstede's framework to enunciate and clarify the importance of the alignment among cultural dimensions, setting criteria for OE, and achieving OE through IS in organizations.

IV. CULTURAL DIMENSIONS AND OE CONNECTIONS

We have examined how OE is defined and achieved, based on the cultural norms and values operating at the societal and organizational levels in different cultures. Broadly speaking, we can conceptualize at least two typologies for defining OE based on the two extremes of the continuum of the masculinity–femininity dimension. There will be several other finer distinctions in the two typologies based on where along the continuum any particular country happens to fit in. Again, taking the extremes of the continua of the other three dimensions, there can be at least eight different culture-specific typologies for achieving OE. For example, countries high on PD, UA, and individualism will achieve OE through IS that are totally different from countries low on all these three dimensions. Because an illustration taking into account all three dimensions might become enormously complex, let us take for illustrative purposes just one of the three other dimensions—the individualism–collectivism dimension—and examine how OE is achieved in extremely masculine and extremely feminine cultures. We can set up four distinct typologies for defining and attaining OE based on combinations of the masculinity–femininity dimension and the individualism–collectivism dimension. Figure 13.1 depicts the four quadrants that will be presently discussed to explain the four typologies.

A. Organizations in the Masculine–Individualism Quadrant

Masculine organizations whose members have individualistic orientations (Quadrant 1 in figure 13.1) will set their OE criteria to encompass profits, return on investment, sales turnover, market share, growth rate,

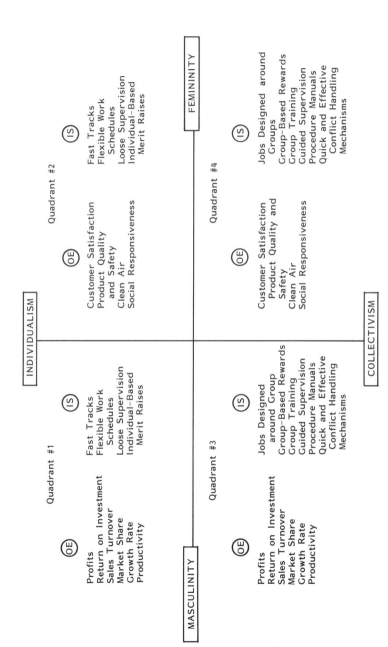

Figure 13.1. Typologies for organizational effectiveness criteria.

productivity, and other achievement and growth-oriented criteria. To achieve OE, they have to develop IS structures such as fast tracks, flexible work schedules, loose supervision, and individualized merit raises, all of which judiciously provide members recognition, challenge, autonomy, and responsibility.

B. Organizations in the Feminine–Individualism Quadrant

Feminine organizations whose members are individualistically oriented (Quadrant 2), will set their OE criteria to include customer satisfaction, product quality and safety, clean air, and social responsibility. The same kinds of IS structures as described for the masculine-individualism quadrant, such as fast tracks, flexible schedules, loose supervision, and individual merit raises that are equitable will help attain OE because such structures will help individual employees to fulfill their aspirations, feel responsible for their challenging jobs, and enjoy their personal time and freedom.

C. Masculine-Collectivistic Organizations

Organizations falling in Quadrant 3 that are masculine and collectivist will have as their criteria for OE profits, return on investment, growth, productivity, and similar criteria that denote monetary growth and bigness. Mechanisms for IS will include designing jobs around work groups, group-based rewards, group training programs, guided supervision, procedural manuals, and structuring mechanisms for conflict handling that lead to group harmony.

D. Feminine-Collectivistic Organizations

Feminine organizations whose members have a collectivist orientation (Quadrant 4) will emphasize customer service and satisfaction, product quality and safety, clean air, and social responsibility for OE (as in Quadrant 2). Integrating systems will however be the same as in Quadrant 3 (jobs designed around work groups, training, etc.).

In summary, we have argued that, broadly speaking, organizations in feminine cultures will tend to rank the overall quality of life for the society in general first and rank the financial criteria somewhat lower. Organizations in extremely masculine cultures, on the other hand, will rank the profit and growth criteria much higher than the quality of life criteria. Organizations having members who are individualistic will structure their IS differently than organizations having collectivistic members in their systems. Countries at various points in the continua on the masculinity–femininity and individualism–collectivism dimensions will thus have an overarching framework for determining their OE and IS criteria for assessing OE, depending upon where along the line they fall on these two dimensions. When we add on the dimensions of high and low PD and strong and weak UA, we can develop 16 typologies and initiate 16 types of structures including hierarchical and decision-making variables and MIS systems variables in the equations pertaining to the definition and attainment of OE criteria.

Some cultures may be more homogeneous, and others may be somewhat heterogenous with subcultures embedded within the nation. Hofstede's cultural dimensions are based on ecological correlations and do not take into account individual differences or regional differences that might exist within the country. But we would not normally expect any violent clashes in organizational values and norms to operate in different business and manufacturing organizations within a country. Our theory then is that OE is more likely to be attained when there is an alignment among the effectiveness criteria set by the organization, the integrating structures in the organization, and the cultural norms and values in which the organization exists and operates.

V. DOES SUCH A THEORY HOLD WATER?—A PRELIMINARY TEST OF THE MODEL

Having conceptualized some culture-specific organizational effectiveness criteria, it will be useful to test the theory using information already known and available about companies in the industrialized world. For this purpose we take four different countries that fall in the four different quadrants as empirically mapped by Hofstede (1980). Figure 13.2 shows where exactly in the four quadrants these four countries—United States (in Quadrant 1—i.e., masculine-individualistic), Sweden (in Quadrant 2—i.e., feminine-individualistic), Japan (in Quadrant 3—i.e., masculine–collectivistic, and Yugoslavia (in Quadrant 4—i.e., feminine collectivistic) fall as per Hofstede's mapping.

The discussions relating to Sweden and Yugoslavia are based primarily on descriptions provided by Miles (1980), among others, and discussions on Japan and the United States are based primarily on descriptions provided by Coral R. Snodgrass and John H. Grant (1986), among others. These will now be detailed.

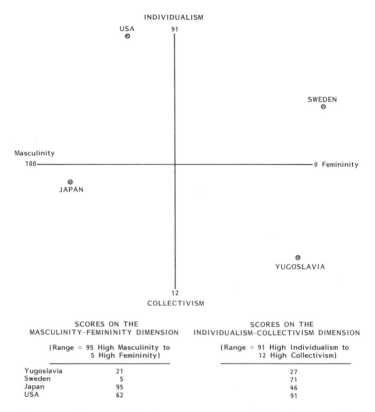

Figure 13.2. Mapping of the four countries as per Hofstede's (1980) data.

	SCORES ON THE MASCULINITY–FEMININITY DIMENSION (Range = 95 High Masculinity to 5 High Femininity)	SCORES ON THE INDIVIDUALISM–COLLECTIVISM DIMENSION (Range = 91 High Individualism to 12 High Collectivism)
Yugoslavia	21	27
Sweden	5	71
Japan	95	46
USA	62	91

A. Yugoslavia

In Hofstede's mapping, Yugoslavia falls in the feminine-collectivism quadrant. As per our theory, Yugoslavia should then have organizations that set OE criteria that would not be primarily geared to profits or other such masculine criteria. Rather, because the culture is feminine, Yugoslavian organizations should seek to achieve socially responsive goals. They would also strive to adopt IS that will satisfy their collectivistically inclined employees through mechanisms such as work groups, training exercises, and collective responsibility. The fact that Yugoslavia is a socialist country is perhaps the natural state that would be expected given Hofstede's typing. A clear implication of the way the organizations in Yugoslavia operate enhances and supports a "Hofstedian" interpretation. As described by Miles (1980), social welfare is indeed an explicitly stated goal of Yugoslav organizations. This takes the form of providing full employment opportunities and worker involvement in the organizations' activities. These goals are enhanced by the political system that seeks a classless social structure and shared ownership of production. Profitability (a masculine goal) is subordinated to equality and cooperation (feminine goals). Worker involvement and nonalienation become more important to organizations than increasing profits. It is also interesting to see that Yugoslav organizations are not run by centralized state planning. Rather, the organizations are "managed" through the collective responsibility of employees. (For more complete discussions on Yugoslav organizations, see Adizes, 1971). Thus the individuals within the organizations are fully integrated into and have total responsibility for the organization. The organization itself is deemed effective in terms of enhancing social welfare. Thus Yugoslavian organizations display characteristics predicted by our model, prioritizing social goals and group-oriented IS. As per our theory, if an organization in Yugoslavia were to structure its IS around individualistically oriented mechanisms such as fast tracks and individually based reward systems, OE will be compromised for the organization.

B. Sweden

Sweden falls in the feminine-individualism quadrant. As per our theory, Swedish organizations should seek to achieve the feminine OE criteria of a good quality of life for society. Further they should have IS mechanisms that permit organizational members to achieve their prized desires of freedom, challenge, and individual responsibility. It is certainly true that Swedish organizations do pursue the goals of social welfare. Although the Social Democrats have achieved the goal of redistribution of wealth, thereby giving Sweden both a high standard of living and comprehensive social welfare system, the Swedish organizations have pursued the goal of full employment, employee satisfaction, and a good quality of life. These are prioritized over profits and achieving a competitive position in the international marketplace. Miles (1980) cites an example that occurred during the recession in 1971–1975. At that time, although unemployment and production slowdowns were the rule worldwide, Swedish organizations (supported by the government) maintained full employment, full production, and even increased wages. The result of this was huge inventories and a highly inflated wage structure, both of which placed Swedish industry in a very unfavorable competitive position (p. 397). However, a favorable international competitive advantage is not a criterion for OE in Sweden! The IS in Swedish organizations allow individuals freedom to do their job and take on individual responsibility. Swedish organizations have instituted new workplace designs characterized by greater autonomy, greater personal challenge on the job, and more individual responsibility (Miles, 1980, pp. 396). Thus Swedish organizations, like Yugoslavian organizations, seek to achieve OE in social welfare terms. However, the IS used to place the individual within the organization are based on individual criteria such as autonomy as opposed to collective criteria such as work group rule. Thus, observed characteristics of Swedish organizations "make sense" in terms of our model. Further, observed similarities and differences between Sweden and Yugoslavia both of which have feminine cultures are rendered understandable by taking the IS into consideration.

C. The United States

The United States is characterized as masculine-individualistic. As per our theory, the U.S. organizations should seek to pursue the goals of profits and growth, and the organizational members should be integrated through mechanisms stressing individual achievement, challenge, and freedom. It is a well-known fact that U.S. organizations are institutionalized with the goal of "maximization of shareholder wealth." Survival and longevity of the organization are aspects of OE that are measured through such criteria as profits and market growth. U.S. firms react to market pressures not by sacrificing profits as Swedish firms have been observed to do but rather by laying off employees and closing down unprofitable units. However, when business is thriving, the organizations provide individual responsibility to the workers and offer them freedom on the job. In that sense, the United States and Swedish organizations are very similar. They both integrate individual members into the organizations by the criteria predicted by our model, that is, individual-based criteria such as autonomy and challenge. However, observed differences between the United States and Sweden on OE criteria (profits in the United States and employee satisfaction in Sweden) also are shown to be appropriate each to its cultural-specific value orientation.

D. Japan

Japan is characterized as masculine-collectivistic. As per our theory, Japanese organizations should pursue goals of growth and profits, although integrating the organizational members through the group. Japanese organizations certainly seek profits and growth. They closely monitor their market share and the changes that take place in the market environment. Most large Japanese companies have financial statements that look no different from their American counterparts (Itami, 1978). Japanese companies are fiercely competitive and measure their competitive strength using the masculine measures of success (Taylor, 1983). As an example, *Business Week* featured a cover article on Toyota's bid to totally dominate car sales (*Business Week*, November 4, 1985). Thus the Japanese clearly use the masculine measures of OE predicted through the Hofstede model. In that sense, Japanese and U.S. organizations are quite similar. However, Japanese and U.S. organizations differ in the IS used to integrate the individual organization members into the organization. In Japan, the individual is subjugated to the group, not separate from it. Anthropological studies of the Japanese indicate that they personally view themselves as a part of a group and *not* as individuals (Nakane, 1972). The IS in Japanese organizations are based on activities such as group decision making, group responsibility, and group evaluation. They have extremely careful screening systems to ensure the quality of the new incoming group members. They also utilize extensive in-house training programs to enhance group performance. Group ostracism becomes the most severe form of punishment in Japanese organizations. Thus Japanese organizations are observed to be just as predicted by the theory. Further, our theory enhances our understanding of the Japanese by clearly articulating both the criteria used for assessing OE (the masculine criteria of growth and profits) and the criteria used for achieving OE through the IS (the collectivistic criteria of group activities). We can now comprehend how the Japanese can be observed to be both ruthlessly and fiercely competitive in the pursuit of market share, whereas at the same time expending considerable organizational resources supporting organizational group members. We in the United States often find the pursuit of profits to be incompatible with concern for our group members. However, the Japanese do not find these two to be incongruent at all. In point of fact, this distinction between Japan and the United States is part of our cultural differences. A vivid, clear, and interesting portrait of a Japanese organization's pursuit of "masculine" goals and the individuals' willing cooperation and subjugation to the group has been presented by Satoshi Kamata (1982).

VI. IMPLICATIONS

The theory of alignment of OE and IS within a cultural perspective is a useful conceptual approach for managers, practitioners, and researchers. The theory helps organizations to explicitly set and attain their criteria for effectiveness rather than operate on a trial-and-error basis. The model is particularly useful for managerial decision making with regard to a number of issues. It is invaluable to managers who have the responsibility for designing appropriate goals for the organization as in the strategic planning function and for designing appropriate IS systems that would be salient to organizational members. MNCs operating in different cultures will also be sensitized to the issue of not having uniform policies, reward systems, and effectiveness criteria irrespective of where they operate. For instance, a Swiss MNC operating in Belgium, France, Italy, Portugal, and Spain would realize that the Swiss manager cannot set the same criteria for effectiveness in all the countries. Although the criteria and IS of the head office may not be totally inappropriate for Belgium and Italy, they may have to be different for France (which is more feminine) and Spain (which is less individualistic), and totally different for Portugal (which is more feminine and collectivistic than any of the other five countries). If the Swiss manager tries to motivate all employees irrespective of the country in which the MNC operates through merit raises, paying scant attention to the quality of life at the workplace, or vice versa, the MNC will be compromising OE in the three countries. If, for some reason, the Swiss MNC wants to establish uniform OE criteria for all its subsidiaries, then Hofstede's mapping would assist the MNC to determine which countries offer greater compatability with respect to all four dimensions. That would eliminate the need to design different systems and different criteria for effectiveness.

This brings us to an earlier issue we had raised about problems with clustering countries into groups based on broad criteria such as the Ronen and Shenkar (1985) classification. Ronen and Shenkar grouped France, Belgium, Italy, Spain, and Portugal under the Latin European cluster, and Switzerland fell into the Germanic cluster. Yet Switzerland is closer to Belgium and France in terms of individual and organizational values on the dimensions considered important here but away from Spain and Portugal. Thus, although broad clusters might lend parsimony and may serve some specific purposes, they lose the richness of insights offered in Hofstede's clustering of countries along the four dimensions.

A. A Word of Caution regarding Managerial Implications

Managers should be aware that our theory is based on dominant tendencies of culture groups, and individuals within groups may display different behavioral tendencies and values. Thus not every single individual in the organization is going to be motivated by appropriate

IS. However, knowing the dominant tendencies is useful for designing systems for total organizations and assists good management decisions.

B. Implications for Research

This chapter makes two suggestions for research. The culture-specific model presented here helps us to get away from universalistic notions and offers fresh insights on how to usefully conceptualize OE from the organizations' perspective. A second contribution made in this chapter is in explicating how individual goals and organizational goals can both be attained by understanding the cultural values on both dimensions. In other words, the theory offers a conceptual scheme on how organizations can design their systems to achieve OE through individuals' motivated efforts. The discussions presented here have implications for both empirical testing and further theory building. With the Japanese currently establishing joint ventures in the United States, an ideal situation presents itself for testing if the Japanese manager in the United States will have IS mechanisms congruent with the individualistically oriented U.S. organizational members, and if there are deviations, what effect they have on OE. Other things that could be tested are the effects of cultural heterogeneity, if any, on the theory, the rate of cultural diffusion on the models proposed here, and the impact of the interactions of other variables such as size and technology on the IS design characteristics, and whether that would mean that OE has to be compromised. OE and its attainment as they are conceptualized here could be the springboard for further ideas and refinements.

VII. CONCLUSION

The conceptualization and operationalization of the organizational effectiveness construct has been a vexing issue among researchers for a long time now. Contingency approaches that have hitherto been suggested have ignored the cultural values that are so integral to the definition of the construct. One of the reasons that there has been prolonged controversy over which of the models is superior and whether an open systems model is viable or not has been due to the fact that the individual has not been explicitly tied to organizational effectiveness in a meaningful way. Additionally, we believe that the confusion has persisted because OE has not been recognized as a value-based construct and that values are essentially nothing other than cultural manifestations of a society's attitudes and beliefs as to how things ought to be. In this chapter we have tried to sort out these issues, using the cultural dimensions delineated by Hofstede, and including culture as a significant variable in defining and operationalizing organizational effectiveness. We hope this preliminary discussion will spur researchers to test, expand, and refine the theory proposed by us here.

The approach we have taken is echoed by Chimzie A. B. Osigweh in Chapter 1, and Cary L. Cooper and Charles J. Cox in Chapter 3, where they have taken the position that certain management principles and practices that account for effectiveness in a specific culture do not necessarily translate to another. This of course, implies that, although some practices can and are universally applicable, others are more particularistic. As an example of the former, Richard C. Hoffman and W. Harvey Hegarty (in Chapter 6) found very little evidence of cultural variation among their sample of Western firms with respect to some of the strategic decisions made. Jeremiah Sullivan, Teruhiko Suzuki, and Yasumasa Kondo (in Chapter 8) also found some dissimilarities as well as similarities between Japan and the United States in performance control, despite significant differences in the culture of these two countries. As illustrations of the latter, Dexter Dunphy and Jeannette Shi's work in Chapter 10 indicates that meaningful differences exist between an Anglo-American style of management and an East Asian style. Wiktor Askanas shows, in Chapter 4, that Western organizational science techniques evoke reverse management practices in centrally planned Warsaw Pact nations. Durhane Wong-Rieger and Fritz Rieger also indicate in Chapter 12 that culture makes a significant difference in the operations of the international airline industry.

So we are back to the basic issue of identifying nomothetic and idiographic characteristics of cultures that have been addressed before (see for example, Sekaran, 1981, 1983). As more and more cross-cultural investigations are undertaken to find answers to different issues revolving around culture, we will have a better handle on those factors that culture does definitely have an impact on and those that are not culture bound.

VIII. REFERENCES

Adizes, I. (1971). *Industrial democracy Yugoslav style*. New York: Free Press.
Argyris, C. (1967). *Integrating the individual and the organization*. New York: Wiley.
Business Week. (1985). Toyota's Fastlane. November 4, pp. 42–44.
Cameron, K. (1981). Domains of organizational effectiveness in colleges and universities. *Academy of Management Journal*, 24(1), 25–27.

Campbell, J. P. (1977). On the nature of organizational effectiveness. In P. S. Goodman, J. M. Pennings & Associates (Eds.), *New perspectives on organizational effectiveness* (pp. 13–55). San Francisco: Jossey-Bass.

Clinebell, S. (1984). Organizational effectiveness: An examination of recent empirical studies and the development of the contingency view. *Midwest Academy of Management Proceedings*, 92–102.

Coulter, P. (1979). Organizational effectiveness in the public sector: The example of municipal fire protection. *Administrative Science Quarterly*, 24(1), 65–81.

Cummings, L. L. (1977). Emergence of the instrumental organization. In P. S. Goodman, J. M. Pennings & Associates, (Eds.), *New perspectives on organizational effectiveness* (pp. 56–62). San Francisco: Jossey-Bass.

Cunningham, J. B. (1977). Approaches to the evaluation of organizational effectiveness. *Academy of Management Review*, 2(3), 463–474.

Etzioni, A. (1960). Two approaches to organizational analysis: A critique and a suggestion. *Administrative Science Quarterly*, 5, 257–278.

Friedlander, F., & Pickle, H. (1968). Components of effectiveness in small organizations. *Administrative Science Quarterly*, 13(2), 289–304.

Georgopoulos, B. S., & Tannenbaum, A. S. (1957). A study of organizational effectiveness. *American Sociological Review*, 22(5), 534–540.

Goodstein, L. D. (1981, Summer). Commentary on: Do American theories apply abroad: American business value and cultural imperialism. *Organizational Dynamics*, 49–54.

Griffeth, R. W., Hom, P. W., Denisi, A., & Kirchner, W. (1980). *A multivariate, multinational comparison of managerial attitudes.* Paper presented at the annual Academy of Management Meeting, Detroit.

Haire, M., Ghiselli, E. E., & Porter, L. W. (1966). *Managerial thinking: An international study.* New York: Wiley.

Hofstede, G. (1976). Nationality and exposed values of managers. *Journal of Applied Psychology*, 61, 148–155.

Hofstede, G. (1980). *Culture's consequences: International differences in culture's work related values.* Beverly Hills, CA: Sage.

Hofstede, G. (1981, Summer). Do American theories apply abroad? *Organizational Dynamics*, 63–68.

Hofstede, G. (1983). National cultures in four dimensions: A research based theory of cultural differences among nations. *International Studies of Management & Organizations*, 13(1-2), 46–74.

Hoy, F., Van Fleet, D. D., & Yetley, M. J. (1984). Comparative organizational effectiveness research leading to an invention strategy. *Journal of Management Studies*, 21(4), 443–462.

Hunt, J. W. (1981, Summer). Commentary on: Do American theories apply abroad: Applying American behavior science—some cross-cultural problems. *Organizational Dynamics*, 55–62.

Inzerilli, G. (1985). *Perceptual models of organization structure in different cultures.* Paper presented at the annual Academy of Management Meeting, San Diego.

Itami, H. (1978). A Japanese-American comparison of management productivity. *Japanese Economic Studies*, 7(1), 3–41.

Jaeger, A. M. (1984). The appropriateness of organization development outside North America. *International Studies of Management & Organization*, 14(1), 23–25.

Kamata, S. (1982). *Japan in the passing lane: An insider's account of life in a Japanese auto factory.* New York: Pantheon Books.

Katz, D., & Kahn, R. L. (1966). *The social psychology of organizations.* New York: Wiley Eastern Pvt. Ltd.

Kluckhohn, F. R., & Strodtbeck, F. L. (1961). *Variations in value orientation.* New York: Row, Peterson & Co.

Merchant, K. A. (1985). *Control in business organizations.* Boston: Pitman.

Miles, R. (1980). *Macro organizational behavior.* Santa Monica: Goodyear Publishing Co.

Nakane, C. (1972). *Japanese society.* Los Angeles: University of California Press.

Pfeffer, J. (1977a). Power and resource allocation in organizations. In B. M. Staw & G. R. Salancik (Eds.), *New directions in organizational behavior* (pp. 235–265). Chicago: St. Clair.

Pfeffer, J. (1977b). Usefulness of the concept. In P. S. Goodman, J. M. Pennings & Associates (Eds.), *New perspectives on organizational effectiveness* (pp. 132–145). San Francisco: Jossey-Bass.

Provan, K. (1980). Board power and organizational effectiveness among human service agencies. *Academy of Management Journal, 23*(2), 221–236.

Ronen, S., & Kraut, A. I. (1977). Similarities among countries based on employee work values and attitudes. *Columbia Journal of World Business, 12*(2), 89–96.

Ronen, S., & Shenkar, O. (1985). Clustering countries on attitudinal dimensions: A review and synthesis. *Academy of Management Review, 10*(3), 435–454.

Sekaran, U. (1981). Are organizational concepts and measures transferable to another culture: An empirical investigation. *Academy of Management Journal, 24*(2), 409–416.

Sekaran, U. (1983). Methodological and theoretical issues and advancements in cross-cultural research. *Journal of International Business Studies, 14*(3), 61–73.

Sirota, D., & Greenwood, J. M. (1971). Understand your overseas workforce. *Harvard Business Review, 49*(1), 53–60.

Snodgrass, C. R., & Grant, J. H. (1986). Cultural influences on strategic planning and control systems. *Advances in Strategic Management, 4,* 205–228.

Sunderarajan, U. (1985). *Organizational effectiveness in an Indian public and private sector organization.* Unpublished doctoral dissertation. New Delhi: Indian Institute of Technology.

Tainio, R., & Santalainen, T. (1984). Some evidence for the cultural reliability of organizational development programs. *Journal of Applied Behavioral Science, 20*(2), 93–111.

Taylor, J. (1983). *Shadows of the rising sun.* New York: William Morrow.

Triandis, H. (1982). Review of culture's consequences: International differences in work-related values. *Human Organization, 41*(1), 86–90.

Yuchtman, E., & Seashore, S. (1967). A systems resource approach to organizational effectiveness. *American Sociological Review, 32*(6), 891–903.

Zammuto, R. F. (1984). A comparison of multiple constituency models of organizational effectiveness. *Academy of Management Review, 9*(4), 606–616.

14

Organizational Science in a Global Environment
Future Directions

Richard M. Steers

I. PROLOGUE

This book has attempted to review much of what is currently known about organizational science in a global environment. As such, it represents a relatively unique perspective by forcing us to consider how cultural and national diversity affects organization design, employee behavior, and organizational effectiveness in different parts of the world. Indeed, if we draw nothing else from the collection of essays in this volume, we should at the very least learn the value of making organizational science international. For too long we have focused on American organizations and American approaches to understanding these organizations. In view of the changing economic and political situation, clearly the time has come to expand our intellectual horizons to incorporate this new dimension into our theories and research.

The chapters contained in this book have a diverse and varied focus. Some are conceptual, whereas others are empirical. Some focus on a single country, whereas others look across different countries. The topics studied include such diverse subjects as participation in decision

Richard M. Steers • Department of Management, Graduate School of Management, University of Oregon, Eugene, Oregon 97403

making, organizational effectiveness, and strategy. Finally—and for-
tunately—the authors themselves come from many countries. As a result, many divergent perspectives are presented.

Although these divergent perspectives may be interesting and indeed useful, their presence nonetheless presents us with a dilemma.
That is, after reviewing internationally-focused chapters such as the
ones presented in this volume, we are forced to confront the uncomfortable fact that we actually know very little about this vital topic. In fact,
from my own perspective, it would appear that at least three issues
confront us in this field that have yet to be dealt with in an effective
manner:

First, there is the problem of defining the major variables under
study and our approach to the study of these variables. We tend to use
such terms as *culture, values,* and *political systems* with alarming casu-
alness. What, in fact, is culture and what are its dimensions? What role
do values play in our research? For example, when we speak of codetermination are we sure this is necessarily a good thing? And when we
speak of central planning economies are we sure these are necessarily
bad? In other words, our first hurdle in improving our approach to
international organizational studies lies in improving the clarity with
which we delineate the particular problem under study and our own
values going into the study. This is a particularly critical problem when
we attempt to take national theories international.

Second, where are all the theories? As we read more and more in
the field of comparative management, we are confronted by the same
few names attached to the same few theories. While the pioneers in the
field deserve respect for showing us the way, clearly considerably more
in the way of theoretical development is warranted if this field is to make
significant progress.

The third problem that confronts us, and one that may help explain
the two problems above, is the extreme difficulty of doing effective
comparative research. We often hear, for example, that international is
not an area for any junior professor desirous of bright career prospects.
In view of the proliferation of research specialists in the general area of
organizational science, perhaps some of these people could be enticed to
help out. One way or another, we must make progress here if this field
is to grow and develop.

If we accept the argument that internationalizing organizational science is a worthy goal and that clear limitations inhibit the attainment of
this goal, then perhaps we should increase the energy with which we
attempt to overcome these hurdles to attain our objective. Although
many paths exist to accomplish this, it appears that a useful beginning in

this search is with the central variable of culture. In almost any aspect of organizational science—macro or micro—culture and cultural differences often emerge as a major moderating variable. As such, I should like to explore briefly some of the ways culture can impact organizational behavior. It is hoped that these examples serve to make the case that for many organizational studies in the future, cultural variation may be a good starting point for analysis.

To understand how central culture is in the study of people at work, consider how most Americans and West Europeans approach family names. When we meet someone from China, Korea, and many other Asian countries, we always want to know why they put their "last" name first. Clearly, in our society the family name goes at the end. We seem to think this is "best" or "appropriate." I might note here that both Americans and many Asians get confused when dealing with someone from Latin America, where one father's family name goes in the middle instead of the beginning or end.

A second example of how important culture can be in business affairs can be seen in the experience of United Airlines when it began service to the Orient. John Zeeman (1987), United's Executive Vice President for Marketing, relates a series of mistakes the airline made when it began service because it had insufficient understanding of the culture in which it was about to do business. Among Mr. Zeeman's many examples, I share with you two. When United began concierge service for its first-class passengers on its Asian routes, it marked the occasion by having its employees proudly wear a white carnation, a well-known oriental symbol for death. Or, take the advertising campaign United used to encourage travel to Australia. United developed an ad campaign around the famous Australian actor Paul Hogan. The theme of the campaign was "Paul Hogan Camps It Up." In other words, they were trying to emphasize the rugged outback nature of Australia, a country you would want to visit. Imagine their surprise when Hogan's lawyer called United to inform them that "camps it up" in Australia refers to someone who boasts of homosexuality. Clearly, words—even in English—don't mean the same thing in different English-speaking countries.

Examples such as these demonstrate how pervasive yet subtle societal differences can be. Such differences have a major impact on human behavior both inside and outside the corporation. In fact, culture affects nearly everything we do from the language and gestures that we use to our patterns of thinking and problem solving to our views about what constitutes acceptable behavior. Culture even affects the direction of the stripes on the ties we wear (most American ties are striped from upper left to lower right, whereas most Asian ties are just the opposite). Yet, despite the importance of culture in determining attitudes and behavior, we seem to pay little attention to this crucial variable in our research and practice in management. The topic has been largely ignored both by managers and researchers.

I would like to advance the argument that the time has come to redress this oversight and to begin putting culture and cultural variation back into our research equations as a central variable worthy of serious study. To make this argument, I should like to explore two related issues: first, why culture is important in research on organizational studies and, second, how we might go about improving our understanding of cultural differences in our research on the management of people at work.

II. CULTURE AS AN EXPLANATORY VARIABLE IN ORGANIZATIONAL SCIENCE

If culture is so central to understanding human attitudes and behavior, then clearly this variable must be considered a potentially useful explanatory variable in organizational research. In fact, it can be argued that culture influences both research and practice in at least three ways: (1) culture helps define the problems we look at in our research on management; (2) culture often defines the methods or approaches we use to study and solve these managerial or organizational problems; and (3) culture often helps define acceptable solutions to the particular problems under study.

A. Culture and Problem Identification

There is a famous quotation by Mr. T. Fujisawa, the co-founder of the Honda Motor Corporation, that "Japanese and American management is 95% the same, and differs in all important respects." That is, although managers in different countries may look the same, their jobs, the problems they face, and their approach to these problems may be radically different.

Consider the case of employee absenteeism. Absenteeism rates vary considerably across national boundaries. For example, absence rates in Western Europe vary from a high of 14% in Italy to a low of 1% in Switzerland and less than 1% in Japan (Yankelovich, 1979). Indeed, things became so bad in Italy that corporations began joking about a new work-related problem: *presemtismo,* which is the problem created when everyone shows up on payday to pick up his or her paycheck.

Because companies routinely employ far more people then they need to keep production lines running in the face of high absence rates, a significant problem emerges when everyone comes to work as there is not sufficient work or space to accommodate everyone. Things got so bad in Italy that in 1982 police began arresting some of the more recalcitrant absentees and a national conference was convened to study the problem. Meanwhile, in the same year, I was asked to give a talk on absenteeism to a group of faculty and business executives in Denmark. After concluding my speech, one gentleman raised his hand and said that he couldn't understand why I was studying absenteeism. It was none of my business why people fail to come to work; that was a personal issue. He went on to say that the only reason someone would study the topic was to discover new ways to squeeze more productivity out of already exploited workers. The contrast between these two countries—both in Western Europe—is enlightening because of the radically divergent definitions as to what constitutes "acceptable" topics for research (Steers, 1987). Although we could argue that these two examples represented isolated events, their existence nevertheless highlights how different people in different cultures view problems of the workplace. Absenteeism is clearly a problem in Western Europe and the United States, yet differences exist as to the perceived magnitude or importance of the problem. Meanwhile, in Japan and several other Asian countries, the problem is not absenteeism but, conversely, how to get workers to take off the time to which they are entitled. Again, different countries and different cultures see the "problem" differently.

Or, consider the way different cultures make use of time. Clearly, the concept of time carries different meanings to people in various societies. In the United States, for example, we often hear the phrase "time is money." People are constantly hurrying to get somewhere. In Latin America, however, or in parts of the Middle East, pressures of time are seldom experienced. As a matter of fact, considerable problems are often encountered by people—native or foreign—who try to rush the system. Hence, when corporate personnel officers are attempting to negotiate a labor contract or resolve a grievance, they are likely to be met with what is seen to be unreasonable resistance, when in fact it may simply reflect divergent opinions about the nature and urgency of the problem. American businesspeople have experienced similar "time warps" when attempting to negotiate contracts in Japan. The problems and the way we use time to understand the problems can be quite different indeed.

A further problem we encounter when trying to define the issue under study is inherent in the language we use. Earlier, I mentioned an example from Australia, but let us look at some other examples. The term *company* means place of work or employer in most Western countries. Yet in Japan, the term takes on family connotations. Hence, when we ask employees about their loyalty to the company, we must understand that significant differences exist in the minds of the employees as to what is being asked. For the American, such a question concerns his or her attachment to that "thing" out there that we call a corporation; it is quite separate from the individual. For a Japanese, however, the question concerns his or her relationship with a familial group. As a result, both individuals may report high levels of loyalty or commitment, but they may mean quite different things. Similar problems exist with many other terms used frequently in humanresources management, such as leadership, performance and equality. The terms, and hence the problems surrounding these terms, simply carry different meanings in different cultures. As a result, efforts to define the problem under study often become muddled and confused.

B. Culture and Approaches to Problem-Solving

Culture can also influence the methods by which we attempt to resolve problems in organizations. Take, for example, the issue of employee participation in decision making. In the United States, employee participation as a concept and as a tool of management had been hotly debated for decades. Considerable controversy emerges from all sides—labor and management—when the topic is proposed as a fundamental approach to management, with managers often expressing fears of loss of control and union leaders ironically often expressing similar fears. We debate whether to allow employee participation in important decisions and, if so, how much. In contrast, in much of Western Europe, we find little debate on this issue. Employee participation is assumed to be an employee right and is often reinforced by federal laws guaranteeing "works councils." In Japan, participation of another form is commonplace in the form of the so-called *ringi* decision-making process that allows widespread involvement by divergent groups in important decisions affecting the firm. In India or Pakistan, by contrast, the issue of participation seldom comes up; it is typically felt that it is management's responsibility to make decisions. If managers are not capable of doing so, then they should be removed. Hence, participation as a problem resolution mechanism is sometimes appropriate, sometimes not.

Or, take the issue of plant closures. In the United States, closing a plant due to inefficiencies or excess capacity is rather commonplace. The company usually issues a formal statement regretting the necessity of the action but pointing out, nevertheless, that the action was essential to corporate survival and competitiveness. The situation in other parts of the world is often somewhat different. As Lester Thurow (1987) notes:

> Recently I was talking with some consultants in a strategic planning firm about situations in which Japanese, European, and American companies find themselves in an industry with excess capacity. The planners said that they always tell their American clients to go out of business. The Japanese mindset, however, is against abandoning an industry; Japanese companies are willing to listen only to strategies for conquering an industry . . . The Europeans are uninterested in strategies for going out of business. They remind their consultants that their government regulations require them to hold on to their employees so long and make it difficult to fire anyone or to close down a facility that it is simply too expensive to go out of business.(p. 8)

Thus, personnel decisions affecting layoffs and plant closures are also constrained by national and cultural variations. Other examples could be cited here. For instance, strike behavior in the United States is often aimed at crippling the company so it will "have" to settle. In several Asian countries, strikes are often shorter in duration and have the purpose of demonstrating to management the importance—and to some extent the commitment—of the workers. Or we could even look at the personnel department itself. In many Asian countries, the personnel department and function are considered very important and represent a powerful influence throughout the corporation. In the United States, by contrast, the personnel department is often relegated to a less influential position in the company. Often, important personnel decisions even get made in other departments. The legal department often makes affirmative action policies and field departments such as marketing often make hiring decisions and then send the "paper" to personnel for processing. The point here, then, is that not only does culture influence our definition of what constitutes an organizational problem, it also influences the manner in which we go about solving the problem.

C. Culture and Problem Resolution

Finally, variations across countries and cultures can have a profound impact on the final outcomes of problem-resolution efforts. Take the case of merit compensation. Merit compensation, or pay for performance programs, are taken as an article of faith by many HRM executives and researchers in the United States. Research demonstrates fairly conclusively that differential rewards based on individual or at least small-group performance can have a profound influence on performance levels. Yet in China, such techniques have failed miserably (Houwink, November 1987, personal communication). Efforts to implement differential rewards in the form of performance bonuses typically led to expressions of inequity in a country that long stressed "equality" and, as a result, soon after implementation the typical Chinese factory gave performance bonuses to around 90% of all employees. Clearly the incentive value had been lost.

Or, take efforts to secure equal employment opportunities for women. In the United States, much has been written about discrimination and unfairness toward women wishing to enter the workplace. Many of the equal opportunity efforts have taken the form of legislation and legal action aimed at achieving "fairness" and "equality." In Japan, equal opportunity is also guaranteed in law but it has been argued that preserving societal harmony, or *wa*, takes precedence over efforts to secure what the West sees as *justice*. Major shifts of women into the managerial ranks, it is said, might disturb the *wa* and as such are avoided. Whatever the reason, Japan even with its laws has one of the smallest percentages of women in significant managerial positions among industrialized societies. However, lest we think that discrimination against women is an "oriental" phenomenon, consider the issue in Western Europe. In West Germany, for example, we hear fairly often that women's place is with *kindern und kuchen*. In the Netherlands (and other countries), structural constraints exist that effectively serve to keep women at home. For example, on a typical school day all children come home for lunch and there are no classes on Wednesday afternoons. Moreover, in contrast to several Scandinavian countries, child care is rare. Hence, many women find it exceedingly difficult to take a job even if someone would hire them and despite the laws that supposedly guarantee equal opportunity.

What do we conclude, then, about the role of cultural variations in organizations? Culture, it would seem, often—although clearly not always—has the capacity to influence how we define a problem, how we go about trying to solve the problem and, finally, the actual solution reached. In view of the myriad of problems facing managers and organizational researchers, it is not surprising that culture emerges as one of the important variables worthy of attention and study, even if it has failed to receive this attention.

III. A PROPOSED AGENDA FOR INTERNATIONALIZING ORGANIZATIONAL SCIENCE

In 1983, Nancy Adler reviewed publications in management research journals for a 10-year period. Her findings are enlightening. She found that only 15% of the articles focused on cross-cultural issues and that only 1% actually investigated interactions between employees of different cultures. In short, we as management researchers are simply not investing the time and resources necessary to explicate this issue with clarity or even a reasonable degree of certainty. I would suggest that the time has come to redress this imbalance and to begin making commitments to incorporate cross-cultural dimensions in future studies of management. To do this we need a full commitment, not just piece-meal efforts to throw in several cultural variables into our future questionnaire research, to rethink how we do research in organizations. There is an ancient Chinese proverb that says that one should not attempt to leap across a chasm in two bounds. We either leap or we don't leap; we do not attempt to leap half way unless we wish disastrous results. I would submit that if organizational science as a field of study has a challenge for the next decade, it is to develop an awareness and understanding of how different cultures and different peoples attempt to solve the human problems of the workplace. Clearly, here is a place where we can learn from each other and contribute to a better work experience for all people.

To begin this task, I suggest several issues we should consider in our research efforts. As you will note, my comments are directed more at how we do research in organizations than on which specific topics are appropriate for study:

1. *Rethinking methodology.* I believe it is not mere coincidence that the decline in serious cross-cultural studies over the past several decades coincides with the increase in the use of sophisticated quantitative analytical techniques. That is, as we have learned more and more about the use of statistics in analyzing behavioral data, we have tended to ignore or render unpublishable serious studies of variables that do not easily lend themselves to such analyses. By and large, cultural variables fall into this category. Thus, our preoccupation with proving our statistical metal has probably served to curtail efforts by serious scholars to explicate the societal factors that provide context for personnel decisions. We must not forget that statistical analyses in the behavioral sciences are more suitable for solving some problems than others. Moreover, we must not forget that after we are done with our statistical analyses on a particular problem, we are not necessarily done with our analysis. There is and there must be room for analyses of a more qualitative nature to add conceptual richness to our search for adequate solutions. The whole point of behavioral science research is to bring together the richness of divergent methodologies to help solve the human problems of the workplace. In this endeavor, I suggest we have been somewhat lacking.

2. *Need for theory.* Second, if we objectively examine the cross-cultural literature that does exist in the area of management, it must be concluded that far too many of the studies are serendipitious in nature. To

be frank, we lack a coherent and systematic body of literature that can be called *cross-cultural* or *comparative* management. We see little in the way of theory development and little attempt by organizational scientists to draw upon the rather extensive relevant research done by anthropologists and sociologists over the decades. The topics chosen for study seem to be highly opportunistic (e.g., surveys of captive foreign students in executive programs, surveys taken because we were in such-and-such country and had a sample available) with samples and study variables seemingly chosen with little regard for their theoretical base or managerial utility. The instruments used are typically existing American instruments hastily translated (and often not back-translated) into another language. The results too often come straight from a computer printout with little effort to get behind the data to understand process dynamics.

I would submit that if we are serious about better understanding the international dimensions of management, the time has come to make a major commitment to developing a systematic and defensible body of literature surrounding this issue. To do this, it may be necessary for many of us to explore new intellectual arenas that we are not familiar with (e.g., cultural anthropology) as a means of developing sufficient theoretical bases upon which to carry out our research efforts. This is no simple task but if we are to be taken seriously by our peers it may be a necessary step. Only when there exists a useful theoretical base and a systematic body of knowledge will the field come into its own as a central area in the study of business administration.

3. *Intracultural differences.* In our search for parsimonious models of comparative management, I suggest one caution. We must be alert not only to differences across cultures and countries, but also to differences within such entities. I believe Singapore provides a good example of a multiculture country that has made an effort to preserve cultural diversity within national purpose and unity. In our search for useful theory, caution must be taken not to ignore or overlook such variations as they have the capacity to represent a major influence on management practices within a single country. Although this complicates our search for parsimony, it is nonetheless a fact of organizational life that we cannot ignore.

4. *Intellectual joint ventures.* Because of several of these problems in research and theory development, a good case can be made for us to rethink the mechanics of comparative research. That is, it may be time to encourage greater use of intellectual joint ventures in which a team of researchers from several countries come together to systematically study particular phenomena. Although it is easy to note the difficulty of this

approach, the fact remains that this approach has been used successfully before, most notably in the Industrial Democracy in Europe (IDE) project of the 1970s. By carefully selecting both team members and research topics, significant work can be accomplished efficiently and effectively that can overcome many of the pitfalls of cross-cultural research. Furthermore, by combining this multiresearcher with a multimethod approach to data collection and analysis, we might eventually hope to see several rather significant international studies that have both the conceptual richness and the intellectual diversity to help us truly understand a particular topic.

5. *Management education.* Finally, in the area of management education, I think we have to admit that we know more about technology transfer than about cultural transfer. Data suggest that among American firms between 20% and 50% of managerial transfers overseas end in premature return and that the figure for managers going to developing nations approaches 70%. If these data are correct, it is estimated that U.S. corporations are losing about $2 billion per year in direct costs (Copeland & Griggs, 1985). However we look at it, the fact remains that most business schools are doing a woefully inadequate job of teaching managers either how to manage successfully overseas or how to manage workers from different cultures at home. In fact, most business schools never address the subject of culture and cross-cultural issues at all in their curriculum or classes, despite constant encouragement to do so from our business school accrediting association. If we don't train managers to be sensitive to cultural differences—at home and abroad—why should we be surprised when they do so poorly in these matters? It is important to business schools that they train future managers to understand accounting principles and financial management; it is far less important to them—unfortunately—that these students understand diversity in human nature as it influences interpersonal behavior and performance at work.

IV. CONCLUDING REMARKS

In conclusion, let me remind you about the Chinese proverb about leaping across chasms in a single bound. If we are to succeed both in international management and in the study of international management, it is essential that we approach this issue collectively with a mind to developing a systematic understanding of the factors that facilitate and inhibit human behavior in the international arena. We cannot approach this subject as this year's "hot topic." We can no longer apply an

American model or a German model or a Japanese model to try to understand global management issues. Instead, what is called for is a long-term commitment and a long-term effort by qualified researchers from many countries working in concert with corporate executives to identify and solve organizational problems for both today and tomorrow. In this search for excellence in the future—both nationally and internationally—there is a clear role to play for organizational scientists interested in applying their craft to this important area.

V. REFERENCES

Adler, N. J. (1983). Cross-cultural management research: The ostrich and the trend. *International Studies of Management and Organization, 8* (2), 226–232.
Copeland, L. & Griggs, L. (1985). *Going international.* New York: Random House.
Steers, R. M. (1987). *The international challenge to management education.* Presidential address, Annual Meeting of the Academy of Management, New Orleans.
Thurow, L. C. (1987). U.S. corporate wisdom: If you can't beat them, quit. *International Herald Tribune,* Aug. 15, p. 8.
Yankelovich, D. (1979). We need new motivational tools. *Industry Week,* Aug. 6, pp. 10–11.
Zeeman, J. R. (1987). *Service: The cutting edge of global competition.* Address, Annual Meeting of the Academy of International Business, Chicago.

Bibliography

[Editor's Note: The following bibliographical compilation is provided as assistance to the delving reader.]

Abegglen, J. (1958). *The Japanese factory: aspects of its social organization*. Glencoe, IL: The Free Press.

Abegglen, J. C. (1984). *The strategy of Japanese business*. Cambridge, MA: Ballinger.

Adams, J. S. (1965). Inequity in social exchange. In L. Berkowitz (Ed.), *Advances in experimental psychology* (pp. 100–235). New York: Academic Press.

Adizes, I. (1971). *Industrial democracy Yugoslav style*. New York: Free Press.

Adler, N. J. (1983a). Cross-cultural management: Issues to be faced. *International Studies of Management and Organization, 13*(1–2), 7–45.

Adler, N. J. (1983b). Organizational development in a multicultural environment. *Journal of Applied Behavioral Science, 19*(3), 350–365.

Adler, N. J. (1983c). Cross-cultural management research. The ostrich and the trend. *International Studies of Management and Organization, 8*(2), 226–232.

Adler, N. J. (1984). Understanding the ways of understanding: Cross-cultural management reviewed. In R. N. Farmer (ed.), *Advances in international comparative management: A research annual* (Vol. 1, pp. 31–67). Greenwich, CT: JAI Press.

Adler, N. J. (1986). *International dimensions of organizational behavior*. Boston: Kent Publishing.

Adler, N. J., & Graham, J. L. (1986). *Cross-cultural interaction: The international comparison fallacy*. Working paper, McGill University, Faculty of Management, Montreal.

Adler, N. J., & Jalinek, M. (1986, Spring). Is "Organizational culture" culture bound? *Human Resource Management, 25*(1), 73–90.

Aiken, M., & Bacharach, S. B. (1979). Culture and organizational structure and process: A comparative study of local government administrative bureaucracies in the Walloon and Flemish regions of Belgium. In C. J. Lammers & D. J. Hickson (Eds.), *Organizations alike and unlike* (pp. 215–250). London: Routledge & Kegan Paul.

Albrecht, S. L. (1980). Politics, bureaucracy, and worker participation: The Swedish case. *Journal of Applied Behavioral Science, 16*(3), 229–317.

Allison, G. T. (1971). *Essence of decision: Explaining the Cuban missle crisis*. Boston: Little, Brown.

Alston, J. P. (1982). Awarding bonuses the Japanese way. *Business Horizons, 25*(5), 46–50.

Ansoff, J. (1984). *Implanting strategic management*. Toronto: Prentice-Hall.

Argyris, C. (1967). *Integrating the individual and the organization.* New York: Wiley.

Askanas, W. (1974). *The impact of technology and R&D on organizational culture.* Warsaw: Polish Academy of Science.

Askanas, W. (1978a). The language of leaders. *Organizational Review 35,* 127–135.

Askanas, W. (1978b). *Spontaneous techniques of management.* Warszawa: TNOIK (Polish Society of Organizational Management).

Askanas, W. (1978c). The obstacle to system management. *Wektory 11,* 47–62.

Azumi, K. (1974). Japanese society: A sociological review. In A. D. Tiedeman (Ed.), *An introduction to Japanese civilization* (pp. 515–535). New York: Columbia University Press.

Azumi, K., & McMillan, C. J. (1975). Culture and organization structure: A comparison of Japanese and British organizations. *International Studies of Management and Organization, 5*(1), 35–47.

Bachrach, S. B., & Aiken, M. (1976). Structural and process constraints on influence in organizations: A level-specific analysis. *Administrative Science Quarterly, 21,* 623–642.

Bain, Trevor. (1983, Winter). Employment readjustments in West Germany, *Columbia Journal of World Business, XVIII*(4), 75–91.

Barnard, C. I. (1938). *The functions of the executive.* Cambridge, MA: Harvard University Press.

Barnet, R. J., & Müller, R. E. (1974). *Global reach: The power of the multinational corporations.* New York: Simon and Schuster.

Barnouw, V. (1963). *Culture and personality.* Homewood, IL: The Dorsey Press.

Barrett, G. V., & Bass, B. M. (1976). Cross-cultural issues in industrial and organizational psychology. In M. D. Dunnette (Ed.), *Handbook of industrial and organizational psychology* (pp. 1639–1686). New York: Rand McNally.

Bass, B., & Eldridge, L. (1973). Accelerated managers' objectives in twelve countries. *Industrial relations, 12,* 158–171.

Bass, B. M., Burger, P. C., Doktor, R., & Barrett, G. V. (1979). *Assessment of managers.* New York: Free Press.

Becker, E. (1971). *The birth and death of meaning* (2nd ed.). New York: Free Press.

Befu, H. (1980). A critique of the group model of Japanese society. *Society Analysis,* No. 5/6, 29–43.

Befu, H. (1983a), Giri and Ninjo. In *Kodansha encyclopedia of Japan* (Vol. 3, p. 34). Tokyo: Kodansha.

Befu, H. (1983b). Groups. In *Kodansha encyclopedia of Japan* (Vol. 3, p. 63). Tokyo: Kodansha.

Befu, H. (1983c). On. In *Kodansha encyclopedia of Japan* (Vol. 6, p. 105). Tokyo: Kodansha.

Benedict, R. (1946). *The chrysanthemum and the sword.* Boston: Houghton Mifflin.

Bennett, M. (1977). Testing management theories cross-culturally. *Journal of Applied Psychology, 62*(5), 578–581.

Benson, J. K. (1983). Paradigm and praxis in organizational behavior. In L. L. Cummings & B. M. Staw (Eds.), *Research in organizational behavior* (Vol. 5, pp. 3–56). Greenwich, CT: JAI Press.

Berne, E. (1961). *Transnational analysis and psychotherapy.* New York: Grove Press.

Berne, E. (1964). *Games people play.* New York: Grove Press.

Bernthal, W. F. (1978, January). Matching German culture and management style: A book review essay. *Academy of Management Review, 3*(1), 75–91.

Berry, J. W. (1969). On cross-cultural comparability. *International Journal of Psychology, 4,* 119–128.

Biddle, B. J., & Thomas, E. J., (1966). *Role theory: Concepts and research.* New York: Wiley.

Birnbaum, P. H., & Wong, G. Y. Y. (1985). *Cultural values of managers in the People's Republic of China and Hong Kong.* Paper presented at the American Academy of Management Meetings, San Diego.

Blanchard, K., & Johnson, S. (1983). *The one minute manager.* Willow Books, London.

Blunt, P. (1973). Cultural and situational determinants of job satisfaction amongst management in South Africa. *Journal of Management Studies, 10*(2), 133–140.

Blunt, P. (1983). *Organizational theory and behaviour.* New York: Longman Group, Ltd.

Boddewyn, J. (1966). *Comparative concepts in management administration and organization.* Mimeo, New York Graduate School of Business Administration.

Bouchner, S., & Ohsako, T. (1977). Ethnic role salience in racially homogeneous and heterogeneous societies. *Journal of Cross-Cultural Psychology, 8,* 455–492.

Bouchner, S., & Perks, R. W. (1971). National role evocation as a function of cross-cultural inter-action. *Journal of Cross-Cultural Psychology, 2,* 157–164.

Bougeois, L. J. (1985). Strategic goals, perceived uncertainty, and economic performance in volatile environments. *Academy of Management Journal, 28,* 548–573.

Bougon, M., Weick, K., & Binkhorst, D. (1977). Cognition in organizations: An analysis of the Utecht Jazz Orchestra. *Administrative science quarterly, 22*(4), 1977.

Breeze, J. D. (1985). Harvest from the archives: The search for Fayol and Carlioz. *Journal of Management, 11*(1), 43–54.

Brett, J. M., & Hammer, T. (1982). Organizational behavior and industrial relations. *Industrial relations research in the 1970's: Review and appraisal.* Madison, WI: Industrial Relations research in the 1970's: Review and appraisal. Madison, WI: Industrial Relations Research Association.

Brislin, R. W., Lonner, W. J., & Thorndike, R. M. (1973). *Cross-cultural research methods.* New York: Plenum Press.

Brossard, M., & Maurice, M. (1976). Is there a universal model of organization structure? *International Studies of Management and Organization, 6*(3), 11–45.

Burns, T., & Stalker, G. M. (1961). *The management of innovation.* London: Tavistock.

Business Week. (1985). An unlikely champion of austerity. January, p. 45.

Business Week. (1985). Suddenly the world doesn't care if you live or die. February 3, pp. 96–98.

Business Week. (1985). Now it's all up to Brazil's young Turks, June 17, pp. 51–54.

Business Week. (1985). Toyota's Fastlane. November 4, pp. 42–44.

Cameron, K. (1981). Domains of organizational effectiveness in colleges and universities. *Academy of Management Journal, 24*(1), 25–27.

Cameron, K. S. (1986). Effectiveness as paradox: Consensus and conflict in conceptions of organizational effectiveness. *Management science, 32,* 539–553.

Cameron, K. S. (1987). Effectiveness and quality in higher education. In M. W. Peterson, & L. A. Mets (Eds.), *Governance, management and Leadership* (pp. 222–242). San Francisco: Jossey-Bass.

Campbell, J. P. (1977). On the nature of organizational effectiveness. In P. S. Goodman, J. M. Pennings & Associates (Eds.), *New perspectives on organizational effectiveness* (pp. 13–55). San Francisco: Jossey-Bass.

Capra, F. (1975). *The tao of physics.* New York: Bantam.

Capelli, P. G. (1983). Concession bargaining in the national economy. *Industrial Relations Research Association Proceedings,* 297–305.

Carroll, M. P. (1982). Culture. In J. Freeman (Ed.), *Introduction to sociology: A Canadian focus* (pp. 19–40). Scarborough, Ontario: Prentice-Hall.

Carroll, S. J., & Gillen, D. J. (1987, January). Are the classical management functions useful in describing managerial work? *Academy of Management Review, 12*(1), 38–51.

Chang, Y. N. (1976). Early Chinese management thought. *California Management Review,*
    19(2), 71–76.
Channon, D. F. (1973). *The strategy and structure of British enterprise.* Boston: Harvard
    University.
Chen, N. R. (1978). Economic modernization in post-Mao China: Policies, problems and
    prospects. In U.S.A. Congress, Joint Economic Committee, *Chinese economy post-Mao*
    (pp. 165–203). Washington, DC: U.S. Government Printing Office.
Child, J. (1981a). The cross national study of organizations. In L. L. Cummings & B. M.
    Staw, (Eds.), *Research in organizational behavior,* (Vol. 3). Greenwich, CT: JAI Press.
Child, J. (1981b). Culture, contingency and capitalism in the cross-national study of orga-
    nizations. In L. L. Cummings & B. M. Staw (Eds.), *Research in organizational behavior*
    (Vol. III, pp. 303–356). Greenwich, CT: JAI Press.
Child, J. (1984). *Organization.* London: Butler.
Child, J. (1985). *Organizations.* London: Harper & Row.
Child, J., & Tayeb, M. (1982–1983). Theoretical perspectives in cross-national organiza-
    tional research. *International Studies of Management and Organizations, 12*(4), 23–70.
Chui, V. C. L. (1977). *Managerial beliefs of Hong Kong managers,* Unpublished master's
    thesis, University of Homg Kong.
Chong, L. E., Cragin, J. P., & Scherling, S. A. (1983). *Manager work-related values in a*
    Chinese corporation. Paper presented to the Academy of International Business, 1983
    Annual Meeting, San Francisco.
Chung, K. H. (1978, October). *A comparative study of managerial characteristics of domestic,*
    international, and governmental institutions in Korea. Paper presented at the Midwest
    Conference in Asian Affairs, Minneapolis.
Cicourrel, A. V. (1972). *Cognitive sociology: Language and meaning in social interaction.* Lon-
    don: Penquin.
Clinebell, S. (1984). Organizational effectiveness: An examination of recent empirical stud-
    ies and the development of the contingency view. *Midwest Academy of Management*
    Proceedings, 92–102.
Cocke, E. C., & Robinson, A. J. (1981). For a new management recipe, China samples a
    Western menu. *Asian Business, 17*(5), 72–75.
Cole, R. E. (1973). Functional alternatives and economic development: An empirical exam-
    ple of permanent employment in Japan. *American Sociological Review, 38,* 424–438.
Cole, R. E. (1979). *Work, mobility, and participation: A comparative study of American and*
    Japanese industry. Berkeley, CA: University of California Press.
Cole, R. E. (1982). Keizai Kyoshitsu. *Nihonkeizai Shinbun,* June 2, p. 13.
Conner, J. W. (1976). Joge Kankei: A key concept for an understanding of Japanese-
    American achievement. *Psychiatry, 39,* 266–279.
Constitution of the People's Republic of China. (1978). Beijing: Foreign Languages Press.
Cooper, C. L. (1979). *Learning from others in groups.* London: Associated Business Press.
Cooper, C. L., & Makin, P. (1984). *Psychology for managers.* London: Macmillan and BPS.
Cooper, C. L., & Robertson, I. T. (1986). *International review of industrial and organizational*
    psychology. London: Wiley.
Copeland, L. & Griggs, L. (1985). *Going international.* New York: Random House.
Coulter, P. (1979). Organizational effectiveness in the public sector: The example of munic-
    ipal fire protection. *Administrative Science Quarterly, 24*(1), 65–81.
Crozier, M. (1964). *The bureaucratic phenomenon.* Chicago: University of Chicago Press.
Culbert, S. A., & McDonough, J. J. (1980). *The invisible war: Pursuing self-interests at work.*
    New York: Wiley
Cullingford, E. M. C. (1977). *Trade unions in West Germany,* Boulder: Westview Press.

Cummings, L. L. (1977). Emergence of the instrumental organization. In P. S. Goodman, J. M. Pennings, & Associates, (Eds.), *New perspectives on organizational effectiveness* (pp. 56–62). San Francisco: Jossey-Bass.

Cummings, L. L., & Schmidt, S. M. (1972). Managerial attitudes of Greeks: The roles of culture and industrialization. *Administrative Science Quarterly, 17*(2), 265–272.

Cummings, L. L. (1983, October). The logics of management. *Academy of Management Review, 8*(4), 532–538.

Cunningham, J. B. (1977). Approaches to the evaluation of organizational effectiveness. *Academy of Management Review, 2*(3), 463–474.

Cyert, R. M., & March, J. G. (1963). *A behavioral theory of the firm.* Englewood Cliffs, NJ: Prentice-Hall.

Davis, R. C. (1928). *The principles of factory organization and management.* New York: Harper & Brothers.

Davis, R. C. (1935). *The principles of business organization and operation.* Columbus, OH: L. H. Hedrick.

Davis, R. C. (1951). *The fundamentals of top management.* New York: Harper & Brothers.

Davis, S. (1968). Managerial resource development in Mexico. In R. Rehder (Ed.), *Latin American management: Development and performance* (pp. 166–179). Reading, MA: Addison-Wesley.

Davis, S. M. (1971). *Comparative management: Cultural and organizational perspectives.* Englewood Cliffs, NJ: Prentice-Hall.

Degler, K. (1971). *Neither black nor white: Slavery and race relations in Brazil and the United States.* New York: Macmillan.

DeNisi, A., & Pritchard, R. D. (1978). Implicit theories of performance as artifacts in survey research: A replication and extension. *Organizational Behavior and Human Performance, 12*, 358–366.

Deustch, M. F. (1984). *Doing business with the Japanese.* New York: New American Library.

DeVos, G. A. (1973). *Socialization for achievement: Essays on the cultural psychology of the Japanese.* Berkeley, CA: University of California Press.

Doi, T. (1962). Amae: A key concept for understanding Japanese personality structure. In R. J. Smith & R. K. Beardsley (Eds.), *Japanese culture* (pp. 253–287). Chicago: Adline.

Doi, T. (1973). *The anatomy of dependence.* Tokyo: Kodansha.

Doktor, R. (1983a). Culture and the management of time: A comparison of Japanese and American top management practice. *Asia Pacific Journal of Management, 1*(1), 65–71.

Doktor, R. (1983b). Some tentative comments on Japanese and American decision making. *Decision Secince, 14*(4), 607–612.

Dore, R. P. (1978). *Shinohata: Portrait of a Japanese village.* New York: Pantheon Books.

Dowling, J. B. (1978). *Organizational legitimacy: The management of meaning.* Unpublished doctoral dissertation, Stanford University: Palo Alto, CA.

Dun & Bradstreet. (1980a). *Million dollar directory.* New York: Dun & Bradstreet.

Dun & Bradstreet. (1980b). *Principal international business.* New York: Dunn & Bradstreet International.

Duncan, R. B. (1972). The characteristics of organizational environments and perceived environmental uncertainty. *Administrative Science Quarterly, 17*, 313–327.

Duncan, R. B. (1973). Multiple decision-making structures in adapting to environmental uncertainty: The impact on organizational effectiveness. *Human Relations, 26*, 273–291.

Dunlop, J. T. (1958). *Industrial relations system.* New York: Holt-Dryden.

Dunphy, D. C. (1987). Convergence and divergence—A temporal review of the literature on the Japanese enterprise and its management. *Academy of Management Review, 12*, 445–459.

Dunphy, D. C., & Shi, J. (1985). *Management and the enterprise in the People's Republic of China: An annotated bibliography.* Informal publication. Sydney, Australia: Australian Graduate School of Management, University of New South Wales.

Dunphy, D. C., & Stening, B. W. (1984). *Japanese organization behaviour and management: An annotated bibliography.* Hong Kong: Asian Research Service.

Drucker, P. (1966). *The concept of corporation.* New York: John Day.

Eckstein, A. (1977). *China's economic revolution.* Cambridge, MA: Cambridge University Press.

Eitman, D. K., & Stonehill, A. I. (1979). *Multinational business finance.* Reading, MA: Addison-Wesley.

Eleventh National Congress of the CCP documents. (1977). Beijing: Foreign Languages Press.

Elliot, O. (1959). *Men at the top.* New York: Harper & Brothers.

England, G. W. (1975). *The manager and his values: An international perspective from the USA, Japan, Korea, India and Australia.* Cambridge, MA: Ballinger.

England, G. W. (1983, Fall). Japanese and American management: Theory Z and beyond. *Journal of International Business Studies, 14*(2), 131–142.

England, G. W., & Harpaz, I. (1983). Some methodological and analytic considerations in cross-national comparative research. *Journal of International Business Studies, 14*(2), 49–59.

England, G. W., & Lee, R. (1971). Organizational goals and expected behavior among American, Japanese, and Korean managers: A comparative study. *Academy of Management Journal, 14*(4), 425–438.

Epstein, S. (1979). The ecological study of emotions in humans. In P. Pliner, K. R. Blankenstein, & I. M. Spigel (Eds.), *Advances in the study of communication and affect: Vol. 5. Perception of emotions in self and others* (pp. 47–247). New York: Plenum Press.

Etzioni, A. (1960). Two approaches to organizational analysis: A critique and a suggestion. *Administrative Science Quarterly, 5,* 257–278.

Evans, P. (1979). *Dependent development: The alliance of multinational, state local capital in Brazil.* Princeton, NJ: Princeton University Press.

Evans, W. M. (1980). *Organization theory.* New York: Wiley.

Everett, J. E., Krishnan, A. R., & Stening, B. W. (1984). *Through a glass darkly: Southeast Asian managers' mutual preceptions of Japanese and local counterparts.* Singapore: Eastern Universities Press.

Farh, J. L., Hoffman, R. C., & Hegarty, W. H. (1984). Assessing environmental scanning at the subunit level: A multitrait-multimethod analysis. *Decision Sciences, 15,* 197–220.

Farmer, R. N. (1968). *New directions in management information transfer.* Bloomington, IN: Cedarwood Press.

Farmer, R. N. & Richman, B. M. (1964, Winter). A model for research in comparative management. *California Management Review, VII*(2), 55–68.

Farmer, R. N., & Richman, B. N. (1965). *Comparative management and economic progress.* Homewood, ILL: Irwin.

Fayol, H. (1916/1949). *General and industrial management* (Constance Storrs, Trans.). London: Pitman.

Fayol, H. (1937). The administrative theory of state (Sarah Greer, Trans.). In L. Gullick & L. Urwick (Eds.), *Papers on the science of administration.* New York: Institute of Public Administration, Columbia University.

Ferris, G. R., Schellenberg, D. A., & Zammuto, R. F. (1984, Winter). Human resource management strategies in declining dinustries. *Human Resource Management, 23*(4), 381–394.

Fiske, S. T., & Linville, P. W. (1980). What does the schema concept buy us? *Personality and social psychology Bulletin, 6,* 543–557.

Fletcher, M. D. (1984). Chinese industrial policy and reforms—Preliminary comparisons with Japan. *Australian Journal of Chinese Affairs, 11*, 121–130.

Flynn, P. (1978). *Brazil: A political analysis.* Boulder, CO: Westview.

Form, W. (1979). Comparative industrial sociology and the convergence hypothesis. *Annual Review of Sociology, 5*, 1–25.

Foy, N., & Gadon, H. (1976). Worker participation contrasts in three countries. *Harvard Business Review, 54*(3), 71–84.

Freedman, A., & Fulmer, W. F. (1982, March/April). Last rites for pattern bargaining. *Harvard Business Review, 60*(2), 30–48.

Friedlander, F., & Pickle, H. (1968). Components of effectiveness in small organizations. *Administrative Science Quarterly, 13*(2), 289–304.

Frieze, I. H., Bar-Tal, D., & Carroll, J. S. (1980). *New approaches to social problems.* San Francisco: Jossey-Bass.

Frost, P. J. (1985, Summer). Special issue on organizational symbolism: Introduction. *Journal of Management, 11*(2), 5–10.

Fujihara, G. (1936). *The spirit of Japanese industry.* Tokyo: The Hokuseido Press.

Fulmer, W. E. (1982). Labor-management relationships in the 1980's: Revolution or evolution. *Industrial Relations Research Association Proceedings*, 397–402.

Garfinkel, H. (1967). *Studies in ethnomethodology.* Englewood Cliffs, NJ: Prentice-Hall.

Geitner, D., & Pulte, P. (1979). *Mitbestimmungs recht.* Müchen: Heyne Verlag.

George, C. S. (1972). *The history of management thought.* Englewood Cliffs, NJ: Prentice-Hall.

Georgopoulos, B. S., & Tannenbaum, A. S. (1957). A study of organizational effectiveness. *American Sociological Review, 22*(5), 534–540.

Ghertman, M. (1976). The strategy formulation process of the foreign subsidiary of a French multinational corporation. *International Studies of Management and Organization, VI*, 27–53.

Gibney, F. (1982). *Miracle by design: The real reasons behind Japan's economic miracle.* New York: Times Books.

Gillin, J. (1960). The middle segments and their values. In R. Adams *et al.* (Eds.), *Social change in Latin America today.* New York: Vintage.

Gimpl, M., & Dakin, S. (1980). *Management and magic.* Australia: University of Canterbury.

Goldsmith, W., & Clutterbuck, K. (1984). *The winning streak.* London: Weidenfeld and Nicholson.

Gonzales, R. F., & McMillan, C. (1961). The universality of American management philosophy. *Academy of Management Journal, 4*(1), 33–41.

Goodstein, L. D. (1981, Summer). Commentary on: Do American theories apply abroad: American business value and cultural imperialism. *Organizational Dynamics*, 49–54.

Goscinski, J. (1981). *Projektowanie organizacji.* Warszawa: PWN.

Gouldner, A. (1984). *Patterns of industrial bureaucracy.* New York: Free Press.

Gouy, M. (1978). Strategic decision making in large European firms. *Long Range Planning, 14*, 41–48.

Graham, J. L. (1985). Cross-cultural marketing negotiations: A laboratory experiment. *Marketing Science, 4*(2), 130–146.

Graham, J. L., & Sano, Y. (1984). *Smart bargaining: Doing business with the Japanese.* Cambridge, MA: Ballinger.

Granick, D. (1972). *Industrial management in four developed countries: France, Britain, United States and Russia.* Cambridge, MA: MIT Press.

Graves, D. (1972). The impact of culture upon managerial attitudes, beliefs and behavior in England and France. *Journal of Management Studies, 10*, 40–56.

Gray, B., Bougon, M. G., & Donnellon, A. (1985, Summer). Organizations as constructions and destructions of meaning. *Journal of Management, 11*(2), 83–98.

Greiner, L. E. (1977). Reflections on O. D. American Style. In C. L. Cooper (Ed.), *Organizational development in the UK and the USA: A joint evaluation*. London: Macmillan.

Griffeth, R. W., Hom, P. W., Denisi, A., & Kirchner, W. (1980). A multivariate, multinational comparison of managerial attituees. Paper presented at the annual Academy of Management Meeting, Detroit.

Grinyer, P. H., & Spender, J. C. (1979). *Turnaround—Managerial recipes for strategic success*. London: Associated Business Press.

Gruenfeld, L. W., & MacEachron, A. E. (1975). A cross-national study of cognitive style among managers and technicians. *International Journal of Psychology*, 10(1), 27–55.

Gulick, L. H. (1937). Notes on the theory of organization. In L. H. Gulick & F. Urwick (Eds.), *Papers on the science of administration*. New York: Institute of Public Administration, Columbia University.

Gurdon, M. A. (1985, Winter). Equity participation by employees: The growing debate in West Germany. *Industrial Relations*, 24(1), 113–129.

Hackman, J. R., & Oldham, F. R. (1976). Motivation through the design of work: Test of a theory. *Organizational Behavior and Human Performance*, 16, 250–279.

Haire, M., Ghiselli, E. E., & Porter, L. W. (1963). Cultural patterns in the role of the manager. *Industrial relations*, 2, 95–117.

Haire, M., Ghiselli, E. E., & Porter, L. W. (1966). *Managerial thinking: An international study*. New York: Wiley.

Hall, A. (1977). Patron-client relations: Concepts and terms. In S. W. Schmidt, J. C. Scott, L. Lande, & L. Guasti (Eds.), *Friends, followers and factions* (pp. 510–512).

Hall, J., & Liedecker, J. (1981, Winter). Is Japanese management anything new? A comparison of Japanese-style management with U.S. participative models. *Human Resource Management*, 14–21.

Hallet, G. (1978). *The social economy of west Germany*. London: The Macmillan Press Limited.

Hambrick, D. C. (1981). Environment, strategy, and power within top management teams. *Administrative Science Quarterly*, 26, 253–276.

Hanada, M. (1980, January). Nihonteki keiei niokeru jyugyoin no kizoku ishiki: genjitsu to kenkyu suijun no hazamade. *Kenkyujo Kiho*, 5, January, 2–13.

Hanada, M. (1981). *Shokuba nkokeru ningenkankei no kokusai hikaku*. Tokyo: Ningen Noryoku Kaihatsu Center.

Hanada, M. (1982). *Gaikokuseiki chishiki rodosha no katsuyo no jittai: uchwgawa karano kokusaika*. Tokyo: Ningen Noryku Kaihatsu Center.

Harbison, F., & Meyers, C. (1959). *Management in the industrial world*. New York: McGraw-Hill.

Harbron, J. (1979). Dorea's executives are not quite "The new Japanese." *The Business Quarterly*, 44(3), 16–19.

Harre, R., & Sekord, P. F. (1972). *The explanation of social behaviour*. Oxford: Blackwell.

Harrigan, K. R. (1980). *Strategies for declining businesses*. Lexington, MA: Lexington Books.

Harris, M. (1964). *Patterns of race in the Americas*. New York: W. W. Norton.

Harris, M. (1980). *Cultural materialism*. New York: Vintage Books.

Harvey, J., Town, J., & Yarkin, K. (1981). How fundamental is the "fundamental attribution error"? *Journal of Personality and Social Psychology*, 40, 346–349.

Hatten, K. J., Schendel, D. E., & Cooper, A. C. (1978). A strategic model of the U.S. brewing industry: 1952–1971. *Academy of Management Journal*, 21, 592–610.

Hazama, H. (1971). Nihonteki keiei no tokushitsu. In H. Hazama (Ed.), *Nihonteki keiei, shudanshugi no kozai* (pp. 9–74). Tokyo: Nihon Keizai Shumbun Sha.

Hazama, H. (1979, October). Comment [on Fruin, 1979]. *Organizational Science*, 13(3), 66–67.

Heider, F. (1958). *The psychology of interpersonal relations*. New York: Wiley.

Healy, J. J. (1965). *Creative collective bargaining*. Englewood Cliffs, NJ: Prentice-Hall.

Heller, R. A., & Wilpert, B. (1979). Managerial decision making: An international comparison. In G. W. England, A. R., Negandhi, & B. Wilpert (Eds.), *Functioning organizations in cross-cultural perspective*. Kent, OH: Kent State University Press.

Heller, F. A., & Wilpert, B. (1981). *Competence and power in managerial decision-making: A study of senior levels of organization in eight countries*. New York: Wiley.

Hemphill, J. K. (1959). Job descriptions for executives. *Harvard Business Review, 37*(3), 55–67.

Herzberg, F. (1966). *Work and the nature of man*. Cleveland, OH: The World Publishing Company.

Hicks, G. L., & Redding, S. G. (1983). The story of the East Asian economic miracle: Part 2, the culture connection. *Euro-Asia Business Review, 2*(2), 18–22.

Hicks, G. L., & Redding, S. G. (n.d.). *Uncovering the sources of East Asian growth*. Unpublished and undated paper, Department of Management, University of Hong Kong.

Hickson, D. J. & McMillan, C. J. (1981). *Organizational and nation: The aston programme IV*. Westmead, Hampshire, England: Gower.

Hickson, D. J., Hinings, C. B., Lee, C. A., Schneck, R. E., & Pennings, J. N. (1971). A strategic contingencies' theory of intraorganizational power. *Administrative Science Quarterly, 16*, 216–229.

Hickson, D. J., Hinnings, C. R., McMillan, C. J. M., & Schwitter, J. P. (1974). The culture-free context of organization structure: A tri-national comparison. *Sociology, 8*, 59–80.

Hickson, D. J., McMillar, C. J., Azumi, K., & Harvath, D. (1979). Grounds for comparative organization theory: Quicksands or hard core? In C. J. Lammers & D. J. Hickson (Eds.), *Organizations alike and unlike* (pp. 25–41). London: Routedge & Kegan Paul.

Hickson, D. J., Pugh, D. S., & Phesey, D. C. (1969). Operations, technology and organization structure. An empirical reappraisal. *Administrative Science Quarterly, 14*, 378–397.

Hinings, C. R., Hickson, D. J., Pennings, J. N., & Schneck, R. E. (1974). Structural conditions of intraorganizational power. *Administrative Science Quarterly, 19*, 22–44.

Hoffman, R. C., & Hegarty, W. H. (1983). A model for development of a data collection instrument. *Proceedings of the Annual Meeting of the Academy of Management*, Dallas, Texas.

Hofheinz, R., & Calder, K. E. (1982). *The East-Asia edge*. New York: Basic Books.

Hofstede, G. (1976). Nationality and exposed values of managers. *Journal of Applied Psychology, 61*, 148–155.

Hofstede, G. (1980a, Summer). Motivation, leadership and organizations. Do American theories apply abroad? *Organizational Dynamics*, 42–63.

Hofstede, G. (1980b). *Culture's consequences. International Differences in work-related values*. Beverly Hills, CA: Sage Publications.

Hofstede, G. (1981, Summer). Do American theories apply abroad? *Organizational Dynamics*, 63–68.

Hofstede, G. (1983). National cultures in four dimensions: A research based theory of cultural differences among nations. *International Studies of Management & Organizations, 13*(1-2), 46–74.

Hofstede, G. (1983, Fall). The cultural relativity of organizational practices and theories. *Journal of International Business Studies, 14*(2), 75–89.

Hofstede, G. (1984). The cultural relativity of the quality of life concept. *Academy of Management Review, 9*, 389–398.

Hoover, J. D., Troub, R. M., Whitehead, C. J., & Flores, L. G. (1978). Social performance goals in the Peruvian and the Yugoslav worker participation systems. In J. Susbauer (Ed.), *Academy of Management Proceedings '78* (pp. 241–246). San Francisco, CA.

Horovitz, J. (1980). *Top management control in Europe*. London: Macmillan.

Howard, A., Shudo, K., & Umeshima, M. (1983). Motivation and values among Japanese and American managers. *Personnel Psychology, 36*, 883–893.

Hoy, F., Van Fleet, D. D., & Yetley, M. J. (1984). Comparative organizational effectiveness research leading to an invention strategy. *Journal of Management Studies, 21*(4), 443–462.

Humble, J. (1965). *Improving management performance*. London: Management Publications.

Hunt, J. W. (1981, Summer). Commentary on: Do American theories apply abroad: Applying American behavior science—some cross-cultural problems. *Organizational Dynamics*, 55–62.

Imaizumi, M. (1984, Spring). Past and present status of quality management in Japan. *Management Japan, 17*(1), 18–22.

International Monetary Fund. (1982). *International financial statistics yearbook*. Washington, DC: Author.

Inzerilli, G. (1985). *Perceptual models of organization structure in different cultures*. Paper presented at the annual Academy of Management Meeting, San Diego.

Ishida, H. (1981, Fall). Human resources management in overseas Japanese firms. *Japanese Economic Studies, X*(1), 53–81.

Ishikawa, A. (1982). A survey of studies in the Japanese style of management. *Economic and Industrial Democracy, 3*, 1–15.

Itami, H. (1978). A Japanese-American comparison of management productivity. *Japanese Economic Studies, 7*(1), 3–14.

Iwata, R. (1977). *Nihonteki keiei no hensei genri*. Tokyo: Bunshindo.

Iwata, R. (1978). *Gendai Nihon no keiei fudo*. Tokyo: Nihonkeizai Shinbunsha.

Iwata, R. (1984). *"Nihonteki keiei" ronso*. Tokyo: Nihonkeizai Shinbunsha.

Jaeger, A. M. (1984). The appropriateness of organization development outside North America. *International Studies of Management & Organization, 14*(1), 23–25.

Jaeger, A. M. (1986). Organization development and national culture. Where's the fit? *Academy of Management Review, 11*, 178–190.

James, W. (1956). *Sentiment of rationality*. New York: Dove.

Jemison, D. E. (1981). Organizational versus environmental sources of influence in strategic decision making. *Strategic Management Journal, 2*, 77–89.

Joynt, P. (1985). Cross-cultural management: The cultural context of micro and macro organizational variables. In P. Joynt & M. Warner, *Managing in different cultures* (pp. 57–68). Oslo, Norway: Universitesforlaget.

Kagono, T., et al. (1980). Mechanistic vs. organic management systems: A comparative study of adaptive patterns of U.S. and Japanese firms. *Kobe Annual Reports*, 115–139.

Kagono, T. Nonaka, I. Sakaibara, K. & Okummura, A. (1981, July). Strategies and structures of U.S. and Japanese firms: An empirical analysis. *Organizational Science, 15*(2), 11–34. In Japanese.

Kagono, T. Nonaka, I. Sakaibara, K. & Okumura, A. (1983–84). Strategic adaptation to environment: Japanese and U.S. firms compared. *Japanese Economic Studies, XII*(2), 33–80.

Kahneman, D., Slovic, P., & Tversky, A. (1982). *Judgment under uncertainty: Heuristics and biases*. Cambridge: Cambridge University Press.

Kamata, S. (1982). *Japan in the passing lane: An insider's account of life in a Japanese auto factory*. New York: Pantheon Books.

Kaminski, A. (1976). *Organizac je a struktura klasowo - warstowa*. Warsaw: PWN.

Kassalow, E. (1984). The crisis in the world steel industry: Union-management responses in four countries. *Industrial Relations Research Association Proceedings*, 341–351.

Kassem, M. S. (1976). Introduction: European versus American organization theories. In G. Hofstede & M. S. Kassem (Eds.), *European contributions to organization theory* (pp. 1– 7). Amsterdam: Van Gorcum.

Katz, D., & Kahn, R. L. (1966). *The social psychology of organizations.* New York: Wiley Eastern Pvt. Ltd.

Katz, D., & Kahn, R. L. (1966/1978). *The social psychology of organizations.* New York: Wiley.

Katz, H., Kochan, T. A., & Weber, M. R. (1985, September). Assessing the effects of industrial relations systems and efforts to improve the quality of working life on organizational effectiveness. *Academy of Management Review, 28*(3), 501–526.

Kawai, H. (1981). *Crisis of the Japanese "hollow structure"* [Nihonteki chuku kozo no kiki]. Tokyo: Chuo Koron.

Keesing, R. M. (1974). Theories of culture. *Annual Review of Anthropology, 3,* 73–97.

Kelley, H. H. (1971). *Attribution in social interaction.* New York: General Learning Press.

Kelley, H. H. (1973). The process of casual attribution. *American Psychologist, 28,* 107–128.

Kelley, H. H., & Michela, J. L. (1980). Attribution theory and research. *Annual Review of Psychology, 31,* 457–501.

Kerlinger, F. N., & Pedhazur, E. J. (1973). *Multiple regression in behavioral research.* New York: Holt, Rinehart & Winston.

Kerr, C. J., Dunlop, T., Harbison, F., & Meyers, C. A. (1952). *Industrialism and industrial man.* Cambridge, MA: Harvard University Press.

Kets de Vires, M. F. R., & Miller, D. (1986, April). Personality, culture, and organization. *Academy of Management Review, 11*(2), 266–279.

Keys, J. B., & Miller, T. R. (1984). The Japanese management theory jungle. *Academy of Management Review, 9,* 342–353.

Khandwalla, P. (1977). *The design of organizations.* New York: Harcourt Brace Jovanovich.

Kido, Y. (1980, August). A study of organizational commitment in Japanese Companies. *Mita Business Review, 23*(3), 132–151. In Japanese.

Kiezun, W. (1980). *Patologie organizac ji.* Warszawa: PWN.

Kluckhohn, F. R., & Strodtbeck, F. L. (1961). *Variations in value orientation.* New York: Row, Peterson.

Kluckhohn, C., & Strodbeck, F. L. (1961). *Variations in values orientations.* Evanston, IL: Row, Peterson.

Kobayashi, N. (1982). The present and future of Japanese multinational enterprise: A comparative analysis of Japanese and U.S.-European multinational management. *International Studies of Management and organization, XII*(1), 38–58.

Kobayashi, S. (1970, November/December). The creative organization—A Japanese experiment. *Personnel,* 8–17.

Korbin, S. J. (1984). *International expertise in American business: How to learn to play with the kids on the street.* I.I.E. Report Number 6. New York: Institute of International Education.

Kochan, T. A. (1980). *Collective bargaining and industrial relations.* Homewood, IL: Richard D. Irwin, Inc.

Koike, K. (1978). Japan's industrial relations: Characteristics and problems. *Japanese Economic Studies, VII*(1), 42–90.

Koike, K. (1983a). Internal labor markets: Workers in large firms. In T. Shirai (Ed.), *Contemporary industrial relations in Japan* (pp. 29–61). Madison: University of Wisconsin Press.

Koike, K. (1983b). Workers in small firms and women in industry. In T. Shirai (Ed.), *Contemporary industrial relations in Japan* (pp. 89–115). Madison: University of Wisconsin Press.

Kono, T. (1981, January). Transferability of Japanese style management to the Japanese affiliated companies outside Japan. *Organizational Science, 18*(4), 38–55.

Kono, T. (1982a, March). Diversification strategy, structure, and performance—A survey. *Organizational Science, 16*(1), 25–40.

Kono, T. (1982b). Japanese management philosophy: Can it be exported? *Long Range Planning, 15*(3), 90–102.

Koontz, H., & O'Donnell, C. (1955). *Principles of Management.* New York: McGraw-Hill.

Kornai, J. (1980). *The economy of shortage.* Amsterdam: North-Holland.

Kroeber, A. L., & Kluckhohn, C. (1952). *Culture: A Critical review of concepts and definitions.* Cambridge, MA: Harvard University Press.

Kroeber, A. L., & Parsons, T. (1958). The concepts of culture and of social systems. *American Sociological Review, 23,* 582–583.

Kuhne, R. J. (1976, Summer). Co-determination: A statutory restructuring of the organization. *Columbia Journal of World Business, XI*(2), 17–25.

Kumagai, H. (1981). A dissection of intimacy: A study of bipolar posturing in Japanese social interaction—Amaeru and amayakasu, indulgence and defence. *Culture, Medicine and Psychiatry, 5,* 249–272.

Kumar, K. (1979). *Bonds without bondage: Explorations in transnational cultural interactions.* Honolulu: University Press of Hawaii.

Kumon, S. (1981). Nihonteki keiei no tokushitsu towa nanika. In *Nihon shakai no tokushitsu* (pp. 99–126). Tokyo: Nihonkeizai Kenkyu center.

Kumon, S. (1984). Some principles governing the thought and behavior of Japanists (contextuals). *Journal of Japanese Studies, 8,* 5–28.

Laaksonen, O. J. (1984). The management and power structure of Chinese enterprises during and after the Cultural Revolution: With empirical data comparing Chinese and European enterprises. *Organization Studies, 5*(1), 1–21.

Lai, T. (George), & Lam, Y. (Constance). (1986). A study on work-related values of managers in the People's Republic of China (Parts I, II, and III). *The Hong Kong Manager* (Dec.–Jan. 1986), 23–41; (Feb.–Mar. 1986), 91–51; (Apr.–May 1986), 7–17.

Lammers, C. J. (1976). Towards the internationalization of the organization sciences. In G. Hofstede & M. S. Kassem (Eds.), *European contributions to organization theory* (pp. 25–42). Amsterdam: Van Gorcum.

Lammers, C. J., & Hickson, D. J. (1979). Towards a comparative sociology of organizations. In C. J. Lammers & D. J. Hickson (Eds.), *Organizations alike and unlike* (pp. 3–20). London: Routledge & Kegan Paul.

Lardy, N. R. (1975). Economic planning in the People's Republic of China: Central-provincial fiscal relations. In U.S.A. Congress, Joint Economic Committee, *China: A reassessment of the economy* (pp. 94–115). Washington, DC: U.S. Government Printing Office.

Lau, A. W., Newman, A. R., & Brodeling, L. A. (1980). The nature of managerial work in the public sector. *Public Management Forum, 19,* 513–521.

Lau, S. (1977). *Managerial style of traditional Chinese firms.* Unpublished master's thesis, University of Hong Kong.

Laurent, A. (1983). The cultural diversity of Western management conceptions. *International Studies of Management and Organization, XIII* (1-2), 75–76.

Lawlor, H. (1985). Education and national development in Brazil. In C. Brock & H. Lawlor (Eds.), *Education in Latin America.* Dover, NH: Croom Helm.

Lawrence, P. R., & Lorsch, J. W. (1969). *Organization and environment.* Homewood, IL: Irwin.

Lebra, T. (1976). *Japanese patterns of behavior.* Honolulu: The University Press of Hawaii.

Lemming, F. (1977). *Street studies in Hong Kong.* Hong Kong: Oxford University Press.

Leventhal, G. S. (1976). The distribution of rewards and resources in groups and organizations. In L. Berkowitz & E. Walster (Eds.), *Advances in experimental social psychology, 9,* 92–133.

Levitt, T. (1983). The globalization of markets. *Harvard Business Review, 83*(3), 92–102.

Likert, R. (1961). *New patterns of management.* New York: McGraw-Hill.

Lincoln, J. R., Hanada, M., & Olson, J. (1981). Cultural orientations and individual reactions to organizations: A study of employees of Japanese-owned firms. *Administrative Science Quarterly, 26,* 93–115.

Lincoln, J., Hanaa, M., & Olson, J. (1981, March). Cultural orientations and individual reactions to organizations. *Administrative Science Quarterly,* 93–114.

Lingnan University Research Institute. (1982). Principles of management in a socialist economy. *International Studies of Management and Organization, 12*(2), 20–44.

Linton, R. (1945). *The cultural background of personality.* New York: Appleton-Century.

Locke, E. A. (1968). Toward a theory of task motivation and incentives. *Organizational Behavior and Human Performance, 3,* 157–189.

Locke, E. A. (1976). The nature and causes of job satisfaction. In M. D. Dunnette (Ed.), *Handbook of industrial and organizational psychology* (pp. 1297–1349). Chicago: Rand McNally.

Locke, E. A. (1978). The ubiquity of goal setting theories of and approach to employee motivation. *Academy of Management Review, 3,* 594–601.

Locke, E. A., Shaw, K. N., Saari, L. M., & Latham, G. P. (1981). Goal setting and task performance: 1969–1980. *Psychological Bulletin, 95,* 125–152.

MacMillan, I. C. (1985). Progress in research on corporate venturing. New York University: Center for Entrepreneurial Studies.

Mannari, H., & Marsh, R. (1980, December). Organizational structure of Japanese factories: A test of technological implication theory. *Organizational Science, 14*(4), 61–75. In Japanese.

Mant, A. (1981). Developing effective managers for the future. In C. L. Cooper (Ed.), *Developing managers for the 1980's.* London: Macmillan.

March, J. G., & Olsen, J. P. (1976). *Ambiguity and choice in organizations.* Bergen, Norway: Universitetsforlaget.

March, J. G., & Simon, H. A. (1958). *Organizations.* New York: Wiley.

Martin, J. (1981). Relative deprivation: A theory of distributive justice for an era of shrinking resources. *Research in Organizational Behavior, 3,* 53–107.

Maruyama, M. (1961, First Quarter). The multilateral mutual causal relationships among the modes of communication, sociometric pattern and the intellectual orientation in the Danish culture. *Phylon: The Atlanta Review of Race and Culture,* 41–58.

Maruyama, M. (1973). Paradigmatology and its application to cross-disciplinary, cross professional and cross-communication. *Dialectica, 29*(3-4), 135–196.

Maruyama, M. (1980). Mindscapes and science theories. *Current Anthropology, 21*(5), 389–600.

Maruyama, M. (1982). New mindscapes for future business policy and management. *Technology Forecasting and Social Change, 21,* 53–76.

Maruyama, M. (1984). Alternative concepts of management: Insights from Asia and Africa. *Asia Pacific Journal of Management, 1*(1), 100–111.

Maslow, A. H. (1964). *Motivation and personality.* New York: Harper and Row.

Maurice, M. & Brossard, M. (1976). Is there a universal model of organization structure? *International Studies of Management and organization, 24,* 612–629.

Mazzolini, R. (1979). *Government controlled enterprises: International strategic and policy decisions.* New York: Wiley.

McGregor, D. M. (1960). *The human side of enterprise.* New York: McGraw-Hill.

Mendenhall, M. E., & Oddou, G. (1986, September). The cognitive, psychological and social contexts of Japanese management. *Asia Pacific Journal of Management, 4*(1), 24–37.

Merchant, K. A. (1985). *Control in business organizations.* Boston: Pitman.

Meyer, J. W., & Rowan, B. (1978). The structure of educational organizations. In M. Meyer (Ed.), *Environments and organizations.* San Francisco: Jossey-Bass.

Miles, R. (1980). *Macro organizational behavior.* Santa Monica: Goodyear Publishing Co.

Miles, R. H. (1982). *Coffin nails and corporate strategies.* Englewood Cliffs, NJ: Prentice-Hall.

Miles, R. E., & Snow, C. C. (1978). *Organizational strategy, structure, and process.* New York: McGraw-Hill.

Miller, D., & Mintzberg, H. (1983). The case for configuration. In G. Morgan (Ed.), *Beyond method: Strategies for social research* (pp. 57–73). Beverly Hills, CA: Sage.

Miller, E. J., & Rice, A. K. (1967). *Systems of organization.* London: Tavistock.

Miller, S. W., & Simonetti, J. L. (1974). Culture and management: Some conceptual considerations. *Management International Review, VII*(6), 87–101.

Mills, T. (1978, November–December). Europe's industrial democracy: An American response. *Harvard Business Review, 56*(6), 143–154.

Minami, H. (1980). *Encyclopedia on human relations of the Japanese* [Nihonjin no Ningen Kankei Jiten]. Tokyo: Kodansha.

Miner, John B. (1982). *Theories of organizational structure and process.* Chicago: Drydey Press.

Miner, J. B. (1984). The validity and usefulness of theories in an emerging organizational science. *Academy of Management Review, 9*(2), 296–306.

Mintzberg, H. (1975, July–August). The manager's job: Folklore and fact. *Harvard Business Review,* 49–61.

Mintzberg, H. (1979). *The structuring of organizations.* Englewood Cliffs, NJ: Prentice-Hall.

Mishler, A. L. (1965). Personal contact in international exchanges. In H. C. Kelman (Ed.), *International behavior: A social-psychological analysis* (pp. 555–561). New York: Holt, Rinehart & Winston.

Misumi, J. (1985). *The behavioral science of leadership.* Ann Arbor: University of Michigan Press.

Misumi, J., & Peterson, M. (1985). The performance-maintenance theory of leadership: Review of a Japanese research program. *Administrative Science Quarterly, 30,* 198–223.

Mitchell, D. J. B. (1984). International convergence with U.S. wage levels. *Industrial Relations Research Association Proceedings,* 76–84.

Mitchell, T. R. (1974). Expectancy models of job satisfaction, occupational preference, and effort. A theoretical, methodological, and empirical appraisal. *Psychological Bulletin, 81,* 1053–1070.

Mitchell, T. R., Green, S. G., & Wood, R. E. (1981). An attribution model of leadership and the poor performing subordinate: Development and validation. *Research in Organizational Behavior, 3,* 197–234.

Mitroff, I. (1983). *Stakeholders of the organizational mind.* San Francisco, CA: Jossey-Bass.

Monsen, J. R., & Walters, K. D. (1983). *Nationalized companies.* New York: McGraw-Hill.

Monson, T., & Snyder, M. (1977). Actors, observers, and the attribution process. *Journal of Experimental Social Psychology, 13,* 89–111.

Mooney, J. D., & Riely, A. C. (1931). *Onward industry!: The principles of organization and their significance to modern industry.* New York: Harper & Row.

Moran, R. T. (1985). *Getting your yen's worth: How to negotiate with Japan, Inc.* Houston, TX.: Gulf Publishing.

Morawski, W. (1976). *Organizac je: socjologia struktur, procesow, rol.* Warszawa: PWN.

Morgan, G. (1983). *Beyond method.* Beverly Hills, CA: Sage.

Morse, E. L. (1971, Summer). Transnational economic processes. *International Organization, XXV*(3), 23–47.

Mouer, R., & Sugimoto, Y. (1983). Internationalization as an ideology in Japanese society. In H. Mannari & H. Befu (Eds.), *The challenge of Japan's internationalization: Organization and culture* (pp. 267–297). Tokyo: Kwansei Gakuin University and Kodansha International.

Nakamura, H. (1964). *Ways of thinking of Eastern peoples.* Honolulu, HI: East-West Center Press.

Nakane, C. (1972). *Japanese society.* Berkeley: University of California Press.

Nam, W. S. (1971). *The traditional pattern of Korean industrial management,* ILCORK Working Paper N. 14, University of Hawaii, Social Science Research Institute.

Naoi, A. & Schooler, C. (1985). Occupational conditions and psychological functioning in Japan. *American Journal of Sociology, 90*(4), 729–749.

Narain, D. (1967, March). Indian national character in the twentieth century. *Annals,* 124–132.

Needham, J. (1978). *The shorter science and civilization in China.* Cambridge: Cambridge University Press.

Negandhi, A. R. (1973). *Management and economic development: The case of Taiwan.* The Hague: Martinus Nijhoff.

Negandhi, A. R. (1975, June). Comparative management and organization theory: A marriage needed. *Academy of Management Journal,* 334–344.

Negandhi, A. R. (1979). Convergence in organizational practices: An empirical study of industrial enterprise in developing countries. In C. J. Lammers & D. J. Hickson (Eds.), *Organizations alike and unlike* (pp. 323–345). London: Routledge & Kegan Paul.

Negandhi, A. R. (1983). Cross-cultural management research: Trend and future directions. *Journal of International Business Studies, 14*(2), 17–28.

Negandhi, A. R. (1985). Management in the Third World. In P. Joynt & M. Warner (Eds.), *Managing in different cultures* (pp. 69–97). Oslo, Norway: Universitesforlaget.

Negandhi, A. R., & Estafen, B. D. (1965). A research model to determine the applicability of American management know-how in different cultures and/or environments. *Academy of Management Journal, 8,* 309–318.

Negandhi, A. R., & Prasad, S. B. (1971). *Comparative management.* New York: Appleton-Century-Crofts.

Nevis, E. C. (1983). Cultural assumptions and productivity: The United States and China. *Sloan Management Review, 24*(3), 17–28.

Newman, W. H. (1951). *Administrative action: The techniques of organization and management.* New York: Prentice-Hall.

Nisbett, R., & Ross, L. (1980). *Human inference: Strategies and short-comings of social judgment.* Englewood Cliffs, NJ: Prentice-Hall.

Nonaka, I., & Johansson, J. (1985). Japanese management: What about the 'hard' skills? *Academy of Management Review,10*(2), 181–191.

Nonaka, I., & Okumura, A. (1984, Spring). A comparison of management in American, Japanese, and European firms (I). *Management Japan, 17*(1), 23–40.

Nonaka, I., & Okumura, A. (1984, Autumn). A comparison of management in American, Japanese, and European firms (II). *Management Japan, 17*(2), 20–37.

Nye, J. S., & Keohane, R. O. (1971). Transnational relations and world politics: An introduction. In R. O. Keohane & J. S. Nye, Jr. (Eds.), *Transnational relations and world politics* (pp. ix–xxix). Cambridge, MA: Harvard University Press.

Oberg, W. (1963). Cross-cultural perspective on management principles. *Academy of Management Journal, 6*(2), 129–143.

O'Connell, J., & Zimmerman, J. W. (1979). Scanning the international environment. *California Management Review, 22,* 15–23.

Odiorne, G. S. (1984). *Strategic management of human resources.* San Francisco: Jossey-Bass.

Okamoto, Y. (1981, Fall). Nihon Kigyo no grand strategy. *Chuo Koron Kiian Mondai,* 277–306.

Okuda, Kenji. (1971a). Managerial evolution in Japan (I) 1911–1925. *Management Japan, 5*(3), 13–19.

Okuda, K. (1971b). Managerial evolution in Japan. [II] 1926–1945. *Management Japan, 6*(4), 16–23.

Ono, T. (1972). A personal survey of the modernization of business administration in Japan. *Management Japan, 6*(1), 20–27. In Japanese.

Osigweh, C. A. B. (1983). *Improving problem-solving participation: The case of local transnational voluntary organizations.* Lanham, Maryland: University Press of America.

Osigweh, C. A. B. (1985a, December). International business and the growth model. *Journal of Economic Development, 10*(2), 123–142.

Osigweh, C. A. B. (1985b). *Professional management: An evolutionary perspective.* Dubuque, IO: Kendall/Hunt Division of W. C. Brown Co.

Osigweh, C. A. B. (1987). *Management as if rights mattered: The challenge of employee rights and management responsibilities.* Working paper. Norfolk, VA: Norfolk State University School of Business. Presented to the First Industrial Congress of the Americas, Quebec, Canada, August 21–27, 1988.

Osigweh, C. A. B. (1988). The challenge of responsibilities: Confronting the revolution in workplace rights in modern organizations. *The Employee Responsibilities and Rights Journal, 1*(1), 5–25.

Ouchi, W. G. (1981). *Theory Z: How American business can meet the Japanese challenge.* Reading MA: Addison-Wesley.

Ouchi, W. G., & Jaeger, A. M. (1978). Type Z organizations: Stability in the midst of mobility. *Academy of Management Review, 3,* 305–314.

Parsons, T. (1951). *The social system.* New York: Free Press.

Parsons, T. (1973). Culture and social system revisited. In L. Schneider & C. M. Benjean (Eds.), *The idea of culture in the social sciences.* Cambridge, England: Cambridge University Press.

Pascale, R. T. (1978). Zen and the art of management. *Harvard Business Review, 56*(2), 153–162.

Pejovich, S. (Ed.). (1978). *The codetermination movement in the West.* Lexington, MA: Lexington Books.

Peters, T. J., & Waterman, R. H., Jr. (1982). *In search of excellence: Lessons from America's best run companies.* New York: Harper & Row.

Peterson, R. B., & Simada, J. Y. (1978). Sources of management problems in Japanese-American joint ventures. *Academy of Management Review, 3,* 796–805.

Pfeffer, J. (1977a). Power and resource allocation in organizations. In B. M. Staw & G. R. Salancik (Eds.), *New directions in organizational behavior* (pp. 235–265). Chicago: St. Clair Press.

Pfeffer, J. (1977b). Usefulness of the concept. In P. S. Goodman, J. M. Pennings, & Associates (Eds.), *New perspectives on organizational effectiveness* (pp. 132–145). San Francisco: Jossey-Bass.

Pfeffer, J. (1981). *Power in organizations.* Marshfield MA: Pitman.

Pfeffer, J. (1982). Organizations and Organization theory. Marshfield, MA: Pitman.

Pfeffer, J., & Salancik, G. (1978). *The external control of the organizations.* New York: Harper & Row.

Pike, K. L. (1967). *Language in relation to an unified theory of the structure of behavior.* The Hague: Mouton.

Polakos, E. D., & Wexley, K. N. (1983). The relationship among perceptual similarity, sex and performance ratings in manager-subordinate dyads. *Academy of Management Journal, 26,* 129–139.

Pondy, L. R. (1978). Leadership is a language game. In W. M. McCall & M. M. Lombardo (Eds.), *Leadership: Where else can we go?* (pp. 87–99). Durham, NC: Duke University Press.

Porter, M. E. (1980). *Comparative strategy.* New York: Free Press. Porter, M. (1985). *Competitive advantage.* New York: Free Press.

Provan, K. (1980). Board power and organizational effectiveness among human service agencies. *Academy of Management Journal, 23*(2), 221–236.

Pugh, D. (1984). *Organization theory.* London: Penguin.

Pyle, T. H. (1981). Reforming Chinese management: The P.R.C. is testing a number of strategies and considering some bold new moves. *China Business Review, 8*(3), 7–19.

Pugh, D., Hickson, D., Hinnings, C., & Turner, C. (1969). The context of organization structures. *Administrative Science Quarterly, 14,* 91–114.

Quinn, J. B. (1980). *Strategies for change: Logical incrementalism.* Homewood, IL: Richard D. Irwin.

Rapp, W. V. (1977). Japan—Its industrial policies and corporate behavior. *Columbia Journal of World Business, 12*(1), 38–48.

Redding, S. G. (1977). Some perceptions of psychological needs among managers in South-East Asia. In Y. H. Poortinga (Ed.), *Basic problems in cross-cultural psychology* (pp. 338–344). Amsterdam: Swets and Zeitlinger.

Redding, S. G. (1980). Cognition as an aspect of culture and its relation to management processes: An exploratory view of the Chinese case. *Journal of Management Studies, 17*(2), 127–148.

Redding, S. G. (1982). Thoughts on causation and research models in comparative management for Asia. *Proceedings of the Academy of International Business Conference on Asia Pacific Dimensions of International Business* (pp. 1–38), University of Hawaii.

Redding, S. G., & Hicks, G. L. (1983, February). *Culture, causation and Chinese Management.* Unpublished paper. Hong Kong: University of Hong Kong, Mongkwok Ping Management Data Bank.

Redding, S. G., Wong, G. (1986). The psychology of Chinese organizational behavior. In M. H. Bond (Ed.), *The psychology of Chinese people.* Hong Kong: Oxford University Press.

Richman, B. M. (1971). Ideology and management: The Chinese oscillate. *Columbia Journal of World Business, 6* 23–33.

Ricks, D. A. (1983). *Big business blunders.* Homewood, IL: Richard D. Irwin.

Richta, R. (1973). *Cywilizac ja na rozdrozu.* Warszawa: PWE.

Rieger, F. (1987). *The influence of national culture on organizational structure, process and strategic decision making: A study of international airlines.* Unpublished PhD dissertation, McGill University.

Roberts, K. (1970). On looking at an elephant: An evaluation of cross-cultural research related to organizations. *Psychological Bulletin, 74*(5), 327–350.

Rohlen, T. (1974). *For harmony and strength: Japanese white collar organization in anthropological perspective.* Berkeley: University of California Press.

Ronen, S., & Kraut, A. I. (1977). Similarities among countries based on employee work values and attitudes. *Columbia Journal of World Business, 12*(2), 89–96.

Ronen, S., & Shenkar, O. (1985). Clustering countries on attitudinal dimensions: A review and synthesis. *Academy of Management Review, 10,* 435–454.

Rosenberg, A. (1967, November). International interaction and the taxonomy of international organization. *International Associations, 19*(11), 721–729.

Russell, B. (1927). *Philosophy.* New York: Norton.

Ryterband, E. C., & Barrett, G. V. (1970). Managers' values and their relationships to the management of tasks: A cross-cultural comparison. In B. M. Bass, R. C. Cooper, & J. A. Hass (Eds.), *Managing for accomplishment*. Lexington, MA: D. C. Health.

Samiee, S. (1984). Transnational data flow constraints: A new challenge for multination corporations. *Journal of International Business Studies, XV*(1), 141–150.

Sampson, E. E. (1980). Justice and social character. In G. Mikila (Ed.), *Justice and social interaction*. New York: Springer-Verlag New York.

Scammon, R. (1972). *The real majority*. Berkeley, CA: Berkeley Publication Corporation.

Schein, E. H. (1985). *Organizational culture and leadership: A dynamic view*. San Francisco, CA: Jossey-Bass.

Schendel, D. E., & Hofer, C. W. (Eds.). (1979). *Strategic management: A new view of business policy and planning*. Boston: Little, Brown.

Schöllhammer, H. (1969, March). The comparative management theory jungle. *Academy of Management Journal*, 81–97.

Schregle, J. (1978, January–February). Co-determination in the Federal Republic of Germany. *International Labor Review, 117*(1), 81–98.

Schwartz, H. S. (1985, Spring). The usefulness of myth and the myth of usefulness: A dilemma for the applied organizational scientist. *Journal of Management, 11*(1) 31–42.

Scott, W. G. (1982, May/June). Barnard on the nature of elitist responsibility. *Public Administration Review*, 197–201.

Scott, W. G. (1985, August). Organizational revolution: An end to managerial orthodoxy. *Administration and Society, 17*(2), 149–170.

Scott, W. G., & Mitchell, T. R. (1986, Autumn). Markets and morals in management education. *Selections: The Magazine of the Graduate Management Admission Council, 11*(2), 3–8.

Segall, M. H. (1979). *Cross-cultural psychology: Human behavior in global perspective*. Monterey, CA: Brooks/Cole.

Sekaran, U. (1981). Are organizational concepts and measures transferable to another culture: An empirical investigation. *Academy of Management Journal, 24*(2), 409–16.

Sekaran, U. (1983). Methodological and theoretical issues and advancements in cross-cultural research. *Journal of International Business Studies, 14*(3), 61–73.

Selznick, P. (1957). *Leadership in administration*. New York: Harper & Row.

Sethi, S. P., Namiki, N., & Swanson, C. L. (1984). *The false promise of the Japanese miracle: Illusions and realities of the Japanese management*. Marshfield, MA: Pitman.

Shaw, M. E., & Iwawaki, S. (1972). Attribution of responsibility by Japanese and Americans as a function of age. *Journal of Cross Cultural Psychology, 3*, 71–81.

Sherif, M., & Hovland, C. I. (1961). *Social judgment: Assimilation and contrast effects in communication and attitude change*. New Haven, CT: Yale University Press.

Shimada, H. (1983). Japanese industrial relations—A new general model? A survey of the English-language literature. In T. Shirai (Ed.), *Contemporary industrial relations in Japan*. Madison: University of Wisconsin Press.

Shinohara, M. (1980). Empirical study of corporate strategy in Japan: Environment-top management strategy. *Mita Business Review, 23*(4), 86–103. In Japanese.

Siehl, C., & Martin, J. (1981). *Learning organizational culture*. Graduate School of Business, Stanford University.

Silin, R. H. (1976). *Leadership and values: The organization of large scale Taiwanese enterprises*. Cambridge, MA: Harvard University Press.

Silverman, D. (1970). *The theory of organizations*. London: Heinemann.

Singer, B. (1980, September/October). Crazy systems. *Social Policy, 2*(4), 25–37.

Sirota, D., & Greenwood, J. M. (1971). Understand your overseas workforce. *Harvard Business Review, 49*(1), 53–60.

Skidmore, T. E., & Smith, P. H. (1984). *Modern Latin America*. New York: Oxford University Press.

Skjelsbaek, K. (1971, Summer). The growth of international non-government organizations in the twentieth century. *International Organization, XXV*(3), 70–92.

Smircich, L. (1983a). Organizations as shared meaning. In L. R. Pondy, P. Frost, G. Morgan, & T. Dandridge (Eds.), *Organizational symbolism* (pp. 160–172). Greenwich, CT: JAI Press.

Smircich, L., & Morgan, G. (1982). Leadership: The management of meaning. *Journal of Applied Behavioral Science, 18*(3), 257–273.

Smircich, L. (1983b). Concepts of culture and organizational analysis. *Administrative Science Quarterly, 28*, 339–358.

Snodgrass, C. R., & Grant, J. H. (1986). Cultural influences on strategic planning and control systems. *Advances in Strategic Management, 4*, pp. 205–228.

Snow, C. C., & Miles, R. E. (1984, Summer). Designing strategic human resources management systems. *Organizational Dynamics, 13*(1), 36–52.

Solange-Peret, M. (1982). *Impact of cultural differences on budget*. Unpublished doctoral dissertation, University of Western Ontario, London, Ontario, Canada.

Somers, Gerand G. (Ed.). (1980). *Collective bargaining: Contemporary American experience*. Madison, WI.: Industrial Relations Research Association.

Sorge, A. (1983a). Cultured organizations. *International Studies of Management and Organization, 12*, 106–138.

Sorge, A. (1983b). Culture's consequences: International differences in work-related values. *Administrative Science Quarterly, 28*, 625–629.

Staniszkis, J. (1984). *Poland's self-limiting revolution*. Princeton: Princeton University Press.

Staw, B. M. (1975). Attribution of the 'cases' of performance: A general alternative interpretation of cross-sectional research on organizations. *Organizational Behavior and Human Performance, 13*, 414–432.

Staw, B. M. (1980). Rationality and justification in organizational life. In B. M. Staw & L. L. Cummings (Eds.), *Research in organizational behavior* (Vol. 2, pp. 45–80). Greenwich, CT: JAI Press.

Steele, F. (1976). Is organizational development work possible in the UK culture? *Journal of European Training, 5*(3), 105–110.

Steers, R. M. (1987). *The international challenge to management education*. Presidential address, Annual Meeting of the Academy of Management, New Orleans.

Stein, S. J., & Stein, B. H. (1970). *The colonial heritage of Latin America*. New York: Oxford University Press.

Steiner, G. A. (1979). *Strategic planning*. New York: Free Press.

Stening, B. W. (1979). Problems in cross-cultural contact: A literature review. *International Journal of Intercultural Relations, 3*, 269–313.

Sterba, R. L. A. (1978). Clandestine management in the Imperial Chinese bureaucracy. *Academy of Management Review, 3*(1), 69–78.

Stinchocombe, A. (1965). Social structure and organizations. In J. G. March (Ed.), *Handbook of organizations* (pp. 142–193). New York: Rand McNally.

Sunderarajan, U. (1985). *Organizational effectiveness in an Indian public and private sector organization*, Unpublished doctoral dissertation, New Delhi, Indian Institute of Technology.

Suzuki, H. (1976). *The transcendents and the climate* [Choetsusha to fudo]. Tokyo: Taimedo.

Tainio, R., & Santalainen, T. (1984). Some evidence for the cultural reliability of organizational development programs. *Journal of Applied Behavioral Science, 20*(2), 93–111.

Taira, K. (1970). *Economic development and the labor market in Japan*. New York: Columbia University Press.

Takahashi, T. (1970). Management information system: A critical appraisal. *Management Japan*, 4(1), 18–23.

Takamiya, M. (1981, Summer). Japanese multinationals in Europe: Internal operations and their public policy implications. *Columbia Journal of World Business*, 5–16.

Takamiya, S. (1983, Spring). Development of Japanese management. *Management Japan*, 16(1), 10–18.

Taku, Y. (1981, July). Strategic business organization. *Organizational Science*, 15(2), 35–48. In Japanese.

Taylor, S. E. (1982). The availability bias in social perception. In K. Jahneman, P. Slovic, & A. Tversky (Eds.), *Judgment under uncertainty* (pp. 190–200). Cambridge: Cambridge University Press.

Taylor, J. (1983). *Shadows of the rising sun*. New York: William Morrow.

Terry, G. R. (1953). *Principles of management*. Homewook, IL: Irwin.

Thimm, A. L. (1976, Spring). Decision making at Volkswagen 1972–1975. *Columbia Journal of World Business*, 16(1), 94–104.

Thompson, J. D. (1967). *Organizations in action*. New York: McGraw-Hill.

Thurow, L. C. (1987). U.S. corporate wisdom: If you can't beat them, quit. *International Herald Tribune*. Aug. 15, p. 8.

Tibaut, J., & Walker, L. (1975). *Procedural justice: A psychological analysis*. Hillsdale, NJ: Erlbaum.

Tichy, N. (1982, Autumn). Managing change strategically: The technical prolitical and cultural keys. *Organization Dynamics*, 59–80.

Tichy, N. (1983). *Managing strategic change*. New York: Wiley.

Triandis, H. (1963). Factors affecting employee selection in two cultures. *Journal of Applied Psychology*, 47(2), 89–96.

Triandis, H. (1972). *The analysis of subjective culture*. New York: Wiley- Interscience.

Triandis, H. C. (1973). Subjective culture and economic development. *International Journal of Psychology*, 8, 163–182.

Triandis, H. (1982). Review of culture's consequences: International differences in work-related values. *Human Organization*, 41(1), 86–90.

Triandis, H. C., Malpas, R. S., & Davidson, A. R. (1973). Psychology and culture. *Annual Review of Psychology*, 24, 355–374.

Tsuchiya, M. (1978). Nihonteki keiei wa Nihonteki ka. prolouge to Moriaki Tsuchiya, *Nihonteki keiei no shinwa* (pp. 11–16). Tokyo: Nihon Keizai Shimubn Sha.

Tsuda, M. (1976). *Nihonteki keiei no yogo*. Tokyo: Toyokeizai Shinposha.

Tsusa, M. (1977). *Nihonteki keiei no ronri*. Tokyo: Chu Kizaisha.

Tsuda, M. (1979). Japanese-style management: Principle and system. *Japanese Economic Studies*, VII, 4(Summer), 3–32.

Tsuda, M. (1981a). *Gendai keiei to kyodo seikatsutai: Nihonteki keiei no riron no tameni*. Tokyo: Dobunkan.

Tsuda, M. (1981b). *Jiniji kanri no gendaiteki kadai*. Tokyo: Zeimu Kyori Kyokai.

Tsuda, M. (1982). *Nihonteki keiei no shinro: keieisha eno issho*. Tokyo: Chuo Keizasha.

Tsunoyama, S. (1978). Government and business: An introductory essay. In International Conference on Business History, Fuji Education Center, *Government and business: Proceedings of the Fifth Fuji Conference* (pp. 1–18). Tokyo: University of Tokyo Press.

Tung, R. L. (1981a). Management practices in China. *China International Business*, 64–105.

Tung, R. L. (1981b). Patterns of motivation in Chinese industrial enterprises. *Academy of Management Review*, 481–489.

Tung, R. L. (1982). *Chinese industrial society after Mao*. Lexington, MA: Lexington Books.

Tung, R. L. (1984). *Business negotiations with the Japanese*. Lexington, MA: Lexington Books.

Tylor, E. B. (1877). *Primitive culture: Researches into the development of mythology, philosophy, religion, language, art and custom* (Vol. 1). New York: Henry Holt.

Uchino, T. (1981, December). On the measurement of interorganizational relations: Focusing on interlocking directorates. *Organizational Science, 154,* 53–63. In Japanese.

Urabe, K. (1978, October). Nihonteki keieiron hihan. *Kokumin Keizai Zasshi, 138,* 1–18.

Urwick, L. F. (1952). *Notes on the theory of organization.* New York: American Management Association.

U.S. Department of Commerce. (1977, February). *Survey of current business.* Washington, D.C.: U.S. Government Printing Office.

U.S. Department of Commerce. (1977, August). *Survey of current business.* Washington, DC: U.S. Government Printing Office.

U.S. Department of Commerce. (1979, August). *Survey of current business.* (Table 3, p. 56). Washington, DC: U.S. Government Printing Office.

U.S. Department of Commerce, Bureau of Census. (1984). *Statistical abstract of the United States – 1984,* 104th edition. Washington, DC: U.S. Government Printing Office.

U.S. Department of Commerce. (1984, October). *Survey of current business.* (p. 38). Washington, DC: U.S. Government Printing Office.

van de Vall, M. (1980). *Labor organizations.* London: Cambridge University Press.

Vassiliou, V., Triandis, H. C., Vassiliou, G., & McGuire, H. (1980). Interpersonal contact and stereotyping. In H. C. Triandis (Ed.), *The analysis of subjective culture* (pp. 89–115). New York: Wiley.

Vickers, S. G. (1965). *The art of judgement.* London: Chapman and Hall.

Vogl, F. (1973). *German business after the economic miracle.* New York: Halsted Press.

Vroom, V. (1964). *Work and motivation.* New York: Wiley.

Wakabayshi, M. Minami, T., Hashimoto, M. Sano, K., Green, G., & Novak, M. (1970). Managerial career development: Japanese style. *International Journal of Intercultural Relations, 4,* 381–419.

Wallich, H. (1960). *Mainsprings of the German revival.* New Haven: Yale University Press.

Waston, A. (1978). Industrial management—Experiments in mass participation. In W. O. Brugger (Ed.), *China: The impact of the cultural revolution* (pp. 171–202). London: Croom Helm.

Webber, R. A. (1969). Convergence or divergence? *Columbia Journal of World Business, IV,* 75–83.

Weick, K. E. (1976). Educational organizations as loosely coupled systems. *Administrative Science Quarterly, 21,* 1–19.

Whitehill, A. & Takezawa, S. (1968). *The other worker.* Honolulu: East-West Center Press.

Willey, R. (1979). *Democracy in the West German trade unions.* Beverly Hills: Sage Publications.

Williamson, O. E. (1986). *The economic institutions of capitalism.* New York: The Free Press.

Witkin, H. A., Dyke, R. B., Faterson, H. F., Goodenough, D. R., & Karp, S. A. (1962). *Psychological differentation.* New York: Wiley.

Woodward, J. (1965). *Industrial organization: Theory and practice.* London: Oxford University Press.

Woodworth, W. (1982). Concession bargaining: What's in it for unions? *Industrial Relations Research Association Proceedings,* 419–424.

Wren, D. A. (1979). *The evolution of management thought.* New York: Wiley.

Wuthunow, R., Hunter, J. D., Bergesen, A., & Kurzweil, E. (1984). *Cultural analysis: The work of Peter L. Berger, Mary Douglas, Michel Faucault, and Jurgen Habermas.* London: Routlege & Kegan Paul.

Xue, M. (1979). *A study on the problems of China's socialist economy.* Beijing: People's Press.

Yamauchi, T. (1974). *Logos and lemma* [Rogosu to remma] Tokyo: Iwaniami Shoten.

Yamada, M. (1980). Beikoku ni miru Nihon-teki keiei. In T. Shishido & the Nikko Research Center (Eds.), *Nihon Kigyo in USA* (pp. 104–131). Tokyo: Tokyo keizai Shimpo Sha.

Yang, H. L. (1973). *The practice of nepotism: A study of sixty Chinese commercial firms in Singapore.* Unpublished manuscript, University of Singapore.

Yankelovich, D. (1979). We need new motivational tools. *Industry Week,* Aug. 6, pp. 10–11.

Yoshihara, H. (1983, September). Cumulative type of management—Japanese management abroad. *Kokumin keizai Zasshi, 148*(3), 119–138. In Japanese.

Yuchtman, E., & Seashore, S. (1967). A systems resource approach to organizational effectiveness. *American Sociological Review, 32*(6), 891–903.

Zaleznik, A., & Kets de Vries, M. F. R. (1980). *Power and the corporate mind.* Boston: Bonus Books.

Zammuto, R. F. (1982). *Assessing organizational effectiveness.* Albany, NY: State University of New York–Albany Press.

Zammuto, R. F. (1984). A comparison of multiple constituency models of organizational effectiveness. *Academy of Management Review, 9*(4), 606–616.

Zeeman, J. R. (1987). *Service: The cutting edge of global competition.* Address, Annual Meeting of the Academy of International Business, Chicago.

About the Authors

Nancy J. Adler is an associate professor of organizational behavior and cross-cultural management at McGill University in Montreal, Canada. Adler received her MBA and PhD from the University of California, Los Angeles. She has published numerous articles in journals such as *Academy of Management Review, Human Resource Management, International Studies of Management and Organization*, and *Journal of Applied Behavioral Science*. She has also produced the film, *A Portable Life*, on the role of the spouse in overseas moves. Her books include *The International Dimensions of Organizational Behavior* (Kent Publishing, 1986) and *Women in Management Worldwide* (M. E. Sharpe, 1987). Adler has taught at the American Graduate School of International Management and at INSEAD, the European Institute of Business Administration, Fontainebleau, France.

Wiktor Askanas is an associate professor of management and policy in the Faculty of Administration at the University of New Brunswick, Canada. Askanas earned his PhD in organization theory at the Polish Academy of Science in Warsaw, Poland. He is the author of *Theory of Organization and Management* (with Mariusz Bratnicki and Jerzy Kurnal, 1980), *Design and Implimentation of MIS* (1978), *The Use of Computers in the Management Process* (1976), and over 30 conference papers, articles, and book chapters. His fourth book, *Organizational Conflicts Resulting from Implementation of MIS* (1978), received the Second Level Award for the Best Published Book in the Field of Management, from the Polish Ministry of Education in 1979. Askanas has worked as a faculty member at Warsaw University and York University, Toronto. He was formerly manager of the Union of Computer Centers (Warsaw) and editor of the Polish Radio and Television Broadcasting Corporation.

William Aussieker received his BS (1968), MBA (1969), and PhD (1974) from the University of California, Berkeley. His research interest in the area of industrial relations has produced about 30 scholarly papers. Aussieker is professor of management at the California Polytechnic and State University.

Schon L. Beechler is currently a PhD candidate in organizational behavior and sociology at the University of Michigan. She has studied in Japan for several years and was in Tokyo for the 1986–1988 academic years on a Fulbright Scholarship to gather her dissertation data on the personnel practices of Japanese multinational corporations.

Kim S. Cameron (PhD, Yale University, 1978) also holds a MA from Yale and a MS and a BS from Brigham Young University. Cameron is associate professor and chairman of the Department of Organizational Behavior and Industrial Relations in the Graduate School of Business Administration at the University of Michigan, where he is also associate professor of higher education in the School of Education. He is author or coauthor of six books, including *Organizational Decline* (Ballinger, 1987), *Paradox and Transformation* (Ballinger, 1987), *Developing Management Skills* (Scott, Foresman, 1984), *Organizational Effectiveness* (Academic Press, 1983), *Coffin Nails and Corporate Strategies* (Prentice-Hall, 1982), and *Management* (Ginn, 1981). He has also published in journals such as *Administrative Science Quarterly, Academy of Management Journal, Research in Higher Education, Journal of Higher Education, Organizational Dynamics,* and *Human Resource Management.* He has consulted with organizations such as the U.S. General Accounting Office, Whirlpool Corporation, State University of New York at Buffalo, American Nurses Association, and General Motors Corporation. Cameron was formerly associate editor of *luman Resource Management* (journal) and consulting editor to the *Journal of Applied Behavioral Science* and *Journal of Higher Education.*

Cary L. Cooper (PhD, University of Leeds, United Kingdom) received his BS and MBA degrees from the University of California, Los Angeles, and an honorary MSc from the University of Manchester in Great Britain. He is professor of organizational psychology and past chairman of the Department of Management Sciences, University of Manchester Institute of Science and Technology. Cooper was the 1985 chairman of the Management Education and Development Division of the (American) Academy of Management. He was elected a Fellow of the British Psychological Society and honored with the Society's Myers Lecture in 1986. Cooper has been an adviser to organizations and governments all over the world. He is editor of the *Journal of Occupational Behaviour* and is on the editorial board of international journals such as the *Journal of Managerial Psychology, Analise Psicologica (Portuguese Journal of Applied Psychology), Employee Responsibilities and Rights Journal, Stress Medicine,* and Leadership and Organization Development Journal. He is author or coauthor of over 42 books and 200 scholarly articles in various areas of management.

Charles J. Cox is lecturer in organizational psychology at the Department of Management Science, University of Manchester Institute of Science and Technology. He holds a BA (Honors) in philosophy and psychology from the University of Bristol, United Kingdom (1954) and was primarily involved in establishing the MSc program in management education and organizational change at the University of Manchester. He is currently course director of the MSc track in organizational psychology. Results of Cox's research have appeared in the *Journal of General Management, Psychology Teaching,* and *Journal of European Training.* Cox is coauthor of three books: *Management Development: Advances in Practice and Theory* (Wiley, 1984), *Introducing Organisational Behaviour* (Macmillan, 1982), and *Advances in Management Education* (Wiley, 1980).

Robert Doktor (PhD, Stanford University, 1970) is professor of management in the College of Business at the University of Hawaii. He has taught at the Wharton School of the University of Pennsylvania, authored one book, *International HRD Annual* (Vol. 1) (American Society for Training and Development, 1985), and coauthored six others: *ISMO: Japanese Insights Concerning Management and Organization in Japan* (Sage, 1985), *Experiencing Management* (Management Publishing Inc., 1980), *Management Advancement: An International Comparison* (Free Press, 1980), *Implimentation of Management Science* (TIMS Studies in Management Science, 1979), *Organizational Behavior* (Prentice-Hall, 1974), and *Managerial Insights: Analysis, Decisions and Implimentation* (Prentice-Hall, 1973). Doktor's research has been published in journals such as *Asian Pacific Journal of Management, Decision Science, Industrial Relations, International Journal of Forecasting, International Studies of Management and Organization, Journal of Applied Behavioral Science, Journal of Management, Management International Reveiw,* and *Organizational Behavior and Human Performance.*

Dexter Dunphy holds the PhD in sociology from Harvard University and the BA (Hons), MEd (Hons) and DipEd from Sydney University, Australia. He is professor of management at the Australian Graduate School of Management and was formerly head and professor of business administration, Department of Organization Behavior in the Faculty of Commerce, University of New South Wales, Australia. Prior to that, Dunphy was an assistant professor of social relations and business administration at Harvard University. He was a 1984 recipient of the Fulbright Senior Scholar Award and has held visiting professorships at Harvard University, Keiko University (Japan), and the National University of Singapore. Dunphy has authored or co-authored 8 books and more than 41 learned articles in management and the social sciences. He is also coauthor of four annotated bibliographies— *Industrial Democracy and Worker Participation* (1979), *Technology and the Workforce* (1981), *Japanese Organization Behaviour and Management* (1984), *Management and the Enterprise in the People's Republic of China* (1985).

Sarah J. Freeman is a doctoral student currently completing her work in organizational behavior at the University of Michigan, School of Business Administration. She also holds the AB and MBA degrees from the University of Michigan. Freeman was formerly director of marketing for a manufacturer of computer peripherals. Her research interests include organizational transformations and organization design and downsizing.

W. Harvey Hegarty is a professor and former dean for professional programs in the Graduate School of Business at Indiana University. He earned an MBA from Indiana University and a PhD from the University of North Carolina, Chapel Hill. His research interests include strategic planning systems, corporate strategies for coping with external publics, business– government relations, and ethics. He has co-authored a book and has published in the *Academy of Management Journal, Planning Review, Journal of Applied Psychology,* and other professional journals. He serves on the editorial boards of the *Journal of Management Case Studies* and the *Strategic Management Journal.* He has taught in Australia, China, Europe, and South America.

Richard C. Hoffman is an assistant professor in the College of Business and Economics at the University of Delaware. He received an MBA from the University of Pennsylvania and a PhD from Indiana University. His research interests include strategic decision making, foreign direct investment, and organizational communications. He has published in journals such as *Decision Science, Long Range Planning,* and the *Journal of International Business Studies.*

Geert Hofstede is professor of organizational anthropology and international management and Director of the Institute of Intercultural Cooperation (IRIC) at the University of Limburg in Maastricht, the Netherlands. He holds an ir. (M.Sc.) degree in mechanical engineering from the Technical University at Delft, and a doctorate (Ph.D.) in social psychology from the University of Groningen. From 1965 to 1971, he founded and managed the Personnel Research Department of IBM Europe. Since then, he has taught and researched at IMEDE (Lausanne, Switzerland), INSEAD (Fontainebleau, France), the European Institute for Advanced Studies in Management (Brussels, Belgium), and IIASA (Laxenburg Castle, Austria). His best known books are *The Game of Budget Control* (Van Gorcum/Tavistock, 1968) and *Culture's Consequences* (Sage, 1980), both of which have also appeared in Japanese and French versions. His articles have been published in the scholarly journals of many countries in Europe, Asia, and North America.

Myung Un Kim is visiting assistant professor of organizational behavior and industrial relations in the School of Business Administration at the University of Michigan. He received his BA in psychology from Seoul National University, Seoul, Korea, MA and PhD in organizational psychology from the University of Michigan. His research interests are in the individual and organizational impacts of dual-career development, spiritual versus transformational leadership, and the relationships among organizational decline, turbulence, culture, strategy, and effectiveness. His recent publications appear in the *Academy of Management Journal, Administrative Science Quarterly,* and *Review of Higher Education.*

Yasumasa Kondo is a professor of accounting in the Department of Commerce at Doshisha University, Kyoto, Japan. Among his books are *Management Accounting* (1983), *Budgetary Control: A Contingency Approach* (1980), and *Problems in Management Accounting* (1986). He has published articles in the *Journal of International Business Studies, Doshisha Business Review,* and *Kaikei.*

Chimezie Anthony Baylon-Pascal Osigweh received his MA, MLHR (master's in labor relations and human resource management) and PhD (1982) from the Ohio State University. He earned his BS degree (*magna cum laude*) in 1978 from East Tennessee State University, after completing the 4-year undergraduate program in 2 years. Osigweh is president of the Council on Employee Responsibilities and Rights (CERR), Virginia Beach, Virginia. He is also professor of management and director of personnel and industrial relations research at Norfolk State University. He was formerly research associate at the Mershon Center and has taught at Northeast Missouri State University and the Ohio State University. He has also served as an occasional reviewer and on the editorial review boards for publications such as the *Journal of Voluntary Action Research* and the international *Journal of Economic Development.* Osigweh is editor-in-chief of the interdisciplinary research and practice quarterly, *The Employee Responsibilities and Rights Journal.* His research in the last 5 years has resulted in the publication of more than 40 articles.

Among his books are *Improving Problem-Solving Participation: The Case of Local Transnational Voluntary Organizations* (University Press of America, 1983); *Petals of Fire* (Poems: Winston-Derek Publishers, 1984); *Professional Management: An Evolutionary Perspective* (Kendall/Hunt division of W. C. Brown Co., 1985); and *Communicating Employee Responsibilities and Rights: A Modern Management Mandate* (Quorum Books, Greenwood-Praeger, 1987). His most recent book, *Managing Employee Rights and Responsibilities* (1988/89), is being released by the Quorum Books Division of Greenwood-Praeger Publishers.

Vladimir Pucik is an assistant professor of international business and organizational behavior at the School of Business Administration, the University of Michigan. He has held visiting academic appointments at IN-SEAD—the European Institute of Business Administration, Fontainebleau (France), and at Otaru School of Commerce (Japan). His research interests include management of multinational firms, strategies for international joint ventures, and comparative management with a particular emphasis on Japan. He has published extensively in academic and professional journals, such as the *Academy of Management Review, Human Resource Management, Japan Economic Journal,* and *Organizational Dynamics.*

S. Gordon Redding holds an MA from Cambridge and a PhD from Manchester Business School. He is professor of management and head of the Department of Management Studies at the University of Hong Kong. Redding has had 10 years executive experience in the U.K. department-store industry and was a visiting professor at the Euro-Asia Center of INSEAD. He has taught at the University of Hawaii and Stockholm School of Economics and is currently visiting professor at the Boston University Institute for the Study of Economic Culture. He is visiting research associate at the Fairbank Center for East Asian Studies, Harvard University. Redding has served as a consultant to organizations such as Cathay, Pacific Airways, Hong Kong Bank, Citicorp, Chase Manhattan, Hutchison Whampoa, the Swire Group, the Mandarin Oriental group, Shangri La, Data General, Fairchild, Hewlett Packard, Kodak, Exxon, Chem, De Beers, Westinghouse, Unisys, Indevo, and SAS. He is the author of *The Working Class Manager,* a study of British managerial beliefs, and is currently completing *The Spirit of Chinese Capitalism.*

Fritz Rieger is an assistant professor of management at the University of Windsor. He holds an MBA from Columbia University and a PhD from McGill University in Canada. His primary research focus is the influence of national culture on organizations, including strategic management in multinational firms and strategy implementation in selected Canadian industries. Rieger's PhD dissertation was a runner-up for the International Management Division of the Academy of Management's best dissertation award and was a finalist in the Academy of International Business dissertation competition.

Rolf E. Rogers is professor of management at California Polytechnic State University, San Luis Obispo. He was formerly professor of management at the University of Alberta and visiting professor of management at the University of Southern California. He received the MA and PhD degrees from the University of Washington, in Seattle. He is a senior member of the American Institute of Industrial Engineers and the Academy of International Business. Rogers is consulting editor of the International Business Series for

Burgess Communications, a division of the Burgess International Group. He is also the author of five books, including *Organization Theory* (Allyn & Bacon, 1975); *Corporate Strategy and Planning* (Grid/Wiley, 1981); and *Organization and Management Theory* (Wiley, 1983). His articles have appeared in the *Academy of Management Review, International Journal of Contemporary Sociology, Personnel Administration, Human Resource Management* (Journal), *Sociological Focus*, and the *Journal of Psychology*.

Uma Sekaran is professor and chairperson of the Department of Management at Southern Illinois University, Carbondale. She received her MBA from the University of Connecticut and PhD (1977) in management from the University of California, Los Angeles. Prior to coming to the United States in 1971, she was a banker in India. Her research in the areas of international management and dual-career families won the Best Paper Award (1981) and the Harlow Outstanding Paper Award (1985) from the Academy of Management. She is the author of *Dual Career Families: Contemporary Organizational and Counseling Issues* (Jossey-Bass, 1986), *Research Methods for Managers* (Wiley, 1984), *Managing Organizational Behavior for Effective Performance* (McGraw-Hill, India, 1988), and coauthor of *Leadership: Beyond Establishment Views* (Southern Illinois University Press, 1981). Sekaran has written over 31 articles in scholarly journals such as the *Administrative Science Quarterly, Academy of Management Journal, Academy of Management Review, Group and Organization Studies, International Review of Applied Psychology, Journal of International Business Studies, Journal of Management, Journal of Occupational Psychology, Indian Journal of Applied Psychology, Journal of Occupational Behavior*, and the *Journal of Vocational Behavior*. She is on the editorial review board of *Management Comparisons*, an international journal.

Jeannette Shi graduated with a BA with majors in economics and Chinese from the University of Sydney. She completed the Diploma of Librarianship in 1969 and the Master of Librarianship in 1975 at the University of New South Wales. Between 1970 and 1982, she worked as a librarian: first at the University of Sydney Library where she was in charge of the Oriental Collection and then from 1973, at the University of New South Wales Library where she held various positions. Since 1983, Shi has worked as a research assistant to Dexter Dunphy at the Australian Graduate School of Management. She is coauthor, with Dunphy, of the annotated bibliography, *Management and the Enterprise in the People's Republic of China* (1985) and an associate author (with Dunphy and B. W. Stening) of the annotated bibliography, *Japanese Organization Behaviour and Management* (1984).

Coral R. Snodgrass is an assistant professor of strategic planning and business policy, in the College of Business and Administration, Southern Illinois University, Carbondale. She received her MBA, and PhD in strategy from the University of Pittsburgh in 1984. She also holds a BA from Duquesne University and has spent some years studying in foreign cultures at the University of Vienna and at Sophia University, Tokyo, Japan. Snodgrass has presented papers and published articles in the areas of strategic management, strategic control, and international management.

Richard M. Steers is a professor of management at the University of Oregon. He has authored twelve books, published over sixty research and professional journal articles, and has served on the editorial boards of the *Academy of Management Review, Journal of Business Research, Administrative Science Quarterly,* and *Academy of Management Journal.* Professor Steers is a fellow of both the American Psychological Association and the Academy of Management, as well as past president of the (American) Academy of Management. He has also taught at Oxford University (England) and the Nijenrode School of Business (The Netherlands). His research interests are in employee motivation, cross-cultural management, and organizational effectiveness.

Jeremiah J. Sullivan is associate professor of business communications in the Department of Marketing and International Business at the University of Washington. He received his PhD in English from New York University in 1970. He also holds the BS, marine transportation (State University of New York, Marine College, 1962), MA, English (New York University), and the MBA (University of Washington, Seattle, 1975). Sullivan has authored two books and coauthored one, including *Handbook of Accounting Communications* (Addison-Wesley, 1983), *Pacific Basin Enterprise and the Changing Law of the Sea* (Lexington Books, 1977), and *Foreign Investment in the U.S. Fishing Industry* (Lexington Books, 1979). He has published articles in the *Academy of Management Journal, Academy of Management Review, Journal of Cross Cultural Psychology, Journal of International Business Studies, Journal of Contemporary Business,* and *Management International Review,* among other publications. Sullivan's interests are focused on cross-cultural studies of managerial behavior and communications.

Teruhiko Suzuki is currently professor of business writing in the Department of Commerce at Doshisha University, Kyoto, Japan. He is a coauthor of five books on business correspondence and communication, including *Case Studies on International Business Communications* (1976), *An Audio-Lingual Approach to Business Communication* (1972), and *Businessman's Correspondence* (1963). Suzuki has also published articles on communication behavior in business organizations in the *Doshisha Business Review.* His research and teaching interests are in the general area of communication behavior in business.

Rosalie L. Tung is professor of business administration and director, International Business Center at the University of Wisconsin, Milwaukee. She was invited as the first foreign expert to teach management at the Foreign Investment Commission (now known as the Ministry of Foreign Economic Relations and Trade), the highest agency under the Chinese State Council that approves all joint ventures and other major forms of foreign investment. Tung is the author of six books: *Management Practices in China* (1980); *U.S.-China Trade Negotiations* (1982); *Chinese Industrial Society after Mao* (1982); *Business Negotiations with the Japanese* (1984); *Key to Japan's Economic Strength: Human Power* (1984); and *Strategic Management in the United States and Japan: A Comparative Analysis* (1986). She has also published widely on the subjects of international management and organizational theory in leading academic journals. Tung is actively involved in management development and consulting activities around the world.

Durhane Wong-Rieger is an assistant professor of applied social psychology at the University of Windsor, where she is also director of the

Human Resources Consultation Unit. She earned her BA in psychology at Barnard College and her MA and PhD in social psychology at McGill University, Montreal, Canada. Her primary interest is the application of research and research methodology to organizational and community problems. Her current areas of research include international management, strategy implementation, individual cross-cultural adjustment, health promotion, and corporate family policies. Wong-Rieger has also consulted with government, business, and social service organizations in the areas of organizational development, strategic planning, and program evaluation.

Index

Absenteeism, 297
Accountability, 215–216
    for goal accomplishment, 216
Adler, N., 4–7
Alitalia Airlines, 235
Ambiguities, 190
American organizational theory, 120
Anaconda, 5
Applied organizational science, 7
Argentina, 7, 14
Askanas, W., 67
Assembly-line approach to training, 58
Attribution theory, 136
Aussieker, W., 81
Australia, 35, 295
Authority distance, 233
Autocracy, 233
Automation, 73
Azumi, K., 34

Barnard, C., 8
Barnet, R., 4
Barrett, G.V., 10
Bass, B.M., 10
Becker, E., 8, 9
Beechler, S., 18, 119
Behavioral processes and relationships, 58
Behaviorist theories, 59
Belief in tradition, 61
Bennett, M., 15
Benson, J.K., 8
Bentham, J., 5
Blunt, P., 19
Boddewyn, J., 12

Bottlenecks in operation, 163
Bougon, M.G., 7
Brazil, 205
    context of, 206
    higher education in, 210
    culture of, 210
Britain, 58
Broedling, L.A., 10
Brossard, M., 7
Bureaucracy in North American organizations, 69
Bureaucratic rigidities, 190

Cadre system, 169
Cameron, K., 19
Capitalist economies, 69
Carlioz, J., 10
Carnation, 295
Carroll, S., 10
Central Committee, 166
Central-planning economies (CPE), 67, 168
Centralization, 69
Child, J., 7
China, 14
    and chasm, 301, 303
    communist party, 165
        enterprise management, 161
        revolutionary values, 194
    National Machinery and Equipment Import and Export Corporation, 182
    political system, 165
    and University of Hong Kong, 182
Chrysler Corporation, 91
Class structure, 63

Clustering analysis, 238
Cognitive theory,
  dispassion, 8
  maps, 32
  meaning, 8
  orientation, 8, 233
Collectivism, 192
Company, connotations of, 298
Comparative management
  paradigm of, 98
  and research in strategic management,
    99
  studies in, 41, 383
Competitiveness of U.S. firms, 81
Confederation of German Employers, 87
Consensus, 234
Constitution, 1978, 169
Control, autonomization of, 73–74
Convergence, 33
  versus divergence, 33
Cooper, C., 16, 290
Copeland, L., 303
Coulter, P.B., 270
Cox, C., 16, 290
Cross-cultural organizational research, 158
Cross-cultural variance, 16, 29
Culbert, S.A., 7
Culture
  and anthropology, 301–302
  corporate, 256
    matrix, 80
  determination of, 16, 30
  hypothesis of, 139
  influence of, 32
  and problem identification, 296–297
  and problem-solving, 298
  and problem resolution, 299–300
  and relativity of effectiveness, 273
  and revolution, 41, 177
Culturalist rollback, 154
Cummings, L.L., 8
Curriculum, 212
  and base budgets, 212

Davidson, A.R., 10
Davis, R., 10
Decentralization of authority, 163
Democratic centralism, 165
Demographic conditions, 207
Denmark, 297

Determinants of performance, 250
Developmental psychology studies, 43
Diffusion, 119
  of American organizational theories in
    Japan, 172
Discussion, 175, 222
Divergence, 34
Diversification, 246
Doktor, R., 16
Donnellon, A., 7
Dowling, J.B., 7
Dun & Bradstreet, 103
Dunphy, D., 19, 179

Economy
  situation of, 63
  systems of, 162
  and sociopolitical system, 162
  and technological stagnation, 162
Eieteman, D.K., and Stonehill, A.I., 6
Electronic data processing, 75
Employee
  participation, 298–299
  stock ownership, 91
England, 9
Enterprise management systems, 169
Environmental bath, 12
Equal Employment Opportunity, 300
  for women, 300
Equality, 300
Epstein, S., 8
Ethnocentric studies, 12
European Economic Community (EEC), 61
European Management Institute, 37
Evocation, 8
  and meaning, 8
  and orientation, 8
Experimental negotiating agreement
  (ENA), 90
External wars, 162
Exxon, 5

Family names, 295
Farmer, R., 11
Fayol, H., 10
Field articulation, 44
Field research, 234
Financial Times, 64
First five-year plan, 162
Foreign direct investment, 5

Foundation for organization research, 271
Four Modernizations, 162, 175
  modernizations efforts and, 163
France, 14, 57
Franchet, A., 10
Freeman, S., 19
Frost, P., 7
Fujisawa, T., ix, 296
Fulbright Distinguished Scholar Program, 204
Fundamental attribution error (FAE), 136

Geographic regions, 242
German Federation of Trade Unions, 85
Ghishelli, E.E., 10
Gillen, D., 10
Goal consciousness, 75
Gonzalez, R.F., 12
Gary, B., 7, 8
Greiner, L., 58
Griggs, L., 303
Group orientation, 233
Groupism, 125
Growth strategies, 246
Guangdon managers, 184
Gulick, L., 11
Guth, W., 4

Harbison, F., 11
Harzburg model, 88
Haire, M., 10
Hegarty, H., 97
Hermes Survey of 1966, 110
Hemphill, J.K., 10
Hickson, D.J., 34
Hoffman, R., 17, 97
Hofstede, Geert, xiv, 9, 180–1, 274–275
Hogan, Paul, 295
Homeostatic casual-loop models, 39
Homo economicus, 158
Homogeneity, 38
Honda Motor Corporation, 296
Horvath, 34
Hoy, F., 270

IBM, 5
Imperialist exploitation, 162
Impersonal rules, 97
Implications for the practice of management, 47

Implicitly structured organization, 236
Incentives, 210
  financial, 210
  for excellent exits, 216
Independent event models, 38
India, 35
Individual management, 164
Individualism–collectivism, 276
Industry performance analysis, 240
Industrial Democracy in Europe project (IDE), 303
Intercultural interaction, 18, 36
Internal strife, 162
International Air Transport Association (IATA), 5
International Civil Aviation Organization, 242
International commerce, 27
International Commission of Jurists, 5
International exchanges, 35
International Monetary Fund, 2, 211
International Olympic Committee (IOC), 5
International Transport Association, 230
International,
  commerce, 27
  exchange, 35
Internationalization of business and industry, 20
Intraorganizational control, 76
Intracultural differences, 302
Internationalizing organizational science, 300
Israel, 100
Italy, 296

Jalinek, M., 4, 10
Japan, 6, 35, 119, 286, 297–298
  Japan Productivity Center, 123
  management systems in, 404
  management techniques of, 81
Jerdee, T.H., 10
Joint-venture investments, 165

Kafka, Franz, 69
Kaiser Steel, 92
Keohane, Robert, 2
Kets de Vries, Manfred, 4
Kim, Myung, 19, 203
Kondo, Yasumasa, 18, 135
Koontz, H., 11

Korbin, Stephen, 5
Korea, 35
Kuhn, Thomas, x

Latin America, 298
Lau, A.W., 10
Laurent, A., 9, 35
Levitt, T., 34
Lilliputian's myth, 9
Locke, Edwin, 4
Loosely coupled systems, 209

Mahoney, T.A., 10
Majority-owned overseas subsidiaries, 6
Malpas, R.S., 10
Management, 64, 75
    education, 64, 303
    by lack of goal consciousness, 75, 76
    by lack of recognition for results, 76, 77
    by prestige and informal authority, 76,
        78
    by traditionalism, 86, 77
Management information systems, 123
Management–labor relationship, 170
Mandated turbulence, 214
Maruyama, M., 4, 38
Marxism, 8
Marxism-Leninism, 177
Marxism-Leninism-Maoism, 167
Masculinity–femininity, 275
Maslow's theory, 175
Massive social disorientation, 162
Maurice, M., 7
McDonnough, J.J., 7
McMillan, C., 12
McMillar, 34
Meaning
    cognitive, 9
    evocative, 8
    myth and, 8–9
    symbolic system of, 8–9
Meiji restoration, 188
Mendenhall, M., 4
Mental programs, x
Merit compensation, 299
Methodology, 234, 13–15
    re-thinking, 301
Meyers, C., 11
Microeconomic theory, 158
Middle East, 298

Miller, D., 4
Miner, J., 10
Mintzberg, H., 8, 9
Mistrust, 71
Misinterpretation
    causes of, 44
    of data across cultures, 44
Mitbestimmung, 85
Mitroff, I., 8
Mitsubishi Corporation, 5
Modern bureaucracy, 234
Muqiao, X., 124
Mooney, J., 10
Moral encouragement, 173
Morgan, G., 7
Morphogenic casual-loop models, 39
Morse, E., 5
Muller, R., 4
Multidinestuc firms, 39
Multinational corporations, 5
Multinational pattern, 172
Multivariate analyses, 242
Myths
    demythologizing organizational, 9–10
    as instruments of denial, 9
    as vehicles of repression, 9

National economy, 165
Nation versus culture, 30
National economic policies, 162
National Foreign Trade Council, 27
National Socialist Party, 185
National private-sector enterprises, 189
Negandhi, A., 7, 10, 15
Negative competition, 72
Newman, A.R., 10
Newman, W.H., 11
Norms, governing work and productivity,
    211–212
Nye, J., 4

O'Donnell, C., 11
Obsession, with position and title, 74
Oddou, G., 4
Open system, 60
Organizational theory
    and behavior, 177
    and effectiveness, 269
    principles of, 177

Organizational theory (*continued*)
  and the transnational business world,
    4–7
Osigweh, C.A.B., 4, 5, 8, 290, xi

Paradigm shift, x
Parallel power, 69
Party branches, 177
Party committees, 165
People's Liberation Army, 165
People's Republic of China, 18, 41, 161
Performance, 248
  correlations of, 251
  and strategy, 251
Performance maintenance (PM) theory of
    leadership, 129
Personnel development, 243
Peters, T.J., 8
Plant closures, 298
Politics
  and chaos, 162
  conditions of, 206
  and entourage, 234
  and graft, 215
  and nepotism, 215
  orientation versus openness of, 62–63
  and pull, 215
Pondy, L.R., 8
Porter, L.W., 10
Power distance, 188, 276
Predicators of performance, 253
Presentismo, 297
Prestige & informal authority, 77
Professional discipline, 213
Proletarian dictatorship, 165
Pucik, V., 18, 119

Quality control (QC), 122
Quantitative analysis, 238
Quasirational foibles, 159

Rational man theory, 148, 156
Redding, G., 16
Rehabilitation years, 162
Reilly, A., 10
Religious homogeneity, 208
Reprimands, 176
Richman, B.N., 11
Roberts, K., 10
Rogers, R., 17, 18

Rosenberg, A., 4
Royal Dutch/Shell group, 5
Runaway inflation, 162

Schein, E., 4
Schollhammer, H., 12
Schwartz, H., 9
Scott, W., 8
Sears Roebuck, 5
Sekaran, U., 269
Senior administrators, 169
Sethi, P., 10
Shi, N., 18
S.I.C., 150
Simplification, of administrative organiza-
    tions, 163
Singapore Airlines, 235
Single culture management studies, 40
Size,
  influence of, 243
  operating strategies, and performance,
    241
Skjelbaek, K., 5
Smircich, L., 7, 8
Snodgrass, C., 269
Society,
  conditions of, 207
  disorientation and, 162
  model for, 154
Socialism,
  and democracy, 165
  economy of, 161
  model for, 166
  and psychology of organizations, 172
Social culture, 229
  airline industry and, 229
  business strategy and, 229
  influence on corporate culture, 229
  performance and, 229
Societal culture configuration model, 231
Societal objectives, 187
Socioeconomic and political systems, 167
Sociological studies, 42
Solange, P., 33
Standard Oil, 122
State and collectively owned enterprises,
    164
State labor department, 169
Steel, 10

Steel industry, employer negotiating committee, 90
Steers, Richard M., 24, 293, 297
Strategic decision, 104
    activities, 104
    influence process, 100, 104
    process, 104
Stratification, 69
Structural overformalization, 74
Sullivan, J., 18, 135
Suspicion, of things foreign, 61
Suzuki, T., 18, 135
Sweden, 213
Symbolic constructions, 8
Symbolism, 7
Synergy, from cultural diversity, 37

Tagiuri, R., 4
Taiwan, 41
Taylor, F., 10
Theory,
    need for, 301
    organizational, 178
    rational man, 148, 156
Thurow, L., 299
Time, use of, 298
Traditional bureaucracy, 234
Traditionalism, 77
Trandis, H., 10
Transnationalism, 3–9
    and environment, 7
    perspective of, 5
    organizational science and, 6, 4–7
Triandis, H., 274
Trojans, 9
Tung, R., 18
Turbulence, mandated, 214

Uncertainty avoidance, 168, 277
United States Department of Commerce, 5
United States enterprises, 174
U.S. Steel, 91
Use of economic means, 163

Union management, 81
    participation in corporate decision-making, 81, 89
Union or employee participation, 89
Unions in China, 194
United Airlines, 295
United Automobile Workers (UAW), 91
United Kingdom, 16
United Rubber Workers, 91
United States, 5, 7, 11, 15, 35
United Steel Workers of America (USWA), 90
Universality myth, 10
Universities, 214

Value differences, 196
Van Fleet, D., 270
Vehicles of repression, 9
Verney, H., 10
Vickers, S.G., 8

Wa, and justice, 300
Warsaw Pact, 74
Waterman, R.H., 8
West Germany, 57, 300
Western ethnocentrism, 204
Western Europe, 297
Western management techniques, and their CPE inverses, 96–98
Wierton Steel, 191
Wiweko's strategies, 258
Workers Representative Congress, 192
Works Constitution Act, 85
World Council of Churches (WCC), 5
World Federation of Trade Unions (WFTU), 5
Wren, Daniel, 10

Yankelovich, D., 296
Yetley, M., 270
Yugoslavia, 14, 284

Zaleznik, A., 4
Zeeman, J., 295